WITHDRAWN 941.085

D0345707

FINEST AND DARKEST

KEVIN JEFFERYS lectures in h⸻
University. He is the author of seve⸻
British politics, including *The Labour Party Since 1945* (1993), *Retreat from New Jerusalem: British Politics 1951–64* (1997), *Anthony Crosland: A New Biography* (1999). He is the editor of *Leading Labour: From Keir Hardie to Tony Blair* (1999).

CONCORD COLLEGE
TAYLOR LIBRARY
ACTON BURNELL HALL

ALSO BY KEVIN JEFFERYS

The Churchill Coaliation and Wartime Politics 1940–45
The Labour Party since 1945
Retreat from New Jerusalem: British Politics 1951–64
Anthony Crosland: A New Biography

EDITED BY KEVIN JEFFERYS

Labour Forces: From Ernest Bevin to Gordon Brown
Leading Labour: From Keir Hardie to Tony Blair

KEVIN JEFFERYS
FINEST AND DARKEST HOURS

The Decisive Events in British Politics
from Churchill to Blair

Atlantic Books
London

First published in Great Britain in 2002 by Atlantic Books,
an imprint of Grove Atlantic Ltd

This paperback edition published by Atlantic Books in 2003

Copyright © Kevin Jefferys 2002

The moral right of Kevin Jefferys to be identified as the author of this
work has been asserted in accordance with the Copyright, Designs and
Patents Act of 1988.

All rights reserved. No part of this publication may be reproduced, stored
in a retrieval system, or transmitted in any form or by any means,
electronic, mechanical, photocopying, recording, or otherwise, without
the prior permission of both the copyright owner and the above publisher
of this book.

1 2 3 4 5 6 7 8 9

A CIP catalogue record for this book is available from the British Library.

ISBN 1 84354 172 6

Printed and bound in Great Britain by
Mackays of Chatham plc, Chatham, Kent

Atlantic Books
An imprint of Grove Atlantic Ltd
Ormond House
26-27 Boswell Street
London WC1N 3JZ

For Margaret Stone

Contents

List of Illustrations

Acknowledgements

I am grateful to many friends and colleagues for their help and guidance in preparing this book. In particular I should like to mention Stuart Ball, Mark Garnett, Rick McLain and Jonathan Wood, the latter of whom provided invaluable assistance in tracking down source material. I am also greatly indebted to Toby Mundy at Atlantic Books, in the first place for asking me to write about 'finest and darkest hours' and then for providing shrewd and pertinent comments on early drafts of the text. Thanks also to Bonnie Chiang and David Atkinson for their assistance. Any responsibility for remaining errors rests, of course, with me alone.

The bulk of the photographs in the book have been taken from the Hulton Archive Picture Collection, and I would particularly like to acknowledge the following for allowing use of material within the Hulton Getty collection: Kurt Hutton (photograph 6), Keystone Press (16), Fox Photos (18), *The Observer* (20 and 26) and Steve Eason (27). Finally, I am grateful to Faber and Faber for allowing me to use an extract from Philip Larkin's poem 'Annus Mirabilis'.

Kevin Jefferys
July 2002

Introduction

In the life of any government, however safe its majority,
there comes a moment when the social movements of
which it had once been the expression turn inexorably
against it . . . After that moment, every mistake it makes
becomes magnified; indeed blunders multiply as if
feeding on themselves; and both outwardly and inwardly
the Government appears to be at the mercy of every wind.

Christopher Booker, author and journalist, The Neophiliacs *(1969)*

Men wiser and more learned than I have discerned in history
a plot, a rhythm, a predetermined pattern. These harmonies
are concealed from me. I can see only one emergency
following upon another as wave follows upon wave, only
one . . . safe rule for the historian: that he should recognise
in the development of human destinies the play of the
contingent and the unforeseen.

H. A. L. Fisher, politician and historian, A History of Europe *(1936)*

When asked about the greatest difficulty of being Prime Minister,
Harold Macmillan famously replied: 'events, dear boy, events.'[1]
This is a book about 'events' in the history of British politics since
the Second World War. It sets out to ask: what have been the
decisive events in British political life since 1939? Which moments
in time have most influenced the direction of politics over the last
sixty years? What have been the key turning points? Each chapter
addresses an incident or period of importance, ranging from

Winston Churchill's accession to the premiership in 1940 through to the emergence of New Labour in 1994. The main aim is to identify and assess the significance of the critical episodes in British political history, including highs like Britain's 'finest hour' in 1940 as well as lows such as Suez and the Profumo affair. Readers will, no doubt, have their own answers to the questions posed above, their own views about the most formative events in living memory.

In drawing up a list of key dates, much depends on what definitions are used and what criteria for inclusion are employed. British politics has a twofold meaning in what follows: the rise and fall of regimes associated with particular Prime Ministers, and the twists and turns of electoral competition between the major parties at Westminster. Events are those developments that arise suddenly, demanding the full attention of the government of the day and often plunging it into crisis. All the moments included here have a limited timescale. Although every chapter attempts to set the scene, the main action is always concentrated in a short time frame, varying from a single day – Black Wednesday in 1992 – to a few months, as in the case of the three-day week and the Falklands War. Any longer than this and the moment becomes something more protracted, losing the urgency and unpredictability that made it distinctive. The events and moments chosen are also deemed to be turning points, having an impact that resonates for years afterwards.

These criteria help to explain my choice of what to focus on and of what to leave out. There is no place to discuss, for instance, the tangled history of Northern Ireland, whether its many bleak moments since the outbreak of the Troubles or its recent step forward with the Good Friday Agreement. I have also limited the field to a dozen key incidents, on the ground that more would diminish the importance of those chosen. This, too, inevitably means that several notable events etched into public consciousness are not included. The 1976 IMF crisis caused considerable short-term damage to Labour, but did not prevent Callaghan's government recovering to a position where re-election was a possibility eighteen months later. This book argues that it was Callaghan's decision not to call an election in the autumn of 1978, followed by the disastrous winter of discontent, that put paid to Labour's electoral prospects and enabled Mrs Thatcher to come to power. Some traumatic episodes, such as the wartime Blitz and the miners' strike of 1984–5, were too long-lasting to qualify as moments. And it is difficult to pinpoint particular turning points that explain the profound social changes since the war – in the role of women, for instance, or the creation of a multicultural society.

What is attempted here is a series of snapshots rather than an overview of British politics since the war. These snapshots set out to combine a reliable narrative of the episode under scrutiny with a consideration of its broader implications. Each chapter also looks at what has shaped our understanding of particular events, how 'myths' arise and become consolidated, and the part played in this process by politicians, by the media and by historians. Two further themes permeate the book. One is to elaborate on the contention that while some regimes prove more lasting than others, each eventually loses its way – as Christopher Booker notes – after a key moment 'when the social movements of which it had once been the expression turn inexorably against it'. The second is to show how historical outcomes are not predetermined, and so to highlight what H. A. L. Fisher calls the role of 'the contingent and the unforeseen'. As John Charmley has written, historians must deal with events as they transpire, but to ask hypothetical questions can add to our understanding and help avoid the temptation to assume 'that what actually happened was inevitable and, therefore, automatically for the best'.[2]

The writing of history as a study of events has a long pedigree, though it has not gone unchallenged. The French historian Fernand Braudel, author of the magisterial work *The Mediterranean in the Age of Philip II*, first published in the late 1940s, dismissed events as 'ephemera', nothing more than waves on the sea of the past. The key features of history, in his view, were the tides and currents: long-term developments such as the slowly evolving pattern of rural life in preindustrial societies. Some social historians after the war developed a 'determinist' view of history, borrowing insights and methodology from the social sciences to claim that historical events are governed by 'laws', for example the driving force of class struggle. More recently the value of narrative history has been reasserted. Simon Schama, presenter of the acclaimed *BBC History of Britain*, pointed out that to write history under headings such as 'nobility' or 'peasantry' is to privilege the explanatory force of these themes. In his 1989 book *Citizens* he argued that the French Revolution was more the product of human agency than it was of structures, ideologies or institutions. On this basis, Schama reasoned, it was essential to let the story unfold as it happened, to provide a chronology that made intelligible the Revolution's complicated twists and turns, and to present events through the eyes of the main historical actors, mirroring the way in which they saw their world. *Finest and Darkest Hours* attempts to follow in this tradition. 'Events', studied in their appropriate context, are a mainspring of history, not only providing colour and drama, but also having lasting and profound consequences. Nowhere is this more obvious than in the case of Winston Churchill's emergence as war leader in 1940.

'In the name of God, go' Chamberlain, Churchill and Britain's 'finest hour', 1940

One thing is certain – [Hitler] missed the bus.

Neville Chamberlain, speech at Central Hall, Westminster,
4 April 1940

[Winston Churchill] mobilized the English language
and sent it into battle.

American broadcaster Ed Murrow, on Churchill in 1940

In the summer of 1940 Britain faced its gravest crisis since Napoleon massed his armies across the Channel nearly one hundred and fifty years earlier. The outline of the story is familiar enough and deeply embedded in popular consciousness as the nation's 'finest hour'. On the day in May 1940 when Winston Churchill replaced Neville Chamberlain as Prime Minister there was an intensification of the war in Europe: Hitler launched his blitzkrieg attack on Holland and Belgium. After the collapse of the French army in June, Britain was left to stand alone against the might of Nazi Germany and, with the prospect of invasion imminent, Churchill played an inspired role in stirring the British people to resist. During July and August the RAF denied Goering's Luftwaffe aerial supremacy in the Battle of Britain, and by the autumn Churchill was confident that Britain had survived its sternest test. Although the civilian population faced untold new horrors in the Blitz, the prospect of invasion had receded for good, as it turned out – and the government could begin considering ways of striking back at the enemy. Victory in the war remained a long way off, and was to be dependent in the long run on American and Russian military might, but Britain had come through its moment of supreme danger. Inevitably, the coalition government formed by Churchill in May 1940 – the only occasion in the twentieth century when the Conservatives and Labour worked together in office – devoted its entire energies to the war effort. 'The situation which faced the members of the new Government,' as the historian Alan Bullock has noted, 'left them no time to think about the future: they needed all their resolution to believe there was going to be a future at all.'[1]

In spite of the extraordinary circumstances of the day, it would be wrong to assume that British politics went entirely into abeyance during the summer of 1940. May 1940 witnessed one of the rare occasions when a British Prime Minister was forced from office, and the impact of Chamberlain's departure was to reverberate for years to come, not only providing the opportunity for Churchill to establish himself as the nation's great war hero but also undermining the pre-war domination of the Conservative Party and marking a vital breakthrough for Labour – one that was to culminate in a famous election victory in 1945. None of these consequences, however, was inevitable or easy to predict when Chamberlain left Downing Street. It was only much later – and with twenty-twenty hindsight – that the significance of 1940 could begin to be appreciated.

The difficulties of assessing Britain's 'finest hour' are compounded by the need to come to terms with the Churchill legend. For many years after 1945 any criticism of Britain's saviour was regarded as almost treasonable. The familiar newsreel images of a defiant Churchill with his trademark hat and cigar, the great man's own influential history of the period (crucially one of the first to appear after the war), and the flattering tone of Martin Gilbert's multi-volume official biography all painted the same picture of an indomitable figure who came to power as the 'man of destiny' and whose bulldog spirit of resistance saved Britain in the nick of time. Only in the last decade, as memories of the war recede, have revisionists put their heads above the parapet. In his book *1940: Myth and Reality*, Clive Ponting snipes at Churchill's personality – talking of his thirst for money and alcohol, among other things – and argues that the untold story of the 'finest hour' was one of disarray among British forces and incompetence 'in relieving the suffering caused by bombing'. For John Charmley, the price of survival in 1940 was post-war subordination to American interests and the demise of the British Empire. 'Churchill's leadership was inspiring,' he writes, 'but at the end it was barren, it led nowhere.'[2]

What follows is an attempt to disentangle the reality from the myths of British politics in the early summer of 1940. As the leader who fell from power, Neville Chamberlain has often been presented unkindly; he was, according to one writer, 'an anachronism, an exhausted old man whose day had passed'.[3] It will be argued in this chapter that there was nothing preordained about Chamberlain's fall from power in May and that, with slightly different handling, he might well have survived to fight another day – with all the consequences this might have had for Britain's war effort. Churchill, it will be suggested, came out on top not because he was 'walking with destiny' – the phrase he used in his own later account – but because he proved most adept and ruthless in exploiting a sudden crisis. The second part of the chapter assesses the new Prime Minister's early weeks in office and again suggests that the reality was more complex than popular mythology allows. It will be shown that in these early days Churchill was by no means a universally acclaimed war leader and that his authority was only built up gradually through good fortune, as well as through immense resolution. None of this is intended to diminish the scale of Churchill's achievement. Rather it is to bring him into sharper focus, avoiding the simple verities of his admirers and detractors alike – making him, in the words of the historian David

Reynolds, 'a more human and thereby a more impressive figure than the two-dimensional bulldog of national mythology. Churchill's greatness is that of a man, not an icon.'[4]

In tracing how Churchill's premiership came about, we need to begin by recognizing that – in spite of the newsreel images of an elderly figure with a top hat and umbrella – Neville Chamberlain was one of the most dominant Prime Ministers in modern British history. His authority stemmed in part from the circumstances he inherited from his predecessor, Stanley Baldwin, in May 1937. The Conservative-dominated National government, in power since 1931, had been re-elected in 1935 with an enormous majority of over 200 parliamentary seats – well in excess of the later landslide victories of premiers such as Margaret Thatcher or Tony Blair. Equally important to Chamberlain's dominance was his personal political style. His considerable following among Tory loyalists, from the Cabinet through to rank-and-file activists, was due both to his widely acclaimed administrative ability, displayed in various high offices of state since the early 1920s, and to his determination to lead from the front. Chamberlain dictated policy in a manner alien to Baldwin's more diffident approach to leadership. He delighted middle-class supporters with his adherence to free-market principles which delivered, after the hardships of the early 1930s, an expanding economy characterized by low taxation and growing home ownership. The regard of Conservatives for their leader was further enhanced by his tough brand of partisan politics. He had no hesitation in scoring points off the Labour Party – only some 150-strong in Parliament – whose leader, Clement Attlee, was widely regarded as an ineffectual, stop-gap figure. Chamberlain never suffered fools gladly and his greatest contempt was reserved for those Labour MPs – 'dirt' as he once called them – who felt that they alone could speak for Britain's industrial heartlands, for the millions of working-class families who had gained little from economic recovery and whose lives continued to be characterized by poverty, poor health, abject housing and high rates of unemployment.

Chamberlain imposed himself on foreign as much as on domestic policy. His strategy towards the European dictators has been the subject of intense scrutiny and controversy among historians; here the intention is simply to make the case that the origins of his downfall should not be sought in the pursuit of appeasement before 1939. The idea of combining increased rearmament with a search for general European peace, although shaped by Chamberlain and his senior colleagues such as Lord Halifax, the Foreign Secretary, met with widespread approval in Conservative ranks. In spite of the controversy about the Munich settlement of September 1938, which conceded Hitler's demands over the Sudetenland in Czechoslovakia, no local party associations registered any public protest; indeed, several constituency parties were still expressing their approval of appeasement in the summer of 1939. There were, naturally enough, doubters in the Tory ranks. Prominent among the critics was Anthony Eden, one of the young aspirants for the future party leadership, who resigned as Foreign Secretary in early 1938, ostensibly over differences with Chamberlain about how far to conciliate Mussolini. The small band of Tory MPs whose private deliberations earned them the name the 'Eden group' (or 'glamour boys', on account of their generally wealthy backgrounds) had growing doubts about the wisdom of Chamberlain's policy. But open rebellion was never seriously considered. Conservative Central Office, tacitly backed by the Prime Minister, encouraged local associations to put pressure on Tory critics to come into line or else face the possibility of deselection. The Eden group, as a result, offered no concerted opposition to the government either before or after Munich. Eden himself, half promised a return to office, remained non-committal in his public statements, and his refusal to adopt an 'I told you so' approach after Hitler's takeover of the remainder of Czechoslovakia in the spring of 1939 removed any doubt about his desire for a recall.[5]

Eden's motives were also apparent in his dealings with the Prime Minister's leading Tory adversary – Winston Churchill. Excluded by successive leaders of the National government in the 1930s, Churchill's concern about Chamberlain's strategy became increasingly vociferous during and after Munich. The prospect of Churchill being invited to join the government was so remote that he was less constrained in his views than many of the younger critics, though he, too, faced considerable pressure from his Epping constituency to toe the party line. Throughout this period, Eden's followers were determined that Churchill and his few associates should not be brought into their discussions. The coolness between Eden and Churchill was partly personal. Before the outbreak of war they had remained equals and rivals; the idea of Eden as Churchill's protégé and successor emerged only after 1940. For the Eden group as a whole there was a wider consideration: association with Churchill was certain to bring with it charges of disloyalty. Churchill had made so many enemies that he was seen in the party as an isolated demagogue: a figure whose poor judgement was demonstrated by the Gallipoli disaster in the First World War; a maverick motivated by personal ambition and bitterness at his exclusion from office. Divisions between the Tory critics clearly made the Prime Minister's task easier. Although Churchill began to attract a measure of press support after Munich, Chamberlain had as yet no reason to feel unduly threatened.

The Prime Minister remained firmly in control in the pre-war period. Hitler's entry into Prague dented Chamberlain's popularity and led to growing demands from all quarters for the reshaping of the government. Even so, British guarantees to protect Poland in the event of attack helped to contain the critics. The Eden and Churchill groups remained reluctant to co-operate either with each other or with the Labour opposition, which had reversed its neo-pacifism of the early 1930s to demand a tough stand against the dictators. Nor was there much evidence that public opinion had turned decisively against the Prime Minister.

The success of an anti-appeasement candidate at the Bridgwater by-election in late 1938 was countered when a Tory critic, the Duchess of Atholl, was defeated after resigning her seat to fight in opposition to Chamberlain's foreign policy. Though public opinion had become increasingly polarized, the best Labour could hope for in the general election scheduled for 1940 was modest inroads into the National government majority. In addition, the Prime Minister's tight and unprecedented control of the lobby system ensured that he continued to receive a favourable press from most national newspapers. In the summer of 1939, with the prospect of war impending, there was no question that if and when hostilities began Neville Chamberlain would be the man at the helm.[6]

It is true that the Prime Minister caused alarm in the Commons by his slow response to Hitler's invasion of Poland on 1 September. MPs gathered at Westminster in anticipation of an immediate declaration of war. But Chamberlain held back, primarily because of difficulties in co-ordinating an Anglo-French ultimatum. The Tory MP for Birmingham Sparkwood, Leo Amery, a fervent imperialist, could not resist an interjection calling on Arthur Greenwood, replying for Labour in the absence of Attlee, to 'speak for England'. By the time Chamberlain made his famous radio broadcast declaring war on the morning of 3 September, many backbenchers were already asking questions about his suitability for the struggle ahead. Yet he showed great resilience in reasserting his authority, and indeed the recovery of Chamberlain's prestige was a striking feature of the early weeks of the so-called 'phoney war'. His handling of erstwhile opponents was crucial in this context. The composition and size of his War Cabinet, at nine strong, gave the Prime Minister scope to control the most important addition to his re-formed administration, Churchill, who became First Lord of the Admiralty. While Churchill was euphoric at this sudden change of fortune, the same could not be said for Eden, who reluctantly accepted a post outside the War Cabinet as Dominions Secretary. These appointments not only silenced the potentially most dangerous sources of party opposition but also left effective power in the hands of Chamberlain and his coterie of senior advisers. The Prime Minister could confidently exclude other leading critics. When the idea was raised of including the likes of Leo Amery, a former Colonial Secretary, Chamberlain dismissed it 'with an irritated snort'.[7] In all, more than two-thirds of ministers from the peace-time government kept their places.

In the early weeks of the war, the Prime Minister continued to look unassailable. The nature of the phoney war also eased pressures on the government. After the defeat of Poland, there were few signs of British forces becoming involved in large-scale military engagements; indeed, it was still widely assumed that Hitler was incapable of waging a long war and that the French army would prevent any further Nazi advance on the Continent. Measures affecting the civilian population, such as evacuation and the blackout, did provoke some disquiet, especially as the reduced level of government activity left backbenchers with more time free to criticize in the House. But Chamberlain was well placed to contain his opponents. Labour had rejected a half-hearted offer to join a coalition and struggled to maintain a policy of 'patriotic opposition' – it supported the war but found itself charged with disloyalty if it exercised its right to criticize. Political opponents of the war, such as the British Fascist Party, remained small in number. And, with the exception of the ageing Lloyd George – the Liberal hero of the Great War, whose attitude contained a strong element of personal bitterness against his long-standing antagonist, Chamberlain – those who pessimistically believed that the war could not be won found little publicity for their views in the press. The majority of proprietors decided that, in spite of misplaced trust in appeasement, it was their patriotic duty to continue supporting the government. Opinion polls in November showed that Chamberlain had reached a new peak in public popularity.[8]

But if the Prime Minister was in a commanding position in late

1939, over the next few months an ebbing of confidence was to take place among even his own supporters; it was a process so imperceptible that government whips were caught completely off guard by the strength of feeling that surfaced in May 1940. In so far as this movement of opinion derived from perceived failures in policy, the major area of concern was the war economy. The Chamberlain government recognized the need to maximize war production on the home front in a manner consistent with providing adequate manpower for the armed forces. To this end, output targets were set in key industries and plans were introduced to raise an army of fifty-five divisions, some of which were soon dispatched to France. For its critics, the government remained too committed to pre-war orthodoxies. Relations with the trade union movement had always been poor and showed only partial improvement, and Labour MPs were able to make a series of telling attacks, especially as unemployment remained at over one million in April 1940. The idea of appointing a powerful Minister for Economic Co-ordination found support well beyond the ranks of the opposition – among sections of the press and from influential figures such as the Cambridge economist John Maynard Keynes. But the Prime Minister remained unmoved. When the suggestion was proposed in the Commons in February 1940 Chamberlain refused to take the idea seriously, candidly admitting that such an appointment would undermine his own authority and that of the Treasury.[9]

These criticisms were not in themselves directly responsible for the fall of Chamberlain. Similar complaints were to persist at least until 'the turn of the tide' in the war effort in late 1942. For many at Westminster, bemoaning production levels represented the best of the limited opportunities available to bolster the war effort. What mattered, as the demand for an economic overlord demonstrated, was the inflexibility of the Prime Minister's response. Chamberlain in wartime had become increasingly intolerant, dismissing the 'opposition riff-raff', and confident that his own party's support would remain solid. 'The House of Commons,'

Churchill's friend Brendan Bracken lamented, 'was no good, the Tory Party were tame yes-men of Chamberlain. 170 had their election expenses paid by Tory Central Office and 100 hoped for jobs.'[10] But by the spring of 1940 Chamberlain's refusal to yield any ground was causing a hardening of feeling. Under the guidance of Leo Amery, the Eden group moved to a more overtly hostile position. More importantly, discontent was spreading. Under the chairmanship of the Liberal MP Clement Davies, an All-Party Parliamentary Action Group committed to a more vigorous prosecution of the war claimed some sixty backbench supporters, and was in touch with both Labour leaders and Tory dissidents. In April the senior Conservative peer Lord Salisbury formed what became known as the 'Watching Committee'. Salisbury's initial purpose was to employ private persuasion in moving ministers to greater urgency, in preference to damaging public dissension. But the committee soon found Chamberlain immune to its constructive criticism; within weeks, Salisbury's group was also becoming more openly critical.[11]

By April 1940 the Prime Minister was faced with considerable, if still hidden, parliamentary opposition. As Hitler's forces ended the phoney war with an attack on Scandinavia, British troops became involved in a hastily conceived and ultimately unsuccessful effort to defend Norway. Early signs that the campaign was not going to plan further heightened tension at Westminster. There was talk of an open political clash between loyal Chamberlainites and the 'glamour boys', and even of Lloyd George seeking to form a new alliance with Labour. More importantly, there was speculation about the first signs of disunity inside the Cabinet, with rumours of Churchill beginning to distance himself from the Prime Minister. Churchill, conscious that he had no party base, was clearly thankful at the outbreak of war to be rescued from the political wilderness. By the spring of 1940, though, he was frustrated in his desire to have overall political responsibility for the conduct of the war. As the Scandinavian campaign, of which he was the chief advocate, began to go wrong, Churchill renewed his demands to be made Minister of Defence or to be given greater control over the powerful Military Co-ordination Committee. After a poor performance in the Commons, which renewed doubts about his leadership qualities, Churchill began to dissociate himself from the Cabinet. The Chamberlainite MP and diarist Sir Henry ('Chips') Channon reported that Churchill, although hitherto loyal, was being tempted to lead a revolt against the Prime Minister. He had been seen consorting in the smoking rooms with senior Labour figures and the opposition Liberal Archie Sinclair, 'the new Shadow Cabinet'.[12] It was against this troubled background that the crucial 'Norway debate' of 7-8 May 1940 was to take place.

In the days before the debate, as news of the evacuation of British forces from Norway came through, parliamentary critics marshalled their forces. Salisbury's Watching Committee was convinced that a new coalition, to include Labour, was now essential. This view was leaked to the press in order to increase pressure on the government. But there was little support for the idea, put to the All-Party Action Group by Clement Davies, that the adjournment debate on events in Norway should be turned into a vote of no confidence in the Prime Minister. Labour leaders in particular feared this would rally Tory support behind Chamberlain and so strengthen his government.[13] The Prime Minister was not, in fact, unduly worried by the prospect of an inquest into the Norwegian campaign and remained confident that his critics would be no more effective than in the past. Most of the doubters, he wrote in a letter to his sister, were enemies of the government who would try to exploit every setback. Others who attacked in order to gratify their partisanship he described as 'traitors just as much as Quisling', the Norwegian fascist. The Tory Chief Whip, David Margesson, was also confident of success: on the eve of the debate he suggested that, if circumstances seemed propitious, the government should itself consider introducing a motion of confidence in order to isolate the critics.[14]

Why, then, did the two-day Norway debate go so badly wrong for the government? With the House in a volatile mood, the Prime Minister in opening proceedings deliberately set out to lower the temperature. He refused to be knocked out of his stride by constant Labour interruptions – mocking his earlier claims that Hitler had 'missed the bus' – and was ineffective only in failing to give assurances that the position in Norway would improve. The first influential attack on the government came from Admiral Sir Roger Keyes who, in the words of the MP Harold Nicolson, was listened to in 'breathless silence' as, bedecked in full military uniform, he lambasted the Naval General Staff for inadequate planning.[15] The most notable criticism on the first day – and in many ways the key contribution of the whole debate – came from Leo Amery, who was almost prevented from rising by the partiality of the Speaker. Amery had not been hitherto known as a compelling parliamentary performer; it had once been said that he might have made Prime Minister if his speeches were half an hour shorter. But on this occasion his carefully prepared critique of his fellow Birmingham MP, Chamberlain, evoked precisely the misgivings of the House. 'I found myself,' he recorded that night in his diary, 'going on to an increasing crescendo of applause. So evident was the whole feeling on our side, as well as on the opposition, ready for a change that I cast prudence to the winds and ended full out with my Cromwellian injunction.' The words that were regarded by one of Chamberlain's aides as 'the dagger in the heart' were those in which Amery echoed Cromwell speaking to the Long Parliament: 'You have sat here too long for any good you have been doing. Depart, I say, and let us have done with you. In the name of God, go.'[16]

Amery's assault articulated and strengthened the dissatisfaction of MPs and encouraged critics to force a division in the Commons. On the morning of 8 May, Labour's National Executive Committee agreed by a narrow majority that the opportunity to discredit Chamberlain could not be missed whatever the danger of rallying support behind the government. In announcing his party's intention to force a division, Herbert Morrison for Labour opened the second day of the debate with a forceful and partisan speech, cleverly designed to rile the Prime Minister. The effect was as intended, noted Labour's Hugh Dalton: visibly angered, 'up jumped Chamberlain, showing his teeth like a rat in a corner'.[17] The Prime Minister had no alternative other than to meet his opponents head on, but by making the issue at stake personal, by calling on his 'friends' to support him in the vote, he shocked the sensibilities of the House. In many ways Chamberlain's short intervention was the most vital factor on the second day; the outcome of the debate was not subsequently influenced to any great degree either by the few loyalists who rallied to the government or by critics such as Lloyd George. The latter's vitriolic language was regarded primarily as an attempt to repay bitter personal scores against Chamberlain, though he did enliven proceedings with his injunction to Churchill not 'to allow himself to be converted into an air-raid shelter to keep the splinters from hitting his colleagues'. The First Lord took this message to heart. In winding up the debate Churchill's chief preoccupation, according to some observers, was to guard against accusations of treachery. This he did with what Chips Channon called a 'magnificent piece of oratory. . . How much of the fire was real . . . we shall never know, but he amused and dazzled everyone with his virtuosity.'[18]

Churchill's triumph, defending the government while distancing himself from responsibility for the failure in Norway, came too late to prevent a serious anti-government revolt. Earlier in the evening, before Churchill spoke, Clement Davies had presided over a meeting of the All-Party Action Group, now joined by Amery and friends. With over a hundred MPs present, the decision was taken to vote en masse against the government. Chamberlain's Parliamentary Private Secretary, who approached some of the critics with an offer to reconstruct the government in return for continued support, was firmly told that things had gone too far, and members of the Watching Committee agreed to ignore

Lord Salisbury's advice to abstain rather than vote against the party leader.[19] Tensions were naturally running high as the debate came to a close. Channon, as a government loyalist, vividly described the scene in his diary:

At last the Speaker called a division, which Winston nearly talked out. I went into the Aye Lobby... and we watched the insurgents file out of the Opposition Lobby . . . 'Quislings', we shouted at them . . . 'Yes-men', they replied. 'We are all right,' I heard someone say, and so it seemed as David Margesson came in and went to the right, the winning side of the table. '281 to 200' he read, and the Speaker repeated the figures. There were shouts of 'Resign-Resign' . . . and that old ape Josh Wedgwood began to wave his arms about and sing 'Rule Britannia'. Neville appeared bowled over by the ominous figures, and was the first to rise.[20]

Chamberlain had every reason to feel crushed by the result. None of his party had voted against the government at the time of the Munich agreement, but forty National MPs now registered a vote of no confidence, and at least thirty more had deliberately abstained, in spite of intense pressure from the whips.

The Prime Minister's initial reaction was to consider resignation. But as the dust settled overnight, he decided to seek means of continuing in office. He was fortified in this resolve by his supporters, and by early signs of contrition among those who had voted against the government. The chairman of the Tory 1922 Committee, Sir Patrick Spens, reassured Chamberlain that he alone had the confidence of the 'great mass' of Conservative opinion at Westminster and beyond, and that his removal would lead within weeks to a 'grand National disaster'.[21] This coded attack on the claims of the Prime Minister's rivals, especially Churchill, tipped the balance and for thirty-six hours Chamberlain desperately sought ways of reconstructing his government in order to remain in office. When he was spurned by Amery he was left with no option but to make a further appeal to Labour, although Attlee and Greenwood in a private meeting made it plain that they would not join a coalition led by Chamberlain. In a decisive move, the Labour leaders left London to consult the party conference, at that moment gathering in Bournemouth, so preventing further talks or the possibility of a government recovery in a reconvened House. News of the German invasion of the Low Countries on the morning of 10 May opened up one final possibility. The Prime Minister tried to claim that any government reconstruction should be postponed in order to meet this intensification of the war in Europe. Rumours about Chamberlain's intentions led Brendan Bracken to note with despair that removing the Prime Minister was like 'trying to get a limpet off a corpse'.[22] But the Labour leadership remained steadfast and by late afternoon on 10 May Attlee had confirmed by telephone from Bournemouth that the party would serve only under another Prime Minister. Within an hour Chamberlain had resigned.

The succession had already been arranged. Political and public opinion was divided between Churchill and Lord Halifax, the urbane Foreign Secretary, considered by London's social and political elite to be the 'safe' choice. Churchill's prolonged silence at a crucial meeting in Chamberlain's office on 9 May, which led Halifax to volunteer that he could not lead a government from the upper chamber, has established the conventional wisdom that Halifax, complaining at the crucial moment of 'stomach ache', effectively ruled himself out in spite of being Chamberlain's chosen successor and enjoying cross-party support.[23] This begs the question, however, of why Chamberlain, never an indecisive leader, called such a meeting rather than simply advising the King of his successor. It may have been that the Prime Minister privately preferred Churchill but did not wish this to be publicly known: Chamberlain harboured thoughts of returning to national leadership after the war, and with this in mind Churchill's age and unpopularity within the Tory party would have made him preferable, in Chamberlain's eyes, to Halifax. It was believed by many within the establishment that a Churchill regime was not likely to last long. This may also help to explain the behaviour of the other senior Conservative minister was instrumental in determining the succession, Kingsley Wood, the Lord Privy Seal. Wood advised Churchill to remain silent at the meeting on 9 May, and he later claimed to have started negotiations around the turn of the year to ensure a Churchill succession. There was the additional advantage for Wood that by swapping horses in midstream he secured high office for himself, as Chancellor of the Exchequer, after Chamberlain's removal.[24]

Although matters came to a head only in May 1940, the crisis that resulted in Chamberlain's downfall had its roots in developments since the outbreak of war, with the final outcome being determined by a wide variety of groups and individuals. The Labour Party played a critical role, both in forcing a division on 8 May and in standing firm against the Prime Minister as the military situation deteriorated. As Hugh Dalton put it, 'the last blow which dislodged the old limpet was struck by us at Bournemouth.'[25] But Labour's role must be kept in perspective: the party was able to act decisively only *after* it became clear that a sea change had taken place on the Conservative benches. The lead in shifting Tory opinion had, over a long period, been taken by the so-called Eden group; from this quarter during the Norway debate came not only Amery's devastating speech but also nearly half of the forty National MPs to vote with the opposition. The established Tory critics, however, had themselves been easily contained by the government until the last moment. What this meant was that they in turn were dependent for their effectiveness on a more general hardening of party feeling against the Prime Minister. A sizeable revolt took place among backbenchers serving in the armed forces. Although twice as many service MPs voted with the government as against it, the sight of sixteen uniformed officers declaring their lack of confidence left a profound impression on those present.[26] Equally importantly, a significant number of hitherto loyal MPs refused to respond when Chamberlain appealed to his 'friends'. A few of these actually voted against the government, while a larger group totalling more than thirty decided to abstain, thereby helping to make the difference between a comfortable victory and the halving of the Prime Minister's majority. A pivotal role in the fall of Neville Chamberlain was played by the abstentionists, an anonymous group of whom no one thought to make a record at the time.[27]

Why, though, had Conservative opinion turned against the Prime Minister? In contrast to the respect and admiration he commanded during the 1930s, the belief gained ground after September 1939 that he was complacent and temperamentally unsuited to the demands of war leadership. Yet this alone does not explain Chamberlain's demise. Churchill himself was to survive a protracted series of military reversals during 1941–2, many of them with strategic consequences at least as serious as those of the Scandinavian campaign. Rather, in explaining the impact of the Norway episode, we must ultimately go back to Chamberlain's political style. Unlike his predecessor Baldwin, Chamberlain, determined to lead from the front, had never taken much trouble to consult party opinion either at Westminster or in the constituencies. Under the pressure of war he became remote even from the constructive criticism of respected Tory loyalists led by Lord Salisbury. To a considerable extent, the Prime Minster brought his fate upon himself by personal failings of man-management. With greater awareness and flexibility there was no reason why he might not have survived in May 1940, just as Asquith as Liberal Prime Minister had survived a first wartime crisis in 1915 before succumbing to Lloyd George in 1916. Instead, Chamberlain failed to recognize that the loyalty of those around him had to be earned and not simply demanded as of right. His own assessment of why he was forced out referred to an 'accumulated mass of grievances' and hostility towards unpopular colleagues. A more accurate conclusion was reached by the Tory MP Cuthbert Headlam, who wrote on the evening of 10 May: 'One is sorry for Neville, but I should imagine that he has only himself to blame.'[28]

Chamberlain's departure was by no means inevitable, at least in the short term, and the same must be said about Churchill's succession, which few were predicting at the start of the Norway debate. Although closely connected, this was in some ways a discrete transition, engineered by a small group of leading ministers. Churchill's role since returning to office had been more ambiguous than his later writings suggest. He had been loyal to the Prime Minister in the early months of the war but by May 1940 he knew he was playing for high stakes, letting it be known via Bracken that he was unlikely to serve under Halifax even before the Norway vote had been taken. Reassurances the following day from another Tory MP, Bob Boothby, about likely support in both main parties enabled him to face the crucial meeting with Chamberlain with greater confidence.[29] Churchill did not come to power, in other words, as the saviour of the nation. Before the collapse of France, the main demand of the disaffected was not for a saviour but for a leader who would bring greater urgency to Britain's military and economic war effort. In the event, Churchill came to the forefront when the opportunity presented itself because his instinct and urge for power greatly outweighed those of his major rival, Halifax. This is not to ascribe to Churchill purely personal motives; he was, more than most, desperately anxious to see the Nazi menace defeated. But the political context in which he operated must not be ignored; far from letting 'events unfold', as he later claimed in his war history, Winston Churchill had to all intents and purposes seized the premiership of wartime Britain.

In assessing the events of early May 1940 we must also acknowledge the impossibility of predicting at the time how profound the consequences would be in the long term. The coalition that Churchill formed between Conservative and Labour forces was eventually to result in military victory abroad and a landslide for Labour at home. Chamberlain's downfall was a first step on the road to 1945 because it undermined the easy Tory ascendancy of the 1930s, providing Labour with a foothold in power and obliging Conservative MPs to follow a Prime Minister whom many distrusted. In spite of the reputation Churchill was to build up as war leader, party loyalists could not forget his contempt for 'appeasers' and his neglect, as a one-time Liberal, of the organizational needs of Central Office. In the long run, Labour was to have the best of all worlds, gaining both from the radical expectations raised by wartime social change and from the aura of responsibility and competence that stemmed from participation in government. But such an outcome seemed remote in May 1940. Aside from the overriding question of how the war would unfold, there was no guarantee that Labour would prove able to exploit its sudden change of fortune. As Churchill went to Buckingham Palace, where he accepted the King's invitation to form a government, the full impact of the Norway campaign could only be a matter for wild speculation. During the desperate weeks that followed, the nation had in any case only one real priority – survival. When Churchill's personal detective wished him luck in the mammoth task ahead, he replied: 'I hope that it is not too late. I am very much afraid that it is.'[30]

Churchill's first action when he returned from Buckingham Palace as Prime Minister was to write to Neville Chamberlain. 'With your help and counsel and with the support of the great party of which you are the leader,' he wrote, 'I trust that I shall succeed . . . To a very large extent I am in your hands – and I feel no fear of that.'[31] This was a striking illustration of Churchill's sense of weakness when he came to power. In forming his government over the next few hectic days, he found his room for manoeuvre limited by the dictates of parliamentary politics. The new War Cabinet, now composed of only five members, was established on strict party lines rather than attempting to promote those deemed most capable of meeting the national emergency. In addition to Chamberlain and Halifax, who remained as Foreign Secretary, Churchill was joined by Attlee, the Labour leader, and his deputy, Arthur Greenwood. At this level, Labour had cause for satisfaction with its representation in the new government. Indeed, Attlee and Greenwood scored an early success. The Prime Minister initially hoped that Chamberlain would be able to serve as Leader of the House of Commons, but this idea aroused great resentment on the Labour side; rumours began to circulate on 11 May that Churchill would have to choose between Chamberlain and the Labour Party. In the event, Chamberlain agreed to avoid further antagonism by accepting office as Lord President of the Council – a post that allowed him, for the time being, to retain considerable influence on the home front.[32]

It would be a mistake to exaggerate the extent to which the coalition marked a break with the past or represented a sudden shift in political power. Labour had not, in practical terms, entered the coalition as equal partners. In the government as a whole, outside the ranks of the War Cabinet, there were only sixteen Labour ministers compared with fifty-two Conservatives. In the short term, the Labour Party had to settle for an immense psychological boost: the result, simply, of taking a share in power at the expense of its hated opponent, Neville Chamberlain. For the time being, Churchill had no option other than to conciliate his former enemies. Orthodox Conservatives still constituted the most dominant force in Parliament and so could ensure a strong element of continuity. David Margesson, who continued as Chief Whip, helped to ensure that there were only limited rewards in the new administration for Tory 'rebels' such as Leo Amery, who went to the India Office.[33] With Chamberlain staying on – unlike Asquith in similar circumstances in 1916 – there was no immediate prospect of the Conservatives being split down the middle as the Liberals had been, with disastrous effects, during the First World War.

Aside from the service ministries, where Churchill appointed amenable colleagues to ensure his control of military strategy, the new Prime Minister took little interest in the personnel of his new administration. His overriding priority, as German forces overran Allied defensive positions on the Continent, was to square up to the Nazi menace. In his early days in power he made repeated trips across the Channel in an attempt to rally British and French troops. At the same time, he sought to instil in the British people a firm resolve to fight on whatever the consequences. To begin with, this meant brave words rather than action; efforts to galvanize the fighting forces abroad and overhaul the war economy at home would take time to have effect. Churchill's task was made more difficult by the insecurity he felt in these early weeks. Hostility towards him remained widespread in Whitehall and Westminster, in private if not in public. Some officials were soon captivated by the astonishing energy displayed by a man of sixty-five. Marian Holmes, working as a secretary, said that it was as if 'a superhuman current of electricity had gone through Number Ten Downing Street'.[34] But many civil servants were not immediately won over by the Prime Minister's working methods – the late-night meetings, the rapid-fire issue of memos and directives, the fondness for taking advice from 'cronies' such as Lord Beaverbrook, the Canadian-born newspaper proprietor appointed as Minister of Aviation. There was a fear that Churchill's tendency to make rash decisions could lead Britain to fresh, untold disaster, and in the House of Commons Chamberlain's humiliation was not something that could be forgotten overnight by Conservative MPs.

Tory distrust of the Prime Minister was partly personal. For many who had loyally followed Chamberlain over the years the ingrained image of Churchill as a dangerous renegade persisted. On the evening of 10 May Rab Butler, no doubt expecting as a staunch Chamberlainite to be removed from his junior post at the Foreign Office, lamented that 'the good clean tradition of English politics' had been sold to a 'half-breed American', the 'greatest adventurer of modern political history'.[35] On top of this, many backbenchers began to have second thoughts about the Norway debate. Neville Chamberlain was soon receiving assurances from Tory MPs that their hostile action had not been directed against him personally but against the composition of his government.

This sense of guilt about Chamberlain's removal turned into anger when it sunk in that government places had to be found for anti-Chamberlainite Tories and Churchill's 'cronies', as well as Labour representatives. Taken together, these feelings explain the Prime Minister's reception when Parliament met to ratify the change of government on 13 May. Churchill was cheered by the Labour benches when he promised 'blood, toil, tears and sweat', but he was listened to in stony silence by Conservative MPs. When Chamberlain appeared the same MPs, as Chips Channon observed, 'shouted; they waved their Order Papers, and his reception was a regular ovation'.[36] Here, then, was a division of loyalty that might not easily be resolved. Chamberlain, to his credit, did not set about rocking the boat in spite of his shattering experience of recent days. But all the same, Churchill was a Prime Minister without a party; it came as no surprise that he decided to turn down Chamberlain's additional offer of resignation from the Conservative leadership.

Churchill's weakness in May 1940 should not, of course, be exaggerated. The very urgency of the military situation concentrated minds on the dangers ahead. There were daily reports of German advances on the Continent: Dutch resistance was quickly overcome; the French Prime Minister Reynaud gloomily phoned Churchill in mid-May to say that 'the battle was lost'; and British troops were being pushed back relentlessly towards the Channel ports. The House of Commons gave an overwhelming vote of confidence to the new government and Churchill was soon rallying support with stirring rhetoric. All the same, the Prime Minister was conscious that the backing of many Tory MPs was conditional upon there being no direct clash involving the party leader. His sense of insecurity was further increased by the tendency of remaining critics to gravitate towards the one major figure left outside the ranks of the government, Lloyd George. Churchill feared that, if anyone, it was his former Liberal colleague who might rally support for the idea of a negotiated peace. In spite of his hectic schedule, the Prime Minister made concerted efforts to tempt Lloyd George into joining the administration. He met with little success, but the invitation was left open subject to the approval of Chamberlain. In a clear indication of his state of mind, Churchill confessed to Lloyd George that 'like you I have no party of my own. I have received a great deal of help from Chamberlain . . . I have joined hands with him, and must act with perfect loyalty.'[37]

What was more, Churchill's hold over his colleagues inside the government did not go unchallenged. With thousands of British troops stranded on the beaches around Dunkirk, the Prime Minister had to take seriously Lord Halifax's claim that peace terms should be considered so long as Britain's independence remained intact. The Foreign Secretary, who commanded much loyalty and respect in Conservative ranks, was highly critical of Churchill's 'frightful rot' about achieving total victory, and he alarmed the Prime Minister by threatening to resign on this point. Over the course of several days, arguments raged inside the War Cabinet, although these were little known at the time.[38] Halifax's view was that Britain must fight for its independence, but if the Empire could be safeguarded then with the war going so badly it might be worth pursuing negotiations for a settlement; the terms on offer were likely to be better than those available down the line. Churchill countered that if Britain joined the French on the 'slippery slope' of negotiation, national morale would collapse; Hitler's terms would put 'us completely at his mercy'. Any private doubts the Prime Minister entertained were cast aside when he appealed directly to ministers outside the War Cabinet, whom he met as a group for the first time on 28 May. Most of those present had served Chamberlain, but none resisted Churchill's exhilarating performance. The insistence that Britain would fight on whatever happened in France was made loud and clear. Hugh Dalton, Minister of Economic Warfare, summed up the reaction in his diary: 'He is quite magnificent. The man, and the only man we have, for this hour . . . There was a murmur of approval round the table, in which I think Amery, Lord Lloyd and I were loudest. Not much more was said. No one expressed even the faintest flicker of dissent . . . It is quite clear that whereas the Old Umbrella [Chamberlain] wanted to run very early, Winston's bias is all the other way.'[39]

Churchill's will-power prevailed over that of Halifax for the second time in a matter of weeks. But his respite could have been short-lived. If the evacuation of troops from Dunkirk were to prove disastrous, leaving the bulk of Britain's professional army in the hands of Hitler, it was difficult to see how the war could be continued, and talk of mediation would inevitably recur. As it was, large numbers made a miraculous escape, thanks to the combination of Hitler's decision to delay an attack, balmy weather conditions, the survival of a pier from which the majority embarked for home, and the skill of the navy and air force in defending the area around Dunkirk. With over 300,000 British and French troops returning safely – more than six times the number originally anticipated – not only did the evacuation rally public opinion to the view that Britain had the means to continue the war, it also isolated those who favoured a negotiated peace. Dunkirk was a deliverance for Churchill, just as it was for the British war effort. The cost had been high. Nearly 70,000 British troops had been killed and many more were captured; six British destroyers had been lost and 475 tanks were left behind as part of the great mass of equipment lost in the French campaign. On 4 June Churchill told the House of Commons that it would be wrong to assign to 'this deliverance the attributes of a victory'. But in what became one of his most famous speeches the Prime Minister could more confidently strike his chosen note of defiance, couched in terms of reviving a glorious past: 'we shall fight on the beaches, we shall fight on the landing grounds, we shall fight in the fields and in the streets, we shall fight in the hills; we shall never surrender.' An apocryphal story developed that Churchill muttered, during a pause in his peroration, that we would 'beat the bastards about the head with bottles: that's all we've got'. On 28 May he had outflanked his critics inside the government; a week later he took a large step in persuading the British people that there was still hope, that it might not all end in defeat.[40]

There was still some way to go before Churchill was fully secure as war leader. National relief about the 'triumph' of the evacuation was rapidly overtaken by a more ominous reaction – the desire to find scapegoats. In taking up complaints of the returning soldiers that the Allied campaign in France had been a shambles, sections of the press embarked upon what became known as the 'attack on the appeasers'. The *Daily Herald* led the way: in a series of stinging editorials, responsibility for the retreat of British forces was placed squarely on the shoulders of the 'men of Munich', notably Chamberlain and Kingsley Wood, who were urged to resign immediately. Some of these complaints were taken up at Westminster, by critics such as Lloyd George and by junior Tory ministers recently brought into office, such as Harold Macmillan and Bob Boothby, who were anxious to improve the speed and efficiency of government decision-making. As discontent mounted, Chamberlain decided to take matters into hand. Convinced that Lloyd George was behind much of the agitation and was 'waiting to inflict a mortal blow on me', the Lord President received confirmation from Margesson as Chief Whip that a major intrigue was building up. As the central target of the various attacks, he determined to seek assurances about his future from the Prime Minister or else resign.[41]

Churchill opposed all demands for recrimination. In the first place, he clearly valued Chamberlain's administrative contribution on the home front; during his frequent visits to France he would politely ask Neville to 'mind the shop'. The Prime Minister was, as a result, prepared to give sympathetic reassurances, though he did at the same time play upon Chamberlain's vulnerability by taking the opportunity to reopen the question of Lloyd George joining the government. The Lord President now agreed to drop his opposition to this idea, subject to the press campaign for his removal being called off. Within days, Churchill had taken steps to ensure that attacks on the 'old gang' were silenced. His interview with Cecil King, director of one of the most critical newspapers, the *Daily Mirror*, highlighted his thinking. Churchill told him that Chamberlain's supporters, 'however unrepresentative of feeling in the country, had to be reckoned with as the ultimate source of power for the duration. If [he] trampled on these men, as he could trample on them, they would set themselves against him, and in such internecine strife lay the Germans' best chance of victory . . . No, he was not going to run a Government of revenge.'[42] The Prime Minister, in short, had no choice but to defend his predecessor. Chamberlain's offer to resign, which was turned down on 8 June, was certain to divide Tory loyalties and provide a fresh focus for discontent; there were grounds for thinking that if Chamberlain went he would soon be followed by others.

With the French army on the verge of collapse, attacks on Chamberlain continued for a while in Parliament, if not in the press. The Prime Minister, told that junior ministers such as Macmillan were pressing for a remodelled War Cabinet, angrily let them know that 'if there is any more of this nonsense they will go'.[43] On 18 June Churchill prepared the nation for bad tidings with his 'finest hour' speech which, with one eye on American opinion, made clear Britain's determination to fight on alone if necessary. 'The whole fury and might of the enemy must soon be turned upon us,' he said; 'Hitler knows that he will have to break us in this island or lose the war.' At the time, the call to 'brace ourselves to our duties' in order that if the Empire lasted for a thousand years, 'men will stay say, "This was their finest hour"' stirred the public, listening on wireless sets to a recording, more than it did the House of Commons, where tensions remained high. Some MPs were not persuaded by Churchill's warning against the 'pernicious process' of attributing blame for the present situation; one shouted to Chamberlain across the floor of the House that 'you ought to be ashamed to come here'.[44] The Prime Minister, moreover, was still receiving a cool response from the majority of Conservative MPs, resentful of Labour and Tory 'rebel' influence in the coalition. As Hugh Dalton wrote in his diary: 'There is some danger in this situation, and it must he watched. One very obvious conclusion is that we must not push the Old Man out of the Government, for he would then become a centre of disaffection and a rallying point for real opposition. Leave him where he is, as a decaying hostage.'[45]

In the event, a month of intense agitation at Westminster failed to dislodge the Conservative leader. 'The attack on Neville and the "men of Munich" comes to nothing,' Lord Beaverbrook wrote to a friend on 6 July.[46] But the 'attack on the appeasers' was to have lasting consequences. In one way, the continuing influence of the Chamberlainite Tories had been highlighted. The reality of parliamentary arithmetic, after all, was at the base of Churchill's insistence that he would stand or fall by the new government. As Rab Butler put it, if the various intrigues were taken any further, 'all we have to do is to pull the string of the toy dog of the 1922 Committee and make it bark. After a few staccato utterances it becomes clear that the Government depends upon the Tory squires for its majority.'[47] On the other hand, Conservative MPs themselves, still reeling from the shock of Chamberlain's downfall, were slow to come to terms with the coalition. They remained on the defensive and proved incapable of preventing permanent damage being done to the reputation of the 'men of Munich'. This process was underlined by the publication of the bestselling satirical pamphlet *Guilty Men*, co-authored by the young left-wing journalist Michael Foot, which clearly struck a chord with the public. In subsequent opinion polls a high percentage of those questioned favoured Chamberlain's removal from the government.[48] The alleged responsibility of Chamberlain for Britain's plight in 1940 was a theme that was to reverberate throughout the war years and beyond.

More immediately, Churchill's authority was strengthened. His hold over the government had increased at Chamberlain's expense, both because of the unpopularity of the 'old gang' and because the Lord President was showing signs of a serious illness that was to result in his death within a matter of months. Nor was there much to fear from critics of the government. By giving such a strong lead, the Prime Minister succeeded in marginalizing those who still favoured a negotiated peace. After the fall of France, there were noticeably fewer efforts to entice Lloyd George into the fold. He had turned down the latest offer, Churchill concluded, and would now be left alone. What was more, the Prime Minister's parliamentary base had become more stable following remarkable scenes in the House of Commons in early July. Chamberlain had been warned by a financial journalist, Paul Einzig, that the lukewarm attitude of Tories towards Churchill was conveying a poor impression of British unity abroad, especially in the United States. Fearing that vital American support might be jeopardized, the Lord President helped to orchestrate a greater show of enthusiasm from Conservative MPs. On 4 July Churchill informed the House that the French fleet had been attacked in North Africa in order to prevent it falling into German hands; over a thousand lost their lives, more than in any single engagement with the Germans so far. Tory backbenchers rose in unison to give prolonged cheers for the Prime Minister. Margesson, the Chief Whip, later denied organizing such a response, though, as one observer present recalled, the speech was no better than several others and 'the occasion – the outbreak of hostilities with our old ally – hardly one for rejoicing'.[49] The hatchet had by no means been buried, and the mutual distrust between Churchill and the party was in many ways to persist throughout the war. But the Tory establishment had at last recognized that the national interest was paramount.

By July 1940, Churchill had become what he was not when he first came to power – a leader of unrivalled authority. For several weeks after the fall of France, a German invasion was in the forefront of people's minds. The 'great invasion scare', the Prime Minister noted on 12 July, was concentrating minds enormously. During August the Luftwaffe began its attempt to establish aerial supremacy over Britain as an essential prerequisite of invasion; it was only later, in the autumn, that Hitler turned to massive bombing raids on the major cities in an attempt to undermine civilian morale. With the might of Nazi Germany directed exclusively against the British, the sense of national unity and determination to survive was greatly heightened. In these circumstances the Prime Minister was reaching a pinnacle of popularity, his approval rating standing at nearly 90 per cent of those questioned by Gallup. His indispensability was all the more obvious after it became clear that Chamberlain's health was deteriorating. The Lord President left the Cabinet for an operation at the end of July, and although he was able briefly to return to office in September he confided in his diary that any likelihood of 'further political activity, and even a possibility of another Premiership after the war, have gone'. Churchill had real fears about Chamberlain's imminent resignation, which he felt might upset the balance and effectiveness of the government. But he could not be oblivious to the implications for his own personal authority. 'There are,' he wrote to a colleague on 30 July, 'no competitors for my job now.'[50]

Winston's Churchill's ascendancy, we might conclude, was not the result of him 'walking with destiny', as he later described it. With less arrogance and more foresight, Neville Chamberlain could have survived the Norway debacle; he might equally have engineered the succession of his close confidant, Lord Halifax. It is quite conceivable, in other words, that there might have been no Churchill premiership in the summer of 1940. With either Chamberlain or Halifax in charge, a negotiated peace was at least on the cards; Britain's 'finest hour' might have become its 'darkest hour'. Nor was Churchill unassailable from the moment he crossed the threshold of Number Ten. Without a firm party base, and conscious that British forces were desperately ill-equipped, he told the American President Roosevelt in June that his was not the only possible administration in Britain – others with less resolve continued to wait in the wings. The consolidation of Churchill's authority also owed much to the unexpected departure of Chamberlain, which removed the acute conflict of loyalty facing Tory supporters since the Norway debate. In October 1940 Churchill was able to accept the Conservative leadership, and shortly afterwards he felt secure enough to dispatch Lord Halifax to Washington, charged as British Ambassador with the task of persuading Roosevelt to join the war. Reluctant to go, the misery of the aristocratic Edward Halifax was compounded by facing Americans who insisted on calling him 'Ed'. At the end of the year it was an American journalist, Ralph Ingersoll, who asked several leading politicians in London who it was felt would become Prime Minister in the event of Churchill succumbing to a stray German bomb. 'Nobody,' the journalist recorded, 'had any idea.'[51]

To say that things could have turned out differently, and that the reality of British politics was more messy than it appears with hindsight, is not to debunk the whole experience of 1940. Critics of Churchill have been able to make telling points. His was a flawed, egotistical personality, and his policy of no surrender was based on instinct as much as logical reasoning; he was incorrect to tell colleagues, as he did in May, that it was worth continuing the fight because America would soon enter the war or because the German war economy was likely to collapse. But in the final reckoning Churchill's achievement cannot be gainsaid. If it was America and Russia that ultimately *won* the war, in 1940 it was Britain that refused to *lose* it. There is little reason to doubt Churchill's view that Hitler's terms for peace would have left Britain humiliated, nor his assertion that with Nazi supremacy Western civilization would have 'sunk into the abyss of a New Dark Age'. The continuation of the war and of British parliamentary democracy would not have been possible without Winston Churchill, the bulldog fighter of popular imagination but also much more: a skilful politician surviving in the most adverse of circumstances, galvanizing the war machine and inspiring a nation to resist by 'mobilizing the English language' or, as Isaiah Berlin put it, speaking to the British people 'as no one ever has before or since'.[52] This is why, sixty years on, biographies continue to appear with titles such as *Churchill: A Study in Greatness*. Britain's 'finest hour' witnessed, quite simply, the single most impressive act of political leadership in the twentieth century.[53]

'The turn of the tide'
El Alamein and Beveridge, 1942–3

Now this is not the end. It is not even the beginning of the end.
But it is, perhaps, the end of the beginning.

Churchill's speech at the Mansion House, London, 10 November 1942

Beveridge is a sinister old man, who wishes to give away
a great deal of other people's money.

Tory minister Rab Butler on his party's view of the Beveridge Report

In the summer of 1945 Winston Churchill looked forward confidently to election victory, to reaping the benefit of presiding over the final defeat of Nazi Germany. Among politicians and political commentators it was widely anticipated that, with the break-up of the wartime coalition, Britain's revered war leader would sweep back to power at the head of a new Conservative administration, just as Lloyd George had triumphed in 1918 as 'the man who won the [Great] war'. Few believed the public would prefer Labour's low-key leader, Clement Attlee – 'Clem the Clam', as the King called him. The best Labour could hope for, it was said, was to improve its standing since the last election, held in 1935, when the party trailed the Tory-dominated National government by a massive margin. But the pundits were wrong. In 1945 Labour famously won a landslide victory, securing nearly half the popular vote and capturing 393 seats, compared with 213 for the Conservatives. In one of the most seismic upsets in modern electoral history, Labour won scores of constituencies across the country, such as Winchester and Wycombe, that had never before returned a Labour member to the House of Commons. As Churchill licked his wounds, Attlee – looking 'very surprised indeed', according to the King – accepted the royal invitation to form an administration, the first Labour government with a clear majority over all other parties combined. The new Prime Minister was not the only one who was taken aback. 'But this is terrible,' a lady diner at the Savoy Hotel was overheard saying, *'they've* elected a Labour government, and *the country* will never stand for that!'[1]

It has long been recognized that a variety of factors contributed to the Conservative defeat in 1945. Neville Chamberlain's downfall in May 1940 was a crucial first blow, providing Labour with an opportunity to demonstrate its electoral credibility through participation in the coalition. The Conservatives also suffered from the implications of the 'people's war'. In the First World War the prevailing ethos on the home front and among the forces was that of service to King and Country, but after 1939 it was widely believed that Hitler was being resisted in the interests of the ordinary citizen. In an atmosphere of upheaval caused by German bombing, mass movements of population and industrial conscription, social distinctions began to break down and the demand for equality of sacrifice became intense. Although it is easy to exaggerate the degree of social levelling that took place in what remained a highly stratified society, the trend towards egalitarianism was a powerful one. In the words of Paul Addison, author of the seminal work *The Road to 1945*, it was a time when Colonel Blimp – David Low's reactionary cartoon creation who represented the 'old gang' – found himself 'pursued through a land of Penguin specials' by the likes of J. B. Priestley, the Yorkshire novelist and playwright who daringly suggested in a series of radio broadcasts that there could be no going back to the social conditions of the 1930s.[2] Even so, the idea of a 'people's war' tells only part of the story. The single most important moment on the road to 1945, it will be argued here, the point at which Tory credibility was undermined irretrievably in the eyes of the electorate, came in early 1943 and was tied up with the government's response, or rather lack of it, to the publication of the Beveridge Report, the harbinger of the post-war welfare state.

Ironically the Beveridge episode, which is explored in the latter part of this chapter, came in the immediate aftermath of what might be called Churchill's second 'finest hour'. The widening of the conflict to a global scale in 1941 marked a crucial moment in the history of the war. With the vast economic and military resources of the Russians and Americans behind the Allied cause, Britain could, after its year of standing alone, be confident of ultimate victory. But British military success was slow in coming. At a time when expectations had been raised, news of continued defeats was doubly difficult to bear and led to a host of tensions inside the coalition. In the event, criticism of the government's war policy disappeared with the 'turn of the tide' at the end of 1942. The Prime Minister's leadership was finally vindicated – and made secure for the rest of the war – by General Montgomery's victory at El Alamein in North Africa, which was soon followed by news of successful Soviet resistance around Stalingrad. On 10 November Churchill told the British people that these events marked not 'the beginning of the end' but perhaps 'the end of the beginning'. As a military forecast, this was quite correct. Henceforth the Axis powers were to be relentlessly pushed back in all theatres of the war. What Churchill did not realize was that the critical months over the winter of 1942–3, while securing his place as war leader for the duration, were also to mark the 'beginning of the end' for his prospects of re-election.

Contrary to popular mythology, Churchill did not remain unchallenged as war leader after his heroics in 1940; indeed, during 1942 his leadership came under serious threat. In order to appreciate why this was so, we first need to understand the decline of his authority after the 'finest hour'. In early 1941 any criticism of the

Prime Minister was muted and ineffective. But the patience of Parliament and the press was tested as military failure became a familiar theme. On top of the horrors of the Blitz and unremitting shipping losses in the Atlantic, British forces were pushed onto the defensive in North Africa and the Balkans. Criticism intensified in the spring of 1941 when defeat in Greece was followed by evacuation from Crete. In some of the fiercest fighting of the war, 13,000 Allied troops were killed as the Germans launched an airborne assault on the island; another 16,000 were evacuated, with the British Expeditionary Force (BEF) acquiring the new nickname of 'Back Every Friday'. At Westminster, it became increasingly difficult to give the Prime Minister the benefit of the doubt. 'On all sides,' wrote Tory MP Chips Channon in his diary on 6 June 1941, 'one hears increasing criticism of Churchill. He is undergoing a noticeable slump in popularity and many of his enemies, long silenced by his personal popularity, are once more vocal. Crete has been a great blow to him.'[3] Matters were not helped by the Prime Minister's evident disdain for any form of criticism, however well intentioned. Churchill's attitude – encapsulated by the remark to his secretary after one episode that he 'didn't give a damn what the House thought as there was a bloody war on' – was resented in Parliament as a repetition of one of Chamberlain's worst failings, arrogance.[4]

The slow sea change in political opinion continued after Hitler's attack on the Soviet Union in the summer of 1941. The Prime Minister's immediate declaration of support for the Soviets helped to bolster his public popularity. But at the same time, with the burden of resistance to Hitler shifting away from Britain, critics of the government felt less inhibited in voicing their concerns, particularly over the handling of war production. Taken as a whole, there was a perceptible change in the political atmosphere during 1941. The *Economist*, in summing this up, made the case that the instinctive unity of 1940 had been lost; criticism among MPs had become more widespread than at any time since the fall of Chamberlain and, in spite of Churchill's immense popularity, the government had been forced onto the backfoot.[5] Nor, in a similar vein, was the Prime Minister's cause helped in the short term by America's entry into the war in December 1941, following the Japanese attack on Pearl Harbor. Instead of bringing a sudden change in war fortunes, it was followed by a series of disastrous military setbacks, with the Japanese threatening to overrun the British Empire in the Far East. The pressure for change was taken up by Chamberlainite Tories at Westminster and became so irresistible that within weeks Churchill was forced to carry out, against his wishes, the most far-reaching government reshuffle since the formation of the coalition.

In early February 1942 the Prime Minister hoped that limited changes in personnel would settle jittery nerves in the House of Commons. To this end, he had already offered the post of Minister of Supply to Sir Stafford Cripps, the recently returned British Ambassador to the Soviet Union. Cripps, a maverick upper-class socialist, was to play a crucial role in the political events of the next few months. He had been serving in Moscow since 1940 and so escaped responsibility for the shortcomings of the coalition. In spite of his association with left-wing extremism in the 1930s, and his expulsion from the Labour Party for advocating a 'popular front' against fascism, Cripps was widely acclaimed by much of the press as the new man of 1942. He arrived back in Britain at a crucial moment in the war effort, his reputation enhanced by his part – much exaggerated – in cementing the Anglo-Soviet military alliance. Sir Stafford was regarded as an austere figure; he was, in the words of historian Angus Calder, 'a teetotaller and vegetarian, and somehow it showed'.[6] But in the circumstances of the moment this served to increase his public appeal, especially for those willing to contemplate further sacrifice if it would only bring an improvement in Britain's war fortunes.

Cripps could not help but be influenced by his astonishing reception; alongside his clear sense of public duty, he harboured the highest personal ambitions. After some thought, he declined to serve at the Ministry of Supply on the ground that this did not involve a seat in the War Cabinet. The Prime Minister had no particular regard for Sir Stafford: a 'lunatic in a country of lunatics', he had said of his role in the Soviet Union. But Churchill recognized that he was faced with a potential rival and did not take kindly to the rejection of his initial offer. According to Hugh Dalton's diary, he could be found 'ramping round denouncing Cripps with every kind of imprecation'.[7] After a powerful speech calling for closer Anglo–Soviet co-operation, surveys showed Sir Stafford making a serious impression on public opinion. Churchill, conscious of the danger of leaving Cripps outside the government where he might rally dissident opinion, was soon looking for ways to 'enlarge the bait' in order to bring him into office.[8]

Pressure on the Prime Minister continued to build as news of fresh military defeats came through. Opinion in the Commons was greatly unsettled when it was confirmed that Japanese advances had resulted in the capture of Singapore, forcing the surrender of thousands of troops in what Churchill later described as the 'greatest disaster in British military history'. Calls by MPs for Churchill either to reduce his own burden of work or else to carry out a reshuffle could no longer be ignored, and on 19 February the composition of a new War Cabinet was announced. Labour's deputy leader Arthur Greenwood was sacked; he had long been considered ineffectual as minister in charge of reconstruction. This move was balanced by the removal from the War Cabinet of the Tory Chancellor, Kingsley Wood, who did, however, remain at the Treasury. Most attention was given to the inclusion of Cripps, who accepted the posts of Lord Privy Seal and Leader of the House of Commons. In private, MPs in both main parties were not enthusiastic. Labour members, said one, felt 'they had been "had" over the dropping of Greenwood', while Tory MPs were alarmed by the exclusion of Kingsley Wood. For the most part, parliamentary opinion was agreed that the new War Cabinet should be given its chance to improve Britain's military fortunes. The full debate in Parliament on the fall of Singapore took place in an atmosphere of anticlimax, and the Conservative MP Beverley Baxter was overheard commenting on the ease with which the Prime Minister had satisfied his critics. 'Never,' he said, 'had so many bears been satisfied by the throwing of so few buns.'[9]

Opinion was divided as to whether the government changes would forestall any further criticism of Churchill's leadership. But, as the *Economist* observed, rarely in political history had the fortunes of an individual been so suddenly transformed: after being for so long an outcast, Cripps 'finds himself with the ball at his feet'.[10] Sir Stafford's first inclination was to run off with the ball. Within weeks of joining the government, he volunteered to go on a personal mission aimed at breaking the constitutional deadlock over Britain's future role in India, which had been made urgent by Japanese advances in the Far East. This decision was greeted with bewilderment in political circles because the promotion of Cripps had been intended to stimulate the war effort on the home front. In the absence of the Lord Privy Seal, critics and friends of the government alike pensively awaited further war news. For the time being, the Prime Minister remained on the defensive. Lord Hankey, one of those removed from office in the February reshuffle, wrote in a letter to Samuel Hoare in March 1942: 'One hears nothing but abuse of Winston wherever one goes – in Clubs, Government offices, Parliamentary lobbies, Fleet Street, private houses, and I am told even in the Services. Absolutely the only thing that keeps the Government in office is the difficulty of finding a successor to the Prime Minister . . . Cripps is the favourite, but he is a dark horse.'[11] The reputation of Cripps was not helped by his failure to persuade Indian leaders to accept British terms for independence. Nevertheless, after returning to England he continued to enjoy a reception in the Commons that equalled that accorded to the Prime Minister, and surveys carried out by the Ministry of Information showed him as the most credible likely successor to Churchill in the public mind after Anthony Eden, well ahead of Labour leaders such as Attlee and Morrison.

In the summer of 1942, with Cripps waiting in the wings, Churchill faced the most open challenge yet to his leadership. On 21 June the North African fortress of Tobruk, with its 30,000 Allied defenders, was captured by the Germans, sending shock waves through the political establishment. This unexpected loss, coming out of the blue after a period of sustained setbacks, provoked renewed doubts about the government's handling of the war. The Prime Minister, visiting the United States as the news filtered through, cannot have been encouraged by reports in the American press predicting the downfall of his government. In the House of Commons wild rumours circulated, and the prominent Tory MP Sir John Wardlaw-Milne declared his intention of moving a vote of no confidence in the government. In his capacity as chairman of the parliamentary Select Committee on National Expenditure, Wardlaw-Milne had become increasingly outspoken about the government's shortcomings in mobilizing the war economy. His decision to confront the Prime Minister openly on the floor of the House was prompted by his Select Committee's recent discovery of appalling deficiencies in tank manufacture. This, he believed, was decisively affecting the North African campaign. When he launched his attack on the government, he was confident of receiving support both from those who had never trusted Churchill and from members of the Select Committee.[12]

The intense unease in the Commons did not escape the attention of the Leader of the House. Cripps believed his moment had arrived. He urged one associate, Malcolm MacDonald, in Britain on leave from his duties as High Commissioner in Canada, to sound out members of the Cabinet about his possible succession to the leadership. He also felt emboldened to write to Churchill saying that 'something is wrong and should be put right without delay'. The Prime Minister reacted furiously to these strictures and there ensued what he later described, with masterful understatement, as a 'stern discussion' between the two men.[13] It soon became evident that Cripps had made his move prematurely. Many Chamberlainite Tories, still harbouring suspicions about

Churchill, favoured some further reduction in the Prime Minister's powers but few wanted the responsibility for a rerun of May 1940, especially as the most likely Tory alternative was the Foreign Secretary Anthony Eden, an equally distrusted figure because of his anti-Chamberlain record and what some considered an effete side to his personality. As one Tory MP acidly remarked, the nation wanted 'a Panzer Government, not a Pansy Government'.[14] The Labour Party also agreed not to press for a fresh investigation into armaments production, and the minority who urged support for the vote of censure were taken to task for rocking the boat by Labour ministers at a heated party meeting. With anger over Tobruk beginning to subside, the Prime Minister had less to fear than had initially seemed likely, though it was with the unexpected outcome of the famous Norway debate in mind that MPs packed into the House to hear Wardlaw-Milne propose his motion on 1 July.

The censure debate of July 1942 was over almost before it had begun. After some fifteen minutes of careful and well-received criticism during which he attacked production failings, Wardlaw-Milne made a celebrated faux pas. The suggestion that the King's brother, the Duke of Gloucester, be appointed Commander-in-Chief of Britain's armed forces provoked a remarkable outburst of sustained ironic cheering. 'I at once saw Winston's face light up,' reported Chips Channon; 'he knew that he was saved.' Although Wardlaw-Milne recovered his composure, the damage was irreparable. In the circumstances, it hardly mattered that Oliver Lyttelton, the Minister of Production, replying for the government, made what he admitted was 'a proper balls of it'.[15] The proceedings broke up in confusion in the early hours of the morning with two MPs coming to blows. The following day the fiery Labour MP for Ebbw Vale, Aneurin Bevan, made biting criticisms of the government, asking how long Churchill could go winning every debate but losing every battle. Bevan knew the outcome of the vote was no longer in doubt. The Prime Minister was sufficiently confident in winding up the debate that he managed to avoid any explanation for the disaster in Libya. The government defeated the motion of censure by 475 votes to twenty-five, with an estimated thirty to forty abstentions.[16]

The Tobruk debate was a resounding triumph for Churchill. He was fascinated to be told of a historical parallel: the minority vote of twenty-five exactly equalled that registered against William Pitt in 1799 after a similarly protracted series of British military defeats. On closer inspection, there were causes for concern. The Prime Minister was aware that the mishandling of the censure motion had persuaded many waverers, notably members of the Select Committee, to rally behind the government. In view of the disastrous mistake made by Wardlaw-Milne, the real surprise was that as many as twenty-five backbenchers were prepared to go into the opposition lobby. Churchill was also fortunate in that the supporters of the censure motion, spread across the parties, lacked any strong sense of unity. Nor, in spite of the vote of confidence, had the doubts of large numbers of MPs been overcome. The Tory backbencher Cuthbert Headlam, who supported the Prime Minister, wrote in his diary that never before 'have so many Members entered a division lobby with so many reservations in their minds'.[17] In this light, the Tobruk debate had only provided the government with a further breathing space. Churchill's Parliamentary Private Secretary was convinced that unless Britain's military fortunes improved dramatically over the next few months, the writing was on the wall.[18]

The political uncertainty that had dogged Churchill since the beginning of the year came to a head in the autumn of 1942. This was the moment when he faced the almost unthinkable: the prospect of falling from power. During August the Prime Minister was out of the country, reorganizing the Allied High Command in the Middle East, making General Montgomery head of the Eighth Army, and informing Stalin that there would be no Second Front in Europe for the foreseeable future. Britain's military strategy – and Churchill's political future – was instead tied up with the fate of Operation Torch, a joint Anglo-American operation designed to push back the German commander, Erwin Rommel, who had advanced to within sixty miles of Alexandria in Egypt. After tough talks, Churchill persuaded President Roosevelt that North Africa, the only place where Britain had a large land force, was the best arena in which to strike hard at the Germans, although the Prime Minister was not confident about the ability of British commanders to launch a counterattack. At one point he said caustically: 'We'd better put an advertisement in the paper, asking for ideas.' Walter Elliot, a senior Tory backbencher, noted in a radio broadcast that Parliament was loath to rise for its annual holiday in August. 'For nobody,' he declared, 'likes the way that things are shaping. Rommel dug in at El Alamein – the Japs reaching up the mountains in New Guinea – and in Russia, the Germans developing a thrust which . . . bids fair to carry them to the Caspian.'[19] But familiar obstacles continued to lie in the path of parliamentary critics. In particular, how could disparate opposition groups be brought together and who could replace the Prime Minister?

Stafford Cripps continued to think he could. Over the summer recess a series of dinners was arranged with the aim, according to Rab Butler, of enabling Sir Stafford to improve his standing among Conservative MPs. At these, Cripps aired his view that the Prime Minister would be pushed aside in due course, lacking as he did any real understanding of the home front. Thereafter, he envisaged a joint government headed by Eden, the Minister of Production Oliver Lyttelton and himself. The Lord Privy Seal was equally open about his ambitions among Labour supporters. During August he was reported to be discussing with family and friends whether he should resign from office, thereby leaving himself free to rally opposition and to voice openly his concerns about coalition policy, in terms of both strategy and what he saw as a lack of genuine commitment to post-war planning.[20] While public support for Cripps had declined from the dizzy heights of the spring, it remained unclear how much backing he could rely on in political circles; his own uncertainty on this point was reflected in the emphasis given in his speeches to the idea of a new centre party, based on progressive elements in both Labour and Conservative ranks. Cripps continued, nevertheless, to figure prominently in speculation about the future. One Labour MP voiced the opinion that the Prime Minister was being left 'high & dry' by successive military defeats and would not be saved by the loyalty of Cabinet colleagues unless matters improved. Of the alternatives, he added, Tory distrust of Eden was still likely to 'bring Cripps to the top'.[21]

When asked years later to reflect on his most anxious period of the war, Churchill did not refer, as might have been expected, to the danger of invasion in 1940 but pointed without hesitation to the months September and October 1942. Certainly, when Parliament reassembled briefly in early September, the Prime Minister was given a rough ride. He was not well received when outlining his negotiations in the Middle East and Moscow, and was caught off guard by an open call for his resignation from Aneurin Bevan. At this stage, the pressure on Churchill was temporarily relieved by a remarkable misjudgement on the part of the Leader of the House. When the Prime Minister finished speaking the following day, MPs left the chamber in large numbers for lunch. Hugh Dalton, taking up the story, noted that 'Cripps – silly ass – instead of saying that this shows the House is completely satisfied . . . preaches a priggish sermon on the duty of MPs to stay and talk. He is rapidly losing all that is left of his "mystique".'[22] Feelings about the intervention of Cripps ran high in all parts of the House. The 1922 Committee responded by making a formal complaint to the Chief Whip, asserting that the prestige of Parliament had been impaired. Labour members were equally angered. One bluntly voiced a common view: that a man who lunched 'on two nuts & half a carrot' had no right to upbraid others for their eating habits. The prospects for Cripps looked less rosy than earlier in the year, although Ministry of Information surveys still found that public reaction to his plain speaking was favourable.[23]

In spite of this episode, the Lord Privy Seal decided to act on his misgivings. He wrote to the Prime Minister detailing a list of concerns that, he said, if not remedied would lead to his resignation; chief among these were the demand for a remodelling of the machinery for handling the war effort to include a War Planning Directorate, and the need for a bold programme of social reconstruction.[24] Cripps did agree, after persuasion from colleagues, to delay his resignation at least until the outcome of the impending battle in North Africa became known. In early October Churchill told Eden that if Operation Torch turned out to be a failure he would be 'done for'. This pessimism was shared by his friend Brendan Bracken, who believed the Prime Minister 'must win his battle in the desert or get out'. When asked whether this exaggerated the position, he retorted that if Cripps 'pulls out, there'll be a hell of a row'. The prospect of a leading minister – and potential rival – resigning in the wake of another military defeat made Churchill more than usually anxious as he awaited news from the battlefront. Was there not one general, he asked in frustration, who could be relied on to deliver a victory?[25]

At first, reports from North Africa were far from encouraging. The Allies had a two to one superiority in men and four to one superiority in tanks and artillery, yet had six times more men killed and wounded than the Germans and Italians. For several days Montgomery's frontal assault was stuck. But finally, in early November, it became clear that British troops had broken through and were overwhelming the Germans. Rommel, outnumbered and outgunned, began to retreat westwards. In terms of military significance, this victory was dwarfed by the success of a massive Soviet counterattack at Stalingrad which began on 19 November and resulted in the German Sixth Army being surrounded by Zhukov's forces. But El Alamein had a decisive and immediate impact on British politics. For the first time in over a year, the Prime Minister could face the Commons confident that there was, as he put it, 'some sugar on the cake'. Critics of the 'higher direction of the war', Hugh Dalton noted, had suddenly sunk out of sight and mind. 'Crazy Cripps,' he went on, 'will have to think again about the prospect of the P.M. falling from power and find some new excuse for his own resignation from the Government.'[26] In the event, resignation was not necessary. Two weeks later Churchill carried out a small ministerial reshuffle: Cripps was removed from the War Cabinet and sent reluctantly to the Ministry of Aircraft Production. The political crisis of 1942 was over.

An obvious question arises from a consideration of the events of 1942: could Winston Churchill have been toppled? The fall of Neville Chamberlain – after only one major reversal in the Norway campaign – resulted from a minority of Conservative MPs deciding to switch their allegiance. For as long as military victory evaded British forces Churchill, like his predecessor, would be vulnerable to even small shifts in parliamentary opinion. As the political atmosphere became more and more highly charged with news of defeat in 1942, so disaffection spread again through Tory ranks: orthodox Chamberlainites, leading peers and Wardlaw-Milne's Select Committee followers all came to have grave doubts, further exacerbated by Churchill's dictatorial style of leadership. The coalition did, it was true, have an extra cushion provided by Labour backing, but this had to be balanced against the possibility of the government coming to grief over a domestic, inter-party controversy. It was in recognition of these underlying realities that the Prime Minister pointed in hindsight to the autumn of 1942 as his most anxious months of the war. The Labour minister Chuter Ede, looking back at the end of the year, commented that after Tobruk 'misgivings were profound' and were not eased by the months of stagnation that followed. 'This apparent inaction,' he added, 'further tried our faith. Had anyone seen an alternative to Churchill the Government would have fallen.'[27]

One of the dominant assumptions of British politics in 1942 is that Churchill was indispensable. Shortly before the Tobruk debate, Chips Channon wrote that 'there *is* nobody else – if only Mr Chamberlain was alive. Many a member who voted against him would now willingly withdraw his vote.'[28] Chamberlain's death, in late 1940, eased Churchill's rise to untrammelled power, though on closer inspection the idea of indispensability could be a double-edged sword. Neville Chamberlain was considered irreplaceable by his own supporters for much of his premiership, whereas Churchill was widely distrusted by the political classes before he assumed the reins of power. In this sense, the shortcomings of Cripps were unimportant, or at least must be balanced against his potential – untested in the event – to take over as an alternative leader committed to new departures abroad and at home. Cripps had no firm party base, but then neither had Churchill before May 1940; and although public enthusiasm for Cripps had waned as he became more identified with the policies of the government, he was still receiving – again like Churchill in 1939 – backing from sections of the press including the editorial columns of the *Times*. The Prime Minister did not believe that Cripps posed a negligible threat, and was conscious that as Britain came to rely more and more on her major allies the notion of his own indispensability was losing ground. The major coalition partners may, of course, have stuck to Churchill even in the event of defeat in North Africa. But it was widely believed that, in concert with the Soviets and Americans, Hitler would ultimately be defeated. The issue at stake, therefore, was how long political opinion in Britain would tolerate defeat on the battlefield before forcing some further change, whatever the consequences.

Although the Prime Minister's war leadership was never again to be questioned after El Alamein, he was powerless to prevent a burgeoning debate, at many different levels of British society, about the shape of the post-war world. Churchill, preoccupied as he was with matters military, believed that discussion about reconstruction was irrelevant until the Nazi menace had been defeated; it was also, he felt, undesirable because it was likely to stimulate further party hostilities. Even so, by the end of the year he could no longer stem the tide. As soon as military victory looked more certain, whatever the timescale involved, it was inevitable that a new phase in the history of the coalition would begin. Instead of military strategy and war production – the themes that had held sway since May 1940 – national attention began to turn to consideration of the domestic future. That this happened so rapidly after the victory at El Alamein, and with such intensity as to set a clear pattern for the remainder of the war years, was due in no small measure to one man – Sir William Beveridge.

After the publication of the Beveridge Report in December 1942, 'reconstruction' – the rebuilding of Britain after the war – became the central theme of British politics. The report has long been seen as a vital turning point in economic and social policy. According to this view, during the second half of the war Churchill's government took up Beveridge's ideas by accepting the goal of full employment, comprehensive social security, a national health service, and improved education and housing. The reforming instincts of the coalition have become deeply embedded in writing about the war years, from Paul Addison's notion of a new consensus emerging between left and right through to Correlli Barnett's lament that the opportunity for wholesale industrial regeneration was lost. 'Instead,' Barnett concludes, 'all the boldness of vision, all the radical planning, all the lavishing of resources, had gone towards working the *social* miracle of the New Jerusalem.'[29] This interpretation has been challenged by revisionist historians, who note that the coalition programme promised more than it delivered. Wartime welfare reforms were not as far-reaching as often supposed, in part because deep-seated differences continued to exist between the main coalition partners. In other words, the idea of a wartime consensus sits uneasily with the strongly partisan disagreement between the Tories and Labour which intensified as the war progressed.[30]

Until the end of 1942 reconstruction struggled to push its way up the political agenda. In this phase of the war the Prime

Minister was, in Hugh Dalton's words, 'allergic to post-war policy'.[31] But there were increasing demands for action. The devastation by bombing of many towns and cities, food shortages and rationing, and the curtailment of leisure and entertainment that came with the familiar ritual of the blackout all caused resentment and led to widespread interest in the need to plan and rebuild for a brighter future. Sections of the press, as well as a multitude of pressure groups, mounted an unofficial campaign designed to promote the cause of a better Britain, one that would 'never again' have to live with the depression and mass unemployment associated with the 1930s. Circulation of the populist *Daily Mirror* was rising sharply, and even establishment papers such as the *Times* joined in, running editorials that attacked 'social and economic privilege' and backed the need for an 'equitable distribution' of resources in the new economic order.

The government was not oblivious to the mood for reform. Planning for change did begin in various parts of Whitehall during 1941–42. But in each case progress was painfully slow. In education, for example, the incumbent Conservative minister was removed in 1941 after publicizing proposals for the reform of schools which had been rejected before the war. The new minister, Rab Butler, was chosen primarily because he seemed less likely to depart from Churchill's injunction that the education department should stick to the task at hand, evacuation. '"You will move poor children from here to here,"' Churchill told Butler, 'and he lifted up and evacuated imaginary children from one side of his blotting pad to the other; "this will be very difficult."'[32] Before the turn of the tide, there was no overall sense of direction or urgency in government planning for reconstruction. The only common theme was the lack of measures that might actually reach the statute book.

Reconstruction planning was constrained not simply by Churchill's hostility to it but also by party differences. The absence of any major initiatives in the first two years of coalition reflected the mood of the Conservative majority in Parliament. Tory backbenchers were resentful of what they saw as the socialistic trend of wartime controls over the economy and were determined to limit, where possible, the influence of Labour ministers. For their part Labour MPs, reflecting the mood of the rank and file away from Westminster, grew increasingly impatient with what they saw as deliberate stonewalling over reconstruction. From mid-1942 onwards the parliamentary party was determined to exhort its representatives in government to secure more tangible results in social policy. In July more than fifty Labour MPs voted to condemn the latest changes to the pensions system – a level of anti-government protest that, if repeated too often, might endanger the continuation of the coalition.

In practical terms, given the composition of the government, Labour was in no position to seize the initiative. Conservatives remained in charge of key departments, in areas such as education and housing, and Attlee and his senior colleagues found themselves in a dilemma: pledged, on the one hand, to defend coalition policy, but forced to recognize, on the other, that sooner or later the Parliamentary Labour Party would demand substantive changes on the home front. The day of reckoning was brought closer once Britain's war fortunes began to show signs of improvement. At the end of 1942 one Labour minister warned privately that the party would create further trouble unless 'something on account' was provided in social policy, adding that Labour MPs feared a repetition of 'the 1918 trick' – keeping them in government until victory was assured and then pushing them out to restore pre-war standards.[33] The battle lines were becoming ever more obvious. In a debate on reconstruction in the autumn of 1942, Aneurin Bevan launched a stinging attack on his coalition partners: 'The British Army are not fighting for the old world. If the hon. Members opposite think we are going through this in order to keep their Malayan swamps, they are making a mistake.'[34] It was against this background that William Beveridge added his voice to the clamour for action.

It was not the original intention that the Beveridge Committee should produce a major blueprint for social reform. Beveridge, whose long career as a civil servant stretched back to the days of the Edwardian Liberal reforms, had been a leading critic of Chamberlain's economic war effort and was subsequently drafted into the Ministry of Labour to provide specialist advice on manpower and labour questions. Ernest Bevin, head of the ministry, soon grew tired of his restless and egotistical charge and decided in 1941 that the best way to occupy Beveridge was to offer him the chairmanship of what appeared to be a minor committee set up to investigate insurance benefits. Bevin telephoned his Labour colleague, Arthur Greenwood, responsible before his sacking for reconstruction policy: 'You remember this 'ere social security business? I've got just the man for you. I'm sending Beveridge round in the morning.'[35]

After recovering from this indignity, Beveridge sensed the opportunity to press for far-reaching reform. Within weeks he was using his personal domination of the new committee to sketch out radical proposals, much to the alarm of his Whitehall colleagues, who dissociated themselves from the eventual findings. Beveridge was not troubled that the report became tied to his name alone. Having cultivated press contacts to ensure wide publicity, his scheme was received with remarkable public acclaim. Apart from the *Daily Telegraph* (which said it would take Britain 'half way to Moscow'), the national press offered enthusiastic support. Beveridge's timing was impeccable. Publication in December 1942 coincided with the moment when improved war fortunes allowed the British people to look forward with real optimism for the first time since the outbreak of war. In total some 635,000 copies of the report were sold.

At the heart of the Beveridge Report was the call for a comprehensive system of social security based on subsistence rate benefits 'from the cradle to the grave'. What made the plan so wide-ranging was the claim that any system could be effective only if accompanied by a new health service and by full employment, though Beveridge left others to work out the details of these additional proposals. In hindsight, the report stands out as the central document in the foundation of Britain's post-war welfare state. But Beveridge's biographer, Jose Harris, has cautioned against exaggerating its significance. The importance of the report, she has shown, lay less in the originality of its ideas than in its successful synthesis and transmission of plans to rationalize the disjointed insurance schemes that existed before the war. Above all, the press and public reaction to the report was such that the coalition came under sustained pressure to give serious, rather than token, attention to the problems of reconstruction.[36]

The initial response of the government and the political parties at Westminster exemplified their attitudes towards social reform in the first half of the war. Among Conservative ministers the Chancellor, Kingsley Wood, as head of the department that had most distanced itself from Beveridge's ideas, spoke out strongly in Cabinet. He argued that no account had been taken in the report of the uncertain post-war economic situation, and that popular expectations might be raised beyond levels that could be satisfied. Labour ministers, in contrast, expressed support for the plan but were anxious that calls for immediate action might pose a threat to the unity of the coalition. The result was prevarication. The Cabinet agreed to welcome the report in principle but also to undertake its own detailed investigation. In the meantime there could be no question of legislation; given the uncertainty of the post-war situation, it was 'impossible at this stage to establish any order of priority or to enter into definite commitments'. This, Churchill told his Parliamentary Private Secretary, was as far as he was prepared to go, adding that the trouble with Beveridge was that he was 'an awful windbag and a dreamer'.[37] In January 1943 the Prime Minister's main priority was securing American agreement to a Mediterranean war strategy at the Casablanca conference; in his later war history he devoted more space to British invasion of Madagascar than he did to Beveridge.[38]

The government's compromise reflected party reactions to the report. With some minor reservations, Labour members responded enthusiastically to what amounted to a more detailed exposition of aims proposed by the party for many years. On the Conservative side Churchill's views – unlike on many issues – were similar to those of the Chamberlainite majority. A committee of Tory back-benchers submitted a secret report to the Prime Minister attacking the whole notion of social security. In the first place, the committee stressed that the major financial priority after the war must be the reduction of wartime levels of taxation, not the redistribution of income implied by the Beveridge scheme. Moreover, there were grave objections to the state assuming overriding responsibility in this area; the uniform provision of subsistence benefits, it was claimed, would undermine the national character by removing incentives to individual initiative.[39] In this way the Beveridge Report brought to the surface underlying tensions between left and right over the nature of the state and social policy. The government had been bounced by Beveridge into modifying its previous policy of playing down reconstruction. But at the same time Churchill had been forcefully reminded by Tory MPs, claiming to represent 90 per cent of backbenchers, that the majority party in the Commons was not prepared to concede ground. In these circumstances, it was not surprising that the government ran into trouble when the report was discussed in Parliament during February 1943.

At the start of the debate, it was intended that MPs would simply welcome the report in general terms as a suitable basis for future action. This approach was reluctantly accepted by most Conservatives, anxious not to be seen blocking a proposal that had such widespread public and press approval. Several spokesmen, however, while professing support, could barely conceal their animosity towards the report and the manner in which it had been produced. A group of Tory industrialists did, in fact, put down an amendment calling for the postponement of legislation, although this was not pressed after government spokesmen, especially Kingsley Wood, gave the strong impression that any such eventuality was unlikely before the end of the war. The party's negative attitude was offset to an extent by the first parliamentary appearance of the more progressive 'Tory Reform Committee', representing the remaining 10 per cent of backbench opinion, whose members urged a more positive approach to Beveridge reform. Tory reformers nevertheless lined up behind the majority of the party when it became clear that Labour members, alarmed by the Chancellor's speech, would press for the immediate introduction of legislation. For Labour, the whole episode sharpened the tension between ministers, who aimed to maximize concessions from within the coalition, and MPs, who were determined to make immediate reform the price of remaining in government. The result was that Labour's amendment calling for 'Beveridge now' produced the largest anti-government vote in the history of the coalition, with Labour ministers and backbenchers marching into different lobbies.[40]

For a short while, the continued participation of Labour in the coalition looked in doubt. A government created ostensibly as a symbol of national unity could not survive many such acts of defiance, and Labour ministers were particularly fearful of the consequences. What backbenchers failed to see, wrote Hugh Dalton in his diary, was that their refusal to support government policy posed the danger of Churchill calling a general election on the question of whether planning for peace was more important than winning the war, with the likely outcome that 'the Labour Party would be scrubbed out as completely as in 1931'.[41] This possibility gradually receded. The Parliamentary Labour Party, which received some stern lectures from Morrison and Bevin, eventually backed down and agreed to accept the government's undertaking to examine further the Beveridge plan. Labour's enthusiasm, in the heat of the moment, rebounded to an extent, although in the longer term, once the immediate crisis had passed, the parliamentary debate proved to have been a critical turning point underlining a wartime swing to the left in public opinion. James Griffiths, the mover of Labour's amendment, commented to Beveridge at the time that the division in the

Commons made the return of a Labour government after the war a certainty.[42]

Churchill's handling of events in early 1943 did indeed produce a long-lasting cynicism about Tory plans for reconstruction. The government's own soundings of popular feeling found that in nearly all parts of the country expectations were raised by the promises of the Beveridge Report. These were soon overlaid by anxiety that reform might never materialize, whether because of government attitudes, vested interests or financial considerations. After the parliamentary debate of February 1943 such anxiety increased. So-called 'Home Intelligence' investigators, working for the Ministry of Information, found that majority opinion deplored what was seen as the shelving of the report. Public feelings were said to vary from anger to despondency at this 'betrayal': 'Why,' it was asked, 'get Beveridge to make a plan at all, if you are going to turn it down?' Home Intelligence reports during the second half of the war were littered with references to scepticism about reconstruction plans, for which the government was squarely blamed.[43] Signs of Conservative unpopularity began to multiply. Opinion polls, although still in their infancy and not regarded as reliable by most politicians, gave Labour a lead of ten percentage points from 1943 onwards. Anti-Tory sentiment was also unmistakable at parliamentary by-elections, notably in early 1944 in West Derbyshire where a Conservative majority of 5000 was easily overturned by an 'independent socialist'.[44]

In spite of these signals, there was no substantive change in coalition policy on reconstruction. The Prime Minister continued to set his face against reform. It is true that in March 1943 Churchill devoted a major radio broadcast to what he called a 'four year plan', outlining his own vision of future economic and social recovery. But it would be misleading to interpret this, as some have, as the first popular proclamation of the new consensus, marking a return to Churchill's Liberal reforming days. The small print of the speech committed the Prime Minister to very little; he envisaged that the plan would begin to operate only when the war ended. Only days after the broadcast, Churchill conceded in a private interview that major legislation was unlikely. He greatly resented, he said, being constantly told about the need for post-war plans when 'we had nothing like won the war. People were always getting ahead of events.'[45] Another committee was established to consider further the government's reaction to the Beveridge plan, but the new machinery proved unwieldy in operation. Some Conservatives did try to create a more positive public image, and at the party's first wartime conference in 1943 Tory reformers were allowed to proceed with a resolution welcoming the Beveridge scheme. But in private little had changed. Several months on, Rab Butler could still be found commenting that there was within the party 'a feeling that Beveridge is a sinister old man, who wishes to give away a great deal of other people's money'.[46]

For the remainder of the war Churchill's government moved only tentatively towards the creation of a 'New Jerusalem'. A new ministry was eventually established and the coalition did outline some objectives for the future, in the shape of White Papers on key areas such as health and employment. This in itself was an advance on pre-war orthodoxy, but 'the White Paper chase' did not imply binding, irreversible commitments for the post-war world. Ideological differences between the parties were still so strong that there was no agreement either on the long-term aims of domestic policy or about the best way to proceed before the war ended. Apart from the 1944 Education Act, reconstruction barely proceeded beyond the planning stage. Much of the national press, having given a lead to the movement for social change, was soon resigning itself to the likelihood that legislation would not be achieved under Churchill, whatever might be said in radio broadcasts or public speeches. In a private letter Beveridge himself wrote in despair: 'It seems to me that any Government under Winston will not do more for social progress than they are driven to by opposition and peace-making.'[47] The reason for such inactivity was simple. Churchill's reputation as war leader made it impossible to believe that a Tory majority of over two hundred seats could be overturned, even if it were to be reduced. In early 1945 Conservative Central Office was still receiving information from agents across the country predicting a three-figure majority.[48] The Prime Minister and his party, anticipating election victory ahead, saw no reason to commit themselves to a brave new world in which they did not believe.

This analysis of the critical months between November 1942 and February 1943 leaves us with two intriguing possibilities. One is that if the outcome at El Alamein had been different, if Montgomery had been unable to break through, it was at least possible that the Prime Minister would have been forced from office. As we have seen, he considered himself to be highly vulnerable after a long series of military defeats. In this eventuality, Churchill's historical reputation would not have risen as it did to such exalted levels; historians would have balanced their accounts of the heroics of 1940 with the setbacks of 1941–42. The dividing line between success and failure was much narrower than the cosy 'walking with destiny' mythology implies. Good fortune in the desert, as well as his own instinct for survival, enabled Churchill to fend off his critics, securing his leadership for the rest of the war – as well as his place in the history books. But what of his part in the handling of reconstruction? If this had been dealt with more skilfully, could he have arrested the swing to the left that resulted in defeat at the polls in 1945? The second counterfactual possibility is that if the Prime Minister had embraced the Beveridge Report, rather than cold-shouldering it, he could have avoided such a stunning rebuff at the hands of the electorate.

It was the case that the Conservative Party had been on the defensive from the moment Neville Chamberlain fell from power. Tory MPs were unhappy with the experience of coalition and found themselves out of tune with the new mood of the 'people's war'. Yet too much importance should not be attached to shifting political attitudes in the early part of the war. Home Intelligence workers found in 1941 that while there was a strong feeling in favour of reducing class distinctions, there was also an 'absence of thought along conventional party lines' and few settled opinions about the expected complexion of Britain's first post-war government.[49] Any signs of Conservative unpopularity before the turn of the tide must also be set against the immense popularity of the Prime Minister. If the Tories had suffered from Chamberlain's appeasement, they had surely gained from Churchill's reputation as the national hero in 1940. Why, when eventually required to choose, would the electorate prefer a Labour alternative the leader of which, Clement Attlee, seemed uninspiring? In this light, the swing to the left before the end of 1942 was by no means irreversible. What made all the difference, deepening the Conservative malaise beyond recovery, was Churchill's shunning of the agenda for social change.

The crucial point, as the writer Tom Harrisson pointed out in the *Political Quarterly* in 1944, was that voters were capable of making a distinction between 'Winston the War Leader, Bulldog of Battle' and the Prime Minister who showed himself 'no man of peace, of domestic policy or human detail'.[50] It was possible to view Churchill, in other words, as a highly regarded war leader *and* as an unsuitable candidate for presiding over a return to peace – a striking reversal of Attlee's public persona. Some voters, of course, were attracted by Labour's positive appeal in 1945 – as a patriotic force, having served loyally in the coalition, and as the party that could best deliver welfare reform. But it would be wrong to exaggerate, as some have done in a misty-eyed way right through to the present day, the extent to which the war created genuine enthusiasm for 'socialism'. More important was the manner in which the Conservatives threw away the opportunity to shape and guide public expectations about the post-war world. Tory defeat in 1945 had much to do with the party's inability to ride with the tide of reconstruction, something for which the Prime Minister bore a large share of responsibility. If Churchill had used Beveridge to forge a popular post-war policy, or even simply had sounded more enthusiastic about the future, wartime suspicions about Conservative intentions might have been partially overcome. This is not to suggest that the Tories would have won in 1945, but it could have been a closer-run thing. As it was, the winter of 1942–3 set the course for victory in the war and for the Labour landslide, so explaining one of the major ironies of Britain's wartime experience: Winston Churchill was the man who both 'won the war' and 'lost the peace'.

3

'The end is Nye'
The demise of Attlee's government, 1951

It is really a fight for the soul of the Labour Party.

Hugh Gaitskell, Labour Chancellor, on his struggle with
Aneurin Bevan over health service charges

. . . the country has got rid of a party it does not want
in favour of one it does not trust.

The News Chronicle, *27 October 1951, on the outcome*
of the 1951 general election

The Attlee governments presided over a series of far-reaching
changes at home and abroad. In domestic affairs, attention
centred on the introduction of a welfare state and a 'mixed' economy of public and privately owned industries. Labour, as it was
constantly to remind voters in later elections, was the party of the
National Health Service. Overseas, these years witnessed the first
phase of a transition from Empire to Commonwealth, and saw
Britain reinforce its wartime relationship with the United States
in order to counter the emerging threat of Soviet expansionism.
Attlee was re-elected with a much reduced majority in 1950 and,
by the time his second, short-lived administration left office in
1951, Labour could claim much of the credit for a new political
order: a 'post-war settlement' that was to remain in place for a
generation to come. Judgements on the end result vary.
Sympathetic observers – and many party activists through to the

present day – believe this was Labour's 'finest hour', combining radicalism and reform, 'hope and public purpose'. Others have been less generous. Left-wing writers see the period as one of wasted opportunity. Instead of a real socialist transformation, fulfilling the hopes of 1945, Labour offered cautious change: insignificant redistribution of wealth together with a foreign policy that tied Britain to the militantly capitalist USA. Some critics writing in the 1970s and 1980s, when much of the post-war settlement unravelled, claimed that Britain took a 'wrong turning' in the aftermath of war. The powers of the state, they alleged, were extended too far, creating levels of social provision that were unsustainable in the long term.[1]

In a period of such momentous change, picking a single defining moment, especially one that marks an electoral turning point, is problematic. One event, however, more than any other shattered the prospect of an extended spell in power, the two full parliamentary terms that remained elusive until the era of 'New Labour': it came in April 1951 with the resignation of Aneurin Bevan, the 'architect' of the NHS. Bevan refused to accept proposals to introduce health service charges put forward by Attlee's third Chancellor of the Exchequer, Hugh Gaitskell, who argued that escalating NHS costs had to be curtailed and priority given to a massive rearmament programme necessitated by Britain's involvement in the Korean War. Bevan's departure was to have more impact on British politics than any other non–prime-ministerial resignation since the war (with the possible exception of Geoffrey Howe's decision to quit the Thatcher government in 1990). What occurred in April 1951 was a prelude not only to electoral defeat in the autumn but also to a period of crippling internal warfare in Labour ranks. The Bevan-Gaitskell dispute, which forms the centrepiece of this chapter, had elements of farce, with part of the clash taking place at Attlee's hospital bedside. It also had overtones of tragedy. In the words of John Campbell, Bevan's biographer:

At the heart of the matter was a real clash of political philosophies . . . Above all there was the rivalry of two contrasting personalities, with the turbulent hero finally brought down by his antagonist's cool exploitation of one fatal defect of character: in this respect Bevan's is a personal tragedy to compare with Antony's or Othello's. Finally there is the consequence: the Labour Party riven in two, doomed to waste itself in fractious opposition for half a generation, until both the principal protagonists were dead. Bevan's defeat was scarcely Gaitskell's victory. Between them they practically destroyed the thing that in their different ways they loved.[2]

It was ironic that Labour should come to grief over the resignation of a senior minister, for until the 1951 crisis broke the Attlee years had been characterized by resilient leadership and unprecedented unity at all levels of the Labour movement. The Prime Minister, as many have pointed out, was an unlikely figurehead to lead the nation in the post-war era. Peter Hennessy, the distinguished pioneer of contemporary history in Britain, wrote that when Attlee spoke, on the 'equivalent of the Richter scale for oratory, the needle scarcely flickered'.[3] Yet far from being 'a modest man with much to be modest about', as his critics alleged, Attlee's considerable inner confidence, the product of his middle-class background and public school training, grew as he showed himself to be a brisk and effective co-ordinator of government business. Those who worked with him were to reflect, as did Treasury minister Douglas Jay, that his combination of 'honesty, common sense and intelligence' made him the ideal foil for the powerful personalities around the Cabinet table.[4] Of his senior colleagues, Ernest Bevin, the Foreign Secretary, stood out. Bevin was hardly traditional Foreign Office material. The semi-literate son of a farm labourer, he was a domineering figure who had made his reputation as Britain's most powerful trade union leader between the wars. With his great physical presence and bullying manner, Bevin was a key influence in the 1945 government. Aside from his vital role in shaping British policy overseas, he helped to maintain trade union support for the government and flatly refused to have any truck with occasional challenges to the Prime Minister's leadership. Attlee and Bevin, both loners in their own ways, developed a relationship that was the closest either had in politics, and it was this alliance that dominated government proceedings until 1950.

The solidity of the Attlee–Bevin axis was a source of frustration for the minister who was third in the pecking order, Herbert Morrison. As the defeated candidate for the party leadership in 1935, Morrison continued to believe he would make a more effective, high-profile leader than Attlee. He was more media-friendly than either Attlee or Bevin although, as with his grandson Peter Mandelson fifty years later, this did not always work to his advantage. His opponents distrusted him as a machine politician, a 'chirpy cockney' more concerned with intrigue than with high policy. Yet Morrison, like Bevin, made an invaluable contribution to the 1945 administration. Appointed as Lord President of the Council and Leader of the House of Commons, his responsibilities ranged from co-ordinating domestic policy to maintaining the morale of the parliamentary party. It was Morrison who orchestrated the early introduction of a massive programme of nationalization, covering industries as diverse as coal, civil aviation, transport and electricity.[5] More broadly, Attlee was able to rely on a talented team of ministers, dominated by loyal and experienced stalwarts while including all shades of party opinion. The most vocal representative of the Labour left in the Cabinet was its youngest member, Aneurin Bevan, the charismatic Minister of Health. Although critical in private of the caution of his colleagues, Bevan was fully engaged in his ministerial duties and showed few signs of rocking the boat before 1951. With backbench revolts a rarity, unity of purpose was not a problem in the early Attlee years. The principal dark cloud on the horizon at this stage came from external economic forces – the prospect that the huge cost of the war might prevent Labour from carrying through its ambitious programme.

Britain had lost almost a quarter of its national wealth in the fight against Hitler. The national debt had increased threefold and British exports had fallen by two-thirds. Aided by the negotiation of a huge loan of $3.75 billion from the USA, ministers were nonetheless determined to press ahead with a full agenda of domestic reform. Much of the lead in the early days was taken by another powerful member of the inner Cabinet, Hugh Dalton, the ebullient old Etonian who, after serving in the wartime coalition, became Chancellor of the Exchequer. Dalton's radical instincts, and his overbearing manner, inspired great hostility on the opposition benches. In the war years Churchill had once been interrupted by loud bellowing from an adjacent room. 'It's Dalton speaking to Glasgow,' an official explained. 'Why doesn't he use the telephone?' asked Churchill. It was Dalton who consciously shaped economic policy to assist lower-paid families, most of whom were still suffering from the biting austerity associated with rationing and war shortages. Food subsidies were kept high in order to hold down living costs, taxation bit hardest on the better off, and regional policy was vigorously pursued to ensure that there was no return to mass unemployment in the pre-war industrial blackspots of the north and west. With the exception of a short period in 1947, unemployment was to remain at far lower levels than between the wars in spite of the return to the job market of millions of service personnel. Through the various difficulties that were to come, Labour's strongest claim on the loyalty of working-class voters was that it had become, in the words of Kenneth Morgan, author of the first full-length historical study of the Attlee years, 'the party of full employment, the party which had exorcised the ghosts of Jarrow, Wigan and Merthyr Tydfil'.[6]

In social policy, the government moved quickly to overhaul the benefits system, basing its new legislation on the principles of the Beveridge Report. The most striking developments in this area, however, were associated with Bevan's tenure at the Ministry of Health. His department retained responsibility for housing as well as health, and there is no doubt that Bevan's housing programme got off to a poor start. With a population enlarged by a million crowded into 700,000 fewer properties, owing to wartime damage or destruction, the minister ran up against intractable problems, not least that of obtaining adequate raw materials for the building of new homes. By 1947 the position was beginning to improve and Bevan's objectives became clearer. In a deliberate attempt to favour the less well-off, attention shifted from private house-building, the priority of the 1930s, towards local authority housing for rent. Four out of five houses built under the Attlee regime were council properties, constructed to more generous specifications than before the war. The minister eventually came to have a defensible record. Over a million homes were built in the six years after 1945 and, if there was disappointment about the initial pace of reform, then part of the reason for this was the priority accorded to what the became the jewel in Labour's welfare crown, the National Health Service.

Medical reform had been exhaustively discussed by Churchill's coalition, but party and professional opinion remained divided over the best way forward, and within weeks of coming to office Bevan indicated his determination to go beyond wartime proposals. In particular, he aimed to bring local authority and independent 'voluntary' hospitals into one state system, a move strongly opposed by the Conservative Party. Many local Tory activists were stalwarts of the voluntary system, and Bevan's plans were attacked as an unnecessary measure of nationalization. Reform of the hospitals became a central plank of the 1946 National Health Service Act, which also introduced for the first time free access to general practitioner treatment and to local authority services such as maternity care. The Act was enthusiastically endorsed by Labour MPs, though the minister had many critics. At one extreme the Socialist Medical Association condemned the failure to introduce a state-salaried GP service; at the other, the British Medical Association, representing the views of many doctors, was bitterly hostile, and the Tories voted against the bill on the grounds that it 'retards the development of hospital services by destroying local ownership'. But Bevan's achievement was beyond question. The NHS was to be the most popular, and enduring, of Labour's welfare reforms. Its impact in improving the lives of working-class families was highlighted by a woman who later recalled how she received a bill for £6 after being delivered of a baby moments before the NHS came into operation in July 1948; had the infant been born fifteen minutes later, there would have been no charge. This situation was reflected in a joke current at the time: what was it that a swan could do easily, a duck couldn't do at all, but a doctor could do after 5 July 1948? Answer: stick his bill up his arse.[7]

After its initial surge of legislative progress, the government began to run into difficulties. If not Labour's 'darkest hour', 1947 was pretty gloomy. The year began with a 'winter crisis', when severe weather and coal shortages combined to produce a temporary industrial standstill, and continued in the summer with a 'convertibility crisis', sparked off when sterling came under intense pressure on the foreign exchanges. Government credibility took a battering. The social survey group Mass Observation recorded the public response. 'I wish I were anywhere but in this goddamned country,' said one young ex-serviceman, 'where there is nothing but queues and restrictions and forms and shortages and no food and cold.'[8] By the end of the year the Prime Minister had been faced with a 'September plot' to oust him from the leadership and with the resignation of his Chancellor, Hugh Dalton, worn down by the economic traumas of recent months and unable to resist pressure to go after he had leaked budget details which appeared in the press before being revealed to Parliament. In the period between the fuel crisis and Dalton's departure ministers were faced with a gradual erosion of public confidence. In August 1947 the Conservatives edged ahead in the opinion polls for the first time since Attlee had come to power, and by-election results showed a pronounced swing to the Tories. The year 1947 marked an important point of transition, from the confidence of the early days to a period when ministers turned to the language of restraint and 'consolidation'.

The so-called 'age of austerity' of the late 1940s became indelibly associated with the figure of Stafford Cripps, Dalton's successor at the Treasury. Until his health gave way under the strain in 1950, Cripps set an example of conscientiousness that few could match. His working day began with a cold bath at 4 a.m. followed by three hours at his desk before breakfast, and he clearly hoped for similar levels of commitment from the nation. He continued with, and sought to make a virtue of, a wartime 'fair shares' policy of food rationing, even though this meant ever-lengthening queues to obtain food of dubious quality. The most notorious example came with the appearance in 1948 of 'snoek', an oily and tasteless South African fish purchased in bulk by the government. The public refused to eat it, and although it was claimed the whole consignment had been sold off rumours persisted that much had been reprocessed as cat food.[9] In several areas of economic policy Labour had made great strides, for example in recovering many of the export markets lost during the war. But Cripps was convinced that without even further increases in productivity it would not be possible to maintain its ambitious programme of social reform. With this in mind, he became a prime exponent of 'consolidation'. During 1948–9 he tightened the belt on welfare expenditure, and in 1949 he decided to devalue sterling against the dollar in order to maintain Britain's export drive.

Aside from external forces, the government was confronted with an increasingly revitalized opposition. The Conservative claim that continuing scarcities in the shops were due to socialist 'bureaucracy' and 'inefficiency' struck a popular chord in the run-up to a general election, called in February 1950. Labour allegations that the post-war settlement would be threatened by the return of Churchill were strenuously denied by Tory leaders, who emphasized their broad acceptance of welfare reform. In the event, a record turn-out helped to ensure that Labour polled more votes than it had in 1945. But so, too, did the Conservatives. The results revealed a swing across the country of 2.9 per cent against the government (compared with 12 per cent against the Tories in

1945), leaving Labour with a majority of just six seats in the House of Commons. Aside from the redrawing of constituency boundaries, which was estimated to have cost the government thirty seats, the regional pattern of results offered the clearest explanation of this narrow victory. Broadly working-class constituencies, especially in the north and west, remained solidly behind the government. But Labour lost ground in seats with a preponderance of middle-class voters, notably in the suburban districts of London and the Home Counties. The party remained in power, but the loss of seventy-eight seats since 1945 made it a hollow victory. Looking back on the 1950 election, many on the Labour side believed that austerity was the primary cause of voter disaffection. 'We proclaimed a just policy of fair shares,' reflected Hugh Dalton, 'but the complaint was not so much that shares were unfair, but that they were too small.'[10]

Attlee was able to stay on at Downing Street, but the omens in February 1950 were not good. In re-forming his administration, the Prime Minister could still count on the loyalty of an experienced Cabinet. Bevin, Cripps and Morrison all returned to their posts, and promotion went primarily to moderate figures such as Hugh Gaitskell, who became the Chancellor's deputy as Minister for Economic Affairs. This was a rapid advancement for the MP for Leeds South, a former economics lecturer and civil servant, whose appointment as Minister of Fuel and Power in 1947 had marked him out as one of the brightest prospects of the 1945 intake. The Cabinet, although at the outset harmonious, was acutely aware of the constraints imposed by a tiny parliamentary majority. As one party official put it, the 'tidal wave' of 1945 had receded.[11] In contrast to the euphoria at the end of the war, there was no dancing in the streets and ministers did not look forward with optimism. The first meeting of the new Cabinet agreed that there was no prospect of introducing controversial legislation outlined in Labour's manifesto, such as the nationalization of sugar, cement and the water supply. According to Hugh Dalton, now

Minister of Town and Country Planning, the election result was the worst of all possible outcomes, for it left Labour in office but 'without authority or power'. Indeed, Dalton recorded in his diary that most ministers believed that the government, unable to take strong executive action, would not last for more than six months.[12]

For a while after the election it seemed that ministerial pessimism might be unwarranted. The first half of 1950 brought a period of sustained economic growth. Opinion polls continued to reflect the result of the general election and Labour held on to two marginal seats at by-elections in the spring of 1950. Backbenchers also remained in defiant mood. Angered by Conservative attempts at harassment through the use of tiring, all-night sessions, Labour MPs closed ranks and made government defeats in the Commons a rarity. Throughout the eighteen months of the 1950–51 parliament, Labour was to lose only five of 234 divisions. Cabinet unity was threatened in April 1950 by one serious disagreement, over the recurring problem of how to control health service costs, which rose from £228 million in 1949–50 to £356 million for 1950–51 and a projected £387 million for 1951–2. In 1949 the government had already taken powers to introduce prescription charges. Nye Bevan accepted this move in order to save his house-building programme, confident that the powers would not be taken up. In 1950 Cripps sought to impose charges on dentures and spectacles, but Bevan resisted in Cabinet discussions any departure from the principle of a free system, which he said would be a 'grave disappointment to Socialist opinion throughout the world'. After several heated meetings, a compromise was reached: Bevan accepted a high ceiling for NHS expenditure in return for the establishment of a Cabinet committee under Attlee to oversee future plans. This formula left unresolved the question of health service charges, although to outward appearances the Cabinet had papered over its disagreements. Above all, ministers were buoyed up by economic growth which held out the prospect of their being able to continue in office for longer than anticipated. 'It looks as though those bastards can stay in as long as they like,' Churchill complained after losing one particularly close vote in the Commons.[13]

In June 1950, however, the government's composure was upset by an unexpected external development – the outbreak of the Korean War. News of an attack by Communist forces from North Korea across the thirty-eighth parallel brought a swift response from Washington and London. The Cabinet, with only Bevan dissenting, was strongly in favour of backing American resistance to North Korean aggression; to allow a blatant violation of international law by Communist forces, it was felt, would be to repeat the folly of 1930s' appeasement. As a result, British forces were soon playing their part in the Far East. Initially, Labour's rank and file supported the government, but by the autumn the mood had changed. Instead of confining United Nations forces to a defence of South Korea, the American commander, General MacArthur, began an offensive that threatened to escalate hostilities by bringing Communist China, North Korea's key ally, into the conflict. Indications that the Americans were considering the use of atomic weapons caused particularly grave concern among Labour MPs, and the Prime Minister was sufficiently alarmed to make a special visit to Washington in December 1950. Attlee returned triumphantly with assurances from President Truman that atomic weapons would not be used, but backbench opinion was becoming ever more concerned that Britain was tying itself to American foreign policy.[14] The clearest indication of this came in January 1951 when the Cabinet agreed to a huge increase in Britain's defence budget. By agreeing to spend £4,700 million over the next three years, ministers imposed a heavier burden of defence costs per capita than the Americans were prepared to contemplate. The result was great strain on the British economy, necessitating a rethink of priorities on the home front.

The task of working out the implications of the rearmament programme fell primarily to a new Chancellor of the Exchequer, Hugh Gaitskell. In the autumn of 1950 Stafford Cripps was forced to resign through ill health. The Prime Minister had little doubt that Gaitskell, having served his apprenticeship as deputy to Cripps, was best equipped for the Treasury. News of the appointment was not unanimously welcomed in Labour ranks. Aneurin Bevan, in particular, felt his record as Minister of Health was sufficient to justify promotion to high office and he greatly resented being passed over in favour of someone with no Cabinet experience. There was a strong element of personal rivalry between the two men; by 1950 they were both regarded as possible future leaders of the party. Gaitskell had already acquired a reputation for economic expertise and administrative competence, though he lacked as yet a base of support outside Westminster. The new Chancellor, Bevan said contemptuously, was still 'young in the Movement'. Bevan, by contrast, was one of the darlings of the constituency activists, renowned for his oratorical skills on the public stage. He was, though, less popular with senior colleagues, who regarded him as a temperamental egotist, often unwilling to accept majority Cabinet opinion. Over and above the personality differences, there were disagreements on policy that left Gaitskell and Bevan at loggerheads. On his first day at the Treasury, Gaitskell told the Prime Minister that increases in defence spending could be met only if economies were made on welfare services, including the NHS. The two men were on a collision course for what became, in Gaitskell's words, 'a fight for the soul of the Labour Party'.[15]

In preparing his first budget, the Chancellor made provision, along the lines of his predecessor, for the imposition of charges for dentures and spectacles and for the introduction of prescription charges. Behind the scenes, in a series of Cabinet committee meetings early in 1951, Bevan made clear his opposition to the abandonment of the principle of a free health service. By this stage he was no longer responsible for policy in health, having reluctantly accepted Attlee's offer to move to the Ministry of Labour in January, a post that brought him into the front line of tackling mounting industrial disputes. His mood was not helped when he was passed over in March 1951 for another senior post, that of Foreign Secretary, which went to Herbert Morrison. Some journalists believed that from this moment onwards Bevan was looking for a pretext to resign.[16] The outgoing Foreign Secretary, Ernest Bevin, had been forced to stand down when his health deteriorated, although he remained in government for a few weeks longer as Lord Privy Seal. In this capacity, Bevin offered a way forward when the Cabinet discussed health service cuts on 22 March. By adopting a slightly higher ceiling for NHS expenditure than the Chancellor proposed, it would be possible to keep the charges on dentures and spectacles but avoid the politically more damaging introduction of prescription charges. This persuaded all but two of those present. Bevan was joined in his dissent by Harold Wilson, President of the Board of Trade, who argued that the defence budget should be cut rather than undermining the welfare state. Bevan's plea that the relatively small sums to be saved from health charges should be trimmed from defence spending fell on deaf ears. He and Wilson were on their own in resisting NHS charges as part of Gaitskell's proposed budget.

In the first week of April 1951 Bevan raised the stakes when he declared, after being provoked at a rowdy public meeting, that he would never be a member of a government that introduced health charges. For the first time, newspapers were alerted to the developing crisis and began running stories about rifts at the highest levels of government. On the eve of the budget, 9 April, the argument raged again around the Cabinet table. Herbert Morrison, asked to deputize for the Prime Minister who was in hospital undergoing treatment for a duodenal ulcer, read out a letter from Attlee warning against the electoral dangers of division but offering no fresh advice on the issues at stake and ultimately agreeing that the Chancellor must prevail on a major issue of policy. Bevan and Wilson gave strong hints that they would resign, but most ministers, convinced that Britain had to stand firm against Communist aggression even if this meant domestic economies, continued to back the Chancellor, who responded with his own veiled threat to go if he did not prevail. The only movement since the Cabinet meeting of 22 March came with the intervention of

George Tomlinson, the Minister of Education, who said the sums of money involved were insignificant in relation to the price that was likely to be paid. Alarmed that the situation was moving out of control, he expressed the hope that his colleagues 'would not press their view to a point which would make these resignations inevitable'.[17] But it was too late; the die was cast.

On the morning of his budget speech, 10 April, Gaitskell visited Attlee in hospital to confirm that he could go ahead with prime ministerial support. Attlee's mumbling led the Chancellor to believe momentarily that he had said 'you will have to go'; he was relieved to realize that Attlee's words had been 'they will have to go'.[18] Later in the day health service charges were included as one element in what turned out to be a generally well-received budget. The NHS was to keep within a ceiling of £400 million – itself an increase on original projections – and henceforth there would be charges for half the cost of false teeth and spectacles, which would bring in £13 million in 1951–2 and £23 million in a full year. At this point in the speech a lone cry of 'shame' came from Jennie Lee, Bevan's wife. Bevan, in the words of Tory MP Chips Channon, 'red in the face and breathing like an angry bull', walked out when Gaitskell finished the passage on health charges. Most Labour MPs, in contrast, were impressed with the Chancellor's skilful balancing of burdens and reliefs. In order to meet the cost of the rearmament programme, sixpence was added to income tax, but this was offset by increased children's and married person's allowances. Over the coming days twenty out of twenty-eight Labour backbenchers who spoke in the budget debate were sympathetic. No one rejected the budget outright, and any reservations on the government benches were more to do with pensions than with health service charges.[19]

After listening to pleas from friends and colleagues, Bevan did not resign immediately. Frantic negotiations, aimed at finding a compromise, took place for another week. The prospect of an eleventh-hour solution appeared to be enhanced by the death of Ernest Bevin only four days after the budget, working in bed with his red box of papers still in front of him. Attlee wrote a note from hospital to Bevan on 18 April saying that the 'death of Ernie has rather overshadowed these differences and I hope everyone will forget them'.[20] But a new Cabinet formula remained elusive. Bevan and Wilson argued for a delay before the bill on health charges was introduced. When Gaitskell resisted this Bevan insisted he could not possibly vote for the measure and at one point attacked the 'Chancellor's bloody obscurantism'.[21] Talk of reviving an earlier idea – that of increasing National Insurance contributions in lieu of charges – failed to persuade any of the main protagonists. Gaitskell toyed with proposing that NHS charges might not be permanent, but Bevan tossed this aside, calling it a 'bromide' and saying he would not be satisfied unless it was left open whether charges would come into force at all. Hugh Dalton in his diary wrote that Bevan was engaging in 'continual nerve war' about his intentions.[22]

Any chance of an amicable agreement was fatally undermined when Bevan's mouthpiece, *Tribune*, launched a scathing personal assault on the Chancellor. Michael Foot, now a Labour MP as well as editor of *Tribune*, penned an article that decried the 'frontal attack on the Health Service' by a Chancellor who was compared to Philip Snowden, second only in Labour demonology to Ramsay MacDonald, the 'traitor' of 1931.[23] *Tribune*'s vitriolic language was greatly resented in party circles and persuaded leading ministers, led by Herbert Morrison, to press Attlee to issue Bevan with an ultimatum. Attlee agreed that 'we cannot go on like this. He must behave properly if he is to remain a Member of the Government.'[24] The Prime Minister wrote to Bevan from hospital saying he must accept collective responsibility or go. On 22 April 1951 Bevan went ahead with his resignation, followed shortly afterwards by Harold Wilson. They were joined by one other junior minister, John Freeman, whose work at the Ministry of Supply gave him a close knowledge of rising raw material costs and led him to endorse doubts about the scale of the government's rearmament programme.

Freed from the constraints of office, Bevan made violent accusations against his erstwhile colleagues, first in the House of Commons and then at a stormy meeting of the parliamentary party, where many of those present were disgusted by his egotistical outburst against attacks on 'my Health Service'. Barbara Castle, the young Labour MP for Blackburn East, later recollected that at the special meeting of the Parliamentary Labour Party in the Grand Committee Room, 'the gloomiest room in the neo-Gothic pile of Westminster', sparks flew when several speakers accused Nye of disloyalty and vanity. 'He reacted,' Castle said, 'like a cornered animal, snarling back.'[25] Whereas Gaitskell made a measured speech, exploiting sympathy that had built up since the publication of the *Tribune* article, Bevan was greeted with derision when he screamed: 'I won't have it.' 'You won't have it?' several MPs called in return. The usually moderate Chuter Ede, Leader of the House, angered by the references to Gaitskell as Philip Snowden, made the inference that Bevan might be another Oswald Mosley in the making. The meeting broke up in acrimony. Press commentators took delight in speaking of a divided administration and a 'Bevanite' challenge to the leadership.[26] From this moment on, Bevan would be treated by his opponents as a wild extremist. 'The internal peace of the Labour Party' as Kenneth Morgan notes, 'would never be the same again.'[27]

The rights and wrongs of this first major split in Labour ranks since 1945 have been hotly contested. Writers and commentators have taken up the cudgels on behalf of both main players. Defenders of the Chancellor, such as his friend and biographer Philip Williams, claim there were good reasons for resisting a compromise. Bevan had made no serious effort to keep within previously agreed limits for NHS spending and charges would therefore not be effective unless included as part of the budget framework. According to this view it was Bevan who behaved erratically, using contradictory arguments, broadening the issue to rearmament when it suited him and seeking to make the health service a sacred cow at a time when all other spending departments accepted the need for economies.[28] In contrast, Bevan's first and most sympathetic biographer, Michael Foot, presented the crisis as a conspiracy by the Chancellor, deliberately aimed at forcing Bevan's resignation. Kenneth Morgan, in his biographical work *Labour People*, uses less impassioned language but agrees that Gaitskell was excessively zealous in his commitment to the Anglo-American alliance, handling the health service issue with an inflexibility that his predecessor Cripps had always avoided when dealing with senior colleagues.[29]

On a personal level, both men can be faulted. Gaitskell showed a streak of rigidity that surprised his closest supporters, some of whom advised him that the small amount of savings envisaged was not worth the trouble caused. Even the Chancellor's mentor, Hugh Dalton, had qualms, recognizing that the government could not afford to lose Bevan's talent. Gaitskell's problem, Dalton wrote in his diary, was that he 'thought too little about the Party & too much about the electorate'.[30] For opponents of Gaitskell, such as Barbara Castle, it was a mixture of 'pedantry and prejudice' that led the Chancellor to make a gross error of judgement.[31] As for Bevan, his strident behaviour alienated even those who agreed with his aims. One minister commented that it was intolerable for Cabinet majorities of eighteen to two to be overturned just because Bevan happened to be one of the two. Indeed, the violence of his language after his resignation strengthened the impression in Labour ranks that Bevan had become an impossible colleague. Hugh Dalton's concerns about Gaitskell were balanced by his diary references to Bevan being 'determined to bend the Cabinet to his will or break it'. According to Dalton, most ministers agreed he was guilty of 'unbearable conceit, crass obstinacy and a totalitarian streak'.[32]

Solely in terms of the issues involved, it must be said that events subsequently vindicated much of Bevan's case. As he predicted, the rearmament programme agreed by the Cabinet was never fully carried out. There were various reasons for this – shortages of labour, scarcity of machine tools and raw materials, and production difficulties in particular industries – all of which had been pointed out at the time. As a relatively inexperienced minister, it could be said in Gaitkell's defence that, even had he wished to do so, he would have found it difficult to stand up to the combined pressure of the Americans and the service chiefs, especially when the Soviet threat to Western Europe was considered serious. Other, more senior, figures in the Cabinet shared Gaitskell's belief that it was crucial to do whatever was necessary to stand up to Communism. 'Nevertheless the fact remains,' as John Campbell has written, 'that on this question Gaitskell and the majority of the Cabinet were wrong and Bevan, Wilson and Freeman were right.'[33] The political judgement may have been a fine one, but it was not clear that rearmament had to be on such a scale as to provoke resignations. Before long it became obvious that the rearmament targets would not be met, and after the Conservatives returned to power the total cost of the programme was to be scaled down by a third.

On the question of health service charges, Gaitskell appears at first sight to be on firmer ground. The Chancellor had a good case for saying that spending on the NHS needed to be checked. His predecessor Cripps had taken the same view. It was only much later, from the 1960s onwards, that the view developed in Labour circles that health spending should be sacrosanct, on the ground that the NHS constituted the finest achievement of the Attlee years. At the time Gaitskell represented the majority view in Cabinet that welfare was not an open-ended commitment. On this view, there was considerable pride in the NHS, but it was seen as only one of several areas of social provision that needed to be given equal treatment. The Chancellor could also point out that Labour had already introduced charges for a number of minor services within the NHS, for example the cost of transport to hospitals in rural areas. While the Cabinet discarded plans for prescription charges, most believed that false teeth and spectacles came in the same category of ancillary services, not central to the notion of free treatment. As George VI reportedly told Gaitskell, he did not see why people should have free false teeth any more than they should have free shoes.[34] To most ministers and Labour MPs, Bevan appeared to have got the issue of teeth and spectacles out of all proportion.

Even so, there are reasons for questioning whether health charges needed to be imposed in the way they were. If events were to vindicate Bevan on rearmament, the same was broadly true on health spending. In 1955 an authoritative report was to dispel the accusation that the NHS had spent extravagantly in its early years, noting that high costs were an inevitable feature of the new service, especially in view of the pent-up demand for various types of medical provision. John Campbell points out that charges for teeth and spectacles were a strange way of attempting to curb health expenditure, combining small levels of savings (lessened further than projected by a last-minute rush to obtain false teeth and glasses while they were free) with public irritation and political controversy. The largest area of NHS spending, and the weakest area of financial control, had hitherto been that of hospital services; the budget proposals of 1951 ignored this and were therefore marginal in terms of potential savings. It thus remains difficult to see why Gaitskell became so fixated on the idea of charges for teeth and spectacles, unless his intention was to provoke Bevan. Once engaged in a power struggle, Campbell notes, he was clearly determined to win at any cost.[35]

Part of the responsibility for the crisis of April 1951 rests with the Prime Minister. Although he could not avoid being in hospital at the critical moment, Attlee had let the dispute drag on for several months. He must have known that Bevan was teetering on the brink of resignation and yet did little to prevent the departure of a minister he on some occasions felt had the potential to be his successor. With Attlee away, Herbert Morrison – no friend of Bevan over the years – gave firm support to the Chancellor. While there is little evidence of a Gaitskell–Morrison conspiracy, the timing of the crisis was critical to Cabinet discussions. Attlee was in hospital, Cripps had retired and Bevin died in the midst of the crisis; if all three had been present, it is quite conceivable that a compromise would have been patched together as in the past. Bevan's key mistake was his failure to recognize that, since the departure of the more sympathetic Cripps, his support in Cabinet was diminished and his chances of countering the 'rigid steel' of Gaitskell were greatly reduced.[36] The balance of power within the Cabinet by April 1951 was such that any middle ground had disappeared. The diaries of Hugh Dalton, an admirer of Gaitskell who recognized the vision and value of Bevan, are marked by mounting frustration that his best efforts persuaded neither man to back down. Dalton spent the days after the budget and prior to Bevan's resignation, as his biographer Ben Pimlott notes, 'in a series of frantic and fruitless errands, dashing from one actor to another'.[37]

Whatever the balance of responsibility, the legacy of the Bevan-Gaitskell clash clouded the remaining months of Attlee's administration. Alarmist predictions that the government would immediately break up did not come to pass. New ministers were found readily enough. Sir Hartley Shawcross replaced Wilson at the Board of Trade and Alfred Robens, a figure with strong trade union credentials, was made Minister of Labour. The parliamentary party rallied behind the new team, and an opposition motion critical of defence policy was comfortably beaten off.[38] After his resignation outbursts, Bevan was restrained in any criticisms he made, although the significance of his departure could not easily be papered over. The crisis underscored the impression that after six years in power, Attlee's government was running out of energy and inspiration. Within the space of six months, the Prime Minister had lost his two most able servants, Stafford Cripps and Ernest Bevin, as well as two of the few high-profile 'younger' ministers, Bevan and Wilson. Attlee, Morrison and Dalton were all in their late sixties; the last said they looked like a government of pensioners. The Festival of Britain, launched on 1 May, with its mixture of science and modern design, did something to lift the mood. But the feeling that this was a tired administration was compounded by fresh economic difficulties in the summer of 1951, sparked off by a deterioration in the balance of payments, a mounting dollar deficit and inflationary wage pressures. As one minister said, it was an 'appallingly gruelling summer', with economic problems, the Bevanites waiting in the wings and an opposition redoubling its efforts to force a knock-out blow with late-night sittings of Parliament. Labour was unable to make any inroads into the clear 10 per cent lead held by the Conservatives in the opinion polls from early 1951 onwards.[39]

In these circumstances, it came as a surprise when Attlee announced the dissolution of Parliament and a general election in October. The Prime Minister's decision was prompted, at least in part, by his concern that the King was scheduled to visit Australia the following spring. George VI had told Attlee he did not wish to embark on a long tour abroad with political affairs so unsettled at home, and the Prime Minister agreed that it would be unreasonable for the monarch to leave the country with the threat of a 'political crisis' looming large. This constitutional propriety did not impress other ministers, such as Hugh Gaitskell, who believed a delay would allow time for economic recovery. But with another leading opponent of an early contest, Morrison, away on a trip to Washington as Foreign Secretary, there was little to prevent Attlee getting his way. Several members of the Cabinet, in any case, believed it was impossible to carry on for another parliamentary term with such a minuscule majority. Hugh Dalton, one of the most experienced campaigners remaining, thought that the longer the government clung on the more discredited it would become.[40]

Labour entered the election of October 1951 on the defensive. Conservative efforts to exploit Labour divisions, using slogans such as 'The end is Nye', were blunted by Bevan's willingness to urge unity. Most of the arguments between the parties had been rehearsed in 1950, and the campaign lacked novelty. Press observers resorted to detailed descriptions of Mrs Attlee's eccentric driving as the Prime Minister busied himself with crossword puzzles in the back of his car on a nationwide tour. Any new ideas came from the Conservative side. Churchill promised to 'set the people free' by removing 'socialist controls', which it was said hampered individual enterprise and perpetuated the miserably low standard of living associated with austerity. In an effort to show trade union voters that 'we are not a class party', two populist initiatives were brought forward by the Tories: the promise of an excess profits tax, and a pledge to outstrip Labour's housing programme by building 300,000 homes every year. Neither proposal was able to dominate the campaign. Unlike in 1950, housing was relegated to the sidelines as Conservative leaders were forced to spend much of their time countering Labour charges that Churchill was a warmonger. More than half of the party's allocated radio broadcast time was spent insisting that Churchill was out to preserve British national prestige, not to embark on fresh military adventures.

The result was closer than many anticipated. On a high turnout, there was a small swing of 1.1 per cent across the country, sufficient to give Churchill a narrow parliamentary majority of seventeen seats, allowing him to form his first peacetime administration. Closer examination of the figures confirmed that although twenty-one seats had been lost, Labour had polled over two hundred thousand more votes than the Tories – the product of huge Labour majorities building up in urban strongholds. Nor was there much evidence of Labour desertions to the Tories, with only an estimated 3 per cent of voters switching allegiance since 1950. The final outcome owed much to reduced Liberal intervention compared with the previous election. With fewer than a hundred candidates in the field, former Liberal voters divided approximately six to four in favour of the Conservatives; seventeen of the twenty-one Tory gains had lost their Liberal candidates since 1950. The clash between Gaitskell and Bevan had clearly not helped Labour's cause, but the importance of rising prices and unsatisfied material expectations was underpinned in the regional pattern of results. Over half the Tory gains were made in the south-east, in constituencies such as Dulwich and Camberwell, where Churchill's rallying cry offering prosperity and opportunity had its greatest appeal.[41]

It would be tempting to conclude that Labour was bound to lose power in 1951 simply because it had run out of steam. Yet British politics in the 1950s could easily have taken a different shape. If a compromise had been found over health charges and if Gaitskell had produced an electorally more appealing budget, then Labour could have faced the electorate with reasonable optimism. Above all, if Attlee had gone for different timing his prospects could have been transformed. The King's proposed tour, a major consideration in the Prime Minister's thinking, never took place; George VI died early in 1952, so compounding Attlee's tactical error in calling for an early election. During 1952–3 the British economy entered a phase of steady growth from which Attlee might well have benefited had he remained longer in office. With the benefit of hindsight, lamented Douglas Jay, one of the ministers who favoured delay, any government was certain to have taken credit for the emergence of Britain's more prosperous 'consumer society' of the 1950s; if Attlee had hung on, he could have 'coasted through to the easy years'.[42]

The closeness of the result in October 1951 confirms the likelihood that better timing could have enabled Attlee to win the prize of successive full-length parliamentary terms. The election was fought against a dark backdrop for the government, with everything pointing to a resounding Churchill victory, and yet Labour's total of nearly fourteen million votes, confirming it as the 'natural party of government' in industrial Britain, was the largest hitherto recorded in British politics; indeed, it remains to this day the largest in Labour's history, exceeding Tony Blair's 13.5 million in 1997. This explains why party stalwarts were not initially downcast. For senior figures such as Hugh Dalton there was relief at being released from the burden of almost a decade in high office. In contrast to his gloom in 1950, Dalton described the outcome in 1951 as 'wonderful', believing that the Conservatives would soon run into electoral difficulties.[43] He was, as it turned out, wide of the mark. Most of Labour's generation of 1945 were never again to return to government. It was not until 1964 that another Labour Prime Minister was to enter Number Ten Downing Street, ironically in the person of Harold Wilson, thirteen years after he resigned from Attlee's Cabinet.

The 1951 crisis had two lasting consequences. One was that Churchill, returning to power, felt that there was no option other than to continue with policies designed to maintain the post-war settlement. Much of what became known as 'consensus politics' in the era between Attlee and Thatcher stemmed from the closeness of the electoral contest in 1951 and the Tory recognition that working-class voters especially would not tolerate the undoing of Labour's economic and social reforms. Whereas Labour had lost the affection of some middle-class voters who had been part of the 1945 'high tide', anecdotal as well as statistical evidence confirmed that class-based voting remained strong and that Conservative support among manual workers, who made up the mass of the electorate, remained stubbornly low. Harold Macmillan, appointed by Churchill to lead the promised housing drive, wrote in his diary that 'wherever I have been, I am impressed by the class solidarity of the Labour vote. They grouse, and tell the Gallup Poll man that they will never vote Socialist again – but when the election comes, they vote the party ticket.'[44] A post-mortem by Tory organizers in a Scottish constituency conceded that the party continued to suffer from its 'hard-faced' image of the 1930s; the fear of unemployment among workers still ran very deep, and if 'unemployment comes back we may be out for a generation'.[45] The *News Chronicle*, lamenting the squeeze on the Liberal Party, summed up the curious nature of the 1951 result by saying the country had 'got rid of a party it does not want in favour of one it does not trust'.

Constrained by the verdict of the electorate and by a bloated defence budget, Churchill was in no position to strike out in new directions. The implications of the election result were apparent in the shaping of the new Cabinet, from which hardline free enterprisers were largely excluded. Aside from the Prime Minister's accepted heir apparent, Anthony Eden, who returned to his wartime role of Foreign Secretary, the key appointment was that of the progressive Tory Rab Butler as Chancellor of the Exchequer. Before the election the favoured candidate for the Treasury was Oliver Lyttelton, a minister in the wartime coalition and considered hawkish on economic policy. What may have tipped the scales, in the view of a knowledgeable Tory backbencher, was that after the narrow election victory 'it would have been more than ever dangerous to have had the other fellow at the Treasury'.[46] Worried about the slenderness of his parliamentary majority, Churchill even gave instructions that not more than five Tory MPs should travel in the same aeroplane, so as not to have 'too many baskets in one egg'.[47] Attlee's post-war experiment thus looked set to continue even after Labour lost power in October 1951, just as Margaret Thatcher's legacy was to remain powerful for many years after she was removed from office in 1990.

If the post-war settlement had come to stay, at least for the time being, the second long-term effect of 1951 was that Labour would be in no position to shape it. Out of office, the gloves came off between the consolidators and radicals in Labour ranks, the Gaitskellites and Bevanites as they became known. The dispute over health charges was only the first round of a lengthy struggle over the future direction of the movement. As the bitterness intensified, Bevan became convinced that 'Hugh is a Tory', prepared to abandon socialist principles for the sake of electoral respectability. For his part, Gaitskell believed that, unless checked, Bevan would break Labour just as Lloyd George had broken the Liberal Party after the Great War.[48] In the power struggle that ensued in the early 1950s Gaitskell again came out on top, establishing the basis for a successful bid to succeed Attlee in 1955. But it was a pyrrhic victory, won at the cost of poisoning the life of the Labour Party for many years to come. Bevan and

Gaitskell were never fully reconciled, and for a generation the Conservative hold on power was buttressed by the claim that Labour was unelectable because of its internal divisions. In the light of what followed, the Bevan-Gaitskell clash of April 1951 cast a long shadow, clouding the achievements of the Attlee years. 'This period,' in the words of the historian David Howell, 'might have been the party's heroic age, but like many feats of heroism it had a devastating effect on the hero.'[49]

4

'The best Prime Minister we have'
Eden and the Suez crisis, 1956

Suez – a smash and grab raid that was all smash and no grab.

Harold Nicolson, politician and writer, in conversation,
November 1956

I am not sure I should have dared to start, but I am sure I should not have dared to stop.

Churchill's verdict on Eden's handling of the Suez episode,
March 1957

Conservative Britain looked set fair in the mid-1950s. For much of the population the legacy of the Second World War was at last fading. Rationing came to an end and austerity gave way to the first stirrings of the 'affluent society'. Two great symbols of prosperity told the story. The numbers of motor cars increased from around 2.3 to 3.3 million between 1951 and 1955, and during the same period ownership of television sets quadrupled to over four million. Churchill's peacetime premiership, after a rocky start, witnessed a renewed sense of national well-being. In the words of the psephologist David Butler, 'Everest had been conquered, an Englishman had been the first to run a four-minute mile, and England had regained, and then held, the Ashes. But far above these, in the summer of 1953, Queen Elizabeth II had been crowned in a flourish of pageantry and amidst bold prophecies of a new Elizabethan age.'[1] What appears with hindsight like a

85

golden age looked set to continue after Churchill retired and made way for Sir Anthony Eden in the spring of 1955. The conventional wisdom was that Eden had everything going for him: film-star good looks and an impeccable record as Foreign Secretary since 1951 made him ideally suited to lead a confident party anticipating electoral victory. 'It is fortunate for Britain that there exists to succeed Sir Winston a leader who is a world statesman in his own right,' wrote the *Yorkshire Post*. (National newspapers were on strike at the time of the announcement of Churchill's retirement.) Eden, the *Yorkshire Post* confidently predicted, would be a success as Prime Minister because he was able to 'command respect in the Cabinet room, in the House and in the country'.[2]

But it all went terribly wrong. Within two years his premiership was sunk in the murky waters of the Suez Canal, in a crisis that was to have major repercussions for Britain's international status as well as for Eden's leadership. He resigned in January 1957, the failure of his aborted military operation in the Middle East leaving a stain on his reputation more indelible even than Chamberlain's association with appeasement. In a 1990s' poll of politicians, journalists and academics on the success of twentieth-century Prime Ministers, Anthony Eden found himself firmly anchored at the bottom of the list, just below Neville Chamberlain.[3] This inability to live up to expectations has rightly been attributed in numerous accounts of the Suez crisis to Eden's personal failings, such as his lack of experience in domestic politics and his volatile temperament. Yet if he proved unexpectedly ill-suited to the demands of the premiership, it was also the case, as sympathetic biographers have pointed out, that Eden's prospects were less rosy in the spring of 1955 than many thought.[4] Aside from his fragile health – always precarious after he underwent major surgery on a bile duct in 1953 – he came to power when Britain's underlying economic weaknesses were becoming impossible to conceal. He also had to work in the shadow of his illustrious predecessor. Whereas Churchill had been almost immune from criticism in his final years, Eden was faced with serious rivals around the Cabinet table. In such circumstances, it was not surprising that he was in trouble well before Suez came to dominate the political agenda in the autumn of 1956.

It all started promisingly enough. Two interrelated questions faced Eden when he took over at Number Ten Downing Street. Should he reconstruct the Cabinet, and should he call an early general election? Conscious that Churchill had carried out a major reshuffle in 1954, the new Prime Minister opted for continuity in personnel. He kept on at the Treasury Rab Butler, who had built a reputation since 1951 for economic competence, if not for straight-talking. Butler was renowned for double-edged remarks which led to accusations that he was 'too clever by half'; anyone who thought they understood Rab, it was once said, was gravely misinformed. The only change of note was the promotion to the Foreign Office of the suave, ambitious Harold Macmillan, whose success as Churchill's housing minister had catapulted him into the reckoning as a serious contender for the future leadership of the party. On the second question he faced, Eden announced after only ten days in office that there would be a general election in late May – a decision requiring a degree of courage. He was aware that the Tories had not out-polled Labour since 1935, and any misjudgement would condemn him to one of the shortest premierships in history. But to offset this, unemployment was low, the balance of payments was favourable and 'electorally', as he said in his memoirs, 'the tide appeared to be with us'.[5] The Prime Minister was, in short, taking only a modest risk, one that he claimed publicly was necessary in order to end uncertainty but that he privately agreed owed much to the fear that rising prices might cause a sterling crisis later in the year. 'As you know,' he confided to Churchill, 'I have been tempted to try to show that we can be a good Administration for at least six months before appealing to the country but I am increasingly compelled to take account of . . . distasteful economic factors.'[6]

A further reason for an early appeal to the country was that the spring budget could provide a launch-pad for the Tory campaign. On 19 April 1955 the Chancellor, to the delight of his back-benchers, announced two highly popular measures: the standard rate of income tax was reduced from nine shillings to eight shillings and sixpence in the pound, and the raising of personal allowances removed over two million people from liability to tax altogether. These changes were criticized as an abandonment of the Cripps approach of refusing to use the budget for overt electioneering. At a time when there were twice as many vacancies as men out of work, extra consumer purchasing power from reduced taxation was also certain to have inflationary effects.[7] Butler claimed in his defence that it was consistent to continue with his past strategy of reducing taxes, especially as more than half the available budget surplus was kept in reserve. The budget certainly provided a strong basis for the Conservative election campaign. Eden's main theme was that since 1951 the Conservatives had delivered unprecedented prosperity; he offered the prospect of Britain doubling its standard of living within twenty-five years. In contrast to Churchill's pugnacious electioneering style, Eden deliberately adopted a low-key approach, conscious that Labour was struggling to mount a forceful challenge. Neither appeals to the memory of the 1945 government nor attacks on rising food prices did much to stir voters. Perhaps the main cause of what Hugh Dalton called the 'most tedious, apathetic, uninteresting' election he had witnessed was the absence of doubt about the outcome. The *Daily Mirror* slogan 'Keep the Tories tame' summed up Labour's defensive-ness throughout; by polling day the opposition seemed less concerned with outright victory than with preventing a government landslide.[8]

In the event Eden secured a solid but not overwhelming victory. On a reduced turn-out (down by 5.7 per cent since 1951 to 76.8 per cent), the Conservatives increased their majority to a comfortable fifty-nine seats. The swing across the country was small but relatively uniform, though the outstanding feature of the result was a drop in Labour support – down by 1.5 million votes since 1951. This amounted to one in ten of those who had previously supported the party. Press observers were agreed about the causes of Eden's triumph. Put simply by the *New Statesman,* 'the nation felt comfortably satisfied and in no mood for a change.' An equally strong theme in newspaper reaction was the impact of Labour's internal warfare between Gaitskellites and Bevanites since its loss of office in 1951.[9] Some Tory officials questioned why, given all the circumstances, the government had not done better still. The total number of Conservative voters was fewer than at the previous election, in spite of the increased size of the electorate, and Labour still commanded over twelve million supporters. The ghost of 1945 had been laid to rest, but there were few signs that the Tories were winning new converts. If affluence was the key to success, it was only slowly driving the working classes into middle-class patterns of voting. As one internal party report concluded, 'it is clear that there are many people at present disillusioned with Socialism who, nevertheless, have a prejudice against voting Conservative.'[10] For a leader only weeks in office such notes of caution paled beside the plaudits he received for securing an increased majority. As far as Eden was concerned, it was so far, so good.

Yet the Prime Minister's honeymoon was to be among the briefest in post-war history. Harold Wilson in 1966 and John Major in 1992, as later chapters show, suffered similar sharp falls in popularity after securing election victories, but unlike Eden they had both been at Number Ten for some time beforehand. In 1955 there were several difficulties facing the new premier. Rab Butler later wrote that Churchill's tardiness in retiring left Eden feeling 'thwarted' and 'stale' by the time he succeeded to the top job, one Churchill had promised him on and off for fifteen years. Whereas Churchill had been unassailable by virtue of his age and reputation, Eden was not immune to criticism from within party ranks, especially as a comfortable majority offered the prospect of several years in power. As Macmillan commented in his diary, it was a 'pretty tough assignment to follow the greatest Englishman of history'.[11]

Neither Macmillan nor Butler showed much sympathy at the time. In the words of Dalton, there was 'no friendship at the top here' among the triumvirate who dominated Conservative politics. With Churchill removed from the scene, Eden, Butler and Macmillan found it difficult to conceal their intense personal rivalries. The Chancellor was reported to have boasted that on domestic issues he would lead the new Prime Minister 'from behind'. Relations between the Prime Minister and his Foreign Secretary were no better. Eden and Macmillan 'simply did not like each other', Macmillan's biographer Alistair Horne notes, and were soon at loggerheads over the direction of British policy towards Europe and the Middle East.[12] Cabinet colleagues in general felt less inclined to accept prime ministerial outbursts of bad temper (not unknown in Churchill's day), compounded by what one called Eden's 'chronic restlessness' – the result partly of fever-filled sleepless nights that went back to the botched operation to clear a bile duct in 1953. One MP said that Eden's temper tantrums and his continued interference in the work of his ministers implied a lack of trust and confidence; this in time was to have a corrosive effect which trickled down via junior ministers to the backbenches.[13]

The electorate at large, to begin with, was less concerned about Eden's brittle temperament than about shortcomings in policy. It was only a matter of months before the economic optimism of the spring was replaced by an atmosphere of crisis. After an election in which the Tory case had been based on the promise of a buoyant economy, it came as a shock to discover that Britain's balance of payments was deteriorating rapidly, reaching a deficit of over £450 million in the first half of 1955. This unsettled the financial markets, with the result that sterling came under pressure on the foreign exchanges. In preparing its response, the government sought both expenditure cuts and increased taxation, although the precise form that these should take proved contentious. After prevaricating over when to act, Eden gave the go-ahead for an emergency budget in October 1955. This proved unpopular, as well as humiliating for a Chancellor recently credited with helping to engineer electoral victory. Sharp cutbacks were announced in local authority building programmes and various forms of indirect taxation were increased. The extension of purchase tax to kitchen and other household goods allowed Butler's package to be labelled the 'pots and pans Budget', which, as Eden reflected, was hardly a rallying cry for his concept of a 'property-owning democracy' (altogether the Chancellor clawed back about two-thirds of the tax reliefs provided in the spring).[14] Hugh Gaitskell, seeking to prove his credentials as favourite to become Labour leader whenever Attlee retired, made a wounding attack in which he accused Butler of deliberately deceiving the nation about the state of the economy at the time of the election. By the end of the year it was clear that things would get worse before they got better, the balance of trade was still in the red and fresh remedies would be needed.

The Prime Minister's popularity was sinking rapidly by the end of 1955, and his cause was not helped by his handling of ministerial changes. By this stage Eden wished he had appointed a more amenable Foreign Secretary; his diary confirmed that he was 'as much irritated by [Macmillan's] patronising tone as by his absence of policy'.[15] On top of this came the problem of a Chancellor whose credibility had been eroded. Eden's solution was to propose moving both his senior colleagues. Well before Butler presented his emergency budget to the Commons – when he received Eden's 'full support' – his job had been offered to Macmillan. In return, Rab was asked to 'lead the Commons and handle the party'. Neither Butler nor Macmillan concurred with enthusiasm. The Chancellor's advisers warned him not to accept anything that smacked of demotion, suggesting that he should stay put until a recovering economy restored his reputation. Macmillan was angry at the prospect of an early departure from the Foreign Office, and his compliance came with strings attached. He insisted that Butler, assuming the titles of Lord Privy

Seal and Leader of the House of Commons, must on no account be appointed Deputy Prime Minister.[16] Wrangling continued behind the scenes for some time before a compromise was reached. Butler was denied the title of Deputy but was empowered to preside over Cabinet in the leader's absence, as he had done since 1952. Shortly before Christmas the reshuffle was announced to lukewarm greetings from the press. In Selwyn Lloyd the Prime Minister gained a compliant Foreign Secretary, but the movement of his two leading colleagues only six months into the new administration suggested something was amiss.

By the beginning of 1956 the Prime Minister's ability to survive was being questioned. Among newspapers usually loyal to the Conservative cause, signs of panic followed hard on the heels of Eden's reshuffle and poor by-election performances of a type unknown during the previous parliament. The *Daily Telegraph*, among the most fulsome in its praise of Eden six months earlier, caused particular consternation by calling for the 'smack of firm government'.[17] Anti-Tory papers gleefully joined in, some running stories that the Prime Minister might resign in favour of Butler or Macmillan. Butler made matters worse when, under persistent questioning from a journalist, he agreed with the view that Eden was the best available leader. This was widely misreported as the claim that Eden 'is the best Prime Minister we have', words that, as the *Manchester Guardian* noted, could easily be interpreted as a 'back-handed compliment'.[18] Ignoring the advice of those who felt he should let things blow over, the Prime Minister confronted his critics. He took the unusual step of issuing a statement saying that rumours of his imminent resignation were false. Then in a speech he turned on 'cantankerous newspapers', adding that 'this country is not on its way down, and this Government is not on its way out'. The barrage of press criticism died down quickly thereafter, especially once Eden had met leading editors to reassure them that his new team was working well.[19] But doubts about the Prime Minister's leadership had hardly been dispelled.

In the first half of 1956 the government continued to drift. Tensions between senior ministers remained obvious; the prosperity of the early 1950s had been replaced by stagnation; and voter disenchantment brought further by-election setbacks and talk of a 'middle-class revolt'. One of the Prime Minister's speeches was so poorly received that a veteran American correspondent noted how Tory backbenchers were 'profoundly gloomy'; there were parallels with the downfall of Neville Chamberlain, for any further reversals might lead to 'the sort of rebellion that I watched in late April and early May 1940'.[20] The impression of a government unable to control events could, it seemed, only be countered either by a strong economic recovery or by a major foreign policy triumph, neither of which seemed likely. In July 1956 the right-wing diarist Harold Nicolson noted how he attended a party at which Labour's Nye Bevan:

talked to me about the decay of the present government. He attributes it entirely to Eden, who, he says, is much disliked, weak and vacillating, and, in fact, hopeless. He was not talking as an Opposition leader, but as a student of politics. I heard the same thing at the Club today . . . To choose Eden had been a mistake, since he was not a strong man. He interfered with his colleagues and did not control them, and gave the impression to the House that he did not know his own mind. Now when I hear a man abused like that, I immediately wish to take his side. But I fear that it is all too true.[21]

On the same day President Nasser of Egypt caused an international crisis by nationalizing the Suez Canal. It was make-or-break time for Eden.

The Suez Canal had long been a vital trade route linking west and east. Egypt had been a protectorate of the Empire from 1914 to 1922, and Britain retained its influence in the region through ownership of a large proportion of shares in the Suez Canal company. After coming to power in the aftermath of a military coup in the early 1950s, Colonel Gamal Abdel Nasser, a champion of Arab nationalism, set much store on the economic development of his country, and in particular on the building of the Aswan Dam on the Nile. In July 1956 the United States withdrew financial backing for this project on the ground that Nasser was not considered a loyal friend, having begun the purchase of weapons from the Soviet bloc. When Britain followed suit, Nasser's response was to nationalize the canal company. The *Times* declared that if Egypt was allowed to get away with it, 'all the British and other Western interests in the Middle East will crumble.'[22] The following day there was sombre agreement in the House of Commons. Eden made a well-received speech in which he firmly denounced Nasser and spoke of 'precautionary measures of a military nature' going ahead. Backing for a firm line came from the opposition, with Hugh Gaitskell, now installed as Labour leader, comparing Nasser's action to that of the fascist dictators in the 1930s. Backbenchers were pleased that all options had been left open. Strong support for the government came from the 'Suez group' of hardline Tory MPs whose leader, Captain Charles Waterhouse, a former officer in the Life Guards, expressed satisfaction that Nasser was 'on the run and he must be kept on the run'. With Parliament due to go into recess until late October, it looked as though the government would not be hampered by political opinion at home in seeking to solve the crisis in the weeks ahead.[23]

Throughout August a series of talks began via intermediaries in an effort to secure a negotiated settlement. In the meantime, Eden prepared for every eventuality. He established a de facto War Cabinet, consisting of senior ministers including the Foreign Secretary and the Chancellor, and he outlined for close associates his main aims: to retake the canal, causing the downfall of Nasser in the process, and to devise a new regime that would stabilize British influence in the Middle East while minimizing the role of the Soviet Union. He stepped up the rhetorical conflict by using a range of arguments against Egypt. Economically, there was a potentially grave threat: two-thirds of the West's oil supplies passed through the canal. Diplomatically, Egypt was regarded as a destabilizing influence, hostile to Israel and unhelpful to France over its war in Algeria. Legally, it was argued that Nasser had no right to seize the property of the canal company. The clear implication was that, if necessary, the Egyptian action would have to be met with force. On 8 August the Prime Minister broadcast to the nation on radio and television, giving his strongest public indication yet of the possible need for military retaliation. While the rationale for force was being built up, urgent talks were taking place behind the scenes with allies such as the French and the Americans, though with a presidential election looming in the United States Eisenhower proved reluctant to give support for military action.[24]

By the time Parliament was recalled in the second week of September the initial sense of unity in Britain was breaking down. Although shipping was continuing to pass through the canal without hindrance – Nasser claiming he would use the income raised to replace lost loans – discussions for a settlement had produced no result and it was difficult to see where to go next. Eden was shouted at by opposition MPs when he spoke not of seeking United Nations support but of establishing a 'Users' Association' for the canal; if this proposal were not accepted, the Prime Minister argued, Britain would be free to take whatever action was required. Gaitskell also received a rough ride when he said the use of force for self-defence was one thing, but 'force is not justified as a solution to this problem'. Although his speech on 2 August had made it clear that Labour would sanction military action only if it were backed by the UN, Tory MPs were bitter at Gaitskell's departure from bipartisanship at a moment of crisis. When the House divided Eden won by 319 to 248, a vote along party lines with the Liberals continuing to give the government the benefit of the doubt. The division in the House reflected sharp differences of opinion in the country as a whole. A Gallup poll indicated overwhelming agreement with the view that Nasser was in the wrong, but in September only 34 per cent approved of using troops, compared with 49 per cent of respondents who disapproved. Several newspapers backed Eden's policy even if it meant war, but other mass-circulation papers such as the *Mirror* and *Herald* were lukewarm. These deep divisions did not augur well for the plans being prepared by Britain's military chiefs. Edward Heath, the youthful Tory Chief Whip, even warned Eden that Tory opponents of force were sufficient in number to put the government into a minority if the crunch came.[25]

The Prime Minister, his health deteriorating under the strain, refused to pull back from the brink. He told Macmillan that it was like Munich all over again, and that he would have none of it. Publicly Eden continued with diplomacy. But on 14 October, only hours after proposing new negotiations in Geneva, he gave his consent to a military plan agreed in secret with French envoys. This was scheduled to begin when Israel, in response to Egyptian raids on its southern border, launched an attack on Nasser. An invasion force of British and French troops would then seize the Suez Canal under the pretext of separating the combatants and protecting international navigation. The risk of incurring American disapproval would simply have to be faced. Although this key decision on the route to war has often been attributed to Eden's desperation as time passed, it may have been the product of a French ultimatum: Britain would either have to join in the French determination to attack or else stand by and watch its influence in the Middle East ebb away.[26] In spite of some serious doubts, the full Cabinet, informed of developments on 25 October, did not dissent from agreement in principle to the scenario that would follow 'in the event of an Israeli attack on Egypt'. On 29 October 1956 the shooting war started, with Israeli troops sweeping across the Sinai peninsula. Two days later Anglo-French bombing of Egypt began and paratroops landed at Port Said, backed up by an invasion fleet sailing from Malta. The landing force quickly moved forward and took over the northern part of the canal. The Egyptians, although pushed onto the defensive with some thousand troops and civilians killed (compared with only forty British and French soldiers), did manage to block the canal with sunken ships.

World opinion was almost uniformly hostile. The UN condemned the attack; the Soviets made veiled threats about nuclear retaliation; Commonwealth nations expressed grave reservations and the US government – not privy to the secret deal between Britain, France and Israel – reacted with indignation. The Americans harassed the allied invasion fleet in the Mediterranean and threatened the exchange value of sterling. Unlike the postwar episode with which Suez was to be most compared, the Falklands War of 1982, there was little international backing for Britain. Nor was there any semblance of political unity after the firing began, as there was to be in 1982. Tempers flared in Parliament to such an extent that a sitting of the House was suspended for the first time since the 1920s. One new MP said the debates that followed the invasion were incredibly exhilarating, and that everything he subsequently experienced in the Commons was an anticlimax.[27] On 1 November the government survived a censure motion, although the Liberals this time switched to support the opposition, and Eden dug a hole for himself by saying that if the UN would separate the combatants the invasion force would pull back. The following day Gaitskell incurred the wrath of the government benches by calling on Tory 'rebels' – known to be about twenty in number, including the likes of Nigel Nicolson and Bob Boothby – to engineer a change in the party leadership. The session ended in turmoil with Labour members howling at the Foreign Secretary, Selwyn Lloyd, calling for his resignation, while Conservative MPs furiously waved their order papers and roared encouragement for the government to continue with the military operation. One journalist recalled that the scenes were more bitter than those at the time of Munich – it was a 'most terrible, terrible spectacle'.[28]

Over the weekend of 3–4 November the divisions in Britain over Suez were starkly highlighted. A rare Saturday sitting of the House of Commons saw further uproar, with Labour MPs this time chanting for the Prime Minister to go. Later in the day Eden gave a television address, the first time a British Prime Minister had used the medium to speak directly to the nation during a time of war. Indeed, the role of television was in the process of being transformed by the crisis. Hitherto the BBC had stuck with the convention that issues due for consideration in Parliament would not appear until a fortnight later. But the new commercial channel ITN struck out on its own, with its chief political presenter Robin Day providing viewers with vivid reports of the passionate debates taking place. Like Churchill before him, Eden had grave reservations about the new medium. The BBC's willingness to report Nasser's statements (not to mention hot lights in the studio) convinced him that the corporation was 'subversive' and out to undermine his government. But in his broadcast on 3 November he came across as sincere and emphatic. He described himself as a man of peace, yet spoke of his utter conviction that it was the right time to act, not to stand aside as Britain had done in the 1930s. A flood of supportive letters and telegrams to Downing Street demonstrated that the Prime Minister had struck a chord. Much to Eden's annoyance, Gaitskell secured the right to reply. His BBC broadcast was seen by admirers as clear and effective, insisting that Britain could not take the moral high ground – 'we have taken the law into our own hands.' In the view of his opponents, the 'traitor' had administered a stab in the back to British soldiers and sailors on eve of battle – a sentiment shared particularly by officers en route to the front.[29]

Further proof that Suez was convulsing the nation, opening up divisions in every class and family, came in the Sunday newspapers on 4 November. It was later claimed that Eden had fought an inept propaganda war, notably with crude threats to censor the BBC, yet the bulk of the national press had hitherto broadly supported his cause. In part this reflected the success of government techniques of persuasion – not only through the selective use of censorship powers but also through the lobby system of non-attributable briefings and by means of personal contacts, particularly with the foreign and deputy editor of the *Times*, Iverach McDonald, who was invited to Downing Street only hours after Nasser's coup in July. As the Suez operation got under way, press support for the government wobbled. McDonald was appalled when he was given confidential knowledge of the collusion plans with Israel, and the *Times* moved to a position of sitting uncomfortably on the fence, holding back from attacking the government as troops went into battle but criticizing the failure to secure American backing. Other papers were less restrained. In addition to those that had been doubtful from the outset, the *Observer* joined the fray by attacking the government's 'crookedness', claiming that Britain and France had acted not as 'policemen but as gangsters'.[30] These sentiments were shared by a crowd of some thirty thousand protestors that gathered later the same day in Trafalgar Square. Displaying banners that urged 'Law, not War', they were addressed by Aneurin Bevan who said that the Prime Minister was either lying in claiming Britain was out to separate the combatants or else 'he is too stupid to be Prime Minister'. Mounted police had to charge to prevent the crowd from reaching Downing Street, where the chants of 'Eden must go' penetrated the Cabinet room.

The meeting inside Number Ten on that Sunday afternoon indicated that ministerial support for continuing the operation was beginning to ebb away. Eden threatened resignation and the breakup of the government: 'if they wouldn't go on he would have to resign.'[31] In the event twelve ministers voted for carrying on, noting that a ceasefire between Israel and Egypt had not yet been agreed; four voted for delay; three for indefinite suspension. By the time the Cabinet met again on the morning of Tuesday 6 November, the balance of the argument had shifted decisively. In spite of his talk of 'dying in the last ditch' only days earlier, Macmillan as Chancellor had taken fright at the prospect of devaluation and the imminent demise of the sterling area. British reserves of foreign currency and gold were dwindling away, and the Americans confirmed that they would obstruct moves to raise funds through a loan or the IMF. Faced with the imminent collapse of the pound, Macmillan's view was now, as he told Selwyn Lloyd, that 'we must stop'.[32] By this time Israel and Egypt confirmed that they had stopped fighting and the UN was pledged to sending a peacekeeping force; the case for halting the operation had become overwhelming. Ministers agreed by late morning that the allies should call a ceasefire. The French, subject to less direct pressure on their currency, reluctantly came into line, and by the evening of 6 November Eden had reported to the House that the troops had been ordered to stop firing, pending confirmation from the UN that any international force would be competent to secure the aims of a resolution that included prompt withdrawal of all combatants behind agreed armistice lines. The news was greeted with cheering from the opposition benches and also from some government supporters. Comparisons were again made with Parliament's reception of the Munich agreement. The Suez operation was over; British and French troops had advanced less than twenty-five miles down the canal.

Inquests into the debacle began almost immediately. The announcement of a ceasefire removed the inhibitions that had restrained some, if not all, critics. Labour tabled a motion of no confidence in the government and Tory opponents of Eden's policy came out of the woodwork. Among those who opposed the military option, Nigel Nicolson led the way with a speech on 7 November saying that the Prime Minister had violated all the axioms of Conservative foreign policy since the war. From the opposite viewpoint, anger within the 'Suez group', stunned by the early ceasefire, was equally intense, and strong pressure had to be applied to persuade disgruntled hardliners to back the government in the vote of confidence. Eden's performance on 8 November – stubbornly maintaining that a bridgehead had been established which might yet be exploited by diplomacy – failed to convince; with every day that passed it was obvious that Anglo-American relations were in cold storage until British and French troops were entirely removed from the canal. Tory advocates of continuing the fight were scathing at the betrayal by Britain's great wartime ally but, as one political journalist noted, the so-called 'tough men' of the right came into line when threatened with the 'unspeakable alternative of a Gaitskell government'.[33] There were only six Tory abstentions at the end of the debate, and the possibility that Eden's majority would fall so far as to endanger his administration, as happened to Chamberlain in 1940, was averted. In the circumstances, government unity held up reasonably well, impaired only by the resignation of two relatively junior ministers, Anthony Nutting and Edward Boyle, and the Press Secretary at Number Ten, who was speeded on his way with an inkpot thrown at him by the Prime Minister.

The pressure on the Cabinet had nevertheless been relentless, with the greatest strain being borne by the triumvirate of senior ministers. As Peter Hennessy has noted, the tensions that built up by early November – with British troops in action, the United States frosty, the Soviets threatening a nuclear response, uproar at the UN, and turmoil in the House of Commons – could have destroyed a fitter, more poised figure than Eden. As it was, his health was increasingly a matter of concern.[34] Suffering from exhaustion, it was decided he should leave the country for a period of complete rest. On 23 November he left to recuperate at the Jamaican residence of the James Bond novelist Ian Fleming. In his absence, Butler and Macmillan were left to pick up the pieces. Secret talks were undertaken with the US government, aimed at establishing on what terms American financial aid to Britain might be resumed. Some ministers toyed with the idea of going down with all guns blazing, resuming the advance down the canal, but the revelation that Britain had lost more than 20 per cent of its foreign currency reserves sealed the issue. The Cabinet agreed to terms that were to bring some \$2 billion of US-backed loans and aid flowing into London over the following few weeks. On 3 December it was left to Selwyn Lloyd to announce to a hostile and raucous House that British troops would withdraw by mid-December. It was impossible to conceal the scale of the humiliation; there would not, as had earlier been hoped, be any preconditions for the negotiations about the future of the canal. Selwyn Lloyd was flanked on his way into the chamber by his taller colleagues, Macmillan and Butler; this was intended as an act of solidarity, though the Foreign Secretary later said it made him feel like a prisoner in handcuffs being taken to the cells.[35]

The curtain had come down on Suez, and it looked as if it would soon come down on Eden's career. As the Chief Whip noted in his memoirs, even a Prime Minister at the pinnacle of power could not afford to be out of the country for long. In Eden's case, Heath said, his absence resulted in a de facto leadership race getting under way.[36] While it was accepted that the Prime Minister needed a break, the decision to travel to an exotic Caribbean island was deeply damaging. Randolph Churchill, one of Eden's long-standing Tory critics, jibed that when German troops were left to fend for themselves at Stalingrad, 'even Hitler did not winter in Jamaica'.[37] Speculation that the Prime Minister might have to resign began to gather pace, not least in the White House where negotiations about renewed aid were based on the assumption that Britain would soon have a new leader. While Eden sunned himself, Rab Butler – as on several occasions over recent years – found himself at the helm, and came to regret being left in charge when the government was so clearly out of step with international opinion. As he later observed, he faced 'the odious duty of withdrawing the troops, re-establishing the pound, salvaging our relations with the US, and bearing the brunt of criticism from private members, constituency worthies and the general public for organizing a withdrawal, which was a collective responsibility'. Butler's notorious ambivalence – formally supporting Eden but indiscreetly expressing reservations behind the scenes – did little for his own reputation. He claimed he was never opposed to the defeat of Nasser, but wherever he went during the difficult weeks of Eden's absence, Butler 'felt the party knives sticking in my innocent back'.[38]

The third key minister during the crisis, Harold Macmillan, ironically found his political standing enhanced. The Chancellor had been confident that Suez would not place undue pressure on sterling, and his belief that the United States would fall into line explained his strong backing for a tough stance. But after playing down warnings from his officials – in a way that for some historians suggests that he deliberately misled the Cabinet – Macmillan was unable to ignore the pressures that threatened to deplete British reserves to the level at which devaluation had been unavoidable in 1949. Within hours he moved, in the acerbic view of Churchill's friend Brendan Bracken, from 'wanting to tear Nasser's scalp off with his own finger nails' to becoming 'leader of the bolters'.[39] The Chancellor was alleged to have threatened resignation unless there was an early ceasefire, and in Eden's absence he championed the view that restoring American backing was more important than holding out for specific terms before withdrawing British troops. This turnaround was interpreted by some as a desire to remedy his misreading of American intentions, a failing he never concealed in his memoirs. Others, including Tory MPs such as Nigel Birch, suspected a deliberate challenge to the Prime Minister, some even claiming that he pushed Eden into Suez in order to hasten his downfall. While this may be an exaggeration, there were signs that Macmillan saw which way the wind was blowing. Unlike Butler, the Chancellor was able to limit his public appearances, so avoiding being linked in the public mind with the decision for British withdrawal. When he did speak, most notably to the 1922 Committee, his language was replete with references to Munich, reminding MPs that Butler had been a supporter of appeasement in the 1930s. The majority of those present were said to have been impressed, though Enoch Powell recalled that the 'sheer devilry of it verged on the disgusting'.[40] On 7 December Bracken wrote that a serious challenge was emerging: 'Macmillan is telling journalists that he intends to retire from politics and go to the morgue [the House of Lords]. His real intentions are to push his boss out of No. 10 and he has a fair following in the Tory party.'[41]

Even so, the resignation of Eden was not a foregone conclusion. When the Prime Minister returned from Jamaica on 14 December, Butler noted, in typically opaque words, that 'he seems very fit, *physically*'; and Bracken reported that Eden had told him that 'he fully intends to brazen this out'.[42] His resolve was shaken by a frosty reception. Besides scathing newspaper headlines, such as 'Prime Minister visits Britain', there were embarrassing scenes in the House of Commons when only one Tory MP cheered Eden's arrival. Things were no better when he met the 1922 Committee on 18 December. Many backbenchers were still angry about the early curtailment of the Suez operation and were not reassured by the Prime Minister's claim that he would act in exactly the same way again. According to one member present, Nigel Nicolson, this remark was greeted 'in almost complete silence'. Instead of striking a chord of defiance, it only confirmed doubts about Eden's judgement: why send the troops in if the operation was not going to be carried through? From this moment, Nicolson said, he must have realized that party support was draining away.[43] Over Christmas Eden asked colleagues individually if they thought he should stay on, and he confided to one his fear about being a 'Prime Minister at half-cock'. It nevertheless required a renewed deterioration in his health to force the issue. Fevers and sleepless nights returned. When asked if he could last out 'till the summer or Easter at the earliest', the opinion of three leading consultants was unanimous: another breakdown was likely within six weeks if he continued in office. On this basis he decided to go. The opinion of the doctors was conveyed in confidence to Butler, Macmillan and Lord Salisbury, Tory leader in the House of Lords, on the morning of 9 January 1957. By five o'clock members of the Cabinet were told that the Prime Minister had resigned.

Historians have generally accepted that this abrupt departure can only be explained on medical grounds. Whatever his reception in December, it was hard to see, prior to the doctors' intervention, what could have toppled him, at least in the short term. Others have been reluctant to conclude that medical advice alone forced Eden to go. One of his biographers claims that Butler initiated moves to persuade the Prime Minister that his position was untenable.[44] Support for this can be found in Bracken's uncorroborated reference to a deputation, led by Butler and Salisbury, which allegedly gave Eden an ultimatum on his return from Jamaica: the Cabinet would remain supportive until Easter but would then seek a change of leader unless the Prime Minister's health was fully restored. 'If,' Bracken wrote to his friend Lord Beaverbrook, 'Churchill had had such a greeting from his colleagues he would have told them to go to the furthermost part of hell, but as you know very well, Eden has none of Churchill's pugnacity.'[45] This might explain Eden pressing his doctors on whether he could continue until 'Easter at the earliest'. While medical advice was paramount, there may have been a further factor at work. On 20 December, in what was to be his final speech in the Commons, the Prime Minister was goaded into saying that he had no prior knowledge of Israel's intention to invade Egypt. It remains difficult to ascertain how worried Eden was that this would be revealed as a lie by one of the few who knew otherwise, whether in Israel, London or Washington, though rumours were widespread even before some of those involved went on the record. The Prime Minister must have been aware that any such revelation would force him to resign in disgrace. Writing in confidence to Beaverbrook, Bracken said that, although Eden's colleagues were willing to put the knife in his back the main reason for his departure was 'a secret stuffed with dynamite'. This was the secret of collusion: 'our friend brought himself down and needless remorse unnerved him.'[46]

Eden was replaced within twenty-four hours. In the days before formal election contests, Tory leaders were expected to 'emerge' – as in 1940 and 1955 – and it fell to two senior government peers, Lord Salisbury (Lord President of the Council) and Lord Kilmuir (the Lord Chancellor), to agree on the procedure to be adopted for the succession. They consulted members of the Cabinet and other leading party dignitaries before advising Queen Elizabeth on the choice between two candidates – Butler and Macmillan. Kilmuir later outlined the sequence of events that followed Eden's resignation on 9 January:

Bobbety [Salisbury] and I asked our colleagues to see us one by one in Bobbety's room in the Privy Council Offices . . . There were two light reliefs. Practically each one began by saying, 'This is like coming to the Headmaster's study.' To each Bobbety said, 'Well, which is it, Wab or Hawold?' As well as seeing the remainder of the ex-Cabinet, we interviewed the Chief Whip and Oliver Poole, the Chairman of the Party. John Morrison, the Chairman of the 1922 Executive, rang me up from Islay the next morning. An overwhelming majority of Cabinet Ministers was in favour of Macmillan as Eden's successor, and back-bench opinion, as reported to us, strongly endorsed this view.[47]

Most newspapers were wide of the mark in predicting Butler as the likely successor on 10 January. By late morning the Queen had received advice from Lord Salisbury and from Winston Churchill, who also went for the older man. Around three o'clock Macmillan, having spent the morning reading Jane Austen's *Pride and Prejudice* – 'very soothing' – was summoned to Buckingham Palace and invited to form a government. During the evening he took the Chief Whip, Edward Heath, to celebrate with champagne and oysters at the Turf Club.

The leadership crisis was swift, although it was by no means free of controversy. In the first place, important questions of procedure were raised. One minister felt Salisbury and Kilmuir had no authority to act at such short notice; another maintained that he was never consulted.[48] Suggestions were also made subsequently that Lord Salisbury, whose personal preference was for Macmillan, influenced the outcome by calling in uncommitted Cabinet members at the end; seeing strong backing for Macmillan on the sheet of paper before them, the pressure to go with the tide became irresistible.[49] No one involved has corroborated this account, however; nor was it obvious who else might carry out the consultation process. Both Salisbury and Kilmuir could claim to be ideally placed, as respected members of the House of Lords, to offer speedy and impartial advice. They could also claim to be following the precedent of 1923, when senior party statesmen stepped in to assist an outgoing Prime Minister, Bonar Law, considered too unwell to take charge of soundings to determine a successor. Clearly a constitutional crisis could have developed, along with a deep split in Tory ranks, had Eden declared a strong preference for Butler. Macmillan states that he 'gathered from Anthony', whom he saw later on 10 January, 'that he had neither been asked for his advice nor had volunteered it'. Some historians have challenged this, citing evidence from Eden's private papers in which he informed the Queen about Butler's success in stepping in during his own absences. But if this was ever intended as an endorsement – which was not clear – it was never repeated in public by Eden.[50]

Controversy also surrounds the question of how far Macmillan's triumph was determined in advance. Although Eden's departure was sudden, his ill health inevitably provoked speculation before Christmas 1956 about a possible change of leadership. In such an event, the Suez group of Tory MPs in particular was determined to block the emergence of Butler. At Cabinet level, as Butler later discovered, there were several younger ministers who were making known their private preference for Macmillan in anticipation of Eden's departure. While Butler was taking comfort from public opinion, which made him the preferred successor, Macmillan was cultivating support where it mattered – inside the party. Edward Heath conceded that there had not been much negotiation but there had been 'contacts'. The distinguished journalist Henry Fairlie went further, claiming that 'while Eden was still Prime Minister, recuperating in the West Indies, his Chancellor of the Exchequer was arranging his removal and his own succession.'[51] Notions of any full-blown conspiracy are, however, difficult to square with Eden's determination, until receiving firm medical advice on 7 January, to remain at the helm. What was more, Butler, though bitterly disappointed by his treatment at the hands of 'our beloved Monarch', could hardly cry foul when his rival was so obviously the party's choice. Whatever system had been used for gauging opinion, it was unlikely to have produced a different outcome. Butler had to accept that his support was minimal among ministers and that even natural 'Butlerite' MPs were switching sides.[52]

The real question is why Macmillan was so overwhelmingly preferred. Butler's key role in helping to deliver electoral victory in 1955 appears to have had no bearing on Conservative opinion. What clearly did was Suez. It was an open secret that Butler shared the view of Churchill. As well as saying he would not have 'dared to stop', Churchill said in private: 'If I had had an operation on my inside I would not have attempted to invade Suez by slow convoy from Malta!'[53] In Eden's absence, it was Rab who became a target for disgruntled members of the Suez group. Unwilling to admit that the operation had been a mistake, backbenchers took out their anger towards Nasser on Butler, who had shown himself, in the words of the *Economist*, to be 'sensible' but not very 'heroic'. By contrast, Macmillan enhanced his standing despite being, in Harold Wilson's jibe, 'first in, first out'. Initial enthusiasm for intervention, followed by recognition that American hostility necessitated withdrawal, at least had the virtue for Tory MPs of demonstrating toughness. In this respect, considerations of character, formed over several years, played their part in determining the leadership question. Whether justly or not, many in the party shared Churchill's belief that 'Harold is more decisive'. Whereas Butler was regarded as a masterful intellectual and administrator, Macmillan, the supreme tactician, was much less content to sit back and let fortune take its course. His rise to the top mirrored that of his mentor Churchill in 1940. Churchill, too, had faced a powerful rival for the succession, Lord Halifax (supported at the time, ironically, by Butler). He also combined public loyalty to the party leader, Neville Chamberlain, with an iron determination to strike when the moment came, even if this meant shuffling off responsibility for failure. Churchill was deeply implicated in the Norway fiasco, just as Macmillan more than anyone else misjudged the likely American response to Suez. In the words of Henry Fairlie: 'it was not surprising that it was with the Chief Whip that Macmillan chose to celebrate on the night of his appointment, for what he had to celebrate was the success of a calculated and ruthless political manoeuvre.'[54]

As the dust settled, it became clear that Suez marked a pivotal moment in Britain's eclipse as a world power. It demonstrated that Britain no longer had the capacity – military or economic – to launch a major operation in defiance of international opinion, especially in the face of American disapproval. Ministers, MPs and newspaper editors alike, all were painfully aware that the attitude of the US government had proved critical. The Americans could have influenced world opinion, deterred the Soviets and supported the pound, but they chose not to. Within a year a new White Paper on defence, foreshadowing the end of conscription, formalized what Suez had made obvious: that the role of world policeman had passed unambiguously to the United States. Relations with major allies such as the Americans and French were to recover, but British prestige and influence in the Middle East never did. Nasser was left as the undisputed champion of Arab nationalism, and British ties with countries such as Iraq and Jordan were broken. Suez, in short, played a key part in the demise of Empire. Some historians have noted that there was no overnight rush to grant independence to Britain's remaining dependent territories. Yet within a decade little remained of the formal Empire. The early 1950s strategy of aiming for looser, more decentralized forms of colonial control was replaced by a new willingness to lower the British flag. Suez provided the catalyst for the last great retreat from Empire.[55]

Why had it happened? It would be a mistake to suggest that

failure was inevitable from the moment Nasser took control of the canal. Before the collusion plans were agreed in mid-October, a negotiated settlement was still feasible. In such an eventuality Britain was certain to have lost face, but not necessarily with the disastrous consequences that followed from an aborted military operation. Without doubt, shortcomings in the machinery of government contributed to the outcome. Military planning did not proceed smoothly; the Treasury was unprepared for massive speculation against the pound; and the Egypt Committee proved ineffective as a War Cabinet. On some occasions ministers were given only twenty minutes' notice of its intention to meet and turned up in the wrong place. Ultimately these failings came back to Eden. Suez, as Peter Hennessy has noted, represents 'the greatest single failure of the premiership in the post-war period'; the lesson of Eden's tenure of the top job, he adds, was quite simple – 'how not to do it'.[56] As Foreign Secretary in the early 1950s, Eden had shown a far-sighted awareness of Britain's changing role in the world, yet as Prime Minister he lost this sense of perspective about the nation's capabilities and limitations. It was difficult to imagine a crisis more ineptly managed, in terms of leadership, political support and the implausibility of Eden's 'cover story'; his was a 'near absurd' attempt to fight a war while ignoring the economic consequences and keeping major allies and the British public in the dark.[57]

Leading colleagues later tried to make out that they suspected Eden might not pass muster all along. Interviewed in old age, Harold Macmillan claimed that 'Winston thought Anthony would wreck it – that's a reason why he held on for so long.'[58] The circumstances of Eden's departure make it difficult to avoid the conclusion that personal failings provide the key to understanding his troubled premiership. According to his detractors, Eden was guilty of everything from indecision and lack of imagination to obsessive vanity. His mismanagement certainly left the party in a state of turmoil. One backbencher noted how weeks of anxiety had produced the danger of an 'absolute split' in Conservative ranks.

The bitterness that resulted was not easily forgotten. The small number of anti-invasion rebels all incurred the wrath of local party activists; one said they were made to feel like officers who had disgraced their regiments. In time, four MPs were deselected and others found their careers blighted.[59] While an 'absolute split', threatening the early breakup of the administration, was ultimately averted, it was difficult to dispute the view of Edward Boyle, one of the two ministers to resign, that the end result brought no credit to the Tory cause: 'Nasser is still there, the canal is blocked, the economic outlook is appallingly black, Stalinism seems to be waxing again, and British influence in the Near East has sunk to a new low point. How any self-respecting Conservative Association can at this juncture circulate pamphlets about Eden entitled "This is his finest hour" I simply cannot imagine.'[60]

While Eden lacked the qualities necessary for successful leadership, it should not be overlooked that he became the scapegoat for ill-conceived decisions that were taken collectively. Aside from being implicated in the Suez fiasco, senior colleagues were responsible for errors of judgement that brought the first appearance of 'stop–go' in the post-war economy. The downturn of 1955–6 has been attributed even by sympathetic writers to short-term expedients, notably a pre-election budget that fuelled inflation and made painful remedial measures unavoidable.[61] Butler was forced to leave the Treasury in humiliation and Macmillan spectacularly misjudged the capacity of Britain's reserves to hold up in an international crisis. On the home front, the Conservative leadership as a whole, and not Eden alone, found itself floundering in the face of changing economic circumstances. Certainly the stagnation of the economy meant that the election victory of May 1955, which afterwards assumed an air of inevitability, was unlikely to have been so easily achieved at any other time during 1955–6. When Eden left office, just as when Churchill had come to power five years earlier, many assumed that Labour would shortly return to office. The problems that had beset and ultimately undone the 'best Prime

Minister we have' were not likely to disappear overnight. His successor was in for a rough ride.

In due course the new leader was able to ride the storm. With half of the 1955 parliament still to run, Macmillan had time to restore Tory fortunes by first mending fences with Britain's allies and then engineering an economic boom which was to convince the electorate that it had 'never had it so good'. In individual terms Harold Macmillan became the chief beneficiary of Suez, his ambition and will-power enabling him to triumph over his adversary Rab Butler. Selwyn Lloyd also lived to fight another day; ' one head on a charger should be enough,' Macmillan said in retaining the Foreign Secretary as part of his new Cabinet.[62] Anthony Eden, although he was to live for many years in retirement, had provided the head on the charger. If he had died on the operating table in 1953, his historical reputation would have been as one of Britain's uncrowned prime ministers, those figures whose potential went unfulfilled through no fault of their own. Instead, Suez meant he would be inescapably regarded, in the words of his friend Noel Coward, as a 'tragic figure who had been cast in a star part well above his capabilities'. The memoirs of Edward Heath capture the personal consequences, describing how he as Chief Whip, with a few colleagues, accompanied Eden and his wife Clarissa as they prepared to set off from Tilbury for New Zealand to recuperate in late January 1957. 'We stood around talking rather awkwardly. There was really nothing to say. We had talked it all out before,' Heath recollected. 'On shore we watched the ship pull away and, with a final wave, turned our backs on a page of history. We were all depressed that what had begun with such high hopes, less than two years before, of a new and younger Prime Minister, so much in tune with his people of the New Elizabethan Age, had come to an end so sadly.'[63]

5

'Sexual intercourse began in 1963'
The Profumo affair

A great party is not to be brought down because of a squalid affair
by a woman of easy virtue and a proved liar.

Lord Hailsham, Tory minister, comments on BBC television,
13 June 1963

Harold Macmillan, whose elevation was achieved by a brutality,
cunning and greed for power normally met only in the conclaves
of Mafia *capi*, said, after he had climbed the greasy pole and
pushed all his rivals off (*takes out handkerchief containing concealed
onion*) that the whole thing was Dead Sea Fruit.

Bernard Levin, commentator, If You Want My Opinion *(1992)*

On 4 June 1963 John Profumo, the Conservative Secretary of
State for War, wrote a letter of resignation to the Prime
Minister, Harold Macmillan. In his letter Profumo admitted he
had lied in the House of Commons about his relationship with a
young woman named Christine Keeler. 'To my very deep regret,'
he said, 'I misled you, and my colleagues, and the House.'
Macmillan replied that this was 'a great tragedy for you, your
family, and your friends', but added that 'in the circumstances' he
had no alternative other than to accept the resignation. 'In the circumstances' was Macmillan's way of referring to the storm that
was about to be unleashed. For weeks to come, the Profumo
episode was to exercise a stranglehold on public life in Britain. At

first sight this seems difficult to explain. The post of War Minister was not important enough to merit inclusion in the Cabinet. Profumo was neither the first nor the last politician to have been 'economical with the truth' in Parliament, or to have committed adultery. Nor was this one of the 'grand passions' of history, in the manner of the affair between Foreign Secretary Lord Curzon and Elinor Glyn after the First World War. Yet throughout the summer newspapers in Britain, and many abroad, pored over the details and repercussions of Profumo's involvement with Keeler. A lengthy inquiry conducted by a senior judge, Lord Denning, became an instant bestseller when its findings were published by Her Majesty's Stationery Office (HMSO) in the autumn. And before the end of the year two full-length books about the case had appeared. 'In the end', wrote the authors of one of these studies, the whole episode 'transcended sanity and threatened to bring down a Prime Minister and his Government, tarred the reputation of the country . . . and left a path of shattered reputations and ruined careers . . . Only a nation harbouring a latent neurosis could have been thrown into such a spasm.'[1]

So why did the scandal become a national obsession in the summer of 1963? The answer lies partly in the rich mix that went to make up the story. Sex, race and class; the worlds of politics, the law and national security; a cast of characters ranging from the aristocratic 'Cliveden set' of Profumo's friend Lord Astor to the shadowy inhabitants of the London criminal scene – all provided irresistible copy for the press as the drama unfolded. The particular timing of the crisis was also crucial. Fleet Street had a major grievance against Macmillan's Conservative government in the aftermath of the so-called 'Vassall case'. In the autumn of 1962 William Vassall, an Admiralty clerk who had been blackmailed for his homosexuality, was convicted of spying for the Soviet Union. The Prime Minister accepted the resignation of Tom Galbraith, an Admiralty minister rumoured to be involved in a sexual relationship with Vassall. But an exhaustive investigation found that there was no basis to the claims and in March 1963 the two journalists who made allegations in the case – from the *Daily Sketch* and the *Daily Mail* – were imprisoned for refusing to disclose their sources. Newspaper editors from the *Times* to the *News of the World* were incensed, believing that the journalists had been made scapegoats by the government. Several papers were only held back from telling what they already knew about Profumo and Keeler by the War Minister's libel threats. As the weeks passed, what Wayland Young, author of the second of the 'instant histories' of the affair, referred to as the 'constipation in Fleet Street', became acute.[2] After the minister came clean in June the floodgates were opened; the press was not going to miss its chance for revenge.

There was, in addition, a broader reason why the Profumo case became all-consuming: it played a vital part in ending Harold Macmillan's premiership. Macmillan was no longer the supremely confident leader – the unflappable 'Supermac' of Vicky's cartoon creation – who had secured a third successive election victory for the Conservatives in 1959. An economic downturn in the early 1960s damaged the credibility of his claims that the nation had 'never had it so good', and much of his personal popularity was forfeited after the sacking of a third of his Cabinet in the 'night of the long knives' in 1962. 'Supermac' became, in the eyes of press commentators, 'Supermacbeth'. This was followed at the beginning of 1963 by what the *Times* called an 'icy blast from Paris' – the French veto over Britain's proposal to join the Common Market, which undermined Macmillan's attempt to give his administration a fresh sense of direction. The Prime Minister, in his late sixties, was increasingly presented as past his best and out of touch, especially in contrast to forty-six-year-old Harold Wilson, who became Labour leader in January 1963 after the sudden death of Hugh Gaitskell. Within weeks of him taking over, Wilson supporters such as the Labour MP Richard Crossman were talking of his dynamism and the effect this was having on the country; one is 'irresistibly driven', Crossman wrote in his diary, 'to clichés of the New Frontier and comparisons of

Harold with Kennedy'.³ In his pomp, Macmillan might have shrugged off Profumo's resignation. By 1963, as this chapter will show, his fragility was already such that, in the words of his biographer Alistair Horne, he could be 'all but ruined by the peccadillo of one junior minister'.⁴

The Profumo affair took place in the context of a rapidly changing social climate. Historians such as Arthur Marwick have noted that the roots of what became the 'permissive society' of the mid- to late 1960s originated in ideas and movements emerging from 1958 onwards. At the heart of what Marwick calls a 'cultural revolution' was a transformation in personal relationships – between the sexes and the generations – one manifestation of which was a new willingness to break the taboo on discussing sex in public. A defining moment in this respect came when Penguin Books was taken to court in 1960 for attempting to print D. H. Lawrence's sexually explicit novel, *Lady Chatterley's Lover*. The prosecution barrister Mervyn Griffith-Jones, who was to figure in the trials associated with the Profumo case, attracted much ridicule when he asked whether it was a book 'that you would . . . wish your wife or your servant to read?' The jury acquitted Penguin Books of obscenity and two million copies of the novel were sold within a year. Although protest groups were formed with the aim of 'defending moral principles', the trial marked a key milestone on the road to a new sexual openness.⁵ Thereafter newspapers and magazines pored over stories about sex in a manner that had been unthinkable in the starchy atmosphere of the mid-1950s. The year 1963 saw the publication of the *Kama Sutra* and *Fanny Hill*, as well as the high-profile divorce case of the Duchess of Argyll, who was accused of taking some ninety lovers, which also became embroiled with the Profumo affair. It was this backdrop that prompted the lines in Philip Larkin's poem:

> *Sexual intercourse began*
> *In nineteen sixty-three . . .*

> *Between the end of the Chatterley ban*
> *And the Beatles' first LP.*[6]

For Profumo and Keeler, sexual intercourse began – and ended – in 1961. John Profumo had the classic pedigree for an aspiring Conservative politician. He came from a wealthy family, was educated at Harrow and Oxford and had a distinguished war record. After his marriage to the actress Valerie Hobson, whose film career included parts in *Kind Hearts and Coronets* and *Great Expectations*, he rose steadily through the party ranks before Macmillan appointed him to the War Office in 1960. His charm and assurance marked him out as a high-flyer, a potential future Foreign Secretary if not leader of the party. In July 1961 Profumo and his wife were at Cliveden among the weekend guests of Lord Astor, a former Tory MP and director of the *Observer* newspaper. Strolling after dinner in the warm summer air, the guests came across the nineteen-year-old Christine Keeler, naked beside the swimming pool. Keeler, who had worked for some time as a show-girl in a London nightclub, was present at the behest of Dr Stephen Ward, an osteopath and socialite who rented a cottage on the Cliveden estate from his friend Astor. Sometime after the encounter at the poolside, Profumo embarked on a brief affair with Keeler, meeting at various locations in London, though it appeared to be over in a matter of weeks. The later scandal would not have assumed the proportions it did but for the presence at Cliveden the same weekend of Captain Yevgeny Ivanov, a naval attaché at the Soviet Embassy in London. Keeler was to claim that at the time of her affair with Profumo she also slept with Ivanov; the potential security risk was enhanced by the possibility that Stephen Ward was also working for the Soviets.

By the autumn of 1962 rumours of the minister's affair, and of Ivanov's involvement, were circulating in London's clubland, at Westminster and in Fleet Street. Matters began to come to a head in early 1963 when Keeler was told she would be called as a witness in the forthcoming trial of Johnny Edgecombe, a West Indian boyfriend, who was arrested following a shooting incident at Stephen Ward's flat in December. At this point Keeler began efforts to interest national newspapers in accounts of her colourful love life – including her liaison with Profumo. Fleet Street editors were wary at the outset, but it was possible that she would refer to the affair when she gave evidence during Edgecombe's trial. As the threat of a scandal loomed, Moscow decided to recall Ivanov. Ministers were also becoming concerned. In late January Profumo was cross-examined by two of the government's senior law officers, the Attorney General, Sir John Hobson, and the Solicitor General, Sir Peter Rawlinson. The latter admitted in his memoirs to having doubts at the time about Profumo's denial of the allegations, but he was pacified by the minister's threat of legal action against anyone going into print.[7] Profumo repeated his version of events – that he was acquainted with the girl but no more – when he was interviewed by Macmillan's Private Secretary, Tim Bligh, and the government Chief Whip, Martin Redmayne. The Prime Minister was first informed of these developments when he returned from a foreign trip at the beginning of February. His dislike of the whole situation was evident in his diary comment that 'all these people move in a raffish, theatrical, bohemian society, where no one really knows anyone and everyone is "darling".' But for the time being he was satisfied with Profumo's assurances.[8]

Macmillan was later to be vilified for taking Profumo's word at face value, yet it is easy to see why he took no action in February 1963. At this stage there was no firm evidence to contradict Profumo's repeated denials. For many senior Conservatives of the generation who served in the war, it was a matter of honour that a colleague should be regarded as innocent until proven guilty. Ministers were deeply angry that Tom Galbraith had been forced to resign in the Vassall case as a result of innuendo and press gossip. Just as the rumours about Profumo were building up, it was becoming obvious that Galbraith was innocent of the charges levelled against him. It was natural that the Tory establishment would wish to protect the War Minister and prevent him from becoming another victim of baseless allegations. The Prime Minister felt the pressure more than anyone. He knew that, politically, his government could not afford another sex and spying scandal. As the Vassall tribunal undermined the case against Galbraith, so Macmillan resolved not to give way for a second time. He felt that he had been precipitate in accepting Galbraith's resignation, setting back the career of one of his colleagues unnecessarily, and he determined that he would not do the same to Profumo. It was while Macmillan was coming to this view that the two journalists were sent to prison for contempt of court in the Vassall affair. Many Conservatives were delighted that Fleet Street had got its comeuppance, but any celebrations were to be short-lived.

The pot continued to simmer in early March when rumours about Profumo were mentioned by the journalist Andrew Roth in *Westminster Confidential,* a newsletter subscribed to mainly by MPs, journalists and London embassies. The minister accepted advice not to sue, agreeing that the circulation of the newsletter was tiny and that a libel action would simply draw more attention to the case. On 14 March, as the trial of Johnny Edgecombe got under way, the mysterious disappearance of Christine Keeler stirred a fresh wave of speculation. Two days later the *Daily Express* sailed closer to the wind by using a picture of Keeler, the missing trial witness, on its front page. Only a few columns away came the claim, presented as a separate story, that the War Minister had offered his resignation for personal reasons but this had been turned down. A week later, on the evening of Thursday 21 March, the issue reached the floor of the House of Commons. Three Labour MPs, led by George Wigg, speaking under the protection of parliamentary privilege, raised the stakes by asking about the 'rumour upon rumour involving a member of the Government'. Ministers immediately sensed an opportunity. As the government now had no choice but to respond to the Labour MPs, this was the chance Profumo needed to clear his name. By coming to the House to make a personal statement, it was believed, he could finally kill off all the talk and prevent a further build-up of the story in the weekend press. Profumo and his solicitor were consequently summoned in the middle of the night to a meeting with five senior ministers at which a form of words was hammered out. The following morning at 11 a.m., flanked by the Prime Minister, Profumo read out his text, which included the denial that he was in any way involved in the disappearance of Keeler as a trial witness. 'There was,' he added, in words that he came to regret, 'no impropriety whatsoever in my acquaintanceship with Miss Keeler.'

Like Macmillan, the five ministers who interviewed Profumo in the early hours of 22 March have been much criticized in hindsight. For some they were not tough enough, failing to ask Profumo to produce a letter sent by the minister to Keeler in 1961 addressed to 'Darling'. For others, including Lord Denning, the ministers were too zealous. It was a 'dreadful thing', Denning reflected, for Profumo to have been dragged from his bed and forced to agree to a statement when he was 'groggy' after taking sleeping tablets. One of those present, the Minister without Portfolio William Deedes, later endorsed Denning's view that it would have been better to have considered things more fully over the weekend, adding that if the police used such methods in a criminal case it would rightly be condemned.[9] Yet it was Deedes who reported at the time that representatives of the press, having access to some of the material, believed the 'Darling' letter was not incriminating; Profumo maintained that this term was commonly used in the circles in which he socialized. Another of the ministers present, Peter Rawlinson, insisted in his memoirs that Profumo gave no impression of drowsiness at the late-night meeting, interjecting to question the wording of the statement at various points. Rawlinson notes that there was still time before the Friday morning statement for the War Minister to recant had he wished; there was no indication that he would have changed his tune over the weekend. Against the backdrop of Galbraith's case, it would have been unjust to enforce resignation in the face of trenchant denials.

All the later talk of sleeping pills, Rawlinson added, had the unfortunate effect of switching 'opprobrium from the deceiver and on to the deceived'. The simple truth, says Rawlinson, was that Profumo gave 'a most brazen and convincing performance'.[10]

The minister certainly gave a convincing performance in the Commons on the morning of 22 March. The Labour MPs who raised the question in the House appeared to have been routed and there was euphoria on the government benches. Jim Prior, one of the 1959 intake of Tory MPs, recalled that he and many others were greatly impressed because an experienced lawyer (Rawlinson), an army man (the Chief Whip, Redmayne) and one of the 'brightest brains in the party' (Iain Macleod) had interviewed Profumo and 'declared him as clean as a whistle'.[11] The Prime Minister was equally convinced that the matter was settled. Profumo concluded his statement with the threat of libel suits, and before long he won actions against two overseas publications, *Paris Match* and *Il Tempo*. Macmillan thought it was hardly credible that the minister would both mislead the House and perjure himself in the courts. Although many newspapers were still bitter about the Vassall case, most fell into line. The *Daily Mail* dutifully ran the headline 'Profumo kills a rumour', showing photographs of the minister going off to the races with his wife after his Commons statement, joining the Queen Mother by prior engagement. One possibility is that publicity about the Edgecombe trial persuaded Profumo to subjugate his 'lesser lie', that of having a brief affair, to the 'larger truth' that he was not involved in Keeler's disappearance. Whatever his thinking, it momentarily looked as if he had triumphed. His victory seemed complete when Stephen Ward, who was better placed than most, went on television to state that 'nothing of a sinister nature' had taken place.[12]

But in the early summer of 1963 the story refused to go away. Indeed, Ward, in spite of what he said on television, was to be crucial in explaining why the time bomb of Profumo's statement eventually blew up in his face. Throughout April and May Stephen Ward was the subject of a detailed police operation conducted by officers based at Marylebone Road station in London. In the most exhaustive study of the Profumo case since the 'instant' histories of the 1960s, the writers Phillip Knightley and Caroline Kennedy found that the Home Secretary of the day, Henry Brooke, initiated a police inquiry even though no specific crime was being investigated, convinced that Profumo would remain under a cloud while the mercurial Ward was at large.[13] If Brooke's intention was to ease the pressure on his colleague, then he miscalculated. Before long Ward, alarmed by persistent police questioning, changed his tune and began telling anyone who would listen that the minister had lied in his Commons statement. One of those Ward wrote to was the opposition leader Harold Wilson, who cleverly increased the pressure on Macmillan by asking for further action on the possibility of security risks. Christine Keeler, in the meantime, was back in the public spotlight. She returned from a hideaway in Spain and apologized to the judge for her non-appearance at the trial of Edgecombe, who was sentenced to seven years' imprisonment for possessing a firearm with intent to endanger life. She then became embroiled in a new case after another West Indian lover, Aloysius 'Lucky' Gordon, was charged with wounding her in a London street. Gordon's story at the Old Bailey was that Keeler was carrying his baby when she went off to Spain and that he was desperately trying to contact her. He was sentenced to three years in prison, although a few weeks later he 'got lucky' when he was released after fresh evidence was presented.

If Macmillan had hitherto acted cautiously and reasonably, accusations that he was too slow in responding to the crisis have more substance from this point onwards. It was obvious by May 1963 that Profumo's parliamentary statement had not 'killed the rumour' as had at first seemed to be the case. The Prime Minister was, moreover, in receipt of new and alarming information. In early May he was made aware of Ward's claims that Profumo was lying, and on 29 May he was told by Sir Roger Hollis, head of MI5, that there was a slight risk that Keeler might have been asked to question Profumo about atomic secrets. Macmillan

decided that the best way forward was to ask another senior colleague, Lord Dilhorne, the Lord Chancellor, to conduct a rapid
investigation into the security aspects of the affair. This allowed
the Prime Minister to stave off Harold Wilson's probing by saying
that a thorough review was under way. But Macmillan seemed
oblivious to the speed at which the noose was tightening around
Profumo's neck and the implications this would have for his
leadership. At the end of the month he left Downing Street for a
ten-day break with his wife in Scotland, determined to make the
most of the respite offered by the Whitsun holiday. Within days
Profumo had resigned. When the news was telephoned through,
Macmillan was taken aback, although he made no plans for an
early return to London. As Wayland Young notes, 'overdoing his
famous unflappability, [he] went on a day-trip to Iona with his
wife'.[14]

Most accounts assume that the War Minister buckled
under the pressure of a fresh inquiry. Lord Dilhorne, Reginald
Manningham-Buller, whose nickname was 'Reggie Bullying
Manner', had a reputation as a fearless lawyer. One of his first
actions was to send a telegram to Profumo – also away on holiday
with his wife, in Venice – summoning him to a meeting planned
for 5 June. Dilhorne's cable, it was claimed in Clive Irving's book
on the crisis, 'indicated that escape was now impossible'.[15]
According to the later Denning Report, before the arrival of the
telegram Profumo had already made what must have been his
most painful confession – to his wife. The couple returned to
England earlier than planned on Monday 3 June and Profumo
immediately requested a meeting with the Prime Minister on
the grounds that there had been a 'serious development'. In
Macmillan's absence, it was arranged that Profumo would see his
Private Secretary, Tim Bligh, and the Chief Whip, Redmayne. At
this meeting on the morning of 4 June the minister came clean,
offering to resign both from the government and as an MP. But
why did Profumo confess at this particular moment? Phillip
Knightley and Caroline Kennedy have argued that Dilhorne's

cable alone may not have tipped the balance. They suggest that the minister might have continued to brazen it out but for the knowledge – transmitted possibly by Henry Brooke, who had access to police information – that Christine Keeler had handed over a series of taped interviews in which she described her affair with Profumo in great detail. Fear that these tapes would blow the whole scandal open may have been the decisive factor. This would be consistent with Profumo returning well ahead of his planned interview with Dilhorne, and with his request for a meeting because of a 'serious development' – wording that supports the notion of outside pressure triggering the resignation.[16]

Whatever the immediate cause of the minister's decision to go, there was no doubting the enormity of its impact. As Macmillan's press adviser Harold Evans wrote in his diary, 'Out of the clear blue sky came the Profumo thunderbolt.'[17] Freed from the threat of legal action, newspaper editors rubbed their hands in glee. In the days after the resignation it was open season on the government. 'What the hell is going on in this country?' asked an editorial in the *Daily Mirror*. 'How can Mr Macmillan be expected to run the nation when he cannot even keep his own henchmen in order?' The weekend press piled on the pressure, giving extensive coverage to the news that Stephen Ward had been arrested and charged with procuring a living from the earnings of prostitutes. The *News of the World* began serializing Christine Keeler's story, including an account of how Ward had playfully thrown her swimming costume aside just as Profumo strolled down to the pool on the fateful evening at Cliveden in 1961. The *Sunday Mirror* published the full text of the 'Darling' letter, signed 'Love J', and also featured what became a famous photograph of Keeler, naked, straddling a small chair. Even traditionally supportive papers such as the *Sunday Telegraph* berated the Prime Minister for not seeing all this coming.[18] Rumours spread suggesting that the Profumo affair was only the tip of an iceberg. There was talk of other ministers calling on the services of expensive call-girls and tales of a notorious 'whipping party' in Mayfair where an important guest had died of a heart attack. Macmillan was shocked by this wave of sensationalism and referred in his diary to the press being 'exultant . . . getting its own back for Vassall. Day after day the attacks developed, chiefly on me – old, incompetent, worn out.'[19]

By the time the Prime Minister returned from Scotland on 10 June, the government was facing a full-blown crisis. Macmillan was reported as saying while he was away that with Parliament in recess the resignation could hardly be a 'major issue'. Back in Downing Street, he belatedly became aware that his own failings were under the spotlight. As Harold Evans confided in his diary, 'There can be no doubt that the Prime Minister's future lies in the balance. Against the wider background, there will be a strong temptation to the Party to jettison him.'[20] Tory MPs, meeting in informal gatherings before Parliament reconvened, were already discussing such a possibility. On 11 June the *Times* fanned the flames of discontent with an editorial, headed 'It *is* a moral issue', that was much quoted in the days to come. 'Eleven years of Conservative rule,' it claimed, 'have brought the nation psychologically and spiritually to a low ebb.' In an effort to build up alternative leaders, the *Times* made much of the alleged misgivings of upright figures such as Enoch Powell, the Minister of Health.[21] Another potential candidate for the leadership, Lord Hailsham, the Minister of Science, did nothing to calm the atmosphere when he burst out on television with the claim that the Tory party would not be ruined by a 'squalid affair'. If Macmillan was to survive this onslaught, his first task was to avoid further damaging resignations. He turned down the Chief Whip's offer to go, made in the immediate aftermath of Profumo's departure. He was then careful to secure the backing of all his leading colleagues, including Powell and Hailsham, although not before a stormy two-day session of the Cabinet at which fierce criticism was directed at the five ministers who had consented to Profumo's personal statement in March. It was revealed that the five ministers knew the contents of the 'Darling' letter and were aware that the War

Minister had been alone with Keeler in Ward's flat on at least two occasions. 'It might well be asked', the Cabinet minutes recorded, why the ministers had not insisted on examining the 'possible implications more deeply'.[22]

Macmillan avoided the danger of internal Cabinet dissension forcing a change of leadership, but he still faced an uphill task in reassuring Tory MPs in a Commons debate on 17 June. His reputation had sunk so far that the *New York Times* said a 'political crisis more profound than the storm over Suez which blew Anthony Eden out of office . . . is now shaking Great Britain to its foundations'. Whereas Suez forced a change of Prime Minister, the present crisis threatened to end the long period of Conservative rule and 'bring to power another Labour government'.[23] It seemed unlikely that Tory backbenchers would precipitate an early election, though it was the case that Harold Wilson's reputation had been enhanced by his handling of the affair. He was in the United States when news came through of the minister's resignation and when asked for his view replied, 'no comment – in glorious technicolour'. This was consistent with the careful line he had taken throughout, pressing Macmillan behind the scenes to set up a judicial inquiry. By keeping a detached dignity, he gave the appearance of putting national before party interests. His task in the parliamentary debate was, even so, not as straightforward as it looked in hindsight. As Neil Kinnock demonstrated much later in a debate over the 'Westland crisis', opposition leaders can easily miss the target when presented with an open goal. Although Wilson had insisted that it was a security matter and not a moral one, no one believed the security risks were serious. He nevertheless had to make such risks sound important without rallying Tory MPs behind their leader. This he did by probing away at Macmillan's slow response to the crisis, painting him as too obsessed with avoiding another Vassall-type scandal. Richard Crossman's view of Wilson's speech was widely shared: it was 'really annihilating, a classical prosecution speech, with weight and self-control'.[24]

By contrast, the Prime Minister looked ill at ease at the dispatch box and was on the defensive throughout his speech. In detailing what he knew about the Profumo case and when, Macmillan argued that he had acted honourably but had been 'grossly deceived'. Plaintively he admitted that he did not 'move among young people'. Even loyal observers such as Harold Evans were under no illusions about his performance. 'Alas,' he wrote in his diary, 'the loss of zest is all too obvious. The substance is good, but the manner weary and dispirited.'[25] Conservative MPs were dismayed, and one who had resigned as a minister and was never recalled by Macmillan, Nigel Birch, took up the charge of incompetence in Downing Street by quoting Robert Browning to great effect: 'Never glad, confident morning again'. Unlike on previous occasions when there had been rumblings of backbench discontent, as after the 'night of the long knives', Tory MPs were prepared to defy the government whips. In what was effectively a vote of confidence, twenty-seven Conservatives abstained on Labour's motion, cutting Macmillan's majority to sixty-nine instead of its maximum of ninety-seven. In scenes reminiscent of the Norway debate in 1940, the Prime Minister left the chamber with head bowed, cries of 'resign, resign' echoing in his ears. It was a crushing blow, especially in view of those involved in the protest: not only 'the usual malcontents', Macmillan acknowledged in his diary, but 'worthy people' swept along by the emotion of the occasion.[26]

In the days after the Commons debate, the government came close to collapsing. On the morning of 18 June Macmillan woke up to apocalyptic headlines. The *Daily Mail*'s 'Mac: The End' vied with the *Telegraph*'s 'Premier likely to resign soon'. Satirists had a field day, depicting the Prime Minister as completely out of touch and employing cruel jibes such as 'I wasn't told' and 'we've never had it so often'.[27] The American ambassador in London wrote to President Kennedy that Macmillan was mortally wounded. His admission that he did not know what was happening at crucial moments was 'pitiable and extremely damaging'; his replacement could not be long delayed as he had become an electoral liability. Ominously, Macmillan's personal rating was the lowest for any Prime Minister since Neville Chamberlain, with only one in five of those polled thinking he should stay on. Inside the parliamentary party there was a sudden upsurge of anti-Macmillan sentiment. Many MPs, including those who had supported the government on Labour's motion, talked to journalists about the need for a new leader. It was strongly felt that there should be a fresh start under a younger figurehead, with much discussion of the prospects of Reginald Maudling, the Chancellor of the Exchequer. There was uproar at a meeting of the backbench 1922 Committee when one MP stated that there were 'too many pimps and prostitutes in high places' and demanded that Macmillan go in the next fortnight.[28]

Panic spread to the ranks of the Cabinet. Amid a fresh bout of speculation about the sexual preferences and behaviour of ministers, a number chose to reveal their indiscretions to the Prime Minister. On 20 June the Colonial and Commonwealth Secretary, Duncan Sandys, Churchill's son-in-law, confessed that he was rumoured to be the 'headless man' in erotic photographs that were used against the Duchess of Argyll in her divorce case. Many years later a television documentary claimed that the particular photograph in question, dating from the late 1950s and showing the Duchess with a lover whose head was 'cut off' by the camera angle, emanated from a type of Polaroid that had been available only at the Ministry of Defence, where Sandys had earlier served as a minister. In the heat of the 1963 crisis Sandys prepared a letter of resignation, but was prevailed upon to stay when it was made clear that the government was certain to fall if another scandal broke. Harold Evans wrote in his diary that it was remarkably fortunate that nothing leaked to the press; 'the situation was saved within a hairsbreadth of disaster.'[29] Other ministers felt the need to go public in order to counter this new wave of scaremongering. Lord Hailsham trenchantly asserted: 'I am not the man without a head, the man in the iron mask, the man who goes about clad only in a Masonic apron, or a visitor to unnamed orgies.'[30] Macmillan was bemused. He was at a low ebb after the Commons debate, with some insiders saying he was talking of resigning, and he was again slow in reacting. Only after an intervention by the Leader of the House, Iain Macleod, who said this was all 'madness', did the Prime Minister tell his colleagues to desist from wild talk. Macleod later recalled that at one meeting Macmillan was in a 'terrible state, going on about a rumour of there having been eight High Court judges involved in some orgy. "One," he said, "perhaps two, conceivably. But eight – I just can't believe it."'[31]

In the short term the Prime Minister recovered sufficiently to defy those who were writing him off. He gained a breathing space by appointing Lord Denning to conduct a full-scale judicial inquiry into the security aspects of the Profumo case and 'rumours affecting the honour and integrity of public life'. As the days passed there was also something of a reaction in Macmillan's favour. The view that he was being made a scapegoat was reflected in a flood of supportive messages sent to Downing Street. In addition, it became clear that Tory malcontents were prepared to wound but not to strike. Inside the Cabinet, Maudling feared that premature action might jeopardize his longer-term leadership prospects. Muttering among MPs was contained by stern warnings from Macmillan loyalists that to oust him would tear the party apart and leave it out of power for a generation. The Prime Minister's reputation was partially restored by the part he played in negotiating a new nuclear test ban treaty. Within weeks, one opinion poll showed a narrowing of Labour's large lead. Harold Evans reported that Macmillan was 'jauntily and firmly back in the saddle'; the 'little crooks' on the backbenches had been put in their place.[32] Press attention shifted to focus on the trial of Stephen Ward, who was absolved from any security offences but convicted of living off immoral earnings. On 3 August, abandoned by his former friends, Ward died from a drug overdose.

The publication of his suicide note, saying he was sorry to 'disappoint the vultures', took much of the remaining heat out of the affair.

There was still Lord Denning's inquiry to consider. Although his critics had not been able to deliver a knockout blow, Macmillan remained fearful that the judge would substantiate allegations against Cabinet ministers, half of whom – as he confided in his diary – appeared to be under suspicion of 'perversion, homosexuality and the like'. If scandal came to the forefront again, he faced the likelihood of his premiership coming to an 'ignoble end'. He did not want to go down in history as the leader 'who had been drowned by filth which had seeped up from the sewers of London'.[33] It was a great relief for Macmillan to find when he read an advance copy of the Denning Report on 17 September that accusations against ministers were dismissed as unfounded. Denning's investigation had in fact discovered that one minister – later named by the writer Richard Lamb as Ernest Marples, the Minister of Transport – had a history of consorting with prostitutes, but it was decided not to make this known because there were no security implications. For the same reason Denning did not publish in full his findings about the Duchess of Argyll and the 'headless man', so removing the need for Duncan Sandys to reconsider his position.[34] Harold Wilson, also permitted as opposition leader to see the report prior to publication, realized immediately that it was not explosive enough to pose a renewed challenge to the Prime Minister. Wilson handed it back to Tim Bligh, Private Secretary at Number Ten, saying there was not 'much in it'. Macmillan sardonically commented that by this Wilson meant 'not much [in it] for me'.[35]

Although – unusually for a publication from HMSO – there were queues in London to get the first copies of the report at midnight on 25 September, the sense of anticlimax was unmistakable. Some of the main findings had been leaked in advance, and most of Denning's recounting of the Profumo episode was already known. Any accusations about security dangers were rejected, and the only real area of concern for Macmillan was the claim that the truth should have been established at an earlier stage. His two senior law officers, John Hobson and Peter Rawlinson, attempted to shoulder responsibility by offering to resign, but the Prime Minister had no intention of opening old wounds and turned them down. Several newspapers highlighted the negative aspects of the report, claiming that ministers had 'failed', although this was not a word used by Denning. On the whole, press criticism was muted and lacked the savagery of the attacks made earlier in the summer.[36] In effect, Profumo had become yesterday's story in Fleet Street. Macmillan had survived against the odds, but he was a wounded, less resilient figure. By the time the Denning Report went on sale he was showing symptoms of a serious illness. On 8 October, with Conservative activists congregating in Blackpool for the party's annual conference, the Cabinet backed the Prime Minister's decision, reached after much agonizing, to continue in office. But as his condition suddenly deteriorated, he was told by his doctors that he must undergo immediate surgery to tackle an inflamed prostate. Instead of making his way to Blackpool, Macmillan sent a message to the conference declaring his intention to resign.

The announcement was followed by the most disputed succession to the Tory leadership since the 1920s, causing much greater bitterness than Macmillan's triumph over Butler in 1957. The whole process was complicated by the lack of an obvious successor. Rab Butler, de facto Deputy Prime Minister, was again the favourite on the basis of his unrivalled experience but, as we have seen, Butler was never close to Macmillan who had tried, without success, to bring on younger pretenders such as Maudling and Macleod. Linked to this was the coincidental passage earlier in 1963 of a measure allowing hereditary peerages to be disclaimed. This had the effect of further broadening the field of contenders, bringing pledges from first Lord Hailsham and then Lord Home, the Foreign Secretary, to renounce their titles and sit in the House of Commons if asked to become party leader. The role played by the outgoing Prime Minister from his sickbed also complicated the plot. Having agreed to go, Macmillan delayed his actual resignation until he was in a position to advise the Queen about a successor; instead of leaving the monarch's advisers to take private soundings, he seemed determined to act as judge and kingmaker.

While Macmillan underwent his operation at the King Edward VII hospital in London, plotting and intrigue were the order of the day in Blackpool. The party conference turned into a 'seaside beauty contest', with the media spotlight highlighting the rival claims of Butler, Maudling and Hailsham.[37] None of them managed to enhance his reputation, however, and as the Prime Minister slowly came round from sedation he found the party in a state of turmoil. With great tenacity for someone emerging from major surgery, he took two decisive steps. In the first place, he 'switched peers in midstream', as the MP Nigel Birch put it: he abandoned Hailsham, his initial preference among the younger candidates, and persuaded his more experienced colleague Lord Home to come forward in the interests of party unity. Secondly, Macmillan dictated the terms on which the party should be consulted about the succession. He insisted that there should be broader soundings than ever before – certainly more extensive than those that had occurred when he came to power in 1957. Within a few days his emissaries reported back with their findings – from ministers, MPs, Tory peers and party activists – which Macmillan summed up by saying that there were strong feelings both for and against Butler and Hailsham, whereas it appeared that 'everyone would rally round Home'.[38] Macmillan's final act as Prime Minister was to compile a memorandum incorporating his findings which he then presented to the Queen on the morning of 18 October. In resigning he advised the monarch to send for Lord Home.

It took more than twenty-four hours before Home was able to complete a new administration. Butler was again gravely disappointed and only reluctantly agreed to serve, accepting Home's offer of the Foreign Secretaryship. Most of the other contenders also came into line. According to Maudling, Lord Hailsham spent some time 'buzzing about like a fly in a bottle', but then capitulated and agreed to continue as Minister of Science.[39] Iain Macleod, however, refused to join the new team, as did Enoch Powell, both claiming that Lord Home's aristocratic background was an insuperable barrier to winning a general election. Three months later Macleod underlined the extent to which the leadership race had scarred the party, launching a blistering attack on the 'magic circle' of Etonians whom he believed had manipulated the consultation process to deny Butler the succession.[40] In later years, after recovering from his illness, Macmillan denied the charge that his purpose was to 'down' Butler. Yet in his diary at the time, in an entry that found no place in his memoirs, he expressed his view that Rab 'has no strength of character or purpose and for this reason should *not* be P.M.'.[41] All the evidence pointed to the outgoing leader controlling the succession from his hospital bed. He not only prevailed upon Lord Home and determined the consultation process, he also refused requests for a full Cabinet meeting, where the strength of Butler's support would have been more evident. Macmillan's premiership was over, but he was as ruthless in quitting the leadership as he had been in acquiring it.

In the fullness of time, it became clear that the events of 1963 had left behind a trail of victims. Macmillan, who lived until well into his nineties, in due course paid tribute to the 'dreadful forfeit' paid by his colleague, John Profumo. He also commended the way in which Profumo, after disappearing from the public arena, devoted the rest of his life to working for charities in the East End of London, a role in which he was loyally supported by his wife. At the same time, Macmillan found it difficult to forgive the damage Proufumo had inflicted on the government, and reflected sadly that if an early admission of the truth had been made the political fallout would have been minimized; an eventual return to office for the War Minister would also have been possible. Christine Keeler, for her part, spent six months in prison for perjury, and went on to experience a series of turbulent relationships which left her with little money and few friends. Many years on she still seemed haunted by her 'fifteen minutes of fame', claiming in her book *The Truth At Last* that she became pregnant by Profumo.[42] Perhaps the main victim of the whole episode was Stephen Ward. According to Phillip Knightley and Caroline Kennedy, Ward may have been a Soviet agent but he was not the highly sexed bohemian he was made out to be in court proceedings. He alone of the chief protagonists, Knightley and Kennedy note, lost his life; in some respects, he was 'the only player to leave the stage with dignity'.[43]

The Prime Minister, in his own way, also suffered as a result of the Profumo case. He may have refused to yield in the first instance to the vitriolic assaults of Fleet Street or to what his colleague Rab Butler called the 'herd instinct' among Tory MPs in favour of a younger leader. But there was no doubt that he was deeply affected, for personal as well as political reasons. His successor at Number Ten, Sir Alec Douglas-Home as he became after renouncing his peerage, later said that it was the only time he could remember Macmillan being 'worsted – he so fundamentally hated the whole thing'. This 'hatred' was not simply a generational trait, the dislike of one who grew up in the Edwardian period for what he called a 'silly scrape'. It also had much to do with his wife, Dorothy Macmillan, having earlier embarked on a long-running affair with another Conservative MP, Bob Boothby; this was rarely spoken about and the cause of great anguish to Macmillan, and he remained with his wife throughout his time as Prime Minister. For some of his associates, this explained Macmillan's refusal to confront Profumo personally. He did not want to face up to what was being rumoured about the War Minister partly because it meant opening himself up to things that had been shut out from his mind for many years. 'To underestimate the "Boothby factor" in Macmillan's handling of Profumo,' writes Alistair Horne, 'would be as misguided as to fail to comprehend just how grievously it hit him.'[44] He may have clung on in the summer of 1963, but the crisis had taken such a toll that the end of his premiership could not be long delayed.

The scandal was more than a near-mortal blow to the Prime Minister of the day; it was also a serious setback to the electoral prospects of the Tory party. In the aftermath of Profumo's resignation, Labour's lead over the government was the largest since the introduction of opinion polling some twenty years earlier. Although he handled the episode adeptly, it was ironic that Harold Wilson should be the chief beneficiary for he, like Macmillan, was highly conventional, even old-fashioned, in his private life and personal tastes. Indeed, voters were not making a moral judgement in reacting to the crisis. Surveys showed that respondents thought Profumo's lie in Parliament was overwhelmingly the most important issue at stake, with adultery ranking below even the potential security risk. Nor was the Profumo affair the only cause of Conservative malaise. It was the latest of several issues that had progressively undermined the government's reputation for competence, part of a pattern that stretched back to the economic downturn of 1961. But coming as it did in the second half of the parliament, it reduced the chances of any Tory recovery. With survival taking precedence over long-term thinking in the middle of 1963, no viable electoral strategy was in sight and time was running short before an election had to be called. Rab Butler – a shrewd judge of electoral opinion over the previous decade – pessimistically concluded that the party had been brought 'to a very bad way': 'it will be with the utmost difficulty that we shall recapture the lost ground.'[45]

Some of the lost ground was made up, but not enough. The best hope for the Conservatives was that Macmillan's resignation would provide a fresh start, just as he himself reinvigorated the party when it was in turmoil after Suez. But Labour's fear that there would be a younger, more assertive leader, capable of challenging opposition claims that it was 'time for a change', was not borne out with the succession of Douglas-Home. This enabled Wilson to maintain his attacks on the 'grouse moor' image of the

Tories, claiming that he represented the future of a more open, meritocratic 'New Britain'. Douglas-Home made inroads into Labour's poll lead, but it was too late to prevent Wilson securing a narrow victory at the general election in October 1964. In explaining this outcome, the verdict on Macmillan, whatever his personal anguish during the Profumo case, must be a harsh one. For someone who believed that power was like Dead Sea fruit – 'when you achieve it, there is nothing there' – he showed great reluctance to relinquish it, and through his handling of the succession in 1963 he missed a final opportunity to show that the government was capable of genuine renewal from within. Douglas-Home did his best to revive Tory fortunes, but was too associated with his predecessor to mark a decisive break with the failures of recent years. It was once said that it was not Churchill who lost the 1945 election for the Conservatives; it was the 'ghost' of Neville Chamberlain and his discredited appeasement policy. By the same token, it was not Sir Alec Douglas-Home who lost the 1964 contest; it was the 'ghost' of Harold Macmillan.

6

'They think it's all over'
The July crisis, 1966

Surely now Harold Wilson would fulfil . . . the personal hope of
millions that he would transcend in achievement the fine work
of Clement Attlee.

*George Wigg, Labour Minister, on Wilson's prospects after the 1966
general election*

I suppose it is the most dramatic decline any modern P.M.
has suffered.

Richard Crossman diary, 24 July 1966

July 1966 was a month of high drama. Much of the nation was
gripped by the spectacle of a small group of men battling desperately against foreign enemies. Throughout the long hot summer days the actions of this valiant band were followed closely on
television screens, every new twist and turn being hotly debated in
the pubs and on street corners. But in the end, the politicians lost;
the 'gnomes of Zurich' proved too strong. England's footballers
were more successful, for July 1966 also witnessed, of course, the
nation's first and only victory in the World Cup. In popular memory it is often assumed that Harold Wilson won the 1966 general
election because it took place at the same time as England's
greatest sporting triumph of the twentieth century, the four-two
victory over Germany in the World Cup final. The reality is that
after eighteen months as Prime Minister with a tiny parliamentary

majority, Wilson triumphantly secured the re-election of his Labour government in March 1966, months before a ball had been kicked. The start of the action in the World Cup coincided with an acute economic crisis, as speculators on the foreign exchanges undermined the value of sterling. Far from overlapping with one of Labour's 'finest hours', the triumph at Wembley took place in the same week as what the diarist Richard Crossman called the 'destruction of the Wilson myth' – the belief that the Prime Minister could sweep all before him.[1] July 1966 produced a new breed of heroes and villains: England's footballers came to be revered, but Wilson's 'New Britain' was stillborn.

History has not been kind to the Wilson governments of 1964–70. For many who placed their faith in Labour's optimistic promises of a brave new world, this was an era of disillusionment – a period that at home brought a lower growth rate than during the 'wasted years' of the Conservatives and abroad saw British backing for unpopular American involvement in the Vietnam War. There were undoubtedly redeeming features. The government did achieve some of its objectives, such as the introduction of comprehensive secondary education, and it could also claim to have supported, if not initiated, moves to liberalize the law on social issues ranging from abortion and equal pay for women to homosexuality. For better or worse, Labour worked with the grain of the new 'permissive society' which was transforming individual and family relationships. Yet the sense of failure persists. Labour in Parliament was hamstrung by internal squabbling, local activists abandoned the party in droves, and traditional supporters voted with their feet. In the lowest turnout since 1935, a million fewer people than in 1964 backed Labour when the party lost power at the 1970 election. Impressive biographies by Ben Pimlott and Philip Ziegler have gone some way towards restoring Wilson's reputation, but the consensus remains that his record looks threadbare, especially when set against the achievements of the Attlee years. Whatever its shortcomings, writes David Howell, there was a feeling at that earlier time that 'great changes were being enacted. After 1964 there were no equivalents.'[2]

In seeking to explain where it all went wrong, this chapter turns the spotlight on the summer of 1966. Part of the reason why Wilson's election triumph in March turned to ashes almost before the ballot boxes had been put away lay in the expectations of the electorate. Labour's campaign at the general election in October 1964 had been based on the view that Britain had lost its way under the outdated leadership of Macmillan and Douglas-Home. It was becoming clear in the early 1960s that Britain's economy, while functioning reasonably when compared with the inter-war period, was failing to keep pace with major international rivals. In 1950 Britain's share in the value of world exports stood at 25 per cent; by 1960 it was down to 16.5 per cent. Living standards were improving, but at a slower rate than elsewhere. The average rate of growth in GDP during the 1950s, at 2.6 per cent, was well below that achieved in France, Germany, Japan and the USA.[3] Wilson encouraged discussion of these problems, and claimed with his 'white heat of technology' rhetoric to have the answers. His character and provincial background – his grammar school education, economic expertise and scientific literacy – symbolized what Labour offered: a new meritocracy to undermine the tired class antagonisms of British society and arrest the nation's slow decline on the global stage. Wilson came to power promising to be one of Britain's most dynamic leaders; he was certain to face trouble if he could not deliver.

For eighteen months after the election in 1964 there were few signs of the disintegration that was to follow. In an effort to leave behind the divisions that had scarred Labour politics in the 1950s, Wilson carefully balanced representatives of different strands of party opinion in his new administration. Most of the senior posts went to followers of the former leader, Hugh Gaitskell. Jim Callaghan became Chancellor of the Exchequer and George Brown headed the Department of Economic Affairs (DEA), a newly formed ministry charged with the task of overseeing long-term economic growth. The claims of former Bevanites were also recognized, notably by the appointment of Frank Cousins who was brought in from the trade union movement to head another forward-looking administrative creation, the Ministry of Technology. This balancing act was not, however, made from the same position of strength as Attlee had enjoyed in 1945. There was nobody in Wilson's team to take on the role played by Ernest Bevin, that of a powerful ally who could help the leader dominate policy and personnel. Indeed, Wilson was aware that most of his Cabinet colleagues had not supported him in the 1963 leadership contest. It was no coincidence that his two rivals in that contest, Callaghan and Brown, were given posts that ensured that much of their energy would be absorbed in interdepartmental rivalry.[4] Yet, in the short term, there were strong incentives to maintain unity. Hopes of creating a 'New Britain' overnight had to be deferred. With a majority of only four seats, controversial measures would never pass through Parliament, and the primary task for Labour was to remain in power long enough to be able to fight another election on its own terms.

In order to achieve this, Wilson had to demonstrate his potential for the high-powered leadership promised in opposition, especially in his handling of economic policy. He faced a stern early test. Unlike in the 1970s when unemployment and inflation came to the forefront, the most pressing concern for economic policy makers for the previous decade had been the balance of trade and the fear that Britain was 'living beyond its means'. In seeking to engineer a pre-election boom in 1964, the Conservatives had allowed imports to outstrip by far any rise in export trade, with the result that Wilson was greeted by officials with the news that Britain had a record balance of payments deficit, estimated to be £800 million. Within days the Prime Minister, in consultation with Callaghan and Brown, ruled out one possible option – a devaluation of sterling aimed at restoring the competitiveness of British goods abroad. In view of the respective strengths of the British and American economies, it was widely felt in the financial markets that at $2.80 the pound was overvalued. But Wilson preferred import controls as the best way forward, and the government moved quickly to impose a temporary surcharge on foreign imports. Although unpopular with Britain's partners in the European Free Trade Area, this move helped to steady market fears and the level of imports began to fall. Wilson had not tripped over the first hurdle.

But the perception that sterling was overvalued would not go away; three years later the government was forced to devalue the pound to the level of $2.40. With hindsight, the decision not to act earlier has been much criticized, especially as devaluation appeared to 'deliver the goods'. Along with other policies, it rectified the trade balance to such an extent that Britain had a £700 million surplus by 1970.[5] There were, however, compelling reasons for not tampering with the exchange rate in October 1964. 'Devaluation would sweep us away,' the Prime Minister told one colleague, implying that Labour would be hard put to win a second election if it were branded as the party that could not maintain sterling parity. Devaluation had already destroyed one Labour government, in 1931, and damaged another, in 1949.[6] There were economic as well as political arguments. Treasury officials thought that devaluation would lead to increased inflation, which Labour had also pledged itself to avoid. Ministers believed, moreover, that pressure on the pound would be eased in the long term only by increasing the productivity of British industry. This required careful central planning and new agreements between employers and unions to ensure a workable prices and incomes policy. These themes were at the heart of an ambitious 'National Plan' announced by the DEA in 1965, which promised an annual growth rate of nearly 4 per cent per annum over the next six years.

There was a further, international, dimension to Wilson's determination to defend the pound. Many poorer countries, especially those in the Commonwealth, held their balances in sterling and so would be hard hit by devaluation. The implication was that if forced to realign its currency, Britain would be unable to maintain its global pretensions. Shortly after coming to power, Wilson proclaimed 'we are a world power . . . or we are nothing.' In spite of decolonization, Wilson was sustained in his view by Britain's military, cultural and economic influence in many parts of the world. Wilson's decision, only days after first entering Downing Street, to go ahead with the purchase of Polaris nuclear submarines confirmed that maintaining any semblance of world power status meant relying on the 'special relationship' with the Americans. With this in mind, the Prime Minister also agreed to hold on, at enormous cost, to British military bases east of Suez – a crucial concern for President Johnson as the United States became embroiled in Vietnam. In 1965 Wilson went so far as to negotiate a secret deal with the Democrat administration in Washington: any devaluation of sterling, which the Americans feared would disrupt their own trade, was ruled out in return for lavish support on the foreign exchanges.[7]

In many ways Wilson was at his best in 1965. He relished the challenge of surviving on a day-to-day basis. As well as blaming economic difficulties on the legacy of his Tory predecessors, he skilfully avoided defeats in the House of Commons and enhanced his reputation as a relaxed and witty performer in the new age of television politics. The same could not be said of Sir Alec Douglas-Home's successor as Tory leader in 1965, Edward Heath, whose wooden style failed to make an early impression on the voting public. For the nation at large, Wilson was still a fresh, populist figure, a man who got things done. The Prime Minister carried out his pledge to abolish prescription charges, introduced by the Tories in the 1950s, and by the end of 1965 the economic indicators were looking generally favourable. An export drive had helped to reduce the balance of payments deficit and unemployment remained at historically low levels, below 2 per cent of the workforce. Early in 1966, Labour won the Hull North by-election with the largest pro-government swing at such a contest for more than a decade.[8] When he called a general election for 31 March on the back of this result, few commentators doubted that it would end in triumph for 'good old Mr Wilson', as he was called by the nation's favourite pop band, The Beatles.

For the first time in twentieth-century politics, March 1966 saw an incumbent Prime Minister secure a second election win with an increased majority. With a cushion of nearly a hundred parliamentary seats, Wilson looked set to achieve his aim of making Labour the 'natural party of government'. The margin between the two main parties in their share of the vote – 47.9 per cent for Labour compared with 41.9 per cent for the Tories – was greater than at any election since the war. The uniformity of the swing across the country enabled the government to capture seats that had eluded Labour even in Attlee's 1945 landslide. These included the likes of Aberdeen South in Scotland, Lancaster and Middleton in northern England, and Hampstead, Oxford and Exeter in the south. In contrast to the 1950s, it was Labour that seemed to represent the future, whereas the Conservatives looked hopelessly out of touch. Looking back on the euphoria that accompanied the election result, one of the Prime Minister's associates, the Paymaster-General, George Wigg, said that Labour had the opportunity to govern for a generation, to stamp its mark as the party of both economic efficiency and social justice. 'Surely now', Wigg believed, Wilson, 'having served his apprenticeship in the highest office of State, would fulfil . . . the personal hope of millions that he would transcend in achievement the fine work of Clement Attlee'.[9]

From the outset, there were those who doubted if it would be possible to satisfy the enormous expectations raised by Labour's victory. Only days after the election Dick Crossman, the Minister of Housing and Local Government, wrote with prescience in his diary that there were major stumbling blocks ahead. It was no longer possible to hide behind the excuses of a small majority and the 'thirteen wasted years' of Tory rule. This made it crucial,

Crossman noted, to resolve the 'Callaghan/Brown conflict' – the ongoing personal and political differences between the Prime Minister's two most senior colleagues. Wilson had hoped for 'creative tension', but the animosity between Callaghan and Brown – both no-nonsense individuals – spilt over into running differences on policy. In spite of Brown's announcement of the National Plan, Callaghan jealously guarded Treasury control over the main levers of policy, and his willingness to keep a tight rein over public spending did not augur well for the hopes of the DEA. In the view of Crossman, the new government would soon face difficulties if it could not settle on an agreed strategy. There was also the challenge of handling the Parliamentary Labour Party. MPs who previously had toed the line because of the narrowness of Labour's majority were likely to feel they were freer to criticize. The Prime Minister, said Crossman, 'needed a Herbert Morrison', someone who could rally the troops in the Commons as in Attlee's day.[10]

Before long, Crossman's fears were borne out. Well in advance of the July crisis ministers were commenting on the sense of anticlimax that followed the election, what Crossman called the 'curious sense of expectations fulfilled'. It soon became apparent that tensions over economic policy remained and that there would be trouble on the Labour backbenches. Tony Benn, the Postmaster-General, organized a tea party for the large intake of new MPs, only to be told that he was the first minister to take the slightest interest in them.[11] With little to show in terms of fresh initiatives, there was growing disillusionment in the parliamentary party. 'Criticism from the usual gang', one minister lamented in his diary. 'They all got themselves elected a few weeks ago on the Government's record and they have kicked us around ever since.'[12] In a meeting at Chequers, Benn bluntly told the Prime Minister that MPs felt the government had suddenly lost its sense of direction. 'Somehow all the magic seems to have rubbed off,' he wrote in his diary. Benn, hitherto an admirer, believed that Wilson had become fatalistic, saying in private that people were bored with politics and wanted

1. Neville Chamberlain announces the outbreak of war, 3 September 1939

2. Winston Churchill on the day he became Prime Minister, 10 May 1940, flanked on the left by Kingsley Wood and on the right by Anthony Eden

3. British and French troops on the beaches at Dunkirk, May 1940

4. *Below*: Churchill leaving Number Ten Downing Street with Brendan Bracken, 19 June 1940

5. Churchill acknowledges the crowds after the 'turn of the tide', December 1942

6. *Below*: Sir William Beveridge, addressing the pressure group the Social
Security League about his 1942 Report

7. Hugh Gaitskell, preparing to deliver his controversial budget, 10 April 1951

8. Aneurin Bevan, leaving his London home on 11 April 1951, shortly before his resignation over health service charges

9. *Left*: *Daily Mirror* front page on election day in October 1951, supporting Attlee and depicting Churchill as a warmonger

10. *Below*: Anthony Eden gives a TV broadcast on the Suez crisis, August 1956

11. British troops patrol Port Said in Egypt, November 1956

12. *Below*: Ships sunk by the Egyptians in the entrance to the Suez canal,
November 1956

13. John Profumo, the War Minister forced to resign in 1963

14. Christine Keeler, pictured during the Profumo scandal

15. Harold Macmillan, arriving back from holiday at Euston Station as the Profumo crisis intensified, 10 June 1963

16. Harold Wilson with his wife Mary, triumphant after the general election of March 1966

to play tennis and clean their cars while the government got on with things. Benn believed it was up to the government to inspire the public and to demonstrate how political issues affected their everyday lives. Otherwise Labour was in danger of drifting into the same shallow 'never had it so good' philosophy as Macmillan.[13]

The issue that went to the heart of the government's malaise in the early summer of 1966 was its relationship with the trade union movement. In April 1965 union leaders had agreed to a voluntary incomes policy which set a 'norm' of 3–3.5 per cent for wage increases, but this had failed to keep pace with inflation, running at over 4 per cent. The pressures this imposed were demonstrated when a protracted strike took place among Britain's merchant seamen. In 1965 the National Union of Seamen (NUS) reached an agreement with employers for a large pay rise, part of which was to cover overtime spent at sea. Some shipowners abused the agreement by giving crews more weekend work; in protest the union demanded a forty-hour week, with weekends paid as overtime. Shortly after the start of the strike in May 1966 over five hundred ships were immobilized. Everyday life was not as yet much disrupted, but the government – determined to show it was not complacent – declared a state of emergency and announced a court of inquiry. The NUS rejected compromise proposals made early in June and the strike dragged on. Supporters of the union were bitter about the government's desire to impress the financial markets by taking a firm stand against the seamen. Wilson further disgusted union critics and many of his own MPs by blaming the stoppage on Communist agitation, and by the time negotiations produced a return to work on 1 July the government had little to show for its efforts. The NUS claimed it was victorious after '47 days of hard-fought strike', gaining the forty-hour week a year earlier than in the 'final offer' made by the employers shortly beforehand.[14] In the meantime relations between the party and the unions were soured in a way that had not occurred in the days of Attlee.

In addition to taking a tough line against the seamen, the

government decided to highlight its concern about wage settlements by introducing new legislation. Unless it could show that its policy of holding down prices and incomes was succeeding, Labour would stand accused of having no credible means of tackling the underlying weaknesses of the economy. But the proposal to initiate statutory delays in wage rises was a step too far for Frank Cousins, the Minister of Technology. Cousins did not have the stature of Bevin, but he was the leading trade unionist of the day, head of the Transport and General Workers' Union, and while in office a symbol of the government's relationship with the unions. Cousins regarded the new plans as 'complete poppycock', interfering in the time-honoured process of free collective bargaining. 'In a free for all,' Cousins believed, 'we [the unions] must be part of the all.'[15] Desperate attempts to talk him round were of no avail. Cousins told the Prime Minister in his resignation letter on 3 July that the new prices and incomes bill was 'fundamentally wrong in its conception and approach'. Political commentators seized on the seriousness of this new blow to the government. It starkly illustrated the breach between the government and its most natural allies and it put back any prospect of an agreed programme of modernization for the trade unions. Without such a programme, many economists believed, Britain would never – as promised in the National Plan – leave behind the damaging 'us and them' mentality that afflicted so many sectors of industry.

After a turbulent few days, the Prime Minister was no doubt relieved to see media attention turn to the eagerly awaited start of the World Cup. Thousands of journalists and fans from all corners of the globe gathered to see how England stars such as Bobby Charlton and Jimmy Greaves would fare when pitted against the world's finest teams. The holders, Brazil, like the organizers, were alarmed when the famous Jules Rimet trophy was stolen earlier in the year, only to be found soon afterwards by a dog named Pickles. As with many sporting occasions, the reality did not match the build-up, at least in the early stages of the tournament. England's opening match on 11 July, a goalless draw with Uruguay, left a capacity crowd at Wembley jeering and whistling at full-time. Elsewhere around the country, the preliminary group matches mostly failed to capture the public imagination. Brazil underperformed, with Pele finding that opponents were determined to nullify his threat by fair means or foul. England's fortunes picked up first with a two-nil win over Mexico and then with victory by the same margin over France, the latter result ensuring the team's qualification for the quarter-finals. There were, nevertheless, concerns about whether England would be good enough to go all the way. The *Daily Mail* observed that England had so far come through with 'composure rather than grandeur' and would have to improve in order to progress in the knockout phase of the tournament.[16]

On the same day that England beat France, the nation was coming to terms with the government's reaction to a sudden economic crisis. Part of this drama was conducted behind closed doors, in fevered discussions between senior ministers, but as the tension mounted so it came increasingly into the open and vied with the football for public attention. The seamen's strike and the resignation of Cousins proved to have a nasty sting in the tail. The former severely disrupted the slow recovery of Britain's balance of payments position which had been taking place since October 1964, while the latter undermined Labour's claim to have a credible incomes policy. In combination, the two factors greatly unsettled the financial markets. Sterling came under pressure, falling to its lowest level for twenty months, and nervousness among exchange dealers was turning into panic. The government's attempt to strengthen the currency by showing its resolve to the markets had backfired. As the *Economist* observed: 'The wolves are now getting uncomfortably close to the door . . . The short-term mess has been allowed to get so out of hand that the country can probably now extricate itself only by using two out of three bitter measures of temporary impoverishment: an incomes freeze, an increase in unemployment, or devaluation.'[17] The July crisis was under way.

Opinion in the senior ranks of government during July 1966 was polarized. Some felt that the best way of meeting the crisis was to imitate the Tory approach of the 1950s – applying the brakes to produce a 'stop' phase in the trade cycle, deflating the economy by higher interest rates and cutting public spending, so demonstrating the government's toughness to the financial markets. Callaghan had already taken this course, on a modest scale, when sterling briefly came under pressure in the summer of 1965. Others believed the time had come to devalue the pound. The three main actors in the drama appeared poised between action and inertia, with rumours that their position was changing by the hour. Ironically the Prime Minister, so often in his career accused of backsliding, was the most firm in his view, which was consistently to oppose the need for devaluation. His reasoning remained the same as it had been since 1964: he believed that a change in parity would be immensely damaging politically, that it would lead to a short-term fall in living standards, whatever its effect in making British exports more competitive in the longer term, and that it would undermine Britain's role on the world stage. The Prime Minister's attitude, in the words of Ben Pimlott, remained 'as fixed as he believed the parity of sterling should be'.[18] Hitherto this had also been true of the Chancellor. Callaghan had backed Wilson in ruling out devaluation in October 1964, since when it had been regarded as the great 'unmentionable' in Cabinet; simply to discuss it was felt to invite its possibility. But Callaghan was badly shaken by the severity of the attacks on sterling in 1966. He was influenced by the visit to London on 7 July of a delegation of French politicians who impressed on him the argument that Britain would be in a stronger position to make a fresh bid to join the European Community with a realigned currency, making the recurrence of destabilizing sterling crises less likely in future. If Callaghan appeared less hostile to devaluation than in the past, then the third main player on the stage, George Brown, had undergone a wholesale change of mind. He, too, had agreed that devaluation was out of the question when Labour first came to power, but since then he had switched camps. By the summer of 1966 Brown was conscious that a straightforward deflation of the economy, slashing public spending and damping down consumer demand, would scupper the programme of expansion to which his department was committed in the National Plan. For as long as the triumvirate of senior ministers was in agreement, devaluation had not been a serious option. But Brown's conversion set alarm bells ringing for Wilson. If Brown could win over the Chancellor then everything the Prime Minister stood for would be in jeopardy. Wilson also sensed that a successful Brown-Callaghan alliance on such a vital issue would undermine, perhaps destroy, his leadership. 'Creative tension,' as Ben Pimlott says, 'was about to give way to creative insurrection.'[19] Brown and Callaghan did not yet see eye to eye. Brown was reluctant to accept the consensus among economists that devaluation, in order to be effective, would itself need to be accompanied by sharp cuts. According to Dick Crossman in his diary, 'the scale of the package [of spending cuts] required to float the pound was not very different from that required to save it.'[20] But a meeting between the three men on 8 July left the Prime Minister with the impression that Callaghan was liable to move in whatever direction the wind was blowing. Wilson decided his best strategy was that of 'divide and rule'. He sought to drive a wedge between his two colleagues, in particular working on Callaghan's inclination to go along with the Treasury wish for orthodox deflation.

On 12 July the Chancellor told Cabinet colleagues of the gloomy economic prospects ahead and of his desire to reduce public spending by £500 million: three times the level of cuts imposed when sterling wobbled in 1965 and more than enough to undermine the Chancellor's reputation for competence. All but one of the ministers who took part in the ensuing discussion voiced their alarm and attacked Callaghan. The Chancellor's feathers were ruffled, and he revealed how far he was wavering by warning the Cabinet that 'we were drifting into devaluation in the worst possible conditions'. The following day the stakes were raised when George Brown told Wilson of his reluctant acceptance of the need for sharp cuts to make devaluation work, so opening the way for full-scale Cabinet discussion of the case for realigning the currency. The Prime Minister was backed into a corner. It appeared that with Callaghan and Brown pulling in the same direction, and with the attitude of the Cabinet uncertain, he would be forced to give way. Ever the master of tactics, Wilson played for time. He told Brown in a private meeting that any decision about immediate cuts should be delayed, and that if the Chancellor would not accept this he would have to resign. Attempting to keep Brown on side, Wilson even dropped hints that he might ask him to take over at the Treasury, rather as Stafford Cripps had been promoted to replace the ailing Labour Chancellor Hugh Dalton in 1947.[21]

Callaghan, although worn down by the strain and muttering about resignation, was prepared to be flexible on the timing of an announcement about cuts. On 14 July Wilson reported to the Cabinet that an urgent reappraisal of strategy was necessary. In the meantime it was proposed to make a holding statement in the Commons, allowing time to work out the details of a new policy. According to the Minister of Transport, Barbara Castle, the Chancellor's statement in the House 'fell limply on an unimpressed audience'. Nor did the pledge to reduce spending by £500 million cut much ice in the financial markets. Although interest rates were raised on the same day as a sign of government resolve, currency dealers were more taken with the news that Britain's trade deficit in June had doubled as a result of the seamen's strike. The flight from sterling continued, and the Prime Minister knew he remained in a fix. He told his long-time ally Barbara Castle in the tearoom that 'there was a great plot on by George and Jim to get rid of him'.[22] On Friday 15 July Wilson woke up to alarmist headlines about splits in the Cabinet. Several newspapers realized that the holding statement indicated that devaluation was being seriously considered. Later in the day there was a fierce row as Brown pressed Wilson again on the need for urgent action. Brown feared that attacks on sterling threatened to ruin the economy for years to come, and he was hoping to pin down the Prime Minister, who was about to leave the country on a long-planned visit to the Soviet Union.

Wilson had agonized for some time over whether to cancel his trip to Moscow, where he was due to discuss Anglo-Soviet trade and the Vietnam War. He eventually decided that cancellation would only add to market jitters. After his departure on Saturday 16 July rumours spread like wildfire through Fleet Street and Westminster. The most lurid story was that of a plot to unseat the Prime Minister hatched at the home of the wealthy society hostess Anne Fleming, former mistress of Hugh Gaitskell and a friend of the Home Secretary, Roy Jenkins. Wilson was told via telegrams that discontent was rife among Labour MPs, with the Defence Secretary Denis Healey allegedly acting as ringleader. The three-day trip to Moscow was to be a crucial turning point in Wilson's premiership. He returned convinced that efforts had been made to remove him, and from this time on his distrust of senior colleagues increased markedly. In reality there was little evidence of a plot. Indeed, the most significant development of the Moscow interlude worked to Wilson's advantage. Callaghan and Brown had argued vehemently and resumed their old rivalry, removing the prospect of them working together to defeat the Prime Minister. Instead, Wilson had to contend with a new danger: the possible resignation of George Brown at a time when it was likely to cause further turmoil on the foreign exchanges. The First Secretary of State for Economic Affairs, as he was officially called, flew into a rage when he realized that Callaghan, after wobbling for a few days, was coming down firmly against devaluation. By sending a telegram to Moscow declaring his intention to resign, Brown forced Wilson to announce that he would cut short his trip and bring forward the date of the government's full statement of policy.

In retrospect, Wilson's fears about the threat to his position were exaggerated. Neither of the main conditions necessary to oust him was in place. There was no concerted action among Labour MPs, and there was no systematic effort inside the Cabinet to promote an alternative leader. There was inevitably much grumbling, but most of the talk among ministers in private was about how to press the case for devaluation. George Brown told Crossman, who had independently come to believe that floating the pound was unavoidable, that the chances of winning the argument were negligible. Brown was similarly pessimistic when he met with Barbara Castle, who was also in the devaluation camp. 'He had drunk enough to be voluble, but not offensive,' Mrs Castle noted in her diary. 'He knew he would lose, and then he would resign.' Brown complained that in his view the Prime Minister was not a free agent, having pledged himself to President Johnson not to devalue in return for American support. When Brown bluntly asked Castle if she would support him as an alternative leader she replied in the negative. This, Brown said, confirmed that Wilson could not be beaten, since he was certain to turn a Cabinet defeat on devaluation into a vote of confidence in his leadership.[23] The so-called 'plot' consisted mostly of loose talk late at night by George Brown, reflecting a recognition that events were moving against him.

Wilson naturally felt vulnerable in his absence from the country, though when he returned from Moscow on Tuesday 19 July he acted decisively to show that he still had the upper hand. He gambled that even if Brown went there would be no mass resignations, such as had occurred in 1931 when the refusal of less than half of the Cabinet to accept cuts precipitated the collapse of Ramsay MacDonald's Labour administration. The Prime Minister sought to flush out his opponents by holding a marathon four-and-a-half-hour session of the Cabinet shortly after he arrived back in London. He opened proceedings by promising to air in a forthcoming trip to Washington the idea of floating the pound. For once Wilson's emollient style did not win over doubters. A succession of ministers argued that a Labour government that constantly resorted to 'stop-go' cycles in the economy would be indistinguishable from its Tory predecessors. Barbara Castle wrote in her diary that the devaluationists appeared to be making ground, but gradually 'one after another the "do nothing" brigade mowed us down.' Towards the end of the discussion Tony Benn did his best to swing the argument back but, in the words of Mrs Castle, 'the others didn't want to know.' When the votes were counted only six of more than twenty hands went up in favour of devaluation – Brown, Crossman, Jenkins, Castle, Benn and Tony Crosland, the Education Secretary. The Prime Minister, in alliance with his Chancellor, had won the day. He confirmed that he was likely to have resigned if the decision had gone the other way.[24]

Wilson's victory was not complete. Before the meeting broke up, George Brown made it clear that he reserved his position. The announcement of the government's agreed policy on the next day, 20 July, was overshadowed by the farcical episode of Brown's 'resignation'. Behind the scenes, Wilson worked hard trying to prevent this, fearing that 'a Brown resignation might have finally pushed us off the pound'.[25] The Prime Minister took the unusual step of returning one of Brown's resignation letters to its sender without a response. When Wilson made his statement of policy in the Commons at 3.30 p.m. his deputy was pointedly absent from his side, and rumours began to spread that Brown was on his way out. In the early evening the nation's favourite soap, *Coronation Street*, was interrupted by a newsflash saying that Brown was leaving the government. As the evening wore on, the mercurial First Secretary was having second thoughts. He was moved to discover that his supporters in the Parliamentary Labour Party had organized a petition, signed by over a hundred MPs, urging him to stay. He also noticed that Wilson had suddenly halted efforts to keep him on board. Exasperated by Brown's antics, the Prime Minister had come to the conclusion that he would be better off without his troublesome colleague, whatever the impact on the markets.

Where soft-soap tactics had not worked, efforts to push Brown over the edge inadvertently brought him round. At midnight he made an appearance in front of the television cameras in Downing Street to tell the nation that his resignation was off.

Newspaper editorials the following day made much of the divisions in the senior ranks of government. The misery was compounded by the hostile reception given to the massive deflationary package announced by the Prime Minister. Although Wilson argued that key programmes such as hospitals, schools and housing would not be affected, there was no disguising the scale of the cuts which amounted to the equivalent of a 1.5 per cent reduction in national income. Cuts in public spending were accompanied by stiff increases in hire-purchase repayment terms, reductions in many areas of public investment, a tightening of foreign exchange controls and – much to the annoyance of trade unionists – a six-month prices and wages freeze, to be followed by a further six months of severe restraint. Labour MPs greeted the statement in stunned silence, and one was later to say that this was the day on which it all fell apart for the Labour government.[26] Overnight the ambitious objectives of the National Plan had been abandoned. Instead of controlled economic growth, the government had opted for financial rectitude and the reining in of consumer demand. The battle between the Treasury and the DEA, which had simmered beneath the surface since 1964, had been settled decisively in favour of the Chancellor. George Brown, who was soon afterwards to leave the discredited DEA, reflected that it was 'undoubtedly the turning point' in the life of the government.[27]

Fortunately for Harold Wilson, there was at least something to cheer on the football field. After the desultory group stage, the tournament came alight during England's fiercely contested quarter-final against Argentina on 23 July. A bad-tempered match was settled by a single goal from Geoff Hurst, the West Ham striker brought in to replace Jimmy Greaves who had been injured in the game against France. Afterwards the England manager Alf Ramsey fanned the flames of controversy by saying that Argentina had played like 'animals'. Three days later another 90,000-strong crowd at Wembley was treated to a far more entertaining encounter when England faced Portugal in the semi-final. Pre-match discussion centred on Alf Ramsey's decision to persist with Hurst up front instead of Greaves, widely regarded as one of the best strikers in international football and one of England's highest-ever goal scorers. Although Greaves insisted he was recovered from injury, Hurst's goal against Argentina persuaded Ramsey to stick with a winning team. His decision was justified when some of his top players finally came good. Bobby Charlton scored twice and Gordon Banks in goal made a series of fine saves. Although he conceded his first goal in five matches, England held on to secure a two-one victory. The stage was set for a final show-down with Germany, who came through their semi-final against the Soviet Union by the same two-one margin.

An estimated one in five of the world's population were watching on television when the teams came out at Wembley on Saturday 30 July. Part of the mythology of the occasion is that the match was a classic from the start. In reality the closeness of the two sides made the game tense and lacking in fluency. An early goal by the Germans was cancelled out when Hurst repaid the manager's trust with an equalizer. Chances were few and far between in the second half before a late strike by Martin Peters. England looked as though they might hold on for a narrow victory, but a last-minute equalizer by Wolfgang Weber sent the match into extra-time. Without this the game would not have been transformed into the stuff of legend. Thirty pulsating minutes of extra time, played in an era when no substitutes were allowed, produced several heroes. The midfielders Alan Ball and 'Nobby' Stiles ran themselves into the ground, socks round their ankles; Jack Charlton and captain Bobby Moore marshalled the English defence superbly; and Geoff Hurst crashed a shot against the underside of the crossbar which the linesman controversially ruled had crossed the line to put England three-two ahead. In the dying moments Moore sent the ball forward for Hurst to seal the victory and to enter the record books by becoming the first player to score a hat-trick in a World Cup final. Wembley went delirious, and the celebrations carried on long into the night around the country. The players went off to a London hotel for their own party; the only notable absentee was Jimmy Greaves, who did not want his teammates to see him overcome with emotion at missing out.

'They think it's all over,' the BBC commentator Kenneth Wolstenholme famously remarked as he spied fans coming onto the pitch in the final seconds of the match, adding 'it is now!' as Hurst crashed in the fourth goal. For England's triumphant team it was, in some respects, only just beginning. The place of England's celebrated win in popular consciousness was to be secured by endless replays of Hurst's third goal, later voted among the top ten television moments of the twentieth century by British viewers. Hurst's number ten shirt was in due course to be auctioned for a staggering £90,000. Kenneth Wolstenholme's words, as well as inspiring a television comedy quiz show, were also pertinent to the fate of Wilson's government. It was not 'all over' in the sense that Labour faced immediate dismissal from office. But Wilson was never able to regain his earlier popularity and authority. By some reckonings, the effects of the July crisis were short-term and superficial. British reporters who accompanied Wilson on his visit to Washington at the end of the month were firmly told that he had no intention of abandoning Britain's world role. The Prime Minister also demonstrated that he remained in charge by carrying out a reshuffle early in August 1966. George Brown moved from the DEA to become Foreign Secretary, a post that gave him less scope to interfere in domestic politics. This move had, for Wilson, the added advantage that it spiked the guns of Callaghan. The Chancellor had infuriated Wilson in the midst of the crisis by telling journalists of his desire to quit the Treasury and go to the Foreign Office himself. Wilson believed this showed the Chancellor's arrogance and ambitions for the leadership; 'he had to be taught a lesson,' Wilson told one colleague. Buoyed up by the American President and by Bobby Moore, it looked as if the Prime Minister had recovered his composure. 'World Cup Harold', as the *Economist* called him, was soon displaying much of his old cockiness.[28]

Behind this façade the crisis had profound and lasting effects, not least on the Prime Minister himself. One of his inner circle confirmed in private that the events of July had 'shaken Harold to the core'.[29] He saw shadows everywhere. At various times over the summer he pointed an accusing finger at Brown, at Callaghan, and at his former Bevanite friends Castle and Crossman for making common cause with the 'European devaluers' Jenkins and Crosland, younger ministers who believed devaluation should be accompanied by British entry into the Common Market. He even believed there was a 'Birmingham conspiracy' of Labour MPs, including the youthful Roy Hattersley, trying to dislodge him.[30] Much of this anxiety was imaginary, but it was important all the same. After July 1966 Wilson's premiership was blighted by his almost obsessive suspicion of his colleagues, and he became more than ever reliant on the advice of a small band of personal advisers, his so-called 'kitchen Cabinet'. Henceforth he could never feel assured that his job was secure. George Brown told Cecil King of the *Daily Mirror* that Wilson was no longer regarded as infallible; for years to come the rival claims of alternative leaders were to be touted in the tearooms and among journalists, thereby reinforcing the Prime Minister's sense of insecurity. As Ben Pimlott has written, Wilson's 'most precious asset, his self-assurance, died in July 1966'.[31]

The public's love affair with the government also came to an abrupt halt. The two major polling companies operating in the 1960s confirmed that Labour's popularity had slumped in the wake of the economic crisis. In May, following the general election triumph, NOP reported a Labour lead of 21 per cent and Gallup 18 per cent. Although this position weakened in June, it was only in July and early August that there was a substantial decline. Following the announcement of the deflationary package on 20 July, NOP showed a fall in Labour's lead from 16.8 per cent on 11 July to 9.3 per cent on 1 August, while Gallup went from a Labour lead of 7.5 per cent on 22 July to a Conservative lead of 0.5 per cent on 5 August. The extent of the damage was especially evident in responses to the question whether people were satisfied or dissatisfied with the way the government was running the country. On this, both polls showed a sharp reversal from the broad levels of satisfaction that had been recorded until June. These findings were reinforced in July when Labour lost a parliamentary by-election at Carmarthen, where a government majority of 9000 votes was comfortably overturned by the Welsh nationalist party Plaid Cymru. Edward Heath, who had so far struggled to make an impression, suddenly seemed a more serious proposition as an alternative leader of the nation. England's football fans were cheering their team on the pitch, but voters at large, the *Economist* noted, were more in the mood to 'kick Mr Wilson up the bottom'. The Prime Minister himself admitted he was 'blown off course'; as one commentator said, he appeared to have entirely 'lost the rudder'.[32]

Wilson may have won the battle against those who questioned his economic policy in 1966, but he did not win the war. During the autumn the pound steadied as the July measures took effect. Those who warned of the danger that Britain would slide from crisis to crisis were nevertheless vindicated by events in 1967; within a year sterling was again under pressure on the foreign exchanges. The July crisis came to be seen as the prelude to months of doomed rearguard action. In November 1967 the Cabinet faced up to the inevitable: the pound was devalued by 14.3 per cent in relation to the dollar. Further massive cutbacks were imposed, including the humiliating reintroduction of prescription charges, and Britain had to abandon its bases east of Suez, so acknowledging its reduced world status. Callaghan resigned as Chancellor and was replaced by Roy Jenkins. The greatest humiliation was reserved for the Prime Minister, whose bizarre claim that the 'pound in your pocket' remained unaffected was exploited mercilessly by a hostile press and a resurgent Tory opposition. Any remaining claim the government had to a credible economic strategy was destroyed. One junior minister summed up the reaction in Labour ranks: 'what the hell was it all for?' The long struggle to avoid devaluation, he concluded, resembled a First World War battle. Instead of securing any new ground, the government ended up making an ignominious and costly retreat.[33]

The decision to devalue in 1967 has been frequently cited by historians who regard the Wilson era as one of paralysis and failure. The more Wilson staked his authority on maintaining the value of sterling – the more he made it a political virility symbol – the greater the cost to his reputation when devaluation became unavoidable. The outcome made it easy to claim that he had been wrong all along. It may have been prudent to avoid tampering with the exchange rate in October 1964, when Labour's narrow majority could have been jeopardized, but the recurrence of the problem meant there was a strong case for facing up to what was necessary in 1966. Instead, the last opportunity to convince voters that devaluation was the product of pre-1964 Tory mismanagement was lost. The government's belated action in November 1967 was, on this view, 'three years and £1500 million of borrowed money too late'.[34] Some recent studies claim this is too harsh a verdict. If Wilson was deluded, he was not uniquely deluded. The weight of opinion in Whitehall was opposed to devaluation in 1966 because it was not an economic panacea; it was certain to have damaging as well as beneficial effects. The July crisis, it has been noted, should not be seen as closing down a fanciful left-wing policy of socialist economic planning, for such an alternative was never seriously on offer.[35]

However much Wilson's 'non-decision' in 1966 can be rationalized, the consequences of that action must be laid at his door.

Going for a crude damping down of the economy meant that ambitious talk of securing sustained growth no longer carried conviction. There were still achievements to come for the Labour government: modest increases in old-age pensions and family allowances, a growing proportion of national wealth spent on education and health, redistributive taxation ensuring that disposable income rose for the lowest paid – all of these continued the Attlee tradition of progressive social reform. But any successes were overshadowed by the failure to produce the promised leap forward in Britain's economic performance. The deflationary measures of 1966 helped to ensure that familiar problems went unresolved. By 1970 unemployment and inflation had crept up to post-war highs, industrial output had increased by an average of only 2 per cent per annum, and it was difficult to avoid the charge that Labour had sacrificed economic growth for an unsustainable exchange rate.[36]

In the long run, July 1966 marks the point when Labour, from being a confident and successful force, entered into a protracted period of decline, uncertain of its identity and future. It was no longer possible to avoid tricky questions about the purpose of the Labour movement. What was the party supposed to stand for if its leaders rested content with the Tory remedy of 'stop-go'? How could it be the party of scientific progress when the 'white heat of technology' had failed to transform the economy? And what was the place of 'planning' when the much-vaunted National Plan had been abandoned? Even Wilson's admirers, such as Dick Crossman, were at a loss to explain what the Prime Minister's objectives were after the summer of 1966. 'His aim,' Crossman wrote in his diary, 'is to stay in office. That's the real thing and for that purpose he will use almost any trick or gimmick.'[37] With no unifying vision on offer other than Wilson's instinct for survival party membership fell sharply, by 15 per cent in six years, a decline almost as great as in the entire thirteen-year period of opposition after 1951. Many of those who remained were turning to more traditional left-wing policies, such as wholesale nationalization, which in turn did little to arrest the unease among mainstream Labour voters, who abstained in large numbers when the Conservatives returned to power in 1970.

In some respects the 1966 crisis undermined the two-party system. The stability of British politics since the war had been based on the resilience of the major parties, which had hitherto commanded an overwhelming majority of all votes cast at general elections. Electoral turn-out had been high, if falling slowly, and there was confidence – as in 1951 and 1964 – that a tired government could be replaced by a viable opposition. But in less than five years both parties had come badly unstuck in their handling of the economy: the Conservatives in 1961 and Labour in 1966. This collective fall from grace by the nation's political leadership helps to explain the opening up of a new, less settled phase in British politics: an era of 'dealignment' which saw a marked rise in support for minority parties, much greater volatility in local and by-election results, and an accelerated trend towards fewer people voting. In the meantime, the chief victim of July 1966 was Harold Wilson who, as Crossman said, had suffered the most 'dramatic decline' of any modern premier. It was more sudden than either Eden or Macmillan before him, and was to be matched in later years only by John Major, who also came to grief over the value of sterling. Unlike his rival on the BBC, the commentator covering the World Cup final for ITN, Hugh Johns, was unable to find inspired words as the game reached its dramatic climax. 'That's it; that's it,' he screamed as Geoff Hurst smashed in the final goal. For Wilson, that was 'it'; his honeymoon with the British public was over.

7

'Who governs?'
The three-day week, 1974

People can clean their teeth in the dark, use the top
of the stove instead of the oven, all sorts of savings,
but they must use less electricity.

Patrick Jenkin, Minister at the Department of Energy,
radio broadcast, 15 January 1974

There are a great many very angry people in the Carlton
Club and White's this week, and even Mr Heath can count
himself lucky that he has so far escaped court martial.

Editorial in the New Statesman, *8 March 1974, following*
Heath's defeat in the general election

Edward Heath came to power in 1970 promising to change the 'course and the history of this nation'. But by 1974 he was out of office, soon to be displaced as Tory leader by Margaret Thatcher and left to embark on what the Robin Oakley, at the time assistant political editor of the *Daily Mail*, called an 'endless sulk'. For over twenty-five years he was to remain an isolated, curmudgeonly figure in the House of Commons, bitter at the disowning of his record by those who served under him. From all sides Heath was vilified, not only for what has been called his 'rigid, humourless, Easter Island-statue personality', but also for his seemingly disastrous record in government.[1] On the left, he was held responsible for provoking the highest level of industrial unrest in Britain since the years immediately after the First World War. Among Mrs Thatcher's acolytes, he was condemned for abandoning laudable right-wing objectives when the going got tough. Instead of the free-market remedies characteristic of his early days in office, Heath reverted to industrial intervention, including subsidies more extensive than those used by Labour in the 1960s. As the historian John Charmley laments, 'instead of the government changing history, history changed the government.'[2] According to some contemporary studies in the 1970s, the unique thing about Heath's premiership was that his failure was 'total'.[3] The whole sorry story culminated in election defeat in February 1974 amid claims by academics and commentators that Britain was becoming 'ungovernable'. For those who lived through the period its most enduring memories are of extensive power cuts, homes lit only by candlelight, and ridicule and anger towards government ministers for suggesting that people should clean their teeth in the dark.

Yet this picture of the Heath era is a caricature. In popular memory the various problems of the early 1970s tend to come under the umbrella label of the 'three-day week', although in fact there were no unexpected power cuts during the three-day week at the beginning of 1974. Homes had been plunged into darkness after the government was caught unprepared in earlier emergencies, notably when power station workers implemented a work-to-rule in 1970. But the placing of industry on short time in 1974 was deliberately designed to prevent a random loss of energy supply. As this chapter will show, Britain was gloomier than usual – it was, literally, a 'darkest hour' – but much of national life proceeded relatively unhindered. With the passage of time there has also been a growing recognition that Heath was gravely constrained by circumstances beyond his control. He lost a powerful ally only a month after coming to power with the sudden death of Iain Macleod, the Chancellor of the Exchequer, arguably the most astute political operator in senior Tory ranks. He faced the full force of escalating violence in Northern Ireland, and he had to deal with economic problems, of rising inflation and unemployment, more intractable than those experienced by any of his post-war predecessors. Above all, he was confronted by an international oil crisis, the scale of which was so great that economies throughout the world lurched suddenly into recession. Against this background, it has been argued, to dismiss Heath's record as one of abject failure is unduly harsh. Although contested as an 'achievement', few can deny that Heath did change the course of history by securing British entry into the European Community in 1973.[4]

A particular emphasis of recent writings on Heath, including John Campbell's acclaimed biography, is that he should not be judged as a proto-Thatcherite, a zealous free-marketeer who failed for lack of political will. Heath was without doubt an advocate of a more competitive market economy. He secured the leadership of the party in 1965 on a platform of modernization which contrasted starkly with Douglas-Home's self-confessed 'matchstick' grasp of economics. But, as John Campbell notes, this did not mean that he intended to break with the one-nation Tory tradition of his mentors, Churchill and Macmillan, the latter of whom had promoted him from the whip's office to various ministerial posts in the early 1960s. Heath was essentially an 'impatient technocrat'. He believed Britain's deep-rooted problems were amenable to rational solutions, notably the comprehensive reform of industrial relations law. He was not seeking, Thatcher-style, to replace the post-war settlement, the cross-party commitment to maintaining full employment, the welfare state and a mixed economy which had held sway since the 1950s. He rather wished to renew that settlement and make it more efficient, enabling both sides of industry to play their part in making Britain a more dynamic state, characterized like many of its European partners by high growth and rising living standards. In this light, Heath was less a compulsive U-turner than a 'somersaulting modernizer', prepared to undertake great leaps of policy in order to find fresh ways of moving in his desired direction.[5] Yet the reconsideration of Heath's reputation should not be taken too far. He may have attempted courageously to reinvigorate the British economy, but it was an effort that ended in defeat and humiliation. The responsibility for this outcome cannot be attributed entirely to 'extenuating circumstances', for the Prime Minister's personal failings contributed greatly to his demise. In the words of John Ramsden, author of a distinguished multi-volume history of the Conservative Party, 'However good the Heath government was at policy, it was certainly not very good at politics.'[6]

Some aspects of British life in the early 1970s smack of an inno-cent age long gone. This was the era of the Woodstock festival, of maxi-skirts and 'tank-tops', a time when the Hillman Avenger was considered a racy car and Babycham a sophisticated drink. But alongside the peace and love message associated with flower power in the late 1960s, it was also an age of confrontation. There were intense clashes between the sexes, with the emergence of a mili-tant feminist movement, between sectarian communities in Northern Ireland, and on the mainland between the social classes, with working-class militancy flaring up in the aftermath of the government's 1971 Industrial Relations Act. Since the war indus-trial relations had been based on voluntary codes of conduct, but the 1971 Act set about providing a comprehensive legal frame-work, proposing, for example, compulsory ballots before any major strike. Trade unions reacted with fury. A series of one-day stoppages was called in protest, and in 1972 the number of working days lost through strike action rose sharply, to nearly twenty-four million compared with 13.5 million the previous year. The Industrial Relations Act was rendered inoperative, but it had greatly soured relationships on the shopfloor. In early 1972 a six-week miners' strike, characterized by violence and intimidation (including the death of a miner, knocked down by a lorry, and the appearance of 'flying pickets', used to prevent the movement of coal), resulted in power cuts for the public and defeat for the gov-ernment, which conceded a pay rise of over 20 per cent, huge by the standards of the day. Heath's early attempts to modernize the economy had run into the sand.

During 1973 the picture began to improve. With unemployment rising towards one million, the Prime Minister had some success in persuading trade unions of the need for wage restraint. He secured broad approval for 'Stages One and Two' of an incomes policy, and hoped the same would apply to 'Stage Three', a phase of restraint involving government-imposed wage increases based on rises in the cost of living. In the first ten months of 1973 the number of working days lost through strike action was down by three-quarters on the corresponding period in 1972. In order to keep the unions on board – and to make the most of the opportunity provided by entry into the European Economic Community – Heath had also prompted his Chancellor, Anthony Barber, to launch a 'dash for growth'. High levels of investment were poured into the economy, notably into local authority services, and unemployment fell back sharply, to half a million by the end of 1973. The *Economist* wrote of Britain being 'two-thirds of the way to an economic miracle'.

There were also signs that voters were being won over. Labour had been ahead in the opinion polls for much of the time since Heath came to power, but had not built up the type of strong lead that pointed to a change of government. Harold Wilson, the opposition leader, was 'spoiled goods', unable to generate much enthusiasm after his own difficulties as Prime Minister. Labour had not captured a single Tory seat at a parliamentary by-election since May 1971, and was itself under threat from a surge in support for the Liberals under Jeremy Thorpe. By the autumn of 1973 the two main parties were level-pegging in most polls, giving Conservatives cause to be reasonably optimistic about the prospect of re-election. 'If no horrors occur,' wrote Douglas Hurd, Heath's Private Secretary, in his diary, 'Autumn 1974 might be best [for an election].'[7]

Before long 'horrors' did occur, destroying the fragile progress made by the government in the first half of 1973. War in the Middle East provided the catalyst. Military forces from Egypt and Syria were overwhelmed by Israel in the conflict that started in

October 1973, but other Arab states had a potent weapon in their control of oil supplies. As well as cutting sharply deliveries to Western industrial nations, the oil producers' group OPEC announced a rapid quadrupling of the price of oil, up to $11.65 per barrel by the end of the year. The period of relatively cheap energy upon which Western prosperity was based came to a shuddering halt. Although the amount of oil being imported was almost back to its previous level within a matter of months, as the effects of the crisis reverberated around the world the British economy was among the worst hit. At a time when North Sea oil had been discovered but was not yet on the market, Britain relied on imported oil for about half of its energy needs, a proportion that had been rising as the coal industry was steadily run down. The government's dash for growth, moreover, had already resulted in sharply rising prices: the inflation rate was up to almost 9 per cent from 6 per cent in 1970, and the hike in the cost of oil piled on inflationary pressure. Heath's ability to maintain a successful counterinflationary strategy was in doubt – something that was not lost on the National Union of Mineworkers (NUM) as it pressed the case for another major pay award, this time of 35 per cent. British miners resented the extent to which their pay trailed their continental counterparts. Despite the 1972 award, they were still some 8 per cent behind the average wage in Britain for factory workers. 'It was not in the end,' writes John Campbell, 'the miners nor the oil crisis alone but the lethal combination of the two which brought the Government to defeat.'[8]

Contrary to later claims, the Prime Minister was not seeking a fresh confrontation with the NUM. In the aftermath of the 1972 strike, efforts had been made to halt the closure of uneconomic pits, a policy pursued with vigour by the previous Labour government. Heath also entered into secret talks with NUM leader Joe Gormley in an effort to find ways of ensuring that the miners, like all workers, complied with Stage Three of his prices and incomes policy. His confidence that a deal could be struck was shattered within days of the outbreak of war in the Middle East.

The National Coal Board (NCB) opened negotiations for the 1974–5 pay round by offering an increase of 16 per cent, the maximum compatible with the government's guidelines. Ministers were dismayed that the NCB had conceded so much so soon. Gormley rejected the offer outright, and made it clear that his members would fight for the full 35 per cent increase demanded by the NUM conference. This was sought, he claimed, not as a direct challenge to government authority, but in order to ensure a flow of new recruits to the industry and to put the miners at the top of the manual workers' wage league where they belonged.[9] Convinced that the NCB could not broker a settlement, Heath then made a disastrous tactical mistake. He stepped in to handle negotiations personally, aiming to demonstrate that Stage Three of the incomes policy had been devised to take account of the miners' concerns but that no exceptions to the strategy could be permitted. By sidelining the employers, the Prime Minister opened the way for a rerun of 1972; unless there was an early agreement, the dispute could develop only in the direction of another major fight between the government and the miners – precisely the outcome that Heath hoped to avoid.

In November 1973 it became clear that there would be no quick settlement. NUM negotiators came away from meetings at Downing Street believing that they had been offered nothing more than 'avocado mousse for lunch'.[10] When one representative asked the Prime Minister why he could not 'pay us for coal what you are willing to pay the Arabs for oil', there was an embarrassed silence. Joe Gormley argued that with 600 men leaving the pits each week, it was not enough to be told that the miners had been made a generous pay offer. In view of the oil crisis, the time had come for a commitment to reverse the long-term decline of the industry. On 12 November an overtime ban came into force; within days, the level of coal production was cut by 40 per cent. Although stocks above ground at various pits remained plentiful, the government was not prepared to risk the accusation that it was doing nothing in the face of impending fuel shortages. The following day Peter Walker, the Minister of Trade and Industry, announced the government's fifth state of emergency since it came to power. In echoes of wartime restrictions, strict limits were imposed on the heating and lighting of shops, offices and schools, the use of energy for advertising purposes was curbed, television broadcasting was to end at 10.30 p.m. every night, and the possible introduction of petrol rationing was signalled. Once again the stakes had been raised, although the Prime Minister still hoped to avoid all-out conflict. He went on television to insist that Stage Three must be upheld but that the way remained open for a negotiated agreement. 'There is,' he maintained, 'absolutely no question of taking on the miners.'[11]

Even so, the longer the dispute dragged on, the more likely it was that there would be no option but to 'take on' the miners. While ministers continued to tread carefully, there were no such inhibitions among Conservative activists, many of whom sensed an opportunity to avenge the defeat at the hands of the miners in 1972. The belief among Tory workers in the existence of an extremist plot was reinforced by the prominence in the NUM of the Scottish Communist, Mick McGahey. At a meeting with the Prime Minister on 28 November McGahey, Gormley's deputy, was alleged to have said to Heath that his aim was to 'get your government out'. Although the precise words used were disputed (McGahey later insisting that he sought a lawful change of government), the meeting was followed by alarmist stories in several newspapers about the threat posed by the miners to the democratic system. Positions on both sides were further entrenched, making it difficult for the Prime Minister to convince the miners that he was genuinely seeking a solution. His preference for conciliation rather than confrontation was evident when he recalled William Whitelaw, at the time busy attempting to secure a political breakthrough in Northern Ireland, and gave him special responsibility for counterinflation policy. It was felt that if anyone could achieve a breakthrough it was the affable Whitelaw. But Whitelaw was exhausted by his endeavours in Northern

Ireland and unfamiliar with the intricacies of the miners' dispute. He soon discovered that there was little room for manoeuvre. Either the NUM had to be given exemption from Stage Three, which Heath firmly ruled out, or they had to be resisted.

As Christmas approached the crisis intensified. Behind the scenes, the government was preparing for a showdown. The so-called Civil Contingencies Unit, set up after the 1972 miners' strike, prepared an emergency structure of regional government, to be introduced in the event of a breakdown of energy supplies. Wild predictions circulated in Whitehall of sewage flowing in the streets, hospitals unable to cope with the resulting epidemics for lack of electricity, and old people dying in their homes of cold and hunger. Leaders of the electricity industry issued a public warning of the 'grave danger' to power supplies, a danger that was underlined after the train drivers' union, ASLEF, announced an overtime ban of its own, so restricting the movement of dwindling coal supplies. On top of all this, monthly trade figures were among the worst on record. The Chancellor, Anthony Barber, told Cabinet colleagues on 12 December that Britain faced its gravest economic crisis since the war, with an estimated balance of payments deficit of £3 billion in 1974.[12] One response was the announcement of a massive package of expenditure cuts, finally bringing down the curtain on the 'Barber boom'. The second major initiative by the government was handled by Heath personally. On 13 December he told a solemn House of Commons that, in order to conserve fuel, electricity supplies would be limited in such a way that industry would be placed on a three-day working week, starting on 1 January 1974. With hindsight, some ministers admitted to another tactical blunder. Coal stocks remained high and deliveries of oil were recovering, and in such circumstances, reflected James Prior, Lord President of the Council, it was 'more difficult to convince people that the situation was really as serious as we claimed.'[13]

After his statement in Parliament, the Prime Minister made a further television broadcast blaming the NUM for the impasse.

He expressed regret that their action would give the nation 'a harder Christmas than we have known since the war'. At last, Heath appeared to be giving ground to the hawks in his party who felt that attack was the best form of defence. Cabinet colleagues such as Prior had consistently argued that the gravity of the crisis should be emphasized; it was the government's duty to show that it was in charge, even to the extent of calling an early general election if necessary. Heath's instinct had hitherto been opposed to presenting the issue openly as a subversive threat to democracy, but he was now persuaded that a three-day week would increase pressure on TUC leaders to push the miners towards a settlement. At the same time, his wooden television broadcast on 13 December, in which he looked ashen with fatigue, was hardly a rallying cry for a full-blooded assault on the NUM. If the government's actions told one story, Heath's rhetoric and body language implied another. As John Campbell notes, appealing for national unity in the face of 'difficulties' was not exactly rousing. The point was that 'he did not *want* to rouse the nation. He simply wanted the nation to demonstrate that it was ready to endure discomfort, in order to shame the miners into accepting the already generous settlement they had been offered . . . He was not looking for confrontation at all, still less to exploit the situation for an early election. He still wanted to believe that reason must eventually prevail.'[14]

The ambiguity in Heath's position had its effect on public perceptions of what was going on. In addition to the miners' dispute, set against the backdrop of the hike in oil prices, there was increasing media hysteria with apocalyptic newspaper headlines accompanied by talk that Britain was becoming 'ungovernable' (a book by the political scientist Anthony King was entitled *Why Is Britain Becoming Harder to Govern?*), capable of being held to ransom by any group with sufficient industrial muscle. Yet reporters on various newspapers and journals who probed behind the headlines had to admit that most people were going about their everyday lives much as before. Pubs, clubs and restaurants were mostly still open, if dimmer and chillier than normal; shops reported feverish Christmas shopping, with retail sales for the final months of 1973 well up, and there were healthy takings in theatres, cinemas and hotels throughout the festive season.

The use of floodlights for professional soccer was curbed, but the Football League managed to continue its full programme of fixtures by resorting to earlier kick-offs. Large numbers of spectators continued to turn up at the top matches, with over forty thousand flocking to Stamford Bridge shortly before Christmas to see First Division leaders Leeds set a post-war record of twenty matches without defeat.[15] In the *New Statesman* Alan Watkins reflected that the government had so far failed to convince the nation that it faced a crisis 'in which individuals are directly involved'. Most people, he added, 'know perfectly well that switching off the odd electric bulb here and there is going to have about as much effect on the power situation as collecting Lord Beaverbrook's ludicrous aluminium saucepans had on the course of the Battle of Britain'. Voters were taking the view, Watkins concluded, that politicians had created the mess and should clear it up; otherwise they would elect another government to do the job.[16]

The possibility of there being another government to 'do the job' came closer as the three-day week got under way in the New Year. For several months opinion had been building in Conservative circles in favour of an early election. By December 1973 speculation was widespread in the press, fuelled by hints from senior figures such as the party chairman, Lord Carrington. Advocates of an early contest reflected the view from the grassroots that there must on no account be a second capitulation to the miners. Far better, it was felt, would be to put to the electorate the issue of 'who governs': the elected parliament or the trade unions? At the turn of the year opinion polls were giving the Conservatives a slender but consistent lead, and private party soundings also suggested that the government would win if it moved quickly. But the Prime Minister hesitated. An opportunist election, designed to take the Labour opposition by surprise and exploit the crisis for partisan ends, was not part of Heath's mindset. He refused at first to discuss election prospects, clinging to the view that it would somehow be possible to work with the unions as 'social partners', and he was not persuaded that a fresh mandate would bring a solution to the crisis. At some point, he reasoned, there would have to be an agreement with the miners. On the other hand, he did not entirely rule out an appeal to the country and refused to kill off the mounting press talk about an election. This indecisiveness threatened the worst of possibilities: no settlement with the NUM in sight, and the government risking that it would be blamed if the crisis caused disruption over a long period.

In the event, the three-day week did not produce the dire results that many predicted. At the outset there were claims that millions of workers would be thrown on the dole and a drastic fall in industrial production would threaten the economy with meltdown. But these catastrophic scenarios went unfulfilled. Exceptionally mild weather throughout January, three degrees above the seasonal average, meant that there were huge savings in fuel consumption. And firms in industry found various ways of mitigating the effects of short-time working. Some maintained high levels of production by offering workers longer hours on the days in the week for which they had power. Others, for example in engineering, switched to old-fashioned methods when they were not allowed to use electricity, using ordinary screwdrivers and spanners to assemble parts and components. Although reports came through of difficulties in particular regions, notably the Midlands and the north-west, many areas reported that firms would survive if the three-day week was not prolonged. In the southern new town of Bracknell, although unemployment rose from virtually nil to 4.8 per cent of the workforce, light industrial companies found production levels down by no more than 10 per cent.[17] The figure across the country was at least double this, but with take-home pay falling only marginally, most observers were surprised that the effects of short-time working were not greater.

As the *Sunday Times* noted, British industry had embarked on the three-day week with 'something approaching gusto', showing 'impressive powers of improvisation' and 'numerous touches of imaginative derring-do'.[18] Within six weeks the CBI reported that output was almost back to normal.

On one level, the limited impact of the three-day week was a triumph for the government. After absorbing the lesson of earlier emergencies, it had shown that with careful planning Britain could come through energy shortages without severe disruption. This time there were no power cuts out of the blue to cause havoc in households across the country. Supermarkets and food stores were exempt from energy restrictions, so there was little panic buying of goods, and in January the nation was even allowed to 'go to the dogs' again, with the resumption of evening greyhound racing. Yet the very success of the three-day week proved to be counterproductive in other ways. As the days passed, it became difficult to maintain a heightened sense of emergency that would help to rally opinion behind the government. This was not for want of trying by some of the Tory-supporting tabloids. The *Daily Mail* claimed that if there were no settlement 'you might as well paper your bathroom wall with your savings'.[19] But the longer the state of emergency went on without causing major hardships, the less necessary it seemed to be. Before Christmas, polling evidence found the public evenly divided on the need for a three-day week; as time passed, the proportion approving of it began to diminish.[20]

There was a second crucial consequence that followed from the limited impact of short-time working. Miners were already angered that the government had gone ahead with plans affecting the whole country on the basis of a single industrial dispute. 'Heath put the country on a three-day week to turn the public against us and make us the villains of this drama,' said the leader of the NUM in Mansfield, Lawrence Foster. He had acted as if it were the Battle of Britain in order to show 'we were holding the country up for ransom'.[21] The suspicions of the NUM were increased on 8 January when Lord Carrington was given charge of a new Department of Energy. As Carrington continued in his role as Tory party chairman the miners, instead of seeing this as a hopeful initiative, viewed the new ministry as a mouthpiece for Conservative Central Office. When it became apparent that the overtime ban was not intensifying pressure on the government, the NUM, far from retreating, became more determined to escalate the dispute towards an all-out strike, as they had done in 1972. In this it reflected the views of ordinary pit workers. As Lawrence Foster argued, 'Heath's decided he's going to have the miners going back on their bellies . . . I've got news for him. We crawl on our bellies all day long and we're sick of it. When we're done with Heath, he'll be the one on his belly.'[22] The continuation of short-time working for several weeks thus hardened attitudes among the main protagonists, with ministers and miners becoming ever more determined that they should not be the first ones to blink.

The effect this had on the prospects of a compromise became clear as the tortuous negotiations to find an agreement continued. On 9 January the possibility of a way forward emerged when representatives of the TUC met with ministers and proposed that, if the government came to terms with the miners, other unions would not exploit any breach of Stage Three to demand corresponding treatment. The TUC offer looked like a face-saving formula all round. It promised the miners their pay demand in full and gave ministers the chance to claim that they had responded flexibly to the new circumstances created by the oil crisis while maintaining a workable incomes policy. But Tony Barber, the Chancellor, gave the TUC proposal a frosty reception. Senior Tories were suspicious that the TUC General Secretary, Len Murray, would not have backed any plan that was not advantageous to the Labour Party. The Prime Minister, although he prided himself on trying to enlist the support of the union movement in the running of the economy, appeared to have run out of patience. He did not believe that member unions would be able to deliver, even if the offer was sincere, and he was not prepared to endorse a solution in which he had no faith. With hindsight, ministers such as Jim Prior believed that a major opportunity for a breakthrough had been missed. The burden of responsibility would have shifted to the unions, leaving the government in a stronger position if they failed to deliver. In the event of success, Heath's reputation would have been enhanced as the leader who had brought the unions on side. This analysis was shared by hardliners on the NUM such as McGahey, who believed moderates on the executive would have welcomed a way out. He, too, agreed that Heath was too inflexible to seize his chance.[23]

For as long as channels of communication with union leaders remained open, Heath resisted calls for an election. Pressure on him from colleagues intensified to such a point that on 11 January he agreed to give Conservative Central Office formal authority to begin making election preparations. At one point Lord Carrington believed he had persuaded the Prime Minister to go the country on 7 February, but the deadline for such a contest passed without an announcement. An angry scene followed when one of the ministers in favour of an election, Prior, told Heath that Labour MPs were cock-a-hoop about the decision, convinced that the government had missed a favourable tide. Prior accused his leader of sitting on the fence, rejecting the Prime Minister's accusation that Tory activists should not have been whipped up into election fever. 'We had already marched the Party's troops up the hill, ready for combat,' Prior recollected, 'and then had to march them down again; it would be much harder to march them up a second time.'[24] Heath had his reasons for refusing to yield to colleagues who favoured an election. Opinion poll evidence suggested that the government might have secured re-election on 7 February but it was by no means cut and dried. In retrospect, the 'non-decision' about an election looked like another wasted opportunity. Expectations of a contest had been raised and then dashed. As public irritation about the three-day week grew, Heath's standing in the polls fell; any election that did come would occur in far less auspicious circumstances.

For a few days the Prime Minister adopted a resolute stance.

On 22 January he stirred Tory MPs with a strong speech standing firm on the miners' pay claim. But the following day the NUM seized back the initiative. Aware that oil supplies were returning to normal and coal stocks holding up well, miners' leaders decided to push for an all-out strike over their claim. The NUM executive agreed by sixteen votes to ten to call a ballot seeking approval for a nationwide stoppage, and when the result was announced on 4 February over 80 per cent of miners backed strike action at a time to be designated by the executive. Last minute attempts to pull back from the brink proved futile. TUC leaders left another lengthy meeting at Downing Street feeling that the whole exercise had been 'a charade'. Heath was desolate, clinging to his belief that if only the miners had gone through proper consultative procedures all sides could have been satisfied. He recognized that the only alternative to a long drawn-out conflict now was an election. He took comfort from continued support for the government's incomes policy and the prospect of opinion rallying when the issues were laid out in an election campaign. On 7 February, the day on which some of his colleagues felt there should have been a contest, the Prime Minister announced that voting would take place at the end of the month.

There was widespread agreement that the key issue of the election in February 1974 was the use or abuse of trade union power in a modern democracy. Many newspapers began their daily coverage of the campaign under headings such as 'the crisis election'. Two assumptions followed. The first was that the contest would be angrily fought, possibly accompanied by scenes of violence on the picket lines; the *Daily Mirror* claimed divisions in society had not run deeper since the 1930s. The second assumption, shared almost without dissent at the start of the campaign, was that the Conservatives would win. Opinion polls pointing to a close outcome tended to be discounted. This was due not only to the unreliability of the polls at the previous election, in 1970, but also to the received wisdom that the public would swing firmly behind

Heath. When confronted with a stark choice, it was expected that voters would turn in droves to the government of the day, just as they had rallied behind the 'National' administration in the crisis of 1931. Yet there was no immediate surge towards the Tories, and the campaign turned out to be a low-key affair; the 'crisis election' was curiously lacking in a crisis atmosphere. This was partly because the public had got used to the three-day week, which continued in force during the election. The weather remained unusually mild and the lifting of the 10.30 p.m. curfew on television also lessened any sense of emergency. Nor did the beginning of the miners' strike on 10 February produce scenes reminiscent of 1972. Conscious of the need to maintain public sympathy, the NUM took steps to ensure that there was no heavy picketing or violence. When ASLEF called off its overtime ban, so ending disruption on the railways, the Prime Minister complained that industrial action was being put on ice in the interests of the opposition.

There was another key reason why the campaign did not become the spectacle predicted at the outset. As Tory doubters about the need for an election suspected, it proved impossible to focus minds right through to polling day on the single question of 'Who governs?' As the days passed, with little new to report on the strike or the three-day week, other issues intruded, usually to the detriment of the government. After a slow start, Labour began to land some heavy punches by concentrating on rising prices and the general state of the economy, both areas that rose in priority for voters during the second half of the campaign. On 15 February official statistics were published showing that retail prices had risen over the previous year at a fastest-ever rate of 20 per cent, although poll findings indicated that most accepted that this was primarily due to international causes. More damaging for the government was the revelation, only three days before voting took place, that January's balance of trade deficit was the largest monthly figure on record. The issue of Europe also came to the forefront when the maverick Tory Enoch Powell, standing down in the Midlands constituency of Wolverhampton South-West in protest against British entry to the European Economic Community, urged voters to support Labour as the best means of securing withdrawal. Powell's insistence that Europe was the major concern of the day was not shared by most of the electorate, but it distracted attention further from the original cause of the contest, dominating the news agenda for much of the last week of the campaign.[25]

There was one final reason why, against expectations, the election turned out to be a subdued affair. Edward Heath, having reluctantly agreed to a contest, refused to turn it into a hostile crusade against the miners. In his opening salvoes, he put the blame for the election squarely on the NUM, and said that the issue at stake was clear enough – whether a strong government had the mandate to conduct its affairs without being held to ransom by one group of workers. But he was determined to show that he was reasonable, as he had been all along, in seeking a settlement within the government's stated procedures. Far from launching an all-out assault on the miners, he agreed on 8 February that their demands should be submitted to the Relativities Board – a new form of independent arbitration machinery – adding that he would accept its adjudication. This announcement was greeted with derision by the opposition. Why, it was asked, could this not have been done earlier, and what was the point of an election if an agreement was in sight via the Relativities Board? Many Conservatives were also dismayed. It made clear that there would be no fight to the finish with the miners, leaving Tories confused as to how they were to conduct the campaign. The Prime Minister could argue that it was the miners who had hitherto been opposed to the pay review machinery; indeed, they refused in advance to submit to its findings. But the NUM's willingness to put its case to the Relativities Board left Heath again looking wrong-footed. In the early days of the contest his time was taken up justifying the need for an election in the first place.

The announcement on 8 February set the tone for Heath's

conduct of his whole campaign. His watchwords throughout were 'firmness' and 'fairness', moderation over confrontation. The Tory manifesto spoke of the need for a strong government to prepare for tough times ahead, although there was little condemnation of the miners. As Heath later said in his memoirs, the election was a 'grim necessity', but his intention was to make it as 'non-divisive as possible'.[26] This approach did nothing to enhance Conservative prospects. Fleet Street stood at the ready to rally opinion behind the government by presenting the fight as a life-and-death struggle for democracy. But newspaper editors lacked ammunition. A few senior Tories spoke of the choice between the rule of reason and the anarchy of a 'Communist regime', but they received no encouragement from Downing Street and scare stories in the press fizzled out. By fighting such a sober campaign, Heath left himself open to counterattack. He was thrown onto the defensive when it was revealed that the Relativities Board had discovered an apparent error in previous calculations about miners' pay. The claim was vigorously denied, but not before an increasingly confident Harold Wilson attacked what looked like 'grave incompetence', suggesting that the whole dispute with the miners was based on faulty figures.

Heath's approach had a further crucial effect. Far from being polarized, the electorate, doubtful of the need for an election and confused by the various claims about miners' pay, turned in large numbers towards the Liberals as a third-party alternative. Under Jeremy Thorpe, the Liberals skilfully developed the theme of 'a plague on both your houses' – a message that struck a particular chord after a Tory attack on Labour leaders produced an undignified spat between the main parties. Instead of being squeezed out, as anticipated, Liberal support rose steadily, though Heath clung to the view that this would more adversely affect Labour. As polling day approached, the Prime Minister remained confident of returning to power on the basis of a steady if slim lead in the polls. His optimism was shattered when news of a large swing to Labour in the West Midlands – Enoch Powell territory – came through. When all the results were announced, Labour emerged as the largest party with 301 seats, compared with 297 for the Conservatives and fourteen for the Liberals. None of Labour's few gains appeared to be directly attributable to an increased Liberal vote; more decisive was an increased turn-out – the highest since 1951 – bolstered by a significant portion of the working population being at home on polling day due to the three-day week. After a failed attempt to form an alliance with Thorpe, Edward Heath resigned and Wilson formed a new minority administration. A week later the NCB and the NUM executive agreed a wage package on the basis of a report by the Relativities Board. By 11 March the miners were back at work.

The question 'Who governs?' had produced no clear-cut answer. For the first time since the 1920s, a general election had resulted in a hung parliament. There was clearly no great enthusiasm for Labour, whose share of the vote, at 37.1 per cent, was the lowest for any post-war administration. Wilson had secured neither the largest number of votes cast nor an overall majority of seats. The Liberals had made the most significant headway, although the voting system gave them only a small number of MPs in proportion to their 19 per cent share of votes cast. If there was doubt about who had 'won' the election, there was no such uncertainty about who had 'lost'. As one political commentator notes, when challenged over 'Who governs?' the country had 'briskly replied that, if he needed to ask the question, then the answer shouldn't be Mr Heath'.[27] The decline in the Tory share of the vote, down from 46.4 per cent to 37.8 per cent, was the largest suffered by any government since 1945. In years to come the feeling was to grow in Conservative circles that, in the words of one junior minister, Heath had been 'stupid to take on the miners'. Although public opinion supported the need for an incomes policy, there was also a sneaking regard for miners, whom many felt to have a good case for rising up the manual workers' wage league.[28] As he left Downing Street, Heath was in a state of shock. The prize of a second term had been snatched away. The knowledge that he had fought a reasoned campaign, rather than blatantly exploiting the crisis for partisan ends, only increased his resentment and his sense that the electorate had let him down. 'Yet in the end,' concludes John Campbell, 'he had no one to blame but himself. He had gambled his job, and he had lost.'[29]

Heath's defeat cast a long shadow over his reputation and the future of British politics. It prepared the ground for many of the myths that developed about the early 1970s. As we have seen, it was not the case that Heath was seeking to take on the miners in order to avenge the defeat of 1972; nor was it true that he lacked consistency in his efforts to modernize the economy. If he had failed to tackle the deeply entrenched problems of British industry and society, he was by no means alone in this; and he could legitimately claim to have encountered a more hostile environment than his predecessors. The oil shock underlined the transition from the post-1945 era of full employment to a period of sharply rising inflation and mounting unemployment. Yet Heath did not help his own cause. It was one thing to sense the need for fundamental change, another to build the necessary support to implement reform. Unlike Harold Wilson, Heath was not a natural communicator in the age of television politics. As the distinguished journalist Robert Taylor has noted, he failed to find the requisite language of persuasion; he lacked the 'intuitive and imaginative grasp' to convince voters of the wisdom of his strategy. He had good relations with several union leaders who welcomed his reforming zeal, but his agenda was never understood on the shopfloor or in the country at large. He did little to prepare the ground, and he failed to understand, in Robert Taylor's words, that most unions were 'neither structurally nor ideologically capable at that time of delivering the kind of agreement he wanted, one which would help in transforming the UK into a European social market economy'.[30]

In the same way, Heath's ignominious departure from Downing Street owed much to his own shortcomings. Perhaps his key mistake was his failure to exploit prime ministerial control over the timing of general elections. Wilson, Macmillan, even Eden – another of the most maligned of post-war leaders – had proved adept at picking moments that maximized their chances of success. Heath, having boxed himself into a corner, opted to go the country with some eighteen months of the parliament still to run. His government had a clear majority and he had suffered no major defeat in the House of Commons. It was not obvious that victory would bring an immediate end to the miners' strike, and he went into the campaign without the unreserved support of his party and large sections of the press. Within months of coming to power in 1970, Heath had almost broken off relations with many political editors, scornful of what he saw as their lack of empathy with his reforming agenda. Although most newspapers were no friends of the miners, Heath had few debts to call in from Fleet Street when the chips were down. By the same token, he suffered when the crunch came for not devoting time to the cultivation of party opinion, either at Westminster or in the constituencies. Tales of his rudeness to MPs were legion, and although party opinion rallied with an election to fight, in private there was a strong feeling among activists that the government had lost touch with Conservative principles. Heath's aloof style, combined with a further defeat at the election in October 1974, ensured that he could no longer escape what the *New Statesman* called 'court martial'. He was defeated when challenged for the party leadership by Margaret Thatcher in 1975.[31]

In due course Mrs Thatcher was to make her reputation as Prime Minister by posing as the antithesis to Heath. Starting from the assumption that he lacked conviction, she made her reform of industrial relations stick and triumphed in her 1980s' battle against the miners. She set about slaying the 1970s' dragon of inflation and shifted the emphasis of Britain's external relations across the Atlantic rather than looking towards Europe.[32] This does not mean, however, that Heath's premiership should be treated as a failed version of the later Thatcher reforms. Another of the myths that has grown up is that Heath had a proto-Thatcherite agenda which he betrayed. In reality no such agenda was on offer in the early 1970s. The prevailing orthodoxy was widely shared – in Whitehall, in the media, and in most parts of the Conservative Party, including the Cabinet where one of the highest spenders after 1970 was Thatcher herself as Education Secretary. It was more the case that Heath's defeat, and his removal from the leadership, paved the way for a radical rethink of Tory priorities. With Thatcher at the helm, lessons began to be drawn from the Heath years: that it might be necessary not to accommodate but to defeat 'trade union power', and that it would no longer be possible to reconcile collective pay bargaining with low inflation and full employment. In order to survive in the new world created by the oil crisis, Tory thinking moved gradually but perceptibly towards tight control of the money supply as a method of curbing union power and creating a more efficient, deregulated labour market. Heath's failure legitimized this agenda, but in the mid-1970s its implementation remained a long way off.

For some observers, the last days of Heath's premiership marked a critical turning point, the demise of Britain's post-war settlement. From this time onwards, it has been suggested, 'the writing was on the handbag'.[33] According to the constitutional historian Vernon Bogdanor, the outcome was surprising given that Heath was so much a child of post-1945 'consensus politics'. The aim of full employment, Bogdanor notes, was not mentioned in Heath's 1970 manifesto because it was taken for granted by politicians of his generation. Similarly, Heath had no sympathy for grassroots Tory opinion which sought moves towards the denationalization of major state-controlled industries. But after February 1974, things could never be the same again. The outcome of the election gave Unionists in Northern Ireland a veto over any constitutional changes in the province, and saw advances for the Scottish Nationalists which challenged the nature of the Union. Future governments would henceforth be confronted with threats to the stability of Britain from the non-English parts

of the United Kingdom. The success of the Liberals also confirmed the new volatility of the electorate and changed the nature
of discussions about reform of the voting system. Above all,
uncertain times lay ahead for the economy. What began to look
like a 'golden age' in the 1950s and 1960s was fading in memory,
and it was not clear that governments could control the economy
when faced with global forces without and the 'trade union problem' within. 'By straining the post-war settlement to its limits',
Vernon Bogdanor claims, Edward Heath, whatever his intentions,
'snapped it in twain'.[34]

This conclusion overstates the case. There was no doubt that
politicians on all sides recognized that chill winds were blowing.
By the mid-1970s both main parties were searching for ways of
coming to terms with the passing of the era of relatively pain-free
economic expansion. Conservatives such as Douglas Hurd were
speaking of 'an end to promises', while one of Wilson's ministers
after 1974, Tony Crosland, coined the phrase 'the party's over'.
But it was not obvious that all aspects of the post-war settlement
were dead and buried. Wilson and his successor as Prime Minister
in 1976, James Callaghan, were still very much conditioned by the
mid-century political and economic culture in which they grew
up, just as Heath was an inheritor of the Tory one-nation tradition. They, like him, regarded the unions as social partners, and
went to great lengths to devise a workable incomes policy based on
agreement with both sides of industry. Although slowly declining,
the proportion of those who agreed that trade unions were a 'good
thing' remained high in the mid-1970s, as it had done since the
1950s. As the next chapter will show, the really decisive moment
for the post-war settlement came when the unions overreached
themselves in the traumatic 'winter of discontent' in 1979. It was
this later event that opened up the way for a fundamental shift in
Britain's political and industrial economy. As far as Edward
Heath's part in this process is concerned, his premiership might
best be described – to paraphrase Winston Churchill – as more
than the end of the beginning; it was the beginning of the end.

8

'Crisis? What crisis?'
The winter of discontent, 1979

I don't think that other people in the world would share the
view that there is mounting chaos.

Prime Minister James Callaghan, on returning to Britain
from a foreign summit, 10 January 1979

There are times, perhaps once every thirty years, when there
is a sea change in politics. It then does not matter what
you say or what you do. There is a shift in what the public
wants and what it approves of. I suspect there is now
such a sea change – and it is for Mrs Thatcher.

Callaghan speaking to a political adviser during the 1979
election campaign

At the height of her power in 1985, Margaret Thatcher posed
a question to her faithful followers at the Conservative Party
conference: 'Do you remember the Labour Britain of 1979? It was
a Britain in which union leaders held their members and our
country to ransom . . . a Britain that was known as the sick man of
Europe and which spoke the language of compassion but which
suffered the winter of discontent.' Most of her audience in the
hall, and millions of television viewers beyond, did remember the
Labour Britain of 1979. The 'winter of discontent' had become
the popular way of describing a period of sustained and sometimes
violent industrial unrest, deeply etched into public consciousness

through newspaper coverage and evocative television pictures, a time when Jim Callaghan's Labour government was seen as helpless in the face of trade union power. Lorry drivers went on strike and petrol deliveries were curtailed. Action on the railways left commuters standing on freezing platforms in the middle of winter. The provision of essential services was threatened when a variety of public sector workers decided to take industrial action – from the office staff of local authorities to refuse collectors, hospital porters, ambulance drivers, school caretakers and, most notoriously of all, gravediggers. Much of the nation, as well as the Conservative rank and file, no doubt shared the view of 1979 presented by Mrs Thatcher: in this darkest of hours, the 'dead were left unburied' in a 'Britain under siege'.

These images were part of the wider picture of the 1970s that gained currency in the Thatcher years. According to this version of events, the winter of discontent – a term used by Callaghan in February 1979 and soon adopted by newspaper headline writers – was the culmination of a decade when inflation stalked the land, destroying the social fabric. It rounded off a long period of union militants 'bullying' the nation with excessive wage demands, thus underpinning the industrial 'disease' that accounted for Britain falling behind its major competitors. Trade unions in general were regarded as the main scapegoats for Britain's relative decline – engines of economic failure and objects of fear and contempt. By successfully rewriting the history of the recent past, the Conservative administrations of the 1980s paved the way for the introduction of what appeared to be the necessary solutions: rolling back the frontiers of the state through an extensive programme of privatization; adherence to monetarism in economic policy; and the reduction of union influence in politics and industry. As Margaret Thatcher went from strength to strength to secure three successive general election victories, so it became easier to argue that her resolution was in contrast to the weakness of her 1970s' predecessors, both Tory and Labour. Jim Callaghan inadvertently lent support to the Thatcherite view of the 1970s with his comment, made to an adviser during the 1979 campaign, that there had been a 'sea change', with British people turning away from post-war collectivism towards the strident individualism of his opponent. Yet, as this chapter will argue, although the winter of discontent was a decisive moment in British politics, it should not be seen as part of an inevitable drift to the right. It was more the case that Labour condemned itself to a long spell in the political wilderness through a series of self-inflicted wounds. All lines in the 1970s did not lead inexorably to the Thatcherite terminus.

After scraping back to power in the spring of 1974, Harold Wilson set out to demonstrate that he, unlike Edward Heath, would be able to work harmoniously with the unions. As well as ending the miners' dispute and the three-day week, the new Labour government abandoned compulsory wage restraint in favour of the 'social contract', an attempt to confront inflationary pressures through voluntary agreements with the unions. For several months – long enough to secure another Labour victory at the general election in October 1974 – the strategy appeared to be delivering results. The social contract brought some modification of wage demands in return for improved welfare benefits, paid for through redistributive taxation and large-scale borrowing. But Britain was not immune to the continuing effects of the international oil crisis, which had plunged most of the industrialized world into deep recession. During 1975 unemployment rose to a higher level than it had reached since the war, some 1.5 million, while inflation, at over 20 per cent, appeared to be out of control. Wilson's abrasive Chancellor, Denis Healey, decided that it was time to change course and resort to the traditional Treasury remedy of deflation. The standard rate of income tax was raised from 33 to 35 per cent (although this was still lower than the 38.75 per cent level of 1971–2), spending programmes were slashed and ministers resorted to a more formal, although still voluntary, pay policy, holding down wage increases across the board. For many, this looked like a rerun of 1966: once again, a Labour government had been 'blown off course', unable to cope with mounting economic chaos.

This was the unfortunate inheritance of Jim Callaghan, who emerged triumphant from the Labour leadership contest after the sudden retirement of Harold Wilson early in 1976. Callaghan did have some advantages over his predecessor. Within Labour ranks, he was regarded as more of a friend to the unions than Wilson, having served as a union official in his early career. Although in his mid-sixties, he was at least a fresh face at the helm after a decade of the Wilson-Heath duopoly. As far as the public was concerned, Callaghan had none of Wilson's 'trickiness' and came across as an avuncular, trustworthy figure – the 'able seaman' who could navigate choppy economic waters. Within months of taking over, Callaghan's resolve was tested to the limit by a fresh crisis. Renewed industrial unrest led to a loss of confidence on the financial markets. Pressure on the pound did not ease even with interest rates pushed up to 15 per cent, leaving the government with little option but to seek a massive loan from the IMF. In return for helping the beleaguered British economy, the IMF demanded draconian cutbacks in public spending. With great skill and patience, Callaghan persuaded first the Cabinet and then the broader Labour movement that there was no alternative to this unpalatable medicine. But he paid a heavy price. The political fall-out from the IMF crisis saw the opposition under Margaret Thatcher open up a massive lead in the opinion polls, while by-election losses during 1975–6 meant that Labour's parliamentary majority was wiped out.

In 1977 Callaghan began to assert himself and staged a notable recovery. He secured a breathing space through negotiation of the 'Lib-Lab pact', which for the time being gave his government a more stable parliamentary base. More importantly, the IMF loan succeeded in calming the foreign exchanges, and with the prolonged world recession coming to an end, and Britain beginning to enjoy the benefits of North Sea oil, the main economic indicators began to look more favourable. Union adherence to a 10 per cent ceiling on pay rises helped to bring inflation down, from its peak of 24 per cent in 1975 to 8 per cent three years later. The value of sterling recovered, the balance of payments moved into surplus, and Chancellor Healey never had to draw on more than half the standby credits available from the IMF. Much earlier than anticipated he was able to celebrate what he called 'Sod off Day' – the moment when Britain became free of IMF control.[1] With his personal popularity rising, Callaghan launched a series of withering attacks on Mrs Thatcher, whom he depicted as untried and dangerous, especially on the issue of industrial relations. A Thatcher government, he said, would mark a return to the power cuts and states of emergency that characterized the Heath years.

By the summer of 1978, economic recovery looked set to produce political dividends. The Conservative lead in the opinion polls, which averaged 10–15 per cent a year earlier, had been whittled away; in August Gallup gave Labour a 4 per cent advantage. In these circumstances, press speculation began to focus on an autumn general election. The Prime Minister was tempted to go early. He consulted widely among ministers, party officials and MPs about the best course of action. He knew that many difficulties lay ahead, not least union reluctance to continue wage restraint. Thinking aloud in a radio interview, Callaghan proposed that wage rises might be restricted to 5 per cent by 1979. When this figure hardened into government policy many union leaders reacted with disbelief, arguing that because of prolonged double-digit inflation the average worker's reduction in purchasing power since 1975 already represented, in the words of one Whitehall official, 'the most severe cut in real wages for twenty years'.[2] Nevertheless, in July 1978 the Cabinet approved a 5 per cent limit on pay deals for the forthcoming year. Ministers calculated that an election, which many were privately urging on Callaghan, was certain to come before the autumn pay round got under way. William Rodgers, the Secretary of State for Transport, recalled that many shared his own view that a 5 per cent pay ceiling was unrealistically low, but that it made sense as pre-election window dressing for an appeal to the country that seemed imminent.[3]

But no election came in the autumn of 1978. After much deliberation at his Sussex farm, Callaghan decided that Labour's position in the marginal constituencies, although it had recovered since the IMF crisis, was not strong enough to ensure a majority. A few more months of economic growth and wage restraint, he figured, would be likely to produce a solid victory in the spring of 1979, avoiding the need for another five years of parliamentary haggling. Senior colleagues such as Healey agreed with the logic of waiting: the government's ability to show that inflation was under control and that Labour could work with the unions might make the difference between victory and defeat. Callaghan's decision has since attracted derision. Although his action made sense on the basis of the evidence available at the time, the Prime Minister's handling of the episode left much to be desired. He conceded in his memoirs that he made a mistake in suggesting that an early election was on the cards, though he added that Cabinet colleagues had been promised that they would be the first to hear his verdict after the summer break.[4] In spite of this, he teased the nation by treating TUC delegates on 1 September 1978 to the words of an old music hall song, 'There was I, waiting at the church'. This was apparently intended to discomfit Mrs Thatcher, implying that she was being kept waiting while Callaghan declared his intention in his own way. But the TUC audience was baffled and press commentators continued to believe that an announcement was imminent. Ministers were stunned when a week later the Prime Minister began Cabinet proceedings by slowly reading out a letter to the Queen stating that there would be no immediate contest. Bill Rodgers recalled that the majority of ministers 'fell off their chairs', most being too taken aback to respond.[5]

Members of the Cabinet were not the only ones who felt let down by 'Jim's little joke'. Union leaders were incensed to find that instead of being a campaigning slogan, the government's

5 per cent wage norm was set to become a reality over the winter. After three years of pay restraint, this was too much to bear. 'You can only stretch an elastic band so far,' argued one delegate as the Labour conference in October voted overwhelmingly to return to free collective bargaining. After the TUC's General Council took a similar view, the green light was given for affiliated unions to seek higher wage settlements. Workers at Ford car plants were the first to demonstrate the strength of feeling on the shopfloor. Ford had announced huge profits for 1978, prompting Moss Evans, head of the Transport and General Workers' Union (TGWU), to declare that a large pay rise was easily affordable. After it became known that senior managers had received rises of up to 80 per cent, car plant workers rejected an offer from the company that fell within the government's guidelines. Although not hitherto known for militancy, Ford workers sustained a nine-week strike before the company settled on a pay package that increased average earnings by 17 per cent. Calls for restraint were dismissed as outside interference with the normal practices of pay bargaining. The result was a crippling blow for the government, setting the benchmark for pay negotiations in both the private and public sectors.

The 5 per cent pay policy was soon in tatters. Only days after Ford came to terms, drivers of tankers from four of the five main oil companies, also members of the TGWU, threatened a national strike in pursuit of a 40 per cent wage claim. Overtime working was banned in December, and television news began to carry pictures of petrol shortages in some areas. Other groups of workers, such as firemen and ventilation engineers, secured pay rises well in excess of the government's formula. On 15 December the government suffered a humiliating defeat in the House of Commons over its plan to impose sanctions against Ford for breaching the pay policy. Although a vote of confidence was survived the following day, ministers had to abandon plans to withdraw subsidies from Ford. Another policy option, that of imposing financial penalties on those who breached the pay norm, was closed off. As

17. Wilson kicking a ball while playing with children on a visit to his Huyton constituency during the 1966 campaign

18. *Below*: Chancellor of the Exchequer Jim Callaghan on budget day, 1966, shortly before the onset of the July crisis

19. Two office workers in Bond Street, London, during the three-day week, January 1974. The women were able to keep themselves warm because they worked for a quilt company

20. *Below*: Edward Heath campaigning in Bexley during the general election of February 1974

21. *Above*: A NUPE rally in Hyde Park at the start of the Winter of Discontent, January 1979

22. *Left*: One of the abiding images of the Winter of Discontent – the garbage mountain in Leicester Square

23. Jim Callaghan leaves Number Ten Downing Street after Labour's defeat at the general election, May 1979

24. *Below*: British troops arriving on the Falklands, May 1982

25. The Royal Navy frigate HMS Antelope is hit in San Carlos bay during the
Falklands War, 26 May 1982

26. Margaret Thatcher
with Cecil Parkinson,
triumphant at the
Conservative party
annual conference,
1982

27. Burning an effigy of Mrs Thatcher in the poll tax demonstrations, May 1990

28. *Below*: Sir Geoffrey Howe delivers his explosive resignation speech,
13 November 1990

29. Margaret Thatcher leaves Downing Street to offer her resignation to the Queen, November 1990

30. *Below*: John Major in happy times – with his wife Norma after victory in the general election, April 1992

31. Chancellor Norman Lamont – 'poor old Badger', as one Tory MP called him – speaks to the media outside the Treasury on Black Wednesday, 16 September 1992

32. *Below*: Tony Blair and Gordon Brown at the Labour Party conference, 1994

Christmas approached, it looked like being a festive season for workers determined to press their pay claims. BBC technicians secured a 15 per cent rise after threatening to black out television screens over the holiday period. One minister admitted privately to a journalist that the Cabinet feared a public backlash in the event of Christmas television schedules being disrupted. Callaghan, the minister added, might be the first Prime Minister to fall from power over the issue of 'yet another repeat of *The Sound of Music*'.[6]

It was in the early weeks of 1979 that the winter of discontent got into full swing. On 3 January 15,000 lorry drivers in Scotland began a strike in pursuit of their pay claim, followed soon after by TGWU members in other parts of the country. With some 80 per cent of goods travelling by road, there was great pressure on the road haulage companies to reach a settlement. Television screens showed images of lorry drivers, huddled around oil-drum braziers to ward off the bitter cold, blocking the entry and exit of goods from docks such as Tilbury. There was much criticism of 'secondary picketing', the blocking of lorries not involved in the dispute by those on strike, with several incidents of violence and intimidation being documented. Hull became known as 'siege city' or, with snow falling, as the 'second Stalingrad'. With only a few main roads into the city, pickets prided themselves on being able to impose a virtual blockade on supplies coming in or out. The efforts of Moss Evans to restrict abuses of secondary picketing were condemned by his detractors as weasel words, and newspapers began to report panic food buying. At this point, with events threatening to get out of control, the Prime Minister took drastic action. He left the country.

Callaghan's trip to the Caribbean island of Guadeloupe for discussions with other Western leaders had been long planned. Any idea of his not attending was regarded as defeatist, though critics were quick to spot the potential for embarrassing the Prime Minister. Newspaper photographs of Callaghan enjoying the sunshine while Britain shivered – especially those of him swimming alongside young air-hostesses – did not go down well. Far more damaging was the Prime Minister's apparently complacent tone when he arrived back at Heathrow Airport on 10 January, relaxed and pleased with the outcome of his wide-ranging talks. One journalist asked what he thought about the growing sense of chaos in Britain while he had been away. This touched a raw nerve and prompted his reply that other people in the world did not believe there was 'mounting chaos'. The following morning, 11 January 1979, Walter Terry, the political editor of the *Sun*, led the charge against the government. 'Sun Tanned Premier Jim Callaghan,' he wrote on the front page, 'breezed back into Britain yesterday and asked: Crisis? What crisis? . . . Not even the threat of up to two million people being laid off work next week worried jaunty Jim. He blandly blamed journalists for talking of "mounting chaos" in strike-battered Britain.'[7] The 'Crisis? What Crisis?' headline had in fact appeared a couple of days earlier in the *Daily Mail*, but it was the *Sun* that used it so vigorously that some voters were convinced Callaghan had actually employed the phrase, as a Labour minister found on the doorstep during the election campaign a few months later.[8]

As the crisis intensified, it seemed that the Prime Minister had lost more than his flair for public relations. His sense of control and authority also deserted him. On 11 January the Secretary of State for Northern Ireland, Roy Mason, reported to the Cabinet that the province was 'bleeding to death' under the impact of the lorry dispute. When he announced that he was about to declare a state of emergency, Shirley Williams, the Education Secretary, muttered: 'Couldn't you take over England as well?'[9] The Cabinet eventually decided not to extend the state of emergency throughout Britain, noting that this tactic had proved ineffective when adopted by Heath in the early 1970s. One unnamed minister, stung by accusations of government paralysis, commented that the public appeared to think that the army could fill the apparently denuded shelves of the supermarkets with Mars bars, if it were only given the chance.[10] In the absence of a state of emergency, ministers waited for a lead from the Prime Minister. But it was slow in coming. He resisted the idea of going on television to steady the nation, thinking that this would be counterproductive, and he remained reluctant to step up attacks on the unions. And so Jim Callaghan, 'keeper of the cloth cap', the former union official who had resisted Barbara Castle's *In Place of Strife* proposals for trade union reform in 1969, was unable to decide what to try next. As he said to one of his advisers, 'How do you announce that the Government's pay policy has completely collapsed?'[11]

Callaghan's continued preference for conciliation was evident in hints that the 5 per cent policy would be modified for low-paid workers, and on 19 January the government announced that it would not prevent road haulage firms from raising their prices to cover increased wage costs. This opened the way for lorry drivers to secure pay rises of 17–20 per cent, amounting to over £60 per week, although this was still some £25 short of the average weekly wage for manual workers. As the press attacked this latest surrender to union demands, Callaghan told colleagues that the agreement reminded him of the Munich settlement in 1938; 'he felt relief and disquiet in equal proportions.'[12] The Prime Minister was mistaken if he thought the worst was over with the ending of the haulage dispute. On 22 January, with blizzards sweeping through much of Scotland and northern England and blocking hundreds of roads, a million and a half public service workers staged a twenty-four hour strike in support of a minimum wage of £60 per week. Major cities such as Glasgow and Birmingham were left without emergency ambulance cover, leaving police and voluntary groups to step in for the day. In what amounted to the most widespread and co-ordinated industrial action since the General Strike of 1926 thousands of demonstrators converged on London, and it was agreed that a series of local strikes would be held until union demands were satisfied. This escalation of public sector disputes left the government with no place to hide. Earlier actions such as those involving Ford could at least be depicted as traditional management versus workers struggles, but for public sector workers the government *was* the employer. It was now directly in the firing line.

A few journals and newspapers put a sympathetic gloss on the actions of the strikers. The *New Statesman* pointed out that while senior executives, including those working for local authorities, had secured pay rises well in excess of the 5 per cent figure, the lowest earning families were being asked to suffer another erosion in relative wage levels. It was estimated that many groups of workers, such as car park attendants, lavatory cleaners and messengers, received less than many families were getting on supplementary benefit. Some space was also given to the plight of individual workers. Under the headline, 'How do they get by on £40 a week?', the *Guardian* highlighted the case of Penny Hibbins, a thirty-four-year-old divorcee with four daughters under the age of fifteen. As a domestic worker at a Devon hospital, she often had to do overtime to supplement her earnings from a normal forty-hour week. Her wage packet as she left the hospital gate each week was usually under £40, and after food and expenses she found herself with £5 a week for clothes and any unexpected bills. 'I can't afford a Sunday joint,' she said. 'I can't afford to take the children on holiday or anywhere else.' The article concluded that Penny Hibbins 'is not alone'. Similar stories were to be found among many of those who were members of the unions coming to public prominence – the health workers in COHSE, the municipal workers in the GMWU and the public employees in NUPE.[13]

Most newspapers, however, presented a very different story, using images and language that was to reverberate for a generation to come. Tony Benn, at the time Secretary of State for Energy, wrote in his diary: 'The press is just full of crises, anarchy, chaos, disruption – bitterly hostile to the trade union movement. I have never seen anything like it in my life.'[14] Tory tabloids, joined by the Maxwell-owned *Daily Mirror*, presented a picture of trade unions on the rampage and willing to penalize the most vulnerable in society. NUPE became a nasty four-letter word, with great

venom being directed at its leader, 'Führer' Alan Fisher, for backing strikes which began to hit the elderly and the infirm. 'Target
for today – Sick Children', ran the headline in the *Daily Mail* after
union members began to picket the entrances to hospitals. There
were plenty of horror stories. Schools were closed when strikes by
caretakers meant that heating systems were not being maintained;
999 calls were left unanswered; frozen roads were not gritted.
Dustbins and bags of rubbish piled up in city centres by the thousand, full of rotting waste. One photographer spent several hours
staked out in central London, charged with the task of taking a
picture of rats among the mounds of rubbish. As the streets emptied at night, the rats duly obliged and within hours the *Evening
Standard*, part of the Trafalgar House group, splashed the picture
on its front cover under the heading 'Rats on the Town'.[15]

The most emotive episode came with the announcement that
municipal workers on Merseyside were refusing to dig graves and
that funerals were being postponed as a result. 'They won't even
let us bury our dead,' screamed the *Daily Mail*, keen to take
advantage of this latest opportunity to attack the unions for cal-
lousness in pursuit of their pay claims. Roy Hattersley, then
Minister for Prices and Consumer Protection, recalled how David
Basnett, secretary of the GMWU, was so appalled by the actions
of some of his members that he broke down in a private meeting
when discussing the gravediggers. He kept repeating plaintively:
'Who could have believed that Liverpool Parks and Cemeteries
Branch would behave like this?'[16] Those on the picket lines
claimed that a strike was the only way to bring attention to their
poor pay and conditions, but they admitted there was much hostility from local residents, fuelled by the determination of journalists to build up the story. As the number of bodies kept in cold
storage in a disused factory rose to over three hundred, the chief
medical officer of Liverpool City Council conceded under persistent questioning that if the dispute went on for months, some
corpses might have to be taken out to sea. The following day 'bodies
to be buried at sea' was made into another chilling newspaper

headline. Some months later, a prime ministerial adviser recalled watching the television pictures of a funeral party being met at the cemetery gates by a group of pickets. They were guarding the entrance, placards aloft. When the cortège was turned back, the Prime Minister's aide sensed that at that moment Labour lost any chance of re-election.[17]

The Prime Minister appeared to share such gloomy sentiments. Tony Benn noted that Callaghan was almost hysterical on 1 February, threatening in turn to give up the leadership and to call an early election: 'Jim asked how the Cabinet was going to survive. We had got to the point where indiscipline was threatening the life of the community and the Government must have a clear line. The situation was extremely grave and the Tories could win, giving Mrs Thatcher a mandate for the most violent anti-trade union policy.'[18] The Prime Minister did, however, rouse himself in pursuit of a 'clear line'. On 14 February he called a press conference to launch a new 'concordat' with the TUC, stating the aim of bringing inflation down to 5 per cent over three years. There was talk of an annual 'national assessment' by the government and both sides of industry, and guidelines were to be issued on picketing and closed shops. Critics were quick to portray it as too little, too late. For the Conservatives, shadow Chancellor Geoffrey Howe used uncharacteristically strong language, calling it 'the same old cobblers', and the *Economist* lambasted an agreement 'which says the unions can do the same all over again if they want to'.[19] It was rumoured that the concordat was bland in tone because union negotiators had threatened to rubbish the document if it made any mention of tough action against those on strike. The agreement certainly did not have the effect of immediately ending the disruption: strike action continued unabated.

The Prime Minister also gave the green light for local authorities to settle their manual workers' claims above the level of the discredited 5 per cent pay norm. This proved acceptable to several unions, but it did not prevent one-day strike action by civil servants and initially it was not enough to satisfy NUPE, which sought to inflict further indignity on the government when Health Secretary David Ennals was admitted to Westminster Hospital in March. Nursing staff pledged to treat the minister according to his medical needs, but the NUPE shop steward at the hospital, Jamie Morris, called the minister 'a legitimate target for industrial action . . . He won't get the little extras our members provide patients. He won't get his locker cleaned or the area around his bed tidied up. He won't get tea or soup.'[20] NUPE members eventually returned to work in the middle of March, accepting a 9 per cent increase with an extra £1 in advance of a promised study of pay comparability. The winter of discontent was finally coming to an end, but retribution was swift. On 28 March the House of Commons passed a motion of no confidence in the government by 311 to 310 votes. The following day the Prime Minister was spied by one political observer in the hall of Number Ten Downing Street, sitting alone and waiting for his car to take him to Buckingham Palace to offer his resignation and announce a general election – the first time a government had been forced to go to the country after an adverse vote in Parliament since 1924. Moments later Callaghan would emerge to wave and show every outward sign of being ready to fight the election. 'But as he sat inside . . . he looked incredibly old and tired.'[21]

The level of disruption witnessed in the early months of 1979 was at the time – and has been subsequently – much overstated. Union leaders rightly complained that tabloid newspapers were guilty of gross exaggeration. In January the *Sun* ran stories under headings such as '1,000 old could die every day' and '3 million face the dole queue'; the actual figure for lay-offs was in the region of two hundred thousand. The scale and scope of the crisis, which left large parts of the country relatively unaffected, can also be gauged from the numbers involved in strike activity. Only one-sixth of all lorry drivers refused to work, and it was estimated that no more than 830 of over 33,000 schools were temporarily closed as a result of action by caretakers.[22] The tanker drivers' dispute was primarily an overtime ban so petrol supplies were never seriously disrupted, and apart from a few medical items essential supplies nearly always got through in spite of hold-ups in the docks. Douglas Smith, a civil servant responsible for activating government machinery to counter the road haulage strike, later recalled that there was no occasion when the threatened use of troops was necessary or would have assisted. He added that the only food shortage he could recollect 'was that Kellogg's Cornflakes were difficult to obtain in some supermarkets!'.[23] Though mostly short-lived, the cases highlighted by the tabloids nevertheless had a powerful impact, setting an agenda that television news found difficult to resist. A specialist unit at Glasgow University monitoring television coverage noted how one journalist, determined to find a new angle on events for viewers, spent a week following up rumours that chickens were dying in blockaded lorries. The reporter admitted that when his crew turned on their lights and cameras inside a chicken coop, twenty-five birds died of shock. 'To his knowledge,' the journalist conceded, 'these were the only chickens to have died in the lorry drivers' dispute.'[24]

There were several reasons why fanciful accounts ran ahead of reality. Some union activists, as in Hull, oblivious to the needs of good PR in an age when politics was less dominated by 'spin', were happy to build up pictures of local communities under siege because this was good for strikers' morale. Tabloid editors, for their part, knew that dramatic stories would increase sales, especially among the bulk of their working-class readership not on strike, even if this meant distorting events on the ground. Under the headline 'Strike Threat to Bone Boy', the *Daily Mirror* referred to a seven-year-old boy waiting for a life-saving bone marrow transplant as cleaners and porters walked out at Westminster Hospital in London. Only at the end of the article was it revealed that the boy was a patient at a different hospital, a unit nearby to which 'the strike is expected to spread'. Above all, many of the tabloids had a political motive in playing up the nature and extent of the disruption. Derek Jameson, the anti-union editor of the *Daily Express*, later boasted that his paper 'pulled out all the stops' to depict the unions as out of control. He and his colleagues, he said, were prepared to do 'whatever was necessary' to destroy Labour and help return a Tory administration. Ministers expected as much from their tabloid opponents in Fleet Street, but were angered that the broadsheets and television news also featured the alarmist, and mostly unfulfilled, predictions of businessmen such as Sir Hector Laing, chairman of United Biscuits and an adviser to Mrs Thatcher, who said that millions would be thrown out of work on the back of strike action.[25]

It follows that care should be taken in endorsing the charge, made with great frequency in the Thatcher years, that the winter of discontent confirmed the notion of British unions as 'overmighty subjects'. Bolstered by developments in the public sector, trade union membership was growing throughout the 1970s, from 11 to 13 million during the course of the decade. But few unions were the highly centralized, 'powerful' bodies that critics allege. With exceptions such as the miners, trade unions were mostly fragmented organizations, vulnerable to the fluctuations of a weak economy. Just as the TUC had limited authority over its affiliates, so most unions could not call on a disciplined body of workers to strike at the drop of a hat. With the spread of workplace bargaining since the 1960s, allegiances were increasingly confined to the immediate workplace. Confirmation that class solidarity was being eroded came from studies of individual plants where many workers were prepared to accept the condemnation by newspapers of other workers' disputes, but not their own. Official statistics indicate, in addition, that the most salient feature of industrial relations since the unrest of the early 1970s had been the unions' general sense of responsibility. Contrary to the notion that strikes were a peculiar feature of the national 'disease', the British pattern had been little different from that of other major industrial powers. The overwhelming majority of pay settlements were agreed without stoppages; even in 1979 the average worker lost little more than a single day through industrial disputes over the whole year. Indeed, the amount of productive time lost through accidents, ill health, absenteeism and unemployment in the 1970s remained at least twice as high as the working time lost through strike action. One academic study concludes that the proportion of all days that could be worked but were lost through strikes was 'minute' at 0.2 per cent, shrinking further to 0.1 per cent in the 1980s and virtually disappearing at 0.001 per cent in the 1990s.[26]

By the same token, the crisis of early 1979 does not validate the view, again propounded vigorously during the Thatcher era, that the whole experience of Labour government since 1974 had been a calamity. As the MEP Phillip Whitehead has written, Callaghan and Wilson have often been portrayed as 'a pair of shabby pragmatists, waiting for something to turn up, the Estragon and Vladimir of degenerate Labourism'.[27] Yet some cautionary notes must be sounded. Both leaders faced the inherited problem of world recession, which made for circumstances that proved too much for Edward Heath. In spite of this, they did manage, according to an exhaustive study of the economy, to adapt to 'the new environment of higher inflation and slower growth', leaving several economic measurements and the policy-making machinery 'in better condition in 1979 than they found them in 1974'.[28] Nor was the record of the government as devoid of achievement in other areas as its detractors claim. In social policy, ministers could point to worthwhile reforms in equal opportunities legislation and to the introduction of a new Commission for Racial Equality. Moreover, the *General Household Survey*, a lengthy report based on interviews with 15,000 families, showed that despite the doom and gloom Britain was a more prosperous place in which to live in the mid-1970s than it had been at the start of the decade, with the nation better housed, better off and having more material possessions than ever before.

This is not to suggest that the winter of discontent was simply a fabrication of right-wing propaganda. The impact was real enough and the consequences were to be profound. Since most strike activity took place in the public services and in transport it caused a degree of dislocation not seen since the 1947 fuel crisis, which had shaken an earlier Labour government and which took place against a similar backdrop of unusually severe winter weather. Even for those not directly involved, tabloid accounts and television pictures were crucial in forging an impression of the period as one of siege and crisis. As Denis Healey remarked in his memoirs, every night screens carried 'film of bearded men in duf-fel coats huddled round braziers. Nervous viewers thought the Revolution had already begun.'[29] By the time the wave of strikes petered out in the spring of 1979, the government's credibility had been irreparably damaged. Labour's anti-inflation strategy lay in ruins, the party's claim that it could work with the unions was destroyed, and the Conservatives had surged ahead in the opinion polls. Gallup had given Labour a five point lead in November 1978; by February 1979 this had turned into a twenty point Tory advantage. Equally significant was the finding of MORI that Callaghan, for the first time, had fallen behind Thatcher in terms of personal popularity. He was, in the words of one minister, 'inescapably responsible' for the sense of government paralysis. In effect, the winter of discontent destroyed Callaghan's premiership just as Profumo had undermined Macmillan and the three-day week had done for Heath. Callaghan acknowledged as much in his autobiography, noting that a tide of disillusionment swept the country, sending the government's fortunes 'cascading downhill, our loss of authority in one field leading to misfortune in others just as the avalanche, gathering speed, sweeps all before it'.[30]

The first major consequence of the winter of discontent was that it prepared the ground for Margaret Thatcher to come to power at the general election in May 1979. The Conservatives went into the campaign promising, as in 1970, to break with a Labour Britain that was said to have resulted in public spending and trade unions out of control. By contrast, Callaghan, rather like Wilson in 1970, opted for safety first. He emphasized the twin themes of competence and conciliation, promising to implement his recently concluded concordat with the unions. Commentators were agreed that the Prime Minister made an impressive personal showing, recovering his composure and seeking to exploit the untried radicalism of his opponent. But the damage had been done. The outcome was a swing to the Conservatives of 5.1 per cent, the largest at any election since the war and more than enough to provide Thatcher with a comfortable majority of forty-three seats, enabling her to become Britain's first woman Prime Minister. The winter of discontent was not, of course, the sole cause of this result, but it played a vital part. The number of voters who thought unions a 'good thing' had declined sharply since 1974, and there had been a continued reduction in the level of support for Labour from trade unionists, down from 66 per cent in 1970 to 55 per cent in the elections of 1974 and a bare majority of 51 per cent in 1979. Regional variations, such as a net swing to Labour in Scotland, provided only a crumb of comfort. In the Midlands, London and the south-east, there were massive defections, especially among women, skilled workers and new voters. There could be no disguising the crushing nature of the defeat. The party's share of the total poll, at 36.9 per cent, was its lowest since the disastrous reversal of 1931.[31]

The second major effect of the events of early 1979 was the rupture it caused within the Labour movement. The alliance between the party and the trade unions, which had helped sustain Labour in office for almost half the period since 1945, was never quite the same again. During the long years in the wilderness after 1979 arguments about who was to blame for the winter of discontent frequently resurfaced, with both sides claiming justification for the stance they adopted. Union leaders said it was no secret that their members disliked the policy of wage restraint the more it went on. The resentments built up most acutely in Labour's own constituency, among the growing battalions of local government, health service and public sector workers whose wages were most directly influenced by central government. Callaghan, it was alleged, chose to ignore the warning signals and instead rubbed salt in the wound by insisting on an unrealistic extension of his incomes policy. Some historians agree that the Prime Minister was the villain of the piece. Apart from his fatal error over the timing of an election, he took the unions for granted, failing to see that union leaders were not in a position to line up their members behind any policy the government proposed, even if they wished to do so. If the TUC had not agreed to the concordat of February 1979, Callaghan would have been left with no line of retreat whatsoever.[32]

Senior Labour politicians, by contrast, maintain that the finger should really be pointed at the 'irrational behaviour' and the 'suicidal lunacy' of those who went on strike. Callaghan had candidly told the TUC that the fate of the government was in their hands and that the alternative was Thatcher, who would 'give them a hell of a time' – as indeed she did. The Prime Minister's adviser Tom McNally said that Callaghan's distress was partly the result of his feeling that he had given the unions great responsibility and influence, but that this had been thrown in his face.[33] In his later reflections Denis Healey accepted that the 5 per cent pay norm was 'provocative' and 'unattainable', saying that a formula under 10 per cent may have got them through the winter. But he, too, reserved his venom for the 'cowardice and irresponsibility' of union leaders and activists whose behaviour left them no grounds for complaining about Mrs Thatcher's subsequent actions against them.[34] Again, some historians concur. Martin Holmes singles out Alan Fisher of NUPE as 'the Conservatives' best election ally since Zinoviev'. Fisher's determination to make a stand against low pay, it has been argued, led him to defend actions of violence and intimidation that outraged a broad mass of the electorate. Agreement on who was to blame remains unlikely. As Phillip Whitehead has written, union leaders 'thought the government would back off, just as it believed they would. But that is how wars are lost.'[35]

It might all have been so different. As we have seen, in the autumn of 1978 there was little indication of the 'sea change' in opinion that Callaghan referred to during the 1979 campaign, by which time he knew the game was up. If as Prime Minister he had called an early election, a winter of industrial turmoil seems unlikely, even in the event of a Tory victory. The Conservatives would have had no mandate for the introduction of anti-trade union laws, and even after the winter of discontent they went into the 1979 election promising only limited changes. Although Tory rhetoric hardened as events unfolded, Mrs Thatcher was well aware of the need to win votes among trade unionists; hence she was careful to stress that there would be no wholesale reform along the lines that Heath had tried without success in 1971. An October election in 1978 might equally have produced a narrow Labour victory, continuing the pattern of 1974. Instead of being regarded as the prelude to disaster, the 1970s might have been seen as a time when trade unions achieved a new level of recognition in the workplace and within society, with membership reaching a post-war peak above thirteen million in 1979–80. In spite of various difficulties, such as a fading sense of collective purpose and a failure to adapt internal procedures, there was no reason why the unions could not have lent their support to building a stronger Labour position in the 1980s.

But the battle was lost. The winter of discontent may not have been the inevitable culmination of the problems of the 1970s, yet its legacy was far-reaching. It represented, in the words of political scientist Colin Hay, '*the* key moment in the pre-history of Thatcherism'.[36] It made possible, if not certain, the backlash that was to come. Without the lorry drivers, without NUPE, without the Liverpool gravediggers, Margaret Thatcher's introduction of restrictive trade union laws would have been far more difficult to implement. What followed was a steep decline in union membership, down almost half by the mid-1990s from the levels of 1979. The winter of discontent also sparked off the chain of events that saw Labour slide towards a still more crushing defeat in 1983.

Over a decade later, in 1992, accusations that a Labour govern-ment would mean a return to the dark days of 1979 still struck a chord with voters, helping the Tories to secure a fourth successive term in office. The spectre of the nation grinding to a halt even came back to haunt 'New Labour' during the fuel crisis of September 2000, when protestors blockaded oil refineries and the petrol stations ran dry, causing a sharp, if only temporary, decline in Tony Blair's popularity. However much distorted, the impres-sion that Britain was on the verge of anarchy in 1979 has proved difficult to shake off. As the historian Nick Tiratsoo writes, over time 'recollection and myth gradually fused to form a new "truth". Britain *had* been collapsing in the 1970s; Labour and the unions *were* to blame; and Thatcher *was* the saviour.'[37] History, the old maxim goes, is written by the winners.

9

'Rejoice, Rejoice'
The Falklands war, 1982

We've lost the Falklands. It's all over. We're a Third World country, no good for anything.

Tory MP Alan Clark, reacting to news of the Argentine invasion of the Falklands, 2 April 1982

The Prime Minister embarks on the last two years of her administration with a store of political capital quite inconceivable three months ago.

The Economist, *19 June 1982*

In 1981 Margaret Thatcher had the distinction of being the most unpopular Prime Minister in the history of opinion polling. Hopes of a new dawn after she came to power, leaving behind the economic misery of the 1970s, had been cruelly frustrated. Her insistence that there was 'no alternative' to the free-market nostrums of sound money and minimal state intervention had helped to plunge Britain into deep recession. Within twelve months of assuming office inflation had jumped sharply, from 10 per cent to 22 per cent, and the Tory election jibe that 'Labour isn't working' had been rendered farcical. Britain's manufacturing base, particularly in the north and west, had been devastated as unemployment rose from 1.3 million to over two million – a figure considered scandalously high by post-war standards. A year later, in the summer of 1981, the jobless total was still rising remorselessly towards the three million mark, and the nation's social fabric appeared to be under threat with rioting on the streets of Brixton in London and Toxteth in Liverpool. The sense of disillusionment among voters was palpable, and the political obituary writers were sharpening their pens. As in the case of Winston Churchill before 1940, Thatcher's career looked as if it would appear in the history books as a 'study in failure'.

In contrast to similar occasions since the war, it was not the main opposition party that benefited from discontent with the government of the day. Demoralized by defeat in 1979, Labour was torn by internal divisions more bitter and lasting than those of the 1950s, its electoral cause not helped when Jim Callaghan resigned and was replaced by the veteran left-winger, Michael Foot. Much of the running in opposing the Thatcher government was being made instead by the newly formed Social Democratic Party (SDP), based around the 'gang of four' ex-ministers who launched a breakaway in protest at Labour 'extremism'. While Thatcher dug herself deeper into a hole, removing leading Cabinet 'wets' who urged a return to more cautious policies, the Liberal-SDP 'Alliance' surged ahead of the main parties in the polls. Although a modest Tory recovery was evident by the spring of 1982, it could not prevent a triumphant return to the House of Commons for Roy Jenkins at the Glasgow Hillhead by-election in March. Political pundits were confident that Jenkins, leader-in-waiting of the SDP, would spearhead a sustained assault on the most reviled administration in living memory. But within weeks the political landscape had changed out of recognition. In April Argentina invaded the Falklands, and by the time the islands were recaptured in June, Mrs Thatcher was in complete command of the Cabinet, her party and the electorate. There was nothing Jenkins or anyone else could do to prevent her going on to a resounding victory in 1983. Since 1945 only Attlee before her had won a second election after serving a full term, and, unlike him, Thatcher did not just scrape home – she won with a thumping majority. The invasion of the Falklands had been regarded as a useful diversion from the internal problems of the military dictatorship in Argentina; it turned out to be an effective diversion for the British government. It became Margaret Thatcher's 'finest hour'.

This was only one of several ironies about the conflict. Twenty years on, the Falklands remains etched in the collective national consciousness. For many, mention of the war conjures up abiding images and phrases, often drawn from television coverage – among them the memorable words of the BBC's Brian Hanrahan, 'I counted them all out and I counted them all back', reporting on British planes launched from the 'task force' in the Atlantic. Yet television coverage from the battle zone was extremely limited; the Falklands was to be one of the least recorded conflicts since the Second World War. It was, in addition, a war Britain did not expect and for which there were no contingency plans. For many years Western strategy had been preoccupied with the threat of the Warsaw Pact and had centred on land and air forces to counter any attack on mainland Europe from the east. The Falklands were outside the main arena of NATO operations and required the Royal Navy, which had suffered most in a recent defence review, to be the lead service.

It was also ironic that a war should be fought over a territory which, unlike Suez, had such little military or economic significance for Britain. When news of an Argentine invasion hit the headlines, a common reaction was one of bemusement. Few people knew the location of the islands 8000 miles away in a cold and inhospitable part of the South Atlantic. Many wondered how Britain could be on the verge of war over an area that had a population of only 1800 people – insufficient to warrant a single local government representative at home. There were almost no finished roads outside the capital Stanley and the population, scattered mainly on thirty to forty sheep-farming settlements, travelled around on horseback as much as by helicopter. The Falklands conflict, in short, was irrelevant to the long-term problems of British society. But war provides a more concentrated test of leadership than day-to-day economic management. Although it was to make Mrs Thatcher, giving her an ascendancy over British politics that was to remain unchallenged for years to come, the war could equally have broken her. As Lawrence Freedman, a leading expert in the history of the conflict, has written, 'The fate of the country was not at stake in the Falklands, but the fate of the Government was.'[1]

At the heart of the dispute lay the issue of sovereignty. When Argentina was created out of former Spanish colonies in the early nineteenth century, it made a claim to include within its jurisdiction the Falklands or 'Malvinas', which lay some three hundred miles from the South American mainland. For many years Spanish and British settlers lived alongside each other, but in 1833 Britain formally claimed the islands as a crown colony. From that time on local residents prided themselves on the British link, though Argentina refused to give up its claim. By the 1960s, when the UN passed a resolution urging both sides to find a peaceful long-term solution, the Foreign Office was of the view that in a postcolonial world British interests in South America as a whole should not be jeopardized by the Falklands. Successive governments were reluctant to commit fresh economic resources to develop the islands. Yet the most obvious way forward, encouraging ties with the country in closest proximity, ran counter to the wishes of the population who insisted there could be no compromise over sovereignty. In 1980 Thatcher's government floated the idea of relinquishing sovereignty in return for Britain maintaining control during a long 'leaseback' period, but this proposal was savaged in the House of Commons. Efforts to coax the islanders into closer co-operation with Argentina came to little, and there were signs of impatience in Buenos Aires. A new military dictatorship under General Galtieri put the Malvinas high on its list of priorities, and it took heart from two developments in 1981. The first was Britain's decision, as part of its defence review, to scrap its only ice-patrol ship in the area, HMS *Endurance*, a vessel with limited military capability but a key symbol of British presence in the South Atlantic. The second was that no special provision was made for residents of the Falklands in a new British Nationality Act, which limited citizenship rights in dependent territories. These gestures helped to persuade Galtieri that the British were unlikely to fight for the Malvinas; the omens, he believed, pointed to Britain preparing the ground to leave.

In the spring of 1982, having run out of patience with talks, and mindful of the forthcoming anniversary of 150 years of British control, the General decided to act. Anxious to divert attention from Argentina's crumbling economy, Galtieri gave orders to prepare an invasion. In March 1982 a group of scrap-metal merchants travelling on an Argentine naval ship landed on the British dependency of South Georgia, 800 miles to the south-east of the Falklands, without following formal procedures. The military junta resisted attempts to have the merchants removed and used the incident as a pretext for a full-scale attack. Residents of the Falklands were stunned when they heard on the radio on the night of 1 April that Argentine troops were about to arrive. John Smith, an islander who lived with his family in Stanley, wrote in his diary that 'something has gone desperately wrong somewhere'. The following day the invasion force rapidly overcame the small detachment of British Marines on the islands. Smith recorded that the Governor of the Falklands, Rex Hunt, had 'met the commander of the Argentines and refused to shake hands with him, which the commander said was discourteous . . . Rex Hunt replied that it was discourteous of him to invade his country.'[2] In the three-hour burst of fighting that accompanied the taking of Government House on the outskirts of Stanley, the British avoided sustaining any casualties while killing five Argentine soldiers and wounding seventeen. 'We came second,' the Marines officer in charge reflected, 'but at least we won the body count.'[3] As the Argentine flag was hoisted and Stanley found itself renamed Puerto Rivero, a political storm began to break in London.

News of the invasion represented a major foreign policy failure for Mrs Thatcher's government. On 2 April the shock waves reverberated throughout the political nation. The horrified reaction of Tory MP Alan Clark – 'We're a Third World country, no good for anything' – was widespread, and echoed in broadsheets and tabloids alike.[4] What followed would clearly be a supreme test of the Prime Minister's leadership, though opinion remains divided over whether she was in danger of losing her job. After the conflict ended, some commentators argued that she was unlikely to have been ousted whatever happened. Peter Kellner in the *New Statesman* agreed that her image was already tarnished by high unemployment, but argued that with an election due before too long Conservative backbenchers were unlikely to risk moves to replace her; in any case her 'lightning raids' on the wets the previous autumn had placed her in 'secure command of Mount Conference and Cabinet Ridge'.[5] But there is a strong case for saying that the crisis had the potential to cause Thatcher's downfall, just as Suez resulted in Eden's demise. Few predicted at the outset of the Suez episode that Eden, with his long experience of international diplomacy, would be toppled in a matter of months. It was impossible to say how the Tory party would react to a bungled response, by a woman leader largely untested in world affairs, especially in view of initial poll findings that placed the blame for the invasion squarely on the government. Only 12 per cent of those questioned by NOP were prepared to absolve the Prime Minister from responsibility, and an ITN poll found that a quarter of respondents thought she should resign. There was, without question, much riding on Mrs Thatcher's handling of the crisis. As Enoch Powell said in the House of Commons, the Prime Minister had been happy to accept the sobriquet of the 'Iron Lady' bestowed on her by the Soviet Union; in the next few weeks, 'the nation and the Right Hon. Lady herself will learn of what metal she is made.'[6]

It was soon evident that one possible reaction, reluctant acceptance of the invasion as a fait accompli, was ruled out. Thatcher could probably have survived at Number Ten with a threefold strategy: accepting ministerial resignations among her Foreign Office team; citing high-level advice that a military response was fraught with difficulty; and pledging to secure the best possible terms for the Falklands through diplomatic means. She would have incurred fury among tabloid editors and many of her own MPs, but was unlikely to have been replaced by a 'task force' Tory leader. If such an option was considered, it was rapidly dismissed. On the evening of Friday 2 April the Cabinet met, as Chancellor of the Exchequer Geoffrey Howe later recalled, in an atmosphere of 'shocked disbelief'. In spite of an assessment from the Chiefs of Staff that a military operation was more likely to fail than to succeed, only one minister, the Defence Secretary John Nott, voted against the decision to use whatever force was necessary to retake the Falklands.[7] Within days the first elements of a hastily assembled task force, including the ships *Invincible*, *Hermes* and *Fearless*, were being cheered off as they left home waters for the South Atlantic. The speed and decisiveness of Thatcher's response, while crucial to her cause in the weeks to come, at the time increased rather than diminished the political dangers she faced. By raising the stakes she was taking an enormous risk, with her own job and possibly with the lives of British servicemen. Although military planning and diplomacy were not mutually exclusive and there was still time for a negotiated settlement, it might yet come to victory or bust. Over dinner after the Cabinet meeting on 2 April Cecil Parkinson, the Tory party chairman, agreed with his ministerial colleague Michael Heseltine that unless 'we succeeded in ousting the Argentinians this incident could destroy the government'.[8]

There was an equally quick response by Britain on the diplomatic stage. On 3 April the British Ambassador to the UN, Sir Anthony Parsons, sought to win over international opinion by securing approval for a resolution that demanded an immediate withdrawal of Argentine forces and called on both sides to negotiate. This was in due course critical, giving a sense of legitimacy to military action, but in the short term it could not prevent a storm of criticism at home. In the parliamentary debate held on the same day – the first such Saturday session of the House of Commons since Suez – the government came in for a rough ride. Demands for vengeance came from all quarters. The Labour leader Michael Foot scored a rare triumph by accusing ministers of 'betraying' the Falklands. In an echo of his 1940 pamphlet *Guilty Men*, he presented the Prime Minister as the 'guilty woman', and he demanded 'actions not words'. Two backbenchers who tried to counsel caution, the Tory Ray Whitney and George Foulkes for Labour, were howled down. Mrs Thatcher, who later described the debate as the most difficult of her career, was listened to respectfully but without much enthusiasm, especially as her speech concentrated on diplomatic as much as military possibilities. The harshest treatment was reserved for John Nott who, in winding up the debate, was jeered and drowned out with cries of 'resign' as he tried to attack Labour's record on defence. Alan Clark was among the many Tory MPs who looked on askance. 'The Lady', he conceded in his diary, was not at her best, 'rattling off far too fast a Foreign Office brief'. Foot had given an 'excellent performance', and Nott had struck entirely the wrong note in taking a partisan stance. 'Poor old Notters', as he called him, was 'a disaster . . . [he] stammered and stuttered and gabbled'.[9]

'Poor old Notters' was a convenient scapegoat in the absence of Lord Carrington, who sat as Foreign Secretary in the House of Lords. There was general agreement in the highly charged atmosphere of the Commons that the Foreign Office was the real villain of the piece, having failed to predict or prevent the Argentine invasion. At a meeting of the Tory 1922 Committee held after the parliamentary debate, Carrington was bitterly criticized. Cecil Parkinson observed that the urbane Foreign Secretary, unused to such cut and thrust, misjudged the mood of Tory MPs and was 'savaged'; the meeting left him 'shattered' and on the verge of resignation.[10] The following day, Mrs Thatcher spent much of her time at Chequers trying to persuade Carrington to stay on. But a wave of hostile newspaper headlines on the morning of Monday

5 April reinforced his view that it was right to resign. Later that day it was announced that the Foreign Secretary had resigned, to be replaced by Francis Pym, the Leader of the House of Commons. It was an indication of how far Thatcher had been thrown off balance that she felt the need to promote one of the leading Cabinet wets. This was the price she thought it necessary to pay to steady Tory nerves. In hindsight, Carrington's departure proved vital to Thatcher's cause. It satisfied the desire of Parliament for retribution, for someone to be held accountable for the disaster, and it helped to focus attention on what needed to happen next rather than on the reasons for the debacle. It provided the Prime Minister with a breathing space, though Conservative backbenchers continued to harbour many anxieties. As the *Economist* observed, 'The mix of Mrs Thatcher, Mr Pym and a politically broken-backed Mr Nott at the core of what will . . . be a cabinet war committee does not inspire confidence, though in the present climate they [Tory MPs] would not dream of saying so.'[11]

Although circumspect in public, behind the scenes many Tories were severely shaken. Some regretted the departure of Carrington, fearing that the loss of his experience would make matters worse. Announcements by the government of a 'maritime exclusion zone' around the Falklands and of a high-level inquiry into events leading up to the invasion were given only a cautious welcome. Alan Clark noted in his diary that the corridors and smoking rooms of Westminster were filled with backbenchers spreading wild rumours, most of which were unfounded. Some were claiming that ships in the task force were not up to the job, and that HMS *Invincible* had left with no operative radar system. Clark himself aired the fallacious story that there may have been some form of collusion with Argentina, and that the Governor of the Falklands had been given secret instructions to order a cease-fire when the invasion started. Why else, it was asked, had the seventy-five Marines on the islands taken no casualties? Clark reflected that, although she had reacted swiftly, there was still great danger ahead for the Prime Minister. Behind much of the chatter, he wrote, was the 'implacable hatred' of senior establishment figures for Mrs Thatcher. They would 'oppose free Campari-sodas for the middle classes if they thought The Lady was in favour. They are within an ace, they think, of bringing her Government down.' By the same token, Clark sensed, it could be the defining moment of her premiership: 'If by some miracle the expedition succeeds they know, and dread, that she will be established for ever as a national hero.'[12]

During the remainder of April 1982 Thatcher confounded her critics by steadily rebuilding her authority. Her case was to argue that all that could be done was being done. The task force, which officially consisted of more than twenty ships under the command of Admiral 'Sandy' Woodward, was being reinforced as it sailed towards and beyond its staging post at Ascension Island. In the meantime the War Cabinet, which in addition to Pym and Nott included Cecil Parkinson and the Home Secretary Willie Whitelaw, set about exploring the possibility of a negotiated settlement. The unstinting efforts of the new Foreign Secretary to find a solution, though some colleagues thought them doomed from the outset, enabled Britain to maintain a high level of international support. American Secretary of State Alexander Haig spent several weeks acting as a mediator, though his proposal that all military forces should withdraw from the Falklands as a prelude to extensive talks found little favour in either London or Buenos Aires. Haig's advisers pressed him to urge compromise on Thatcher, but she refused to budge from the position that the task force would turn round only when Argentine forces had withdrawn. 'That's a hell of a tough lady,' he was heard telling his advisers at one point.[13] The Prime Minister's cause was also helped by an early success in the South Atlantic. After initial difficulties which saw two helicopters crash, a short operation led to the recapture of South Georgia on 25 April; there was little resistance from the small Argentine garrison, and 180 prisoners were taken. Announcing this news in Downing Street alongside John Nott, Mrs Thatcher was irritated by what she regarded as grudging questions from journalists. 'Just rejoice at that news,' she said, 'rejoice' – comments that led critics to claim she was glorying in conflict. Shortly afterwards Haig conceded that his mission had failed, and the United States declared that, in contrast to Suez, it would fully support Britain.

In the first week of May the prospect of a peaceful resolution receded further. Hostilities began in and around the Falklands. Stanley airfield came under bombardment from the British; Argentine Skyhawks began attacking the task force; and on 2 May, in what became the most controversial incident of the war, a British submarine sank the Argentine cruiser the *General Belgrano*, causing the loss of some three hundred and sixty lives. The government's initial explanation, that the *Belgrano* was closing on the task force, was soon exposed as misleading, with the result that many assumed at the time and have since that the real motive must have been more sinister. Thatcher, it has been alleged, was by this time spoiling for a fight, and so agreed to the attack in the absence of her Foreign Secretary, who was actively pursuing fresh peace plans.[14] Mystery still surrounds some aspects of the episode, for example why there was a delay before the government made it clear that it would not interfere with rescue operations. Britain had also muddied the waters with its 200-mile exclusion zone, falsely implying that Argentine forces outside this area, as the *Belgrano* was when it was sunk, would not come under attack. Yet there is little evidence to challenge the view, forcefully expressed by ministers in later years, that the cruiser was sunk for operational not political reasons. As Cecil Parkinson recalled, it was regarded simply as a threat to the task force; if it had been allowed to escape and subsequently sank British ships, the government would have been vilified. The captain of the *Belgrano*, Parkinson adds, later admitted that, although he was outside the exclusion zone, he had orders to attack British forces.[15] On 4 May, as the War Cabinet was discussing how to counter unfavourable world reaction to the sinking, news arrived of the Argentine response. The destroyer HMS *Sheffield* had been hit by a French-made Exocet missile. Twenty-one British troops were killed and the *Sheffield* sank a few days later. What had hitherto been mainly a war of words had become a full-blown shooting war.

The controversy over the escalation of the conflict in the first week of May only momentarily interrupted the growing confidence of the Prime Minister. After its shaky start to the crisis, the government drew comfort from increasingly clear signals of public support. Opinion polls showed that those satisfied with the government's handling of the issue outnumbered those unhappy by a margin of two to one, although a majority continued to agree that the invasion should have been averted in the first place. Labour's satisfaction rating, by contrast, had fallen sharply after showing up well in early April. Although newspaper headlines exaggerated the scale of success, the war helped to rally Conservative voters at the local elections in early May. The leader of one district council, on hearing that every Tory seat was being defended in an area where there had been disastrous reverses in 1980–81, publicly thanked the Falklands task force.[16] The conflict was already having a discernible impact on political reputations. Michael Foot was seen to be floundering, uneasy about the loss of lives but unable to withdraw support for the task force after his tub-thumping speech on 3 April. Tony Benn was waiting in the wings as unofficial leader of the 'peace party', well placed to take advantage of any disaster in the South Atlantic. Roy Jenkins, contrary to expectations, had failed to make any impression following his return to the Commons and was being overshadowed in SDP ranks by the bellicose ex-Foreign Secretary, David Owen. As the historian Peter Clarke has written, Owen missed no opportunity 'to wrap himself in those remnants of the flag which were not already draping Thatcher'.[17] In spite of this, support for the Alliance was in decline. After a disappointing performance in the local elections, widespread media coverage was given to a by-election in June at Mitcham and Morden where the sitting Labour

MP was beaten into second place by the Conservatives when he stood as an SDP candidate.

There were several factors at work behind the growing tide of opinion in favour of the government. Aside from Thatcher's handling of the dispute and the heightened sense of crisis that came with the outbreak of hostilities, it helped that Britain was able to maintain support on the international stage. Initial sympathy at the UN began to wane with the sinking of the *Belgrano*, but the loss of HMS *Sheffield* swung opinion back in Britain's favour. From that moment until the end of the conflict, Galtieri struggled to counter the impression that he had spurned opportunities for a settlement. There was, in turn, little difficulty in persuading the British public that the enemy was entirely in the wrong. A further and related factor was the lack of coherent or widespread opposition in the country. Protest marches attracted nothing like Suez levels of anti-government support, and only about thirty Labour MPs openly backed Tony Benn's call for the withdrawal of the task force and the handing over of the issue to the UN. One of the prominent Labour dissidents, Tam Dalyell, lost his job as an opposition spokesman when he refused to adopt the official party line. In response to unease among Labour activists, Michael Foot and his deputy, Denis Healey, put increasing emphasis on the need for a diplomatic solution, but they knew that to object to military activity would leave them open to charges of being unpatriotic. The modification of Labour's initially firm stance towards a more equivocal position threatened the worst of all worlds. As one study of the left's attitude to the war concludes, 'In a period of crisis that was popularly seen to require above all things decisive leadership and national unity, this display of vacillation by Labour did the Party enormous electoral harm and was almost certainly one of the underlying reasons for Thatcher's crushing victory a year later.'[18]

Another crucial influence on the trend of opinion was the role adopted by the media. Much has been written subsequently about the distrust between the military, who believed the task force would be endangered by information leaking out prematurely, and journalists eager to satisfy an insatiable public appetite for news of what was happening in the South Atlantic. Admiral Woodward was reported as saying that, if he had his way, the public would find out about the fighting only when it was all over. Television and newspaper editors had to fight hard before it was agreed that no more than thirty pressmen could travel with the task force. Relations on board were tense. Journalists resented restrictions on their reporting, believing the military wanted them to provide Second World War-style propaganda; some recalled that they were called traitors or 'Argie' intelligence officers. Officers for their part claimed that breaches of confidentiality and irresponsible behaviour, such as 'doorstepping' outside their cabins by tabloid reporters, posed a serious threat to naval operations. The Ministry of Defence maintained a notoriously tight control over the use of television pictures which, owing to technical difficulties, were shown in Britain up to two weeks after the events they described. Viewers had to wait longer to see film of HMS *Sheffield* than readers of the *Times* had had to wait for a report on the Charge of the Light Brigade in 1854. Matters were not helped by the 'Dalek-type delivery' of the deputy director of public relations at the ministry, Ian McDonald.[19] Michael Nicholson of ITN recollected that the Falklands was the most censored of all the many conflicts he covered in his career. He estimated that only about fifteen minutes of genuine war footage was filmed; most fighting took place at night when television cameras were unable to operate. The great irony of the constraints imposed on television coverage, Nicholson noted, was that those reports that did get back reflected extremely favourably on British forces; they helped to shore up support for the government and could have been exploited much more fully.[20]

As far as national and provincial newspapers were concerned, backing for the task force was overwhelming. A few left-wing journals, reflecting the views of their readers, struck a defiant note. The *New Statesman* described the conflict as a dubious imperial exercise, scornfully referring to what it called 'a game of blind-man's buff at the other end of the world'. During the 1970s, it argued, Britain had provided nearly one-third of all major weapons purchased by Argentina, including missiles that could be used against the British fleet. No serious efforts were made, the *New Statesman* claimed, to exert financial pressure on Argentina, which owed some £18 billion in debts; the implication was that military sacrifices were more acceptable than financial losses, blood more expendable than profit.[21] As the war intensified, however, voices of dissent were drowned out by the nationalistic fervour of most coverage. The *New Statesman* complained that the patriotic rhetoric of newspapers such as the *Times* and *Daily Mail* gave the impression that Britain faced an evil comparable to Nazi Germany in the 1930s. The *Sun*, as it had done during the winter of discontent, took the lead with its use of striking headlines, the most provocative of which were 'Stick this up your junta!' and 'Gotcha', which followed the sinking of the *Belgrano*. Contrary to the spoof claim of *Private Eye*, the *Sun* did not say 'Kill an Argie and win a Mini Metro', but it came close; it did run a 'sponsor a Sidewinder' feature and urged its readers to send in abusive jokes about Argentina. Although liberal opinion was offended, there was little doubt that this type of aggressive nationalism struck a chord, underpinning the growing numbers across all ages and social classes who backed the military operation.

None of this meant that the Prime Minister was as yet invulnerable. For as long as the potential for disaster remained, the jury was still out on her leadership. Ministers were aware by the middle of May that the main invasion force was arriving in the South Atlantic, and that troops could only be held on board for a short period in the main battle zone as the southern hemisphere winter approached. Mrs Thatcher recalled in her memoirs that 'perhaps the crucial moment' came on 18 May when the War Cabinet met with the Chiefs of Staff to decide whether to go ahead with the invasion. 'None of us doubted what must be done,' though great difficulties were made clear.[22] In hindsight these difficulties have

tended to be overlooked. The sinking of the *Belgrano* had the beneficial effect for the task force of persuading the Argentine navy to
remain in home ports, although the threat of a breakout could not
be discounted. It also encouraged greater caution among leaders
of the enemy's most potent weapon, its air force, which had been
underestimated by the British in the early stages of the war. This
meant that any invasion would have to take place in the absence of
what was considered an essential precondition, control of the
skies. British ships attempting a landing would be within easy
range of air attack from the Argentine mainland; their positions
would be impossible to conceal, making an invasion a hazardous
enterprise. It was also acknowledged that international pressure
for a ceasefire would grow once British troops were on the
Falklands. Unless there was a swift victory, it would be difficult to
maintain support for a war of attrition on land. But politically it
was unthinkable for the government to consider abandoning the
operation with the job half done. The great risk had therefore to
be taken of defying the accepted rules for the conduct of amphibi-
ous warfare – attempting a landing that would be vulnerable to
air attack and that risked costly and humiliating defeat on the
beaches.[23] The moment of truth had arrived.

On 21 May, with diversionary attacks taking place around the
Falklands, British troops disembarked in large numbers at
San Carlos bay, which proved to be an inspired choice. It was virtually undefended, the Argentines expecting an assault closer to
Stanley, and its deep waters allowed British warships in close to
defend the landing, so minimizing the risk from enemy aerial
attacks. Although British ships came under heavy fire in the days
that followed, the Argentine air force lost some forty planes in its
raids over San Carlos, a rate of attrition that left it incapable of
seriously threatening British forces thereafter. The landing succeeded beyond expectations, with 4000 men of 3 Commando
Brigade under Brigadier Julian Thompson being brought ashore
with few casualties. This triumph was followed by a period that
more than any other tested the nerve of politicians back in

London. Confidence in Thompson began to erode when there was no immediate attempt to break out of the bridgehead; instead the emphasis was placed on bringing ashore supplies of equipment and munitions. Willie Whitelaw, the Home Secretary, admitted he was 'lying awake at night with visions of Suez', and another unnamed minister later said he could not understand 'what the hell was going on down there. We were losing a ship a day and nothing on land was moving.'[24] It was another week before the settlements of Darwin and Goose Green were captured after the first and arguably most intense land battle of the war. In one of the most celebrated episodes of the conflict Colonel 'H' Jones, the commander of 2 Para, lost his life leading the attack on heavily fortified Argentine positions. Some twenty British and an estimated two hundred and fifty Argentinians died, with 1400 more captured.

Victory at Goose Green opened the way for the British to move across East Falkland towards Stanley. After the belated arrival of General Jeremy Moore, in overall command of land forces, it was decided to launch what was referred to as a 'no-nonsense Warminster style attack' – a reference to the methods of attacking a well-dug-in enemy as taught at the Warminster military base. In echoes of infantry campaigns going back to the First World War, British forces proceeded to pound enemy positions and then engage them in fierce night-time combat. The land battle was won and lost not at Darwin and Goose Green, important though these much-publicized encounters were, but on the hills outside Stanley – on Mount Tumbledown, Wireless Ridge, Mount William and Sapper Hill.[25] In his diary the Falklands resident John Smith vividly described the chaos and deafening noise as British forces closed in on the capital, backed up by heavy artillery and aerial bombardment. Houses were hit, killing three elderly islanders, and the local church was reduced to a 'pathetic mess, with pools of mud and water on the floor; smelling dank with the sweat and fear of the troops'. On the evening of 14 June many residents were huddled together in Stanley's West Store, a designated safe area, when a British officer entered by the back door and announced with sangfroid: 'Hullo, I'm Jeremy Moore. Sorry it's taken rather a long time to get here.' Confirmation that the Argentine commander, General Menendez, had surrendered was followed by wild cheering. Moore was hoisted aloft onto shoulders and toasts were drunk to Mrs Thatcher, the Queen and the task force; no one could quite remember in what order.[26] After seventy-four days of Argentine occupation, the British flag flew once more over Government House in Stanley.

Ever since the guns fell silent, arguments have raged over whether the conflict was justifiable. The majority view at the time, underlined in the memoirs later written by Conservative ministers, was that self-determination was paramount: the government had no choice but to reclaim a territory the inhabitants of which regarded themselves as British. World opinion on the whole supported the case that Argentina must be held accountable for flouting international law. Others believe that while it was right to send the task force as a sign of Britain's determination to act, much greater effort should have been made to secure a diplomatic solution before lives were lost. The response of Tory ministers to this charge is that the military junta was at no stage seriously interested in peace. Some writers, reflecting the minority view in 1982, continued to regard the war as an expensive, futile adventure. The cost of maintaining a large British garrison and extending the runway at Stanley, allowing rapid aerial reinforcement in the event of a further crisis, was estimated at £2 million per islander per year by the end of the 1980s. In view of Britain's prior willingness to relinquish the Falklands, it was ridiculous to pour so much effort into their recapture. In the view of the distinguished South American writer Jorge Luis Borges, it was like 'a fight between two bald men over a comb'. There was, in addition, the price paid by those most directly involved: islanders who had to contend with thousands of unexploded devices and who found their former way of life disrupted; hundreds of troops on both sides left with appalling injuries; above all, those killed in action, 255 British and an estimated seven hundred and fifty Argentinians. The comments of the widow of one British serviceman reflected, simultaneously, anger at her loss and acceptance that the cause may have been just: 'They had to do it. Ah . . . the price my family paid. No one will ever know . . . exactly what price we paid. Perhaps it was worth it for Britain's sake.'[27]

The rights and wrongs of the campaign were not widely discussed in the atmosphere of euphoria that followed victory. During the summer and autumn of 1982 flag-waving crowds flocked to Southampton, Portsmouth and Plymouth to welcome home the task force. Television news, starved of live action during the war itself, made amends by giving extensive coverage to the returning ships, each greeted with the singing of 'Rule Britannia'. The British triumph was underlined by the fall of the Galtieri regime in Buenos Aires, and Mrs Thatcher could not resist a note of jingoism. 'We rejoice,' she said, 'that Britain has rekindled that spirit which has fired her for generations past and which has begun to burn as brightly as before. Britain found herself again in the South Atlantic and will not look back from the victory she has won.'[28] The Prime Minister spoke of a 'Falklands spirit' pervading all corners of national life. For a few weeks there was heavy demand for 'Up your junta!' T-shirts, and impromptu sing-songs were reported around the military bandstand at Royal Ascot. But these types of celebration were short-lived and struck the wrong note in many quarters, including among some British troops who returned home distressed by their experiences and preoccupied with the memory of friends and colleagues lost. Recruitment to the forces increased only modestly in the aftermath of the war, and at a commemoration service held in St Paul's Cathedral the Archbishop of Canterbury, to the annoyance of Mrs Thatcher, avoided triumphalism and said that the dead on all sides should be remembered.[29]

The effect of the war on Britain's place in the world was also not as long-lasting as has been claimed. The Prime Minister believed that success in the South Atlantic reversed a long period of decline: 'Since the Suez fiasco in 1956, British foreign policy had been one long retreat . . . Victory in the Falklands changed that. Everywhere I went after the war, Britain's name meant something more than it had.'[30] Thatcher, like many, was fond of drawing comparisons between the Falklands and Suez, although the differences between the two conflicts were more striking than the parallels. While both saw parliamentary unity break down in the face of armed struggle, many more lives were lost in 1982, and Thatcher could count on international support which did not exist in 1956 when it was Britain that was regarded as the unbridled aggressor. The Falklands War did little to change the reality of Britain's much-reduced role on the world stage. What remained of the Empire was small and fragmentary, consisting of fewer than twenty dependent territories around the globe; most found that, like the Falklands, their interests barely registered in Britain. Aside from Hong Kong, which was later to revert to China, the combined population of the dependent territories numbered just 150,000. War in the South Atlantic only temporarily distracted from what had been the central concern of British foreign policy for many years past – how to preserve the semblance of a 'special relationship' with America while clarifying Britain's place within the European Community. This issue was to dog Mrs Thatcher long after memories of the Falklands began to fade.

This is not to downplay the significance of the war, which was to have serious consequences for politics in Britain. The first and most important impact was on the Prime Minister herself. Max Hastings, who as a journalist with the task force was among the first to arrive in Stanley, later wrote in his account of the conflict, co-authored with Simon Jenkins: 'The figure of Margaret Thatcher towers over the Falklands drama from its inception to the euphoria of the final triumph . . . Her single-mindedness, her belief in the futility of negotiations, even her arch phraseology at moments of crisis, all seemed to armour her against any suspicion that this might be a dangerous, even absurd adventure.'[31] Within the space of weeks, one of the least regarded of post-war leaders had become the most popular, with an approval rating that had never seemed remotely possible before April 1982.

The knock-on effect of this was that any opposition within Conservative ranks was silenced overnight. Inside the Cabinet Thatcher's authority henceforth went unchallenged. Francis Pym remained as a Foreign Secretary who was tolerated, but the wets were no longer in a position to urge caution. As Peter Kellner wrote in the *New Statesman*, if anyone dared to suggest that she was misjudging the public mood, she would have 'little difficulty in telling them to get lost'. Inside the parliamentary party, opponents of the Prime Minister would have to keep their heads down for the foreseeable future. In the words of the MP Alan Clark, 'The Lady's autocracy is complete.'[32] Her self-esteem bolstered by a personal triumph against the odds, Mrs Thatcher's valuation of herself, as a leader who towered above colleagues and opponents alike, came to be shared by many at Westminster and beyond. She no longer had anything to fear from claims that she was responsible for failing to prevent the invasion in the first place. The inquiry into the background to the crisis, headed by Lord Franks, far from providing an indictment of ministers, concluded in 1983 that the government could neither have anticipated nor prevented the original attack. The *Guardian* columnist Hugo Young lamented that it was a 'state paper written by the establishment for the benefit of the establishment'.[33]

The Falklands conflict was also a crucial turning point in the electoral history of the 1980s. It remains widely accepted today that the 'Falklands factor' helped the Conservatives to secure re-election in 1983 with a much-increased majority. In her memoirs Thatcher voiced what became a commonplace assumption. Although a recovery was already taking place in early 1982, she said, the effect of the conflict was 'real enough. I could feel the impact of victory wherever I went . . . without any prompting from us, people saw the connection between the resolution we had shown in economic policy and that demonstrated in the handling of the Falklands crisis.'[34] Opinion polls, at first glance, told an incontrovertible story. On the eve of the war all three parties were neck and neck, each claiming the support of just over 30 per cent of voters. Between April and June there was a surge of support for the Tories, up to over 50 per cent in many polls, putting the government well ahead. In the second half of the year this fell back slightly and stabilized at around 45 per cent, with Labour on 30 per cent and the Alliance just above 20 per cent. Unable to claw back this deficit during the remainder of the parliament, there was no doubt that the Falklands had seriously undermined the prospects of the opposition. Labour's uncertain stance showed that the party had no distinctive view of Britain's place in the world and had failed to address the issues of nationalism raised by the war. While many railed against government 'manipulation', some on the left acknowledged that Thatcher had exploited, not created, nationalist sentiment among voters whom Labour needed to attract. The Alliance, for its part, had been stopped in its tracks. Not only did its poll rating slump but so, too, did its membership; recruitment of new members to the SDP, essential to building up a broad-based party, had been steady in the early months of 1982 but was cut in half during the war and never recovered thereafter.[35]

In spite of such evidence, a team of political scientists from Essex University later put forward the claim that Thatcher's victory in 1983 was much less dependent on the Falklands than was popularly supposed. It was noted that several studies attempting to quantify differences of opinion before and after the war, while underlining the existence of a Falklands factor, had come to widely divergent conclusions about its precise impact. By employing a new methodology, the Essex team argued that increased government popularity in mid-1982 owed less to the war than to a growing awareness that economic fortunes were improving. A jump in popularity would have occurred without the conflict in the wake of Geoffrey Howe's spring budget, which was much more expansionary than those he had previously introduced since 1979. Interest rates were falling, consumer spending was rising and, most crucial of all, confidence about the soundness of the economy in the months ahead was rising sharply. On this basis, the Essex team proposed, any Falklands effect was small (worth no more than 3 per cent additional government popularity) and short-lived (lasting for only a few months over the summer). While it was conceded that many were impressed with Thatcher's handling of the crisis, this did not necessarily lead to a change of voting intention – in the same way that Churchill was admired by many who refused to vote for him in 1945. The key to explaining the 1983 election result was the recovery of the economy following the recession of the early Thatcher years: 'Jolly good wars abroad hardly entered into it at all.'[36]

These claims have failed to persuade the majority in the academic community and beyond. The Essex team has been attacked for a research design said to include so many economic variables that it was bound to find something other than the Falklands to explain changing government fortunes. It has also been accused of ignoring polling evidence that showed the Falklands replacing unemployment as the key issue in voters' minds in mid-1982; a surge in support for the Tories was highly unlikely at that time in the absence of the war. Subsequent studies claim that the key difference after mid-1982 was the perception of Mrs Thatcher's leadership. Her handling of the war, one such academic study concludes, 'dramatically altered public judgements about her competence as prime minister, and thereby prompted the development of more sanguine expectations about the future course of the nation's economy under her stewardship'. While the economy recovered its place as the crucial issue for voters by the time the 1983 election was held, it was the Falklands that had pushed her beyond the reach of the other parties.[37] Certainly, Labour references to the war during the 1983 campaign proved to be counterproductive. Denis Healey was vilified in the tabloids as 'wild and embittered' for commenting that Thatcher was 'glorying in slaughter', exploiting the sacrifice of servicemen for party advantage. And Neil Kinnock, soon to replace Foot as Labour leader, was obliged to write to bereaved families to apologize for any offence caused by his remark, in response to a heckler who said that Thatcher had guts, that it was 'a pity people had to leave theirs on Goose Green in order to prove it'.[38]

It cannot be known if the Conservatives would have won the 1983 election without the Falklands episode. If the war had gone badly, victory at the polls may still have been possible under a new leader, just as Macmillan triumphed in 1959 after replacing a predecessor discredited by a failed overseas adventure. Economic recovery was a potent electoral force. But in view of Thatcher's difficulties in the early years of her premiership, and the suddenness of the turnaround in her fortunes, it seems reasonable to conclude that her ascendancy owed much to General Galtieri. It should not be forgotten that victory in the South Atlantic was due to good luck as much as it was to Thatcher's resolute leadership. The odds against the task force succeeding were considerable, and if the junta had waited a few weeks more before attacking the Falklands, winter conditions in the southern hemisphere would have made a military response impossible to contemplate, at least in the short term. As it was, the professionalism of British forces, the choice of San Carlos waters for an invasion, and the superiority of British weapons systems were just enough to hold the tactical balance in a situation where disaster could have struck almost up to the last moment. In the event of such a disaster, there may have been more Tory administrations in the 1980s but it is unlikely that there would have been second and third Thatcher terms with all that flowed from them. Like two of her predecessors, Eden in 1956 and Heath in 1974, Margaret Thatcher took a huge gamble with the premiership; unlike them, she won. 'To the victor,' said the nineteenth-century writer W. L. Marcy, 'belong the spoils.'

10

'I fight on, I fight to win'
Margaret Thatcher's downfall, 1990

The conflict of loyalty, of loyalty to my Right Honourable friend
the Prime Minister . . . and of loyalty to what I perceive to be
the true interests of the nation, has become all too great. I no
longer believe it possible to resolve that conflict from within this
government. That is why I have resigned . . . The time has come
for others to consider their own response to the tragic conflict of
loyalties with which I have myself wrestled for perhaps too long.

Sir Geoffrey Howe, speech in the House of Commons,
13 November 1990

You know those maps on the Paris Metro that light up when
you press a button to go from A to B? Well, it was like that.
Someone pressed a button, and all the connections lit up.

Tory MP and minister John Biffen on the events that led to
Thatcher's downfall

M argaret Thatcher's legacy towers over modern-day British
politics. When she fell from power in November 1990 she
entered the history books as the longest-serving Prime
Minister of the twentieth century, with an unprecedented three
successive election victories to her name. Ten years later the journalist Andrew Rawnsley was able to comment that both main
party leaders at the start of the twenty-first century, Tony Blair
and William Hague, were 'creations of her era'. To an extent that

neither was comfortable acknowledging, they were 'Sons of Thatcherism'.[1] Media interest on the tenth anniversary of her downfall was such that many newspapers ran features allowing people to recall how they had reacted to her departure from Downing Street. Long after she had ceased to be Prime Minister, Mrs Thatcher continued to evoke mixed feelings; for some she was a heroine, while for others she remained a hate-figure. One retired secretary from Didsbury said that people in her local pub cheered on that Tuesday in 1990 when the news came on a television screen; she protested and shouted back, 'she's the best thing that ever happened to this country.' The academic and writer A. C. Grayling was at home and said he 'went delirious with joy and quite literally danced about the room'. Footage of her tears as she left Downing Street 'did nothing to soften me', Grayling said:

I saw in those tears a contemptibly self-regarding and very pale reflection of the anxiety, difficulty and often real suffering of the millions who lost jobs, opportunities [and] . . . their homes when mortgages went through the roof . . . In short, I thought only of her 'no such thing as society' war on human lives in the name of market economics, and rejoiced mightily that the lecturing, hectoring, callous succuba had been forced to go at last. A very good riddance!'[2]

For the historian, the events of November 1990 present something of a mystery. It had long been accepted among academic observers of British politics that a Prime Minister with a strong parliamentary majority and in good health, enjoying the considerable advantages of patronage and access to the media, was virtually impregnable.[3] No Conservative leader since Neville Chamberlain, who was confronted by the test of full-scale war, had been forced to leave office other than at the behest of the electorate or on the advice of the doctors. Yet it happened to Margaret Thatcher, despite her being the most commanding British political leader since Churchill. Besides her record of being unbeaten in three general elections, she remained in vigorous health at the age of sixty-five and possessed one of the largest Commons majorities since the war. She had not suffered any major reverse in the House, as Chamberlain did in 1940, and only two days before her resignation she was demonstrating her experience on the global stage, deliberating with other European leaders at a conference on security. Less than a week before that Michael Heseltine, her challenger for the Tory leadership, was still repeating in public his mantra of several years past that there were 'no circumstances' in which he could envisage taking on the Prime Minister. So what caused Thatcher's fall from power? And why did it occur with a swiftness seen before only in wartime conditions? Should the events of November 1990 be seen as a 'murder mystery', and if so, who carried out the crime? Or was the demise of the Iron Lady more a case of 'death by misadventure', attributable mainly to her own failings?

Existing accounts have noted that there was no single, overriding cause of Thatcher's downfall.[4] Various factors played a part: the unpopularity of key policies such as the Community Charge or poll tax; party divisions over Europe; the beginnings of a prolonged economic recession; criticisms of Thatcher's increasingly 'remote' style of leadership; the resignation of leading Cabinet figures such as Nigel Lawson and Geoffrey Howe; the availability of a credible challenger in Michael Heseltine; and fears among Tory MPs that the Prime Minister had become an electoral liability, incapable of repeating her earlier victories at the polls. But what was the balance between these factors? Most studies of the crisis, whether by journalists, academics or Tory insiders looking back, tend to present the outcome as unavoidable. The accumulated resentments of the late 1980s were such, the argument goes, that Thatcher was certain to be ousted. Yet her departure was a messy and unpredictable process. In the words of one of those who remained loyal to the Prime Minister to the end, Kenneth Baker, the Conservative Party chairman:

The flickering lamps of history will show many ruts in the road, many stones, winding diversions, cunning traps and treacherous slopes. They will not reveal a highway leading directly to a given destination. There was . . . nothing inevitable about the events of autumn 1990 which led to Margaret's fall. That came about through an amazing mixture of accident, mistake, ambition, intrigue, slighted pride, misplaced optimism and faulty judgement.[5]

Where should the origins of Thatcher's departure from Number Ten Downing Street be sought? Not, it would seem, in her record or performance before 1987. The Falklands War, the election triumph of 1983 and, above all, victory in the protracted miners' strike of 1984–5 had set the scene for the introduction of what became known as 'Thatcherism'. The curbing of trade union influence was confirmed by restrictive legislation; council house sales proceeded apace; and ownership of shares soared as much of nationalized industry was returned to the private sector. In retrospect, the mid-1980s marked the zenith of Thatcher's power, a time when almost any social change was equated with her influence. 'If brash young bankers started using cordless phones in restaurants, or if working-class people spent more time at home watching videos,' an editorial in the *Spectator* was to observe, 'these changes were attributed to "Thatcherism" almost as if the Prime Minister had invented the technology herself.'[6]

In 1986 Mrs Thatcher faced a barrage of criticism after her Defence Secretary, Michael Heseltine, resigned over the Westland helicopter crisis. Any political damage was short-lived, however. The Prime Minister brazened out the affair and 'Tarzan' – as Heseltine was dubbed on account of his flowing hair and all-action style – was left to wander the political undergrowth, ostracized by the Tory hierarchy. With the economy in good shape the government rapidly recovered from its mid-term blues. Although the opposition parties made gains at the 1987 general election, the Conservative majority of 101 seats was still the second largest since the war, bettered only by the landslide of 1983. Under the leadership of Neil Kinnock, Labour avoided the prospect of being eclipsed by the Alliance, but any return to power looked a long way off. One of Thatcher's ministers, William Waldegrave, said that after 1987 it was possible to talk of the most 'all-pervasive personal government since Churchill as a war leader'.[7] In fine fettle and determined to continue with her programme of economic liberalization, there appeared to be little that could prevent Thatcher – as was rumoured to be her intention – from going 'on and on'.

But things did not go to plan during the 1987 parliament. In the first place, the government was beset by economic difficulties. The tax-cutting budget of Chancellor Nigel Lawson in the spring of 1988 was greeted with great acclaim by Tory MPs. Lawson, an intellectually formidable figure at the Treasury in the mould of Denis Healey, was credited with achieving a British 'economic miracle'. Yet within months the Chancellor was under attack for permitting, even encouraging, a resurgence of inflation. In mid-1986 inflation stood at 2.4 per cent, but by 1989 it was three times that level. Interest rates were increased sharply amid talk of middle Britain suffering from 'mortgage misery'. Differences between Thatcher and Lawson, particularly over the Chancellor's desire to use sterling to shadow the value of the Deutschmark, intensified and proved impossible to contain. Lawson resigned amid great acrimony in October 1989 after six years at Number Eleven Downing Street. Bernard Ingham, Thatcher's ultra-loyal press secretary, claimed in his memoirs that the economy was the 'most important' element in the Prime Minister's eventual demise. He warned in private that economic policy had become 'far too loose and slack and the Government would live to regret it'.[8] Without doubt, the onset of recession in the late 1980s damaged the unity and popularity of the Tory regime. It allowed Labour to surge ahead in the polls and it bred discontent on the backbenches of a sort that Thatcher had not encountered before. Even so, economic problems did not make her fall inevitable, or even likely. Many post-war governments, including the first two Thatcher administrations, had recovered from downturns to secure re-election, and there was every hope that this might happen again, especially as survey evidence showed that voters continued to trust the Tories ahead of Labour on the key issue of economic management.

A second reason why the Prime Minister found herself on the defensive after 1987 was growing disquiet about her style of leadership. Backbenchers noted that Thatcher increasingly refused to brook any criticism and had become heavily reliant on unelected courtiers at Number Ten, such as Ingham. After the retirement in 1988 of her emollient troubleshooter, William Whitelaw ('every Prime Minister needs a Willie,' she said), there was, in the words of Nigel Lawson, 'no restraint on her at all'.[9] In the aftermath of Lawson's resignation, murmurings among MPs were such that one 'stalking horse' candidate, Sir Anthony Meyer, decided to bid for the leadership of the party, a development that would have been unthinkable in the mid-1980s. While party rules required Thatcher to submit herself annually to MPs for re-election, no one had come forward to make a challenge in her fourteen years as leader. In reply to the standard question of who would take over if the Prime Minister was to be hit by a bus, one minister had remarked that the bus would never dare. Anthony Meyer's challenge was beaten off easily enough, by 314 votes to thirty-three, although another twenty-seven MPs abstained or spoiled their papers. The government whip Tristan Garel-Jones warned Thatcher that a further one hundred MPs had given only conditional support, and that unless she changed her 'tone', they would 'be back'.[10] The Prime Minister was confident that she had lanced the boil. Michael Heseltine remained the only potential leader over the water, having travelled the 'rubber chicken' circuit of local Tory associations tirelessly since his resignation, building up his reputation as a figure of substance. But Heseltine knew that any leadership challenge would involve accusations of disloyalty, and he maintained that he could not envisage standing against Thatcher. His refusal to take up the cudgel in place of Sir Anthony Meyer led to speculation that he may have missed his best chance.

Contrary to her expectations, matters got worse for the Prime Minister in the months after the 1989 leadership contest. The principal reason for this was the huge unpopularity of the so-called 'flagship' policy of her third administration. Mrs Thatcher had been a long-standing opponent of the British system of local taxation. She wrote in her memoirs that she 'always disliked the rates intensely', sharing the view of many critics that a system based on the notional rental value of property unfairly obliged a single pensioner to pay the same as an adjacent household containing several working adults.[11] In 1984 the Prime Minister ordered an investigation of rate reform, and in the spring of 1985 a ministerial review group met at Chequers and heard the case for the introduction of a 'Community Charge'. Thatcher was soon persuaded of its advantages. It would, its supporters claimed, avoid looming revaluations that were certain to alienate Tory voters by pushing up rates; as a tax on people rather than property it would make everyone contribute, whereas in some areas only one-third of adults paid full rates; and it would curb the excesses of 'extravagant' Labour local authorities, encouraging voters to plump for low-spending Conservative councils.

Nigel Lawson, absent from the Chequers meeting, was sufficiently alarmed when he heard of the proposals to outline the likely objections. A flat-rate 'poll tax', he told colleagues, would be 'politically catastrophic'. By requiring everyone to pay the same, it would hit the poor much harder than the rich, and instead of increasing accountability it would be used as an excuse by local authorities to raise spending levels, with central government taking the blame for higher charges.[12] Lawson's warning was ignored. By coincidence, the full Cabinet discussed the new scheme for the first time on 11 January 1986, the day of Michael Heseltine's resignation. This gave Heseltine scope to claim he had no part in what followed. With attention fixed on the dramatic walkout over Westland, the single most controversial policy of the Thatcher years was able to take shape without the media or the political world really noticing. The poll tax had 'emerged almost without trace'.[13]

The 1987 election victory cleared the way for reform of local taxation to come to the top of the political agenda. In a wave of triumphalism, it was announced at the Tory annual conference later in the year that the Community Charge would be introduced more rapidly than initially intended. From this moment onwards, as the implications of the new system became the subject of greater scrutiny, voices of concern began to be heard. In the spring of 1988 the Conservative backbencher Michael Mates, a close friend of Heseltine, sought to amend the legislation so that the tax might be banded according to ability to pay. His amendment was defeated, but despite promises that there would be generous rebates for the less well-off, the reduction of the government's majority from 101 to twenty-five indicated a growing level of disquiet. Early predictions that the average Community Charge would come in at £200 looked to be a serious underestimate. By the time the poll tax – as almost everyone apart from the Prime Minister called it – was introduced in Scotland in April 1989, a year earlier than in England and Wales, its unpopularity was not in doubt. In the first year of operation, warrants for non-payment were taken out against over 1.2 million individuals; some estimates claimed that almost half of all adults in Scotland withheld at least part of their payment.[14] Yet instead of prompting a complete rethink, ministers concluded that the Scottish experience showed only the need to adjust and improve the efficiency of the system. The flagship was heading for the rocks.

In the early months of 1990 there were widespread protests on the streets against the poll tax. With inflation at 8 per cent (and rising towards 10 per cent later in the year), local authorities were continuing to revise their required tax levels upwards. The first bills that went out in England and Wales averaged £363, in spite of government proposals to cushion the blow through 'transitional relief'. Newspapers widely reported that the Duke of Westminster, who previously had paid over £10,000 in rates on his estate, got a bill for £417, the same as his housekeeper. Much media attention was also given to the violent clashes that took place between police and protestors in places such as Bristol, Colchester and Norwich. The demonstrations culminated in London on 31 March, when some two hundred thousand protestors turned up from hastily formed 'Anti-Poll-Tax Unions' across the country. Hours of rioting took place in and around Trafalgar Square, with cars overturned, windows smashed and shops looted. March organizers blamed heavy-handed tactics by the police; ministers pointed the finger at anarchist extremists. Either way, there were nearly three hundred and fifty arrests, with hundreds left injured, and pictures of pitched battles in central London were given prominence in television news for days afterwards.[15] Elsewhere large-scale demonstrations were more peaceful – many, it was noted, taking place in areas of strong Tory support such as Plymouth, Taunton and Weymouth. In some cases protestors used humour to make their point. A meeting to set the level of the poll tax in Nottingham was interrupted and broken up by the arrival of demonstrators dressed up as Robin Hood and his Merry Men, armed with imitation custard pies. Several councillors were hit in the face as the pies flew around the council chamber; the Sheriff in his ceremonial robes managed to take evasive action.[16]

All of this, needless to say, did enormous harm to the government's reputation. Surveys in March 1990 showed that some 70 per cent of those questioned disapproved of the poll tax; about half said that it was the key issue determining how they would vote in a general election. Discontent with the new system underpinned a huge swing against the Tories at the Mid-Staffordshire by-election, held only ten days before the London riots, representing Labour's best by-election performance for nearly half a century. The Prime Minister's personal association with the policy inevitably damaged her reputation. Her satisfaction rating fell to only a quarter of those questioned, exceeding her own earlier record for unpopularity at the height of the 1981 recession. Journalists eagerly picked up Westminster rumours that there would be another Tory leadership contest later in the year. In the wake of the London demonstrations, *Tribune* expressed a widely held view: 'It seems that the poll tax is what will bring Mrs Thatcher down. How appropriate, for we were all brought up on those romantic stories of wicked monarchs taxing the people unfairly and being dethroned.'[17] Later accounts often take a similar line, naming the poll tax as the single most important factor in Thatcher's downfall. One academic study, extending the nautical metaphor of the flagship, called the poll tax 'the iceberg that sank her'; 'its unpopularity proved to be her undoing.'[18] John Cole, the BBC's political editor at the time, argued in his memoirs that it 'lethally' undermined the Prime Minister's leadership. After ministerial tinkering with relief systems failed to take the sting out of the issue, Cole claims, 'her fate was sealed'.[19]

Yet the role of the poll tax in explaining Thatcher's fall can be overstated. In the spring of 1990 the Prime Minister was obviously regarded by many Tory MPs as an electoral liability. While postbags bulged with complaints from traditional supporters, the Iron Lady remained unrepentant. In her memoirs she stuck resolutely to the view that 'given time', the Community Charge could have become one of the most 'beneficial reforms ever made in the working of local government'.[20] But if the poll tax, like the economic downturn, made her vulnerable, it did not follow automatically that the Prime Minister was finished. Much of the electorate had never warmed to her in the first place, and she remained confident of riding out the storm, just as she had come through bouts of serious criticism in 1981 and 1986. The immediate pressure on her leadership was eased when the government did not perform as badly as expected at the local elections in May 1990. At the instigation of party chairman Kenneth Baker, newspaper reaction centred not on Tory losses but on gains in the 'flagship' London councils of Wandsworth and Westminster, both of which had set low poll tax rates. Over the summer Labour's lead in opinion polls fell as some of the initial anger about the tax abated. By the autumn it was being named by far fewer voters as the issue that would determine voting preference. In early October Thatcher received a nine-minute standing ovation at the end of a successful party conference. The poll tax by itself had thus been insufficient to dislodge the Prime Minister. Talk of another leadership challenge had largely disappeared. If there were to be any threat in the autumn of 1990, there would have to be something with even greater potency than the poll tax; there would need to be, as one academic study puts it, 'a major issue and a trigger'.[21] In the event, both of these were to come courtesy of the most unlikely of sources – Sir Geoffrey Howe, the Deputy Prime Minister.

Geoffrey Howe had been a central figure in Conservative politics for many years, serving as Chancellor of the Exchequer during the first Thatcher administration and as Foreign Secretary since 1983. Aside from his doleful style of speech – famously mocked by Denis Healey, who said that being attacked by Howe was like being savaged by a dead sheep – Sir Geoffrey was best known as an ardent pro-European. As Solicitor-General in the Heath government he had played a key role in helping to draft the legislation to secure British entry into the European Community. It was an open secret in Westminster circles that the relationship between Thatcher and Howe had steadily deteriorated since the 1987 election, with Europe at the heart of their disagreements. After the 1986 Single European Act, Thatcher increasingly gave vent to her dislike of what she saw as the centralism of the European Community, a sentiment shared by a sizeable number of Tory MPs. Howe believed his leader was undermining the pragmatic approach he sought to adopt as Foreign Secretary. For her part, the Prime Minister disliked Howe's 'misty Europeanism' and his defiant support for Nigel Lawson in the debates over the shadowing of the Deutschmark. With growing regularity, Howe was humiliated in front of Cabinet colleagues by Thatcher – who treated him, in Lawson's words, like a cross between a doormat and a punchbag – and in 1989 he was moved from the Foreign Office to become Leader of the House of Commons. Although he was accorded the title of Deputy Prime Minister, as a mark of his seniority, he had none of the status or influence of Thatcher's former de facto deputy, Willie Whitelaw.

In late October 1990, just when it seemed that the Prime Minister had survived the worst of her troubles, Sir Geoffrey decided he had had enough. After returning from a European Council meeting in Rome, Thatcher reported back to the House of Commons at first in a low-key tone, reading from a prepared text. But under questioning from Eurosceptic Tory MPs she became more and more animated, ending with a memorable response to what she regarded as three unacceptable elements of the vision of Commission President, Jacques Delors. 'No!, No!, No!' she said of Delors's proposals, words that were given pride of place in television and press coverage of the speech. Sitting next to the Prime Minister on the front bench, Howe was appalled. This not only breached carefully crafted Cabinet positions on Europe, it also bordered on unthinking hostility towards the Community. 'Each answer was more reckless than the last,' he wrote in his memoirs, and within twenty-four hours he had reached 'the regretful conclusion that it was time for me to leave'.[22] Thatcher earned plaudits from many commentators impressed by her confident parliamentary performance. But on 1 November she paid the price: Sir Geoffrey announced his resignation. While a shock, it was not enough to puncture the view that the Prime Minister would survive. The *Times* claimed that her leadership remained 'robust, undaunted and unchallenged', and Hugo Young in the *Guardian* said that sudden resignations had become such a feature of recent years that 'Howe's is no longer one capable of shaking the Thatcher world'.[23]

For several days it looked as if the Prime Minister had little to worry about. With the annual deadline for the party leadership contest looming, there was speculation that Michael Heseltine might at last be emboldened to challenge. On the evening of 1 November Heseltine telephoned Sir Geoffrey to suggest otherwise: he did not think 'his undoubtedly courageous decision had materially altered my own position'.[24] With media interest mounting, Heseltine did, however, test the waters on 3 November by writing an open letter to his constituency association chairman, detailing his concerns with the direction of government policy. Four days later he got a frosty response, urging him not to rock the boat by standing for the leadership. The *Economist* reflected what was a common view. Howe's resignation had not caused any immediate revolt, and Heseltine had 'been feinting for so long that most ministers guess he will not bring himself to strike now'.[25] Confident that things were going their way, the Prime Minister and her advisers made a series of crucial mistakes. At the behest of Bernard Ingham, Tory-supporting newspapers put pressure on Heseltine to 'put up or shut up'. In addition, the date for nominations for the party leadership was brought forward to 15 November, with voting among MPs to take place five days later. As Heseltine wrote in his memoirs, these moves 'raised the game' and left him little room for manoeuvre; facing Downing Street-inspired claims that he was 'glamour without substance', he moved closer to a decision to stand.[26] On the evening of 12 November, in a speech at the Guildhall in London, Thatcher made a further error, using words she was soon to regret. Aware that Howe was a keen cricket fan, she said she was still at the crease; she refused to duck the bouncers and had every intention of hitting the bowling all round the ground.

Sir Geoffrey, in the meantime, had been keeping his own counsel. He refused media requests for interviews and spent his time preparing a resignation speech. This was delayed as Parliament had gone into a short recess before reconvening to hear the Queen's Speech on 13 November. Although the occasion of the opening of a new session ensured that the House and press gallery were full to capacity when Howe rose, few anticipated the fireworks that were about to happen. On his past record, Thatcher and most of those present never believed Howe was capable of the captivating performance he delivered. Listened to in silence, as was the custom with resignation speeches, he won over his audience by first introducing a light touch. If Downing Street press releases of the past few days were to be believed, he said, he was the only minister ever to have resigned while being in full agreement with government policy. He then proceeded to outline the basis of his very real differences with the Prime Minister over both Europe and the economy, arguing that leading ministers had found themselves constantly undermined by her methods. Picking up the cricket theme, Howe said that it was like the best batsmen in a team being sent to the crease only to find that their bats 'had been broken before the game' by the captain. The journalist Alan Watkins later commented that Thatcher rather invited this by having used cricket imagery the previous evening when she clearly knew little about the game. 'Bernard Ingham, a Yorkshireman,' he said, 'should at least have been able to tell her that ducking was precisely what one did with bouncers.'[27] Sir Geoffrey went on to make a compelling assault on the Prime Minister's refusal to tolerate differences of opinion inside the Cabinet, and he ended with an implicit call for Michael Heseltine to take up the gauntlet – 'for others to consider their own response to the tragic conflict of loyalties with which I have myself wrestled for perhaps too long'. In his *Spectator* column a few days later, Alan Watkins neatly summed up: 'The past master of code,' he said, 'was writing with an aerosol in block capitals.'[28]

Howe's speech was soon being compared with earlier attacks by MPs that had gravely damaged Tory leaders, such as Nigel Birch's assault on Macmillan during the Profumo crisis of 1963. What made Sir Geoffrey's performance unique, and added greatly to its impact, was the advent of televised proceedings from the Commons. Audiences across the country were able to see and hear, either live or on the evening news, every nuance of the unfolding drama. Peter Hennessy was to describe it as an unrivalled moment in British 'televisual politics' in his lifetime.[29] Tory MPs could be seen wincing at the savagery of some of Howe's wording. The reaction on the other side was very different. Alan Clark described in his diary how the 'Labour benches loved it', lapping up every fresh insinuation. 'Grinning from ear to ear they "oooh'd and aaah'd" dead on cue.'[30] The nation was equally able to see Nigel Lawson, sitting below Sir Geoffrey, nodding his grave approval, while on the front bench the faint smile on the Prime Minister's face at the outset soon disappeared. As one of those in the press gallery wrote, 'Politely, cheerfully, repeatedly, and to her face, he [Howe] knifed his former leader. At first she hardly felt the blade slip in, and smiled at his joking. As he continued, her face became a set mask of misery.'[31] The metaphor of the knife was to be repeated frequently, pointing to the most apt historical parallel. Just as Leo Amery's 'In the name of God, go' speech was called 'the dagger in the heart' of Neville Chamberlain in 1940, so Howe had dealt a mortal blow to Margaret Thatcher. Within ten days she would be staring resignation in the face.

Howe's resignation speech instantly revived doubts about the Prime Minister's ability to survive. As MPs spilled out into the lobbies and corridors of Westminster, many were overheard saying 'the game is up for her' and she was 'dead in the water'.[32] Talk of a leadership challenge came back with a vengeance; the newspapers on 14 November made grim reading in Downing Street. Headlines such as 'bowled middle stump', 'much worse than Westland' and 'foundering' were littered across the front pages. As the morning papers were going on sale, the most crucial impact of the speech became evident: it persuaded Michael Heseltine to declare himself a contender. An hour after Howe finished speaking in the Commons, Heseltine met with his old friend and Thatcher loyalist, Cecil Parkinson, who argued that party unity would be jeopardized if a challenge were made. Heseltine simply replied: 'Cecil, she is finished. After Geoffrey's speech, she's finished.'[33] In his memoirs Heseltine admitted that the pressure to make a bid became irresistible at this point. Journalists and MPs were besieging his home, and one Tory colleague asked him bluntly: 'Have you got the balls for it?' The die was cast. Aware that it would be in his interests to allow the headlines to be dominated by Howe's speech, he delayed a statement overnight. Early on the morning of 14 November, just hours before the deadline for nominations was reached, Heseltine gave a press conference on the steps of his house in Chapel Street, combining an announcement of his decision to challenge Mrs Thatcher with a commitment to 'review' the poll tax.[34]

As the short leadership campaign got under way, the two contenders approached the task in very different ways. With less than a week to go before balloting took place, Heseltine took to the television and radio studios as frequently as possible, highlighting the poll tax and Europe as the chief issues that needed a fresh approach. In the past he had never cared greatly for the 'social life' of the Commons, but now, one of his opponents noted, 'he was everywhere' around the bars and dining rooms of Westminster.[35] His campaign team worked assiduously to persuade MPs that it was time for a change, and his prospects were enhanced when opinion polls suggested that he would bolster electoral support for the government. Instead of trailing Labour, the indications were that a majority of voters would back a Heseltine-led Conservative Party. The Prime Minister, by contrast, chose to stand above the fray, attempting to demonstrate that she was getting on with running the country. She made no major media appearances, consenting only to a few interviews with sympathetic newspaper journalists, and she made no personal calls to secure the votes of wavering backbenchers. Instead she left operations to her Parliamentary Private Secretary, Peter Morrison, who in the words of Hugo Young, was 'known for his loyalty' but not for 'his ability to count'.[36] Morrison advised Thatcher that she would get 230–240 votes, easily enough to secure outright victory. On this basis the Prime Minister decided, contrary to some advice she was given, that she should go ahead on Sunday 18 November with a planned visit to Paris for a security conference, confident that her absence would not affect the outcome. Other supporters were not so sure. Alan Clark in his diary lamented that there was not 'a single person working for her who cuts any ice at all . . . The Lady herself is away. It's absolute madness. There is no Party mileage whatever in being at the Paris summit. It just makes her seem snooty and remote.'[37]

With the Prime Minister away, Westminster became consumed with talk about the vote and its possible aftermath. Under the rules for the contest, if neither candidate had the required majority it would be necessary to go to a second ballot. In such circumstances, Thatcher and Heseltine could stand again, but new candidates could also come forward. There was much discussion among MPs about who might be the best 'stop Heseltine' candidate in the event of Thatcher being unable to secure a first-round triumph. The Prime Minister had been nominated by her Foreign Secretary, Douglas Hurd, and seconded by her Chancellor, John Major, but both men were said to have leadership ambitions of their own. The febrile atmosphere of the last days of the campaign was intensified after Hurd intimated that he would be willing to stand if it came to a second ballot. With the arm-twisting over, Tory MPs crowded into a small committee room in the Commons at 6.30 on the evening of Tuesday 20 November to hear the result declared by the chairman of the 1922 Committee, Cranley Onslow. Alan Clark noted that there was a typical 'balls-up over the figures', with MPs hearing the result in the corridor before Onslow spoke.[38] Heseltine had secured a better than anticipated 152 votes, with Mrs Thatcher out ahead on 204 – a tantalizing four short of the amount required to avoid a second ballot. By any reckoning it was a damaging result for the Prime Minister; some 45 per cent of her backbenchers had refused to support her. In his memoirs Heseltine described the implications with a note of bitterness: 'To anyone with the faintest knowledge of how Westminister politics work, her position was manifestly untenable. It says much for Mrs Thatcher's capacity for self-delusion that at first she stubbornly refused to recognize that fact.'[39]

Far from standing aside, the Prime Minister intimated within minutes that she would contest a second ballot, even if it meant fighting new contenders. In one of the most memorable moments of the crisis, she bustled down the steps of the British Embassy in

Paris where the BBC's political correspondent, John Sergeant, was talking to viewers about her likely reaction. Bernard Ingham pushed Sergeant aside, looking for a microphone set up for the waiting contingent of newspaper reporters, but with great speed and aplomb Sergeant offered his own microphone and secured an exclusive. In a specially prepared statement, the Prime Minister proceeded to say that she was pleased to have received the backing of more than half of the parliamentary party, and that she could confirm her intention to stand in the next round of voting. While intended to show her decisiveness, the consensus was that the television shots from Paris did more harm than good. John Sergeant reflected that this farcical incident symbolized the disintegration of Thatcher's regime, the principal actors having 'no idea where they should go' as they emerged from the Embassy. Kenneth Baker later said that it gave the impression that she had reached her decision 'all alone; it was typical of her style, and far too gung-ho. The speed and brusqueness of the announcement represented all that her critics found wrong with her style.'[40] The statement was certainly not sufficient to prevent the frenzy that gripped the political world back in London, where Tory MPs began to come to terms with the likelihood that Thatcher would be unable to win a second ballot. The loyalist Alan Clark wrote in his diary late at night that by failing to secure a clear victory she had been fatally wounded and would find it difficult to re-establish her authority. 'But this wastage of time in Paris is sheer lunacy,' he added; 'Harold at Stamford Bridge.'[41]

In the hours after the result was announced, gatherings of ministers and Tory MPs took place across London to discuss what should happen next. Nothing comparable had been seen in the capital since the war, for the last such infighting over the leadership – after Macmillan announced he would resign in 1963 – had been concentrated in Blackpool where the party was gathered for its annual conference. One crucial meeting took place at the home of the Deputy Chief Whip, Tristan Garel-Jones, and was attended by five members of the Cabinet, including Chris Patten,

Malcolm Rifkind and Norman Lamont, as well as several junior ministers. The feeling of the meeting was that Thatcher was so unlikely to win a second ballot that she should be dissuaded from standing; at all costs, a Heseltine triumph had to be averted. Meeting with some of the group later that night, Kenneth Baker got the impression that they were 'searching for an executioner', but he, as party chairman, refused to play ball. Baker noted how a line that was to be frequently repeated the following day was already taking shape: ministers, he was told, would of course still vote for the Prime Minister, but if she did not withdraw she would suffer a humiliating defeat. In his memoirs Baker wrote that those present always denied they were 'plotting', though to him it amounted to the same thing. 'While daggers were not issued, guns not loaded, gunpowder barrels not installed', the group had clearly decided on a 'collective course of action', and so had that 'sense of purpose which every plot has to have . . . Of such stuff is modern political assassination made.'[42]

When Thatcher returned to Downing Street from Paris on the morning of 21 November, however, it was not clear who, if anyone, would inform her that support was ebbing away. There was much speculation in the press that senior party dignitaries – the 'men in grey suits' – would tell her to go. The 'men in grey suits' had long been part of the mythology of Tory politics. In reality, Conservatives were more inclined to wear dark blue, pinstripe suits, and there had been no previous occasion when a group of elders had actually forced the resignation of a leader. According to one historian of the party, Stuart Ball, the arrival of men in grey suits was about as likely as the arrival in Downing Street of a deputation of 'little green men from Mars'.[43] Yet at lunchtime on 21 November the Prime Minister did receive such a visitation. Among those who came to report on opinion inside the party were the Chief Whip, Tim Renton, and the head of the 1922 Committee, Onslow, as well as loyalist ministers such as Kenneth Baker and John Wakeham, the Secretary of State for Energy. The problem was that no one present was prepared to spell out the bleakness of the Prime Minister's position. While a slippage of support among MPs was noted, Thatcher was given reassurances that she remained the best available candidate to take on Heseltine. As the journalist Andy McSmith puts it, the legendary 'men in grey suits' had given 'a passable impression of men in brown trousers'.[44] Buoyed up by the outcome of the lunchtime meeting, the Prime Minister left for the Commons to make a statement on the Paris summit. Pausing on the steps of Number Ten, she declared for the waiting television cameras: 'I fight on, I fight to win.'

As a sign of her resolve, Thatcher also appointed a new campaign team led by John Wakeham. On his advice, she agreed to meet with members of the Cabinet individually later in the day to confirm their willingness to back her in a second ballot. This proved to be a critical error. Ministers were kept waiting until the early evening before they were able to see Thatcher in her room at the House of Commons, and many used the time to agree among themselves what needed to be said. In her memoirs she spoke of how they mostly stuck to the same 'line', namely that as loyal followers they would back her in a second ballot but that they did not believe she could win. 'Almost to a man they used the same formula.'[45] Several ministers were in tears in these tense face-to-face meetings. Alan Watkins wrote that the whole crisis was 'distinguished by lachrymosity as by general sobriety', although not in the case of Education Secretary Kenneth Clarke, who was 'no blubber'.[46] The plain-speaking Clarke – 'Ken Bloke' as he was later called – was the first to puncture the optimism that Thatcher had maintained since the announcement of the result the previous evening. He bluntly told his leader that if she stood again she would hand the premiership to her hated enemy, Heseltine, and that it would be far better to release her backers, Hurd and Major, from their obligation not to stand. Altogether eleven out of fifteen Cabinet ministers consulted advised her that the cause was lost.[47]

The tide had turned with remarkable speed. As the evening wore on Thatcher was visited by a few loyalists who urged her to carry on. 'What a way to go!' Alan Clark told her; 'Unbeaten in three elections, never rejected by the people. Brought down by nonentities!' They, like she, realized the game was up. This was underlined when Wakeham reported back that support among backbenchers had collapsed during the day. Nothing could now reverse 'the laws of arithmetic', as Hugo Young puts it, or the influence of Thatcher's husband Denis, whose desire at this juncture was to ensure that 'his heroic wife did not end her public life in humiliation'.[48] At a Cabinet meeting held at the unusually early hour of 9 a.m. the following morning, 22 November, the Prime Minister struggled through tears to read a resignation statement. She concluded that the unity of the party would be best served by her standing aside for others to come forward in a second ballot. Still in a state of shock, she added: 'It's a funny old world.' In her final days at Number Ten, awaiting the result of the second ballot, she devoted herself to ensuring that Michael Heseltine did not become her successor. Heseltine found that after the announcement of Thatcher's intention to go, there was a new mood among Tory MPs. He knew that he would be held accountable for forcing the Prime Minister to quit, and that he had little chance of succeeding against the new candidates, Douglas Hurd and John Major. By way of atonement many MPs felt it important to vote for Major as Thatcher's preferred candidate, and he came out ahead when the result of the second ballot was declared on 27 November. Heseltine and Hurd immediately conceded defeat and John Major became Britain's new, 'unknown Prime Minister'.

The Thatcher premiership had come to an abrupt end, though not the Thatcher era. It was widely agreed that the changes wrought in the 1980s could not easily be set aside. Thatcher's successors at Number Ten, Conservative and Labour, accepted much of her legacy: a market economy free from the constraints of 1970s-style corporatism and trade union influence, income tax levels below the European average, and a resolute approach to matters of war and peace. There was one notable departure in policy. Michael Heseltine, rewarded in the new administration with the post of Environment Secretary, replaced the poll tax with a less contentious, property-based 'council tax', reverting to the type of local taxation tried and tested over hundreds of years. But for the most part, Margaret Thatcher's successor as Tory leader was noted for changes of style rather than substance. John Major's low-key approach to leadership was soon being described by journalists as 'Thatcherism with a human face'. Despite the great trauma it caused in the party, the crisis of November 1990 proved beneficial to the Tory electoral cause in the short run. Labour strategy was based on the assumption that any coming contest would be fought against a discredited Thatcher regime. Joy at the departure of 'That Bloody Woman' was quickly overtaken by a recognition that Major would be difficult to beat. For many voters, a change of leader was more important than a change of government – a feeling that persisted through to the general election of 1992, when the Conservatives secured an unlikely fourth successive victory. Thereafter, the downside of November 1990 became more evident: from the sidelines, Thatcher was unable to resist frequent off-the-record complaints that her successor lacked resolve, especially over Europe.

In semi-retirement, Lady Thatcher, as she had become, also had plenty of time to ponder on why she had fallen from power. Former colleagues, journalists and academics – others too – reflected on the events of November 1990. In terms of issues, most emphasis came to be placed on the view that economic difficulties, combined with the poll tax, ruined Thatcher's credibility with the electorate. This, in turn, persuaded Conservative MPs that she was an electoral liability and would have to go. By contrast, Europe is said to have provided the spark, but it did not figure prominently during the leadership campaign itself. In the view of Tory historian Lord Blake, 'She was ousted because she was believed to be a vote-loser, not because of arcane differences about the EC.'[49] Yet, as we have seen, the Prime Minister survived the introduction of the poll tax, damaging as it was, and, according to some of her advisers, might have been persuaded to amend it had she come through the battle against Heseltine.[50] It was the nature of Britain's relationship with the rest of Europe, though not high among the priorities of voters, that was arguably the central connecting issue from 1987 onwards. It was increasingly divisive at all levels of the Tory party and it underpinned several ministerial departures, including that of Thatcher's most likeminded ally in the Cabinet, Nicholas Ridley, who was forced to go after unacceptably blunt anti-German comments in the summer of 1990. The European question was a key ingredient in the resignations of Lawson and Howe, and even the Westland crisis that prompted Heseltine's walkout in 1986 stemmed from arguments over whether Europe needed the capacity to manufacture its own defence equipment.

This leads to a consideration of *who* most influenced the Prime Minister's demise. The loss of three powerful pro-European ministers after 1986 clearly had a cumulative, debilitating effect on Thatcher's premiership. Her dismissal was to be described by one ex-minister, John Biffen, as 'the revenge of the unburied dead'.[51] Of the disaffected triumvirate, Lawson's departure led to the first, unsuccessful challenge to the Prime Minister in the autumn of 1989, though he was not directly implicated in the 1990 crisis. A more central role was, of course, played by Michael Heseltine. His candidature provided something that had been missing on all previous occasions when Thatcher's leadership had been called into question – a credible alternative. When the time came, he fought a skilful campaign, one that did not bring him the top prize but did guarantee his place in a post-Thatcher administration. It became usual to say that it was Heseltine who 'brought down' the Prime Minister. Yet Geoffrey Howe's part in the drama was even more decisive. The unexpected ferocity of his resignation speech was the catalyst for everything that followed, as even the loyal party chairman Kenneth Baker recognized. 'If it had not been for the provocation of Geoffrey Howe's resignation speech,' Baker said, 'then there would have been no leadership contest.' Sir

Geoffrey, to return to John Biffen's comparison with a map of the Paris Metro on which 'all the connections lit up', was the 'someone' who pressed the button.[52]

This is not to deny that other groups and individuals also played a part in bringing down the Prime Minister. In her memoirs Lady Thatcher poured scorn on those Cabinet colleagues who warned her on the evening of 21 November against standing in a second ballot. Until that point she had been determined to carry on; 'what grieved me,' she wrote, 'was the desertion of those I had always considered friends and allies and the weasel words whereby they had transmuted their betrayal into frank advice and concern for my fate.'[53] This view of the Cabinet's importance, shared by some seasoned political commentators, was one that Thatcher first formed at the time of her resignation. When Cecil Parkinson said to her that he and others were determined to 'pin regicide on Heseltine', she looked puzzled and replied: 'Oh no, it wasn't Heseltine, it was the Cabinet.'[54] But if the erosion of support among Cabinet colleagues was vital in persuading Thatcher that she could not go on, this only came into play at the eleventh hour. The Cabinet was not in the first place responsible for such a desperate situation having arisen. The 'fatal procession' of ministers on 21 November was responding not to any bold tendency to rebellion, which it had never possessed, but to the same instinct for survival as was being displayed by many MPs. 'It was, in that sense,' as Hugo Young notes, 'the party and not the Cabinet that pushed its leader out.'[55]

Support for the Prime Minister, in other words, had decayed from the outside inwards, not vice versa. Her popularity had declined sharply in the constituencies, not among Tory activists – who remained strongly supportive, even after the first ballot – but among floating and disaffected voters angered by the government's performance since 1987. In these circumstances party grandees, often dependent on the leader for positions of power and influence, were reluctant to give clear warnings about the drift of opinion. This helps to explain why, in the words of Douglas

Hurd, 'the greybeards . . . failed to deliver the message' in their lunchtime meeting with Thatcher on 21 November.[56] The 'men in suits', of whatever colour, played only a minor role in bringing down the Prime Minister. In contrast, MPs in marginal seats were those who felt most threatened by voter revolt. Many of these were emboldened in November 1990 to combine with the pro-Europeans who had backed Sir Anthony Meyer's challenge the previous year. Hence an essential part in the undermining of Thatcher was played by Tory backbenchers who had lost faith in their leader well before the Cabinet weighed in with its advice. But again this must be seen in perspective. The number of hardline critics had always been relatively small, and Mrs Thatcher did, after all, win the first ballot. As she pointed out in her memoirs, she received more votes in defeat from Tory MPs than John Major did in his second-ballot victory.[57]

In determining who caused Thatcher's downfall, the finger of responsibility must ultimately be pointed at the Prime Minister herself. Like Neville Chamberlain in 1940, she was the author of her own misfortune. Some commentators noted that it might have been better to have retired gracefully in 1989 on her tenth anniversary of coming to power; after that, it was inevitable that voters would tire of her. Thatcher not only preferred to go 'on and on'; she also exacerbated the feeling that she had outstayed her welcome. If in the early days her forceful personality won over more voters than it alienated, then by the late 1980s the balance had shifted. As a close observer of the Prime Minister, John Cole of the BBC later wrote that her struggles to impose herself on party and country, on the enemy within and the enemy without, had produced a leader driven 'not just by ideology, but by an immanent sense of being right. She now believed that she knew better than almost anyone what was right and what was wrong.' While admirers continued to admire, for an increasing proportion of the population she was, John Cole said, 'insensitive, narrow, [and] humourless, with growing signs of arrogance, intolerance, even megalomania'.[58] The effects of this were damaging well before she fell from power. Many Tory MPs came to share the doubts of the public, noting that she visited the tearoom at Westminster only when in trouble, and even then without really listening to their concerns. 'Margaret was on transmit, not receive,' it was said of one such visitation.[59]

Throughout the crisis that led to her fall, Thatcher made errors that underlined how out of touch she had become. Her style of management – which she once admitted was to 'explode and have my way' – did not permit her to contemplate any return to government for ministers who had resigned. Michael Heseltine was allowed to build up a power base on the backbenches irrespective of the danger that might pose to her own position. In the aftermath of Howe's resignation, Thatcher then allowed her advisers to goad Heseltine into making a challenge, again apparently blind to the damage he could cause. Her conduct of the leadership campaign was by turns complacent and misguided. She made the mistake of leaving the country at the critical juncture; she made counterproductive attacks on her opponent as 'little more than a socialist'; and she refused to make personal efforts to win over wavering MPs. ITN's Michael Brunson wrote that she made a revealing confession about her attitude to garnering backbench support in an interview some time later. 'Did they really expect me,' she said, 'to go around begging for their votes?' This, Brunson added, said much about what had gone wrong.[60] Thatcher's premature statement of her intention to stand again after the result of the first ballot was announced compounded her earlier errors, as did her willingness to see Cabinet ministers individually on the evening of 21 November. In the same way that governments lose elections rather than oppositions winning them, so it might be said that incumbents lose leadership campaigns, challengers do not win them.

In spite of all this, it was a close-run thing. The Prime Minister almost survived the crisis of November 1990. Her distinguished record and the reserves of loyalty upon which she could call enabled her to come within a few votes of outright victory on the first ballot. With just a little more support, she might have been able to brazen things out, battered but defiant. As Kenneth Baker has written, it is not difficult to envisage a scenario of the 'Warrior Queen' coming into her element again in the Gulf War, which began only weeks later. 'In a head-to-head battle with Neil Kinnock,' Baker speculates, 'Margaret would have won a fourth successive term, albeit with a reduced majority.'[61] Uncertain as it was until the last moment, Thatcher's fall was not a Greek tragedy, its outcome predetermined and written in the stars. There was no deep-laid plot in Tory ranks, no evidence of a Heseltine-Howe conspiracy ('Tarzan on Mogadon', in the cutting description of Bernard Ingham). Cabinet ministers had not engaged over a long period in careful planning to oust the leader and the idea that MPs saw in a clear-eyed way that she could not win again looks like a rationalization after the event.[62] The fall of the Prime Minister was more akin to a Shakespearian tragedy, in which nemesis follows hubris. It was an unfolding tale of opportunities spurned and bad luck, with Howe's resignation coming at the one time of the year when a leadership challenge could be mounted. The Prime Minister convinced herself that it all amounted to political 'murder' by her senior colleagues; 'treachery', she said, 'with a smile on its face'.[63] In the final reckoning, Thatcher's own failings made it a case of death by misadventure. To have survived, she would have needed greater subtlety and flexibility; she would have needed to make concessions and compromises that were alien to her nature. The Lady was not for turning.

'. . . an extremely difficult and turbulent day' Black Wednesday, 1992

At least the nation can comfort itself that it was only money that was poured away, not blood. National pride has too often been paid for with the lives of young men in war. Nonetheless Mr Major's quixotic battle with the speculators still seems the economic equivalent of the Charge of the Light Brigade: half a billion, half a billion, half a billion onwards . . .

The Times, *19 September 1992*

It was at that moment we lost the 1997 election . . .
There was never any real hope after that.

*John Major, reflecting on Black Wednesday, quoted in
Robin Oakley,* Inside Track *(2001)*

The weakness of the contemporary Conservative Party, humiliated in the general elections of 1997 and 2001, can be traced back to a single day almost a decade ago. On what swiftly became known as 'Black Wednesday', 16 September 1992, John Major's government was confronted by a financial crisis from which it never recovered. For all those involved the overwhelming emotions, as interest rates swung up and down and as sterling faced devaluation, were those of disbelief, impotence and a terrible sense of failure. Britain had, of course, experienced similar situations before, but none had engulfed a government with such startling speed, and most had been associated with Labour administrations. After earlier devaluations of the pound, Labour had narrowly managed to secure re-election in 1950, and recovered some lost ground prior to defeat in 1970. But after September 1992, the Tories never looked remotely capable of winning a fifth successive term of office. The Conservative reputation for sound management, whether justified or not, was destroyed at a stroke, and the party plunged to the modest level of public support at which it has remained stuck ever since. Black Wednesday, in short, stands out as the single most debilitating event in Tory politics since the war. Its impact was more devastating to the party's electoral fortunes than any of the earlier crises it had confronted – Suez, Profumo, the three-day week and the downfall of Thatcher among them. In order to understand why this was so, we need to appreciate the particular circumstances of 1992, especially what the distinguished financial writer Philip Stephens calls the lethal combination and crossover between 'the economics of the pound and the politics of Europe'.[1]

John Major had only entered the Cabinet as Chief Secretary to the Treasury in 1987, and spent a brief spell at the Foreign Office before becoming Chancellor in October 1989. After the downfall of Thatcher, he triumphed in the Conservative leadership contest to become, until Tony Blair after him, the youngest Prime Minister of the twentieth century. Within a year he had successfully negotiated a compromise over Europe acceptable to an increasingly fractious Tory party at the small Dutch town of Maastricht, and within eighteen months he had triumphed against the odds by securing a fourth successive Conservative victory at the 1992 general election. A slim but workable majority of twenty-one seats was achieved in spite of a prolonged recession. When the nation went to the polls, it was difficult to detect the 'green shoots of recovery' referred to by the intense figure of Norman Lamont, Chancellor of the Exchequer. On the day Major went to Number Ten in 1990 unemployment stood at 1.75 million, but it rose remorselessly towards three million, bringing personal hardship to many families as bankruptcies multiplied and 'negative equity' trapped those who had bought their homes in the boom years of the mid-1980s.[2] The 1992 victory also occasioned surprise because the Prime Minister faced accusations that his voice and vocabulary made him a grey, uninspiring leader. 'So John Major turned out to be Clark Kent after all,' began one startled newspaper editorial after the election.[3]

Two themes were picked out by political commentators to explain the surprise result. One was that the departure of Thatcher and the change to a more consensual leadership style under Major remained welcome. The second was that the Prime Minister's qualities, superhuman or otherwise, were less important than continuing fear of the Labour alternative. With the economy in poor shape, it was a case of 'better the devil you know' for many voters. The Labour opposition continued to suffer from Neil Kinnock's 'Welsh boyo' image and from relentless charges in the tabloids that it, unlike the Tories, would raise taxes. Despite taking some forty seats, Labour was unable to recapture the hearts and minds of 'Essex man' – symbolized by the voters of Basildon, a vital target seat for Kinnock held by the Tories early on election night. Major's honeymoon as Prime Minister looked set to continue. Whatever critics among the chattering classes might say, his personal popularity was high and had been sufficient to see off Neil Kinnock, who resigned and was replaced by John Smith in the aftermath of the April election. Yet within six months Major was to be regarded as a spent force. His reputation was torn to shreds by the events that took place in mid-September – events that vindicated the prediction of those, like the *Observer*, that claimed that Britain's fragile economy made 1992 a 'good election to lose'.[4]

It was in the autumn of 1990, while Major was Chancellor, that Britain had joined the so-called exchange rate mechanism (ERM) of the European Monetary System. The ERM was a central feature of the system that linked the currencies of the European

Union and had been devised as a first step towards the eventual establishment of monetary union. The Eurosceptic wing of the Conservative Party was strongly opposed to the idea of a single currency, regarding sterling as a badge of British sovereignty; in order to maintain party unity Major, after becoming Prime Minister, sought and secured an 'opt-out' for Britain on this aspect of the Maastricht Treaty. But he was convinced, as he had been as Chancellor, that membership of the ERM was vital to British interests. It would, he argued, link sterling with the most inflation-resistant currency in Europe, the Deutschmark, and so in due course rid Britain of the inflationary disease that had underlain the economic ills of earlier decades. In spite of resistance from Thatcher, in the death throes of her premiership, Major was able to announce Britain's entry to the ERM at the level of DM2.95 to the pound. This was too high according to some economists, but, as Major noted in his memoirs, it was the only level permissible in the eyes of Britain's European partners.[5] Other European nations regarded the ERM as a fixed system – no significant realignment of currencies had taken place since 1987 – and it was widely assumed that Britain would stick with the rate at which it had joined. This assumption was called into question when in June 1992 the Danish electorate rejected the Maastricht Treaty, which Major had yet to pilot through the House of Commons. Instead of steady progress towards monetary union, prospects for European integration had been thrown into doubt; financial markets could no longer be certain that existing parities would hold, still less that the ERM would lead seamlessly to a single currency.

Over the summer of 1992 pressure on the weaker European currencies, including sterling, increased significantly. In the aftermath of the Danish referendum, two factors further eroded market confidence in the ERM. One was uncertainty about the outcome of a referendum in France, scheduled for late September; a rejection of Maastricht by one of the leading players in the European Union was likely to damage irrevocably moves towards economic and monetary union. The second was resistance from the Bundesbank to calls from other European leaders for the reduction of high levels of German interest rates, felt to be necessary in the wake of reunification with the east. John Major, like other leaders, made several unsuccessful attempts to persuade his German counterpart, Helmut Kohl, to take steps that would allow the rest of Europe to follow suit in reducing rates, so helping to provide the continent with a desperately needed escape from recession. In private, the Prime Minister discussed with key advisers possible alternatives, such as seeking a realignment or devaluation of sterling within the ERM. None of the options, however, looked feasible. 'We had looked over the precipice,' Major later said, 'and decided not to jump.'[6] Norman Lamont, who had been rewarded for his part in helping Major secure the leadership in 1990 by being made Chancellor, was no fan of the system he found in place when he went to the Treasury. He later claimed that he tried to put the case for leaving the ERM altogether but found that Major did not want to 'discuss that at all'.[7] In public, Major and Lamont presented a united front, conscious that any lack of certainty in British policy would further damage sterling. In August the Bank of England began to use its reserves on a large scale to defend the pound, and the Chancellor issued a statement saying that the government would do 'whatever is necessary' to protect the existing parity.

At the beginning of September the Bank, in a further attempt to show that it was determined to resist speculative attacks on sterling, announced that it had secured a large foreign currency loan of 10 billion ecus (over £7 billion). Hopes were pinned on a successful outcome at the next six-monthly gathering of EC finance ministers and central bank governors, meeting under Lamont's chairmanship in Bath over the weekend of 4–5 September. With Helmut Schlesinger, President of the Bundesbank, in attendance, it was a golden opportunity for European leaders to put pressure on Germany to cut interest rates. The British Chancellor spoke bluntly. He asked Schlesinger directly to cut rates four times; after the last request Schlesinger got up and made for the exit, only to be prevented from leaving by a colleague. Long hours of negotiations in the eighteenth-century Assembly Rooms ended with little progress. The Prime Minister was spending his Saturday watching cricket at Lord's, where he received the message: 'no realignment, no interest rates cut, lots of bad blood'.[8] Schlesinger was greatly offended by Lamont's approach and only reluctantly agreed to issue a statement saying that the Bundesbank had no intention of further raising German rates 'in present circumstances'. As it was the weekend, efforts had to be made to keep Downing Street officials, away in various parts of the country, informed of the deteriorating situation in Bath. Major's adviser Sarah Hogg was walking in the Scottish hills and had difficulty persuading local police of her need for a secure phone line to London. Once connected, she bawled down the crackly line, 'Prime Minister, I don't think we can rely on the Germans.' Two policemen nearby, knowing nothing of the context, responded in unison: 'Dead right'.[9]

By the time the Cabinet assembled for its first meeting since the summer holidays, on Thursday 10 September, the Italian lira was under sustained attack on the foreign exchanges. The Prime Minister told colleagues that any realignment of sterling was out of the question, a message he repeated in public to the Scottish CBI during a speech in Glasgow later in the day. Major used words that were to come back to haunt him within a week: 'All my adult life I have seen British governments driven off their virtuous pursuit of low inflation by market problems or political pressures. I was under no illusion when I took Britain into the ERM. I said at the time that membership was no soft option. The soft option, the devaluers' option, the inflationary option, would be a betrayal of our future.'[10] Some of the Prime Minister's advisers, including Sarah Hogg, had suggested a softer line. But Major refused to budge. He was deeply opposed to devaluation, which he regarded as a failing that afflicted only Labour governments. He also knew that his reputation was on the line: not only had he taken sterling into the ERM but he also believed, as he had told Andrew Neil of the *Sunday Times* and other newspaper editors only weeks earlier, that in time the pound could eclipse the Deutschmark to become the strongest currency in Europe. There were also tactical considerations. 'If I equivocate the market will smell it,' he said, hoping that sterling would survive until the French referendum on 20 September, after which the whole situation might look very different.[11]

The following day, Friday 11 September, there was some good news when the Bundesbank made a tiny reduction in interest rates. The Prime Minister was later to describe this as 'distressingly small' and 'miserly', although a signal that German policy was at last easing.[12] But over the weekend, which Major and his wife spent at Balmoral, a telephone call came through from Giuliano Amato, the Italian Prime Minister, to say the lira would be devalued by 7 per cent. Asked about sterling, Major was resolute: the British would not follow suit. Over the next couple of days, as it became clear that the pound was next in the firing line for speculators, a series of crisis meetings were held involving Major, Lamont and officials from the Bank of England and the Treasury. By Tuesday 15 September the Bank was intervening heavily in the markets to prop up sterling, which was sliding towards its lowest permissible level within the terms of the ERM, DM2.77. Tensions were heightened when it was announced that the Prime Minister was cancelling a scheduled visit to Spain, prompting recollections of Denis Healey's decision to turn back from Heathrow airport to confront the IMF crisis in 1976.[13] Worse was to follow in the evening when news reached Downing Street that Helmut Schlesinger had made comments implying that sterling should have been devalued at the same time as the lira. Major and Lamont were dumbstruck, later describing these words as 'deeply unhelpful', 'cavalier' and 'devastating'.[14] As one newspaper was to comment: 'Short of John Major rushing naked into the streets screaming "Sell! Sell", it is hard to imagine an event which could have done the currency more harm.'[15] Within hours of Schlesinger's comments, the pound fell through its DM2.77 floor on the New York financial markets and ministers knew that the following day would see no let-up. The scene was set for what was to become the worst twenty-four hours in the Major premiership.

As London woke to a bright and sunny morning on 16 September the trend started in New York continued in the City. By 9 a.m., the Bank of England had already spent £1 billion attempting to shore up sterling. While the Bank and other European central banks were buying pounds, at a rate of tens of millions every few minutes, commercial banks and fund managers were selling at DM2.77. Traders knew that once the value of the currency had fallen, as it was bound to do under sustained pressure, sterling could be bought back at a new, cheaper rate, so producing large profits at the government's expense. By selling massive volumes of sterling, the foreign exchange dealers – described by the *Times* as 'the City's equivalent of serial killers' – were inflicting huge, unsustainable losses on the government. 'I can't stress enough the scale of the selling,' said one Bank of England insider. 'This generation at the Bank had never seen anything like it.'[16] Once the speculators got to work, it was no contest. The Bank of England's total holdings of foreign exchange amounted to only around 10 per cent of the average daily turnover in the London markets, giving it little chance of holding out. Even so, the government was determined that the effort would be made. It was later calculated that during the course of 15–16 September the Bank used over £15 billion of its reserves, the largest level of intervention in its history. The total cost to the taxpayer was to be £3–4 billion, equivalent to £20 per head of the population in the UK.[17]

The only other weapon in the government armoury was the raising of interest rates. In retrospect, the first key mistake on 16 September was that no rate rise was in place when the London markets opened. Shortly before 9 a.m. Norman Lamont telephoned the Prime Minister to say that an increase was unavoidable, whatever further damage it might do in delaying recovery from the recession. Major was determined that his most senior Cabinet colleagues – Home Secretary Kenneth Clarke, Trade Minister Michael Heseltine and Foreign Secretary Douglas Hurd – should be involved in all the subsequent key decisions, no doubt anxious that they be tied to any changes in policy. In the vivid phrase later used by Ken Clarke, their presence was required so that they should have their 'hands dipped in the blood'.[18] All three happened to be present for a meeting at Admiralty House, the eighteenth-century porticoed building overlooking Whitehall where the Prime Minister was temporarily based while contractors carried out building works on Number Ten Downing Street. By 10.45 a.m. the so-called 'big beasts' of the Cabinet had been told by the Prime Minister that there would be a 2 per cent interest rate rise, taking the level up to 12 per cent. The announcement was made at 11 a.m., but had no impact in stemming the run on the pound. The speculative avalanche continued and sterling remained sunk below its ERM floor. In desperation the Governor of the Bank of England, Robin Leigh-Pemberton, telephoned his counterparts in Europe to see if they could do anything to ease the pressure, hoping against hope that the Bundesbank might come in with a large-scale cut in German rates. For Norman Lamont, glued to the money market screens, this was the moment when 'I knew the game was up. I later told a journalist I felt like a TV surgeon in *Casualty* watching a heart monitor and realizing that the patient was dead; all we needed to do now was to unplug the system.'[19]

'Unplugging the system' in Lamont's eyes meant suspending Britain's membership of the ERM, allowing the pound to float and so removing the need to drain the reserves. In his memoirs Lamont says that he regarded this as imperative once the interest rate rise had failed to work, and his retelling of the story from this point onwards becomes highly critical of John Major's tardiness in facing up to what was necessary. In the days to follow rumours circulated that the Prime Minister had temporarily lost his nerve or 'wobbled' on 16 September. Various witnesses agree that these accusations were completely unfounded, and that Major – despite occasional flashes of anger, often directed at the Germans – remained calm and in control throughout.[20] Lamont's criticism was to be exactly the reverse: 'he was far too calm, and slow to take the difficult decisions that we needed. He seemed unwilling to face up to the issue.'[21] The Chancellor claims he was unable to get an early response to his telephone requests for another urgent meeting with the Prime Minister. In frustration he eventually took himself, along with the Governor of the Bank and Treasury officials, across from Number Eleven Downing Street to Admiralty House, only to find that Major was busy, fulfilling a long-planned engagement with a group of Conservative MPs. The deputation of senior figures was kept waiting impatiently at the door as the Prime Minister, perhaps aiming to convey an impression of 'business as usual', extended his meeting with backbenchers to nearly half an hour instead of ushering them out after the allocated ten minutes. It was not until 12.45 p.m. that another emergency meeting got under way, Major and Lamont being rejoined by Heseltine, Clarke and Hurd, as well as leading officials.

As the 11 a.m. rate rise had proved ineffective, the Prime Minister outlined the remaining options, each of which was highly unpalatable. Interest rates could be raised further, an attempt might be made to realign sterling within the ERM – a government-led devaluation – or British membership of the system could be suspended with immediate effect. The Chancellor forcefully opposed another rate increase, believing it would lack credibility in the markets. 'We are losing tens of millions of pounds for every few minutes that we are going on talking,' he exclaimed, arguing that suspension of ERM membership was now the only viable course. Accounts of the meeting vary as to who first dissented from this viewpoint, but Heseltine, Clarke and Hurd as Euro-enthusiasts all agreed that the government should not be seen, in Hurd's words, to have 'thrown in the towel at the first squall'. Suspension of ERM membership should only be a very last resort, and it was therefore worth trying a further interest rate hike. If this too failed, the situation could be reviewed after 4 p.m., when European trading officially closed for the day. For the Prime Minister, it was a moment of agonizing decision. Was he to back his Chancellor, dismayed to find decisions about interest rates moving beyond the traditional control of the Treasury, or was he to support his senior colleagues who wanted one final attempt to avoid suspension, and probable long-term abandonment, of membership of the ERM? In the end he plumped for the latter. Fifteen minutes after the meeting ended at 2 p.m. the Bank announced that interest rates would go up to a staggering 15 per cent, the only concession to Treasury opinion being that the increase would take effect not immediately but the following morning.[22]

The failure of this further movement on interest rates, and the astonished response it produced, help to explain why the lunchtime meeting of senior ministers was, in the fullness of time, to lead to bitter recriminations. Heseltine later claimed that he was given no briefing for the session, adding that, like his colleagues, he was alarmed at the lack of reliable information. No Reuters monitors charting developments in the markets had been installed in Admiralty House, and at one stage ministers found themselves in an anteroom without even a television screen to allow them to follow developments. If Lamont had made it clearer that ERM-suspension was imperative, Heseltine said, he would have supported the Chancellor; but presented with alternatives, the 'tough it out' approach seemed best at the time.[23] By contrast, Lamont in his memoirs described himself as 'astounded' that senior colleagues were first called in and then given options by the Prime Minister. Far from being there to sign on the dotted line, as Ken Clarke was to assert, it was the politicians who took over from the technicians at the key moment, 'making things even worse with their amateur and bungling intervention'. A television, Lamont said, was hardly necessary to gauge the scale of the catastrophe that was unfolding.[24] For his part, Major was to describe Lamont's complaints about bringing in the 'big beasts' as 'outrageous': senior colleagues had every right to be involved, and in any case they agreed with the Prime Minister's own view that a rate rise to 15 per cent should be attempted. It was small wonder that relations between Major and Lamont were severely damaged by this crucial meeting, so much so that the two men would not exchange another word subsequent to Lamont's eventual sacking in May 1993.[25]

As the afternoon wore on there was some gallows humour at Admiralty House. Kenneth Clarke commented at one stage that the only hope was that European governments might establish a single currency 'pretty damn quick'. But when the principal protagonists gathered together again at 5 p.m. the mood was 'dire', according to one of those present. 'We were all . . . clear that the whole thing had been an unmitigated disaster.'[26] The discussion turned to how the news of Britain's inevitable withdrawal from ERM membership would be presented. The Chancellor was reluctant to announce that the 15 per cent interest rate level would not, in consequence, come into force the following day; instead the rate would stay at 12 per cent. He wrote in his memoirs that he had been made to look a 'complete fool' with the second increase of the day; this reversion he felt would only compound the misery. Eventually he included the agreed formula on interest rates as part of a statement that was made in the glare of world media attention outside the Treasury at 7.30 p.m. Looking pale and drawn, the Chancellor began: 'Today has been an extremely difficult and turbulent day.' The government, he said, had concluded that Britain should suspend its membership of the exchange rate mechanism, but would rejoin 'as soon as circumstances allowed'.[27] The Tory MP Gyles Brandreth, watching on television, wrote in his diary that 'poor old Badger', as he called him, looked 'blanched [and] puffy-eyed', but had 'made as dignified a fist of it as he could'.[28]

As the evening wore on the Tory party chairman, Norman

Fowler, did the rounds of the radio and television studios, attempting to start the process of damage limitation. Ministers were under no illusion about the fact that it would be a near-impossible task. As Ken Clarke observed, the impression had been given that the government was 'utterly out of control of events. The market was going to devalue the pound, which it sure as hell did.'[29] By the end of the day the pound had fallen to DM2.63, an effective devaluation of 11 per cent; advance knowledge that the unemployment figures for August would increase at twice the expected rate only added to the sense of despair. At Admiralty House the Prime Minister began to chew over with his advisers just how serious the crisis would prove to his government and to party unity. He had regarded ERM entry as the key achievement of his brief Chancellorship, while the success of the Maastricht Treaty was essential to his strategy towards Europe. In a matter of hours, Britain had been forced out of the ERM and the future of Maastricht had been called into doubt. Robin Leigh-Pemberton, Governor of the Bank, later recalled that he went to bed that night feeling he had suffered the most crushing defeat of his professional life. His thoughts turned to John Major who he said during the course of the day looked ever more crushed as the policy on which he had staked his reputation collapsed before his eyes.[30]

The Prime Minister had a fair idea of what the press would make of it all. Late on the evening of 16 September he spoke on the phone to Kelvin MacKenzie, editor of the *Sun*, who told him bluntly: 'John, I'm holding a bucket of shit in my hands and tomorrow morning it's going to be emptied over your head.'[31] The *Sun* duly obliged on the morning of 17 September when it declared itself 'outraged' by the interest rate ups and downs of 'Black Wednesday', as it was already being called. 'Now we've ALL been screwed by the Cabinet', its front-page headline ran. Major was accused of betraying the trust of the nation, although the real venom was reserved for the Chancellor. 'Like King Canute trying to hold back the tide,' the paper declared, 'Mr

Lamont tossed away a fortune.' He should resign immediately, having lied to the electorate about 'green shoots of recovery'. There were, the *Sun* concluded, 'more green shoots in a Pot Noodle'.[32] Other tabloids were equally brutal, including natural Tory-supporting newspapers such as the *Daily Mail*, which described Lamont on its front page as the 'devalued Chancellor'; in spite of doing his best, 'he must go'. Support for the Prime Minister at the *Mail* also went into sharp decline, with calls for Major to 'get a grip' on his party.[33]

Comment in the broadsheets and quality press underlined the scale of the disaster and the possibility that, for the first time in a generation, newspaper sympathies were shifting against the Conservatives. Journalists on the political left could not resist the opportunity to pour scorn on the government. Major and Lamont were compared to Laurel and Hardy and described as the co-stars of a new production, 'Honey I Shrunk the £'. The whole episode, the *New Statesman* claimed, was like a Whitehall farce, with John Major being left 'trouserless in Europe'.[34] More significantly, the strongest language in the broadsheets came from those within the Tory fold. 'Yesterday,' wrote William Rees-Mogg, 'was one of the most grotesque days in the history of British finance, a day of crisis, disorder, confusion and mismanagement.'[35] The *Times* was scathing, saying in its editorial that Mr Major had 'showed the courage for which he is famous without also showing the common sense that made him prime minister. The result was sadly ridiculous.' In line with most newspaper comment, the *Times* nevertheless thought that Major's position was not under immediate threat. It was rather the Chancellor's future that was 'called into question'.[36] Max Hastings, editor of the *Daily Telegraph*, took the same line and went one stage further when in a face-to-face meeting on 17 September he told the Chancellor he should go. Lamont disagreed and the meeting broke up in acrimony. In this case fences were never mended. The *Telegraph* sniped at Lamont until he was sacked several months later.[37]

In the short term the Chancellor saw no reason why he should carry the can. It was an open secret in Whitehall that Lamont was a critic of the ERM. He privately agreed with a protester he once saw carrying a placard that read 'ERM – Extending Recession Mechanism'. He could claim that he had done his best to make the system work and that, if any single individual was responsible for the fiasco, it was the Prime Minister. Major, after all, had taken Britain into the ERM and had also decided, against Lamont's wishes, to push ahead with the disastrous decision to raise interest rates to 15 per cent. In later years, when writing his memoirs, Lamont rejected the view that his refusal to resign showed that standards of ministerial behaviour had changed for the worse. Max Hastings in his meeting with the Chancellor pointed out that Lord Carrington had done the honourable thing in 1982 by accepting blame for the loss of the Falklands. Lamont argued that there was no convention that Chancellors always resigned in the wake of financial crises. Cripps stayed on after the 1949 devaluation, Callaghan 'skilfully changed jobs' in 1967 and Healey survived in 1976. Unlike 1967, which was a purely British crisis, Lamont said Black Wednesday was more a case of 'an international system collapsing under its own contradictions', with many other currencies suffering the same fate as sterling. In none of the other affected countries, he noted, did a finance minister resign. Contrary to mythology, Lamont did not sing in his bath on the morning of 17 September, but he did remark to one colleague on his way in to a three-hour emergency Cabinet session, 'Now I have got the economic policy I want, I don't see why I should resign.'[38] Emboldened by the support of ministers, the Chancellor came out of the meeting and greeted reporters with the message that he was to repeat over the coming days – he had been operating the policy of the whole government and was not going to stand down.

The Prime Minister was in no position to demand Lamont's departure. He almost certainly told the Chancellor on the evening of Black Wednesday that he was safe, conscious that Lamont's resignation would make his own position more vulnerable. With the

Chancellor out of the way, critics were certain to move on to the argument that the ERM policy was Major's own creation, one for which he also should pay the price. Some Treasury officials believed that the overruling of Lamont at the crucial lunchtime meeting on 16 September was critical in explaining Major's attitude. His opponents would have a field day if it became known, in the aftermath of a Lamont resignation, that the Chancellor's wish to suspend ERM membership had initially been turned down. Hence at the Cabinet meeting on 17 September the Prime Minister echoed the words used by Lloyd George of Churchill in May 1940, saying the Chancellor should not be turned into 'an air-raid shelter', taking all the flak for a policy supported by the full Cabinet.[39] Once the decision to defend Lamont had been taken, Major did in fact spend several days contemplating his own future. His memoirs later described how he suffered conflicting emotions. On the one hand, he calculated that his resignation might jeopardize the survival of the Conservative government. There would be a leadership vacuum, with no obvious successor in sight, at a time when firm decisions about rebuilding economic policy were needed. On the other hand his instinct was for going, recognizing that the collapse of sterling was a 'catastrophic defeat' from which his reputation might never recover. The doubts nagged away sufficiently for Major to draft a resignation speech. When asked, one of his advisers refused to read it, later saying that had he done so he would have got involved in a textual analysis that would have reinforced the likelihood of the Prime Minister resigning. 'I was never certain then that I was right', Major wrote in 1999, 'nor am I now.'[40]

As he deliberated, the Prime Minister faced the most uncomfortable few days of his career. Relations with EC leaders deteriorated sharply when he made public his view that German intransigence was at the root of the crisis; his Italian counterpart accused Major of behaving like a three-year-old child trying to blame others. At home the Prime Minister was not only mauled by the press but also confronted by anger in Tory ranks at

Westminster, especially among those who had never wanted to enter the ERM in the first place. The faces of Eurosceptic MPs, according to one of their number, Teresa Gorman, 'positively glowed' when they gathered for an emergency debate in the House of Commons, recalled early from its summer break.[41] Margaret Thatcher, in Washington for a speech, was unable to resist claiming that she had been right all along. As the *Times* noted, Thatcher made herself the most prominent member of the 'I told you so' brigade, much to the fury of her detractors. The idea that Thatcher, the Iron Lady, had been duped into joining the ERM was one that some government loyalists found laughable, not to say hypocritical.[42] The Eurosceptic case was bolstered when the French referendum on 20 September produced a tiny majority in favour of the Maastricht Treaty. For Major, this was the worst possible result, neither giving Maastricht a renewed lease of life nor undermining it irrevocably.

When Parliament discussed the events of Black Wednesday on 24 September, the Prime Minister began confidently enough, reminding the House that nearly all sections of political and industrial opinion had supported the decision to enter the ERM. But as he attempted to outline future policy – arguing that the government remained committed to a low tax, low inflation economy – he was knocked out of his stride by a series of interruptions from his own side. When one Eurosceptic Tory, Michael Spicer, asked whether a free vote would be granted on the Maastricht bill, Major was rattled and replied acidly that the bill was included in the manifesto on which Spicer and his friends had been re-elected only a few months beforehand. Salt was rubbed into the wounds by John Smith, who in making his first speech in parliament as Labour leader gave a riproaring performance, taunting Major for his comments earlier in the year about sterling becoming the strongest currency in Europe and describing him as the 'devalued prime minister of a devalued government'. Tory MPs such as Gyles Brandreth admitted that Smith was 'magnificent: dry, droll, devastating', and Major later agreed in his memoirs that it was a 'brilliant debating performance . . . Presented with an open goal, he joyfully smashed the ball into the net.'[43] Although the Prime Minister secured a solid majority of twenty-six on a motion to 'support the economic policy of Her Majesty's Government', it had been a rough ride, and the following day large numbers of Eurosceptics supported an early day motion critical of official policy towards Europe. As Teresa Gorman noted, on this basis some forty-five Tories had voted with the government but against their consciences the previous day.[44] A terrible week was rounded off when David Mellor, the Heritage Minister, resigned after weeks of revelations in the press about his extramarital activities. 'For the tabloids,' Brandreth wrote in his diary, 'this is a lot more fun than poor old Badger and the ERM.'[45]

It was also obvious by this time that Black Wednesday had damaged profoundly the government's political standing. A MORI telephone poll for the *Sunday Times* on 21 September showed that only 35 per cent of respondents approved of the Prime Minister's leadership, compared with 58 per cent thinking he was doing a 'bad job'. In August Major had had a plus rating for his popularity; the slump in his personal standing was the biggest suffered in a single month by any Prime Minister. Similarly, Lamont had the lowest satisfaction rating for any Chancellor in polling history. A Harris poll in the *Observer* the same weekend also showed a sharp turnaround in voting intention, with Labour jumping to an eight point lead.[46] The trend was to continue over the coming weeks. In the three months from June to August 1992, the average standing of the parties in the polls gave Labour a narrow 2.5 per cent advantage over the Conservatives. In the three months from October to December, this rose to 17.8 per cent. Confidence in Major as Prime Minister, in the government's overall record and in the future of the economy all collapsed together.[47] Most crucially, the Tory reputation for competent economic management was shattered overnight. Throughout the 1980s, even when Labour had been ahead in the polls, the Conservatives had always been preferred as the best party for handling the economy. This vital distinction was suddenly forfeited, and it had not been recovered a decade later.

Could it all have been avoided? Critics of the ERM, particularly among Tory Eurosceptics, later developed the case they made in the days after Britain's hasty exit from the system: disintegration was bound to happen, they claimed, because sterling was overvalued at the outset. Further support for this viewpoint appeared to come when the ERM effectively broke down less than a year later, in the summer of 1993. After the French franc came under pressure, the size of the 'bands' within which currencies could fluctuate was increased so broadly as to render the original system untenable. Yet this may not have been due simply to inbuilt failings of the ERM; it could have been that Black Wednesday produced currency problems that had not existed in the same form before September 1992.[48] As the individual most associated with British entry, John Major later took the lead in rejecting the view that 'random events have some kind of structural inevitability . . . The rigidities of the Exchange Rate Mechanism were certainly bound to cause frictions, subterranean pressures and tremors, but there was no inevitability about the earthquake. It was precipitated by a combination – to a degree haphazard – of circumstances.' In his memoirs Major mixed metaphors by reflecting on the 'witches' brew' of circumstances that caused the 'earthquake': British economic weakness (the legacy, he said, of mistakes in the Lawson era of the late 1980s), fear in the markets that the Maastricht Treaty would fall with the French referendum, and the consequences of German reunification. The ERM, Major concluded, was the 'medicine', not the 'ailment'; it was the precursor to years of sustained growth without high inflation and those who claimed that sterling was overvalued needed to note how it stabilized well above its ERM ceiling after 1992.[49]

If failure of the system was not inevitable, it follows that some action or set of actions could have averted breakdown. On this John Major claimed, at the time of the crisis and in his memoirs, that it was the Germans who should have adopted a more flexible approach. While the strength of the Deutschmark clearly made life difficult for recession-hit Europe, it did not, however, follow that Germany, which faced its own huge political and economic challenges, was to blame for the plight of sterling. Major's account has little to say about his own government's failings or Britain's share of responsibility for the collapse of the ERM. Some of the arguments directed at the Prime Minister's handling of policy can and have been rebutted. The notion that sterling should have been devalued independently within the ERM has been analysed and found wanting. Aside from its enormous political consequences, it was by no means certain that the markets would have reacted favourably. In the short term a humiliating government-led deval-uation would have been liable to have deepened market turbu-lence.[50] Nor should credence be given to the idea that a general realignment of currencies was jeopardized by Norman Lamont's inept handling of the meeting with European ministers and offi-cials at Bath. One thing on which Major and Lamont agreed in later years was that no easy solution was on offer at Bath. While there was little to lose by putting pressure on the Bundesbank, it was known that Germany would not give way on interest rates without a wider realignment of currencies; this, in turn, was opposed by other EC partners, notably the French who were determined to protect the value of the franc. In Major's words, the Chancellor may have caused irritation by his handling of events at Bath, but this did not mean that it was a last chance to save the ERM.[51]

Two key British mistakes nevertheless stand out. In the first place, if the parity of sterling was to be maintained, any scintilla of doubt that ministers would do 'whatever is necessary' had to be removed from the markets. Yet interest rates had fallen slowly since Britain joined the ERM, and when the pound came under pressure in late 1991 the Treasury indicated that it would not come to its aid with higher borrowing costs. From this moment, Britain's commitment to maintain the DM2.95 level for sterling lacked credibility in the markets. Whereas other European nations had developed mechanisms for temporarily raising the cost of borrowing without affecting their broader economies (for example, by raising interest rates in the financial markets to 100 per cent while leaving other rates unchanged), no such techniques existed in Britain. Major's second and most critical error was, in the words of Philip Stephens of the *Financial Times*, 'the elevation of the exchange rate parity into a badge of pride'. Stephens notes that the steady depreciation of sterling since the war meant that it was as much a symptom as a cause of economic decline; the exchange rate had little bearing on key structural problems such as Britain's weak manufacturing base and low levels of industrial investment. A credible anti-inflation strategy was necessary for economic success, but was not sufficient on its own; in spite of this, sterling parity was elevated above other considerations despite its propensity to rebound and cause grave political damage. It was not even the case for Britain, as it was for others such as the French, that maintenance of a particular exchange rate was required in order to secure the aim of a single currency.[52] In his obsession with sterling, Major made exactly the same misjudgement as Harold Wilson in the mid-1960s. The *Economist* could not resist noting the strong parallels: both men saw themselves as astute party managers with a great eye for detail, but both failed on the broader stage. 'Harold Major', the *Economist* speculated, could well suffer the same fate as his 1960s' predecessor.[53]

This prediction was borne out in due course. After September 1992, the Major government set new records for unpopularity, whether measured by opinion polls, parliamentary by-elections or local and European election results. Labour moved into a lead in voter intention that was not relinquished after the 1997 election. As the political scientist Paul Whiteley comments, 'in a real sense, the Conservatives won an election (in 1992) and then lost another election [1997] in the same year.'[54] John Major and his ministers hoped that the damage caused by Black Wednesday would gradually diminish; that an economic recovery would produce a corresponding revival of confidence, as it had done for earlier governments, sufficient to produce yet another election victory. Indeed, what followed Britain's departure from the ERM was in the medium term an almost textbook recovery of the economy, with low inflation accompanied by an export-led rise in output. But none of this cut much ice with the electorate. Norman Lamont, sidelined after his sacking in 1993, sniped in his memoirs that the government could have won again with more conviction, its enunciation of the message of recovery at the time of the 1997 election being 'pathetic'.[55] This view, however, underestimates not only the scale of the setback suffered in 1992, but also its lasting consequences.

There were several reasons why the impact of Black Wednesday proved so difficult to shake off, and why voters were reluctant to give John Major credit for the recovery of the mid-1990s. As the polling evidence during the crisis itself indicated, the suddenness with which the government was overwhelmed undermined fatally the Prime Minister's reputation. As Peter Riddell noted in the *Times*, during the course of twenty-four hours Major and Lamont appeared completely to have 'lost control of events, the worst possible position for any Prime Minister and Chancellor to be in'.[56] It was also a case of once bitten, twice shy. The electorate had given the Conservatives the benefit of the doubt at the 1992 election, in spite of the recession, but Black Wednesday strained loyalty beyond breaking point. Nor were voters in much doubt about who to blame. Attempts by ministers to shuffle responsibility onto the Germans carried little weight. Many newspaper commentators were incensed by efforts to turn the spotlight on the Bundesbank which, it was noted, did not play the role of a European central bank; its job, at which it had proved highly successful, was to defeat inflation in Germany. Traditionally loyalist papers like the *Times* agreed that the crisis reflected the weakness of a British economy presided over by the Tories for more than a decade. It was, moreover, the Prime Minister's very personal policy that exploded. Even previous Labour Chancellors, the *Times* said, had not suffered the humiliation of seeing interest rates upped twice on the same day before admitting that 'it had all been a mistake'.[57]

The refusal of the electorate to forgive and forget was due, in addition, to the attitude adopted by the government after Black Wednesday. Many newspaper editorials argued that John Major should first apologize and then move on. In spite of what was widely regarded as the inescapable responsibility of ministers, there was no inquiry into what went wrong, still less an apology. Sarah Baxter in the *New Statesman* noted that the Citizen's Charter, which Major had introduced and of which he was so proud, said that when things went wrong people were entitled to 'a good explanation, or an apology'. 'We,' she wrote, 'have had neither.'[58] The Prime Minister's line was to remain the one he used in the parliamentary debate: the government was right to enter the ERM and had been the unfortunate victim of circumstances. The Chancellor, far from resigning, adopted an unrepentant tone, accompanied by an insistence that departure from the ERM 'does not mean that we are changing policy at all'. Simon Heffer in the *Spectator* reported that morale among the Tory faithful was not helped by the collective ministerial refusal to admit to any errors, preferring instead to adopt 'fantasies'. One party activist summed up the messages being sent and the reaction they induced: 'First, that we haven't had a devaluation. Second, that there hasn't been a change of policy. And third, that it's business as usual. We're not sharing the same planet.'[59]

This last comment pointed to a further reason why Major's government suffered from more sustained unpopularity than any of its post-war predecessors. From Black Wednesday onwards, an image of deep Tory division was added to its association with economic failure. As Michael Heseltine wrote in his memoirs, Eurosceptic MPs and their allies in Fleet Street gained a massive boost in confidence, stimulating the 'civil war into which they were plunging the Conservatives with increasing bitterness'.[60] For much of the remainder of the parliament, the Prime Minister was to be hounded by 'the bastards' in his Cabinet – middle-ranking ministers such as Michael Howard and John Redwood who became increasingly bold in defying official policy. Several Tory backbenchers were to be denied the party whip for their outspoken views on Europe, forcing the government, already nursing a small majority, to walk a tightrope on important Commons votes. Political observers struggled to recall the last time fissures in Conservative ranks were so obvious. Even the rifts at the time of Suez had healed relatively quickly. Edward Pearce in the *New Statesman* wrote perceptively in September 1992 that Tory divisions had 'Bevanite potential' – the capacity, as was to prove the case, for keeping the affected party out of power for a generation.[61]

John Major's inability to recover owed much, finally, to the boost that Black Wednesday gave to the morale, purpose and standing of the Labour Party. After 16 September 1992, the Prime Minister awoke every day to a combination of circumstances that his predecessor Margaret Thatcher had never encountered: a shaky majority in the House; open rebellion on the government benches, and a revitalized opposition. It seemed that his hold on power could hardly become more precarious. Yet after 1994 it did, thanks to events that were sparked off, ironically, by a personal and political tragedy: the death of the Labour leader, John Smith.

'The people have lost a friend'
The emergence of New Labour, 1994

What has been striking over the last dark week has not been
the tributes of the great and good – handsome as they have been
– but the sadness, the dismay, the sense of loss across the range of
our community. The people have lost a friend – someone who was
on their side, and they know it.

Donald Dewar MP, funeral oration for John Smith, 20 May 1994

Blair has yet to deny that he agreed with Gordon [Brown] not to
fight more than two elections as leader. That is because he did,
on Tuesday 31 May 1994.

Labour official Derek Draper, letter to the Guardian, *22 May 2001*

O n the afternoon of Thursday 12 May 1994 the Speaker of
the House of Commons, Betty Boothroyd, made a short
announcement to a packed, silent chamber: 'I regret to have to
report to the House,' she said, 'the death of the Right Honourable
John Smith QC, member for Monklands East.' The leader of the
opposition, aged fifty-five, had suffered a heart attack in the bathroom of his London flat, on the thirty-fifth floor of the Barbican
complex, shortly after 8 a.m. that morning. Smith's wife,
Elizabeth, attempted to revive him, but to no avail, and called her
husband's driver, waiting below, who also attempted resuscitation
in vain. Within minutes a paramedic was on the scene and Mr
Smith was rushed to nearby St Bartholomew's, one of London's

prestigious teaching hospitals, where a cardiac crash team made final efforts to save him. By 9.15 a.m. he was pronounced dead. News of the story began to spread as journalists and photographers gathered at the hospital entrance, but confirmation was delayed while efforts were made to contact immediate family members. Within an hour two of the Smiths' three daughters had been reached (the third was on holiday in California and took longer to locate), and at 10.35 a.m. the announcement was made public. What followed was remarkable. While first and foremost a private tragedy for the Smith family, reactions to the death of the leader of the opposition went far beyond formal expressions of grief. Smith's death, in the words of his biographer Andy McSmith, came to mark 'a defining moment in the political life of the United Kingdom.'[1] It was such a moment, the most recent in British politics to have such profound effects, for two main reasons: it enhanced the credibility of the opposition as an alternative government, and it opened the way for the unexpected emergence of 'New Labour'. Both were developments that undermined further the hapless Major administration. If the end of Tory rule was a good bet after Black Wednesday, after the summer of 1994 it was a racing certainty.

When Neil Kinnock resigned in the wake of Labour's 1992 election defeat, John Smith was the obvious choice as leader. His background in the party and his personal qualities put him in a stronger position than any rival. Unlike others, he could claim the advantage of ministerial experience, having served as a member of the Callaghan government in the late 1970s. His loyalty to the party was beyond question; like most Labour moderates from a Scottish background, he had distanced himself from the defections associated with the SDP in the early 1980s. In opposition to the Thatcher governments, he had made a name for himself as shadow Trade and Industry Secretary by a series of effective speeches during the Westland crisis of 1986; several commentators contrasted Smith's performances with the ineffectual interventions of Kinnock. Although criticized in the run-up to the 1992 election for a shadow budget that left Labour open to charges that it would 'tax and spend' as of old, Smith's time as shadow Chancellor after 1987 had generally enhanced his reputation as a figure of substance. His legal training and public image as a dependable 'bank manager' type gave him a gravitas which consistently eluded Kinnock, and at the age of fifty-three he seemed ideally placed to face the challenges of leadership. Although he had suffered a serious heart attack in 1988, Smith's recovery, underpinned by a healthier diet and regular exercise, appeared to be complete. His claims to the job were so strong that calls were made for him to be accepted unopposed, so avoiding the need for a lengthy leadership contest.[2]

In the event, Smith was challenged by the New Zealand-born Bryan Gould, a prominent 'soft left' figure in the Kinnock years, who built his campaign around opposition to the ERM. Gould argued that any form of fixed exchange rate would prevent a future Labour government from adopting the programme of Keynesian expansion necessary, he felt, for the achievement of full employment and social justice. This stance enabled him to attract limited support on the Labour left, but it was soon obvious that he had little chance of defeating Smith. Gould, unable to match his rival's experience and roots in the party, rejected calls to withdraw from the race, using the contest as an opportunity to sketch out an alternative to what he regarded as Smith's uncritical pro-Europeanism. When the votes were counted Smith amassed an overwhelming 91 per cent level of support from Labour's 'electoral college'. This included 97.7 per cent of Constituency Labour Party votes and 96.2 per cent of union votes. Gould fared marginally better among MPs, but even here Smith took 77.3 per cent. Nor was Gould able to claim the consolation prize of the deputy leadership. Smith's preferred candidate, Margaret Beckett, shadow Chief Secretary to the Treasury since 1989, gave the impression of both gender and political balance – being regarded as a one-time member of the 'hard left' – and was able to secure a comfortable victory. Within months Gould was to resign from the shadow Cabinet and leave British politics altogether to return to academic life in New Zealand.[3]

Smith inherited a party demoralized by four successive election defeats, but his task was made easier by the difficulties that beset John Major from the summer of 1992 onwards. Even before Black Wednesday destroyed the Tory reputation for sound management, the Prime Minister was on the defensive. As the recession continued to hit middle-class families, the government found it necessary to introduce a range of higher indirect taxes, giving a hollow ring to Tory election pledges of only months before. 'Sleaze' became a prominent issue following tabloid exposure of the private lives of ministers, and concerted broadsheet investigations into allegations about illegal arms sales to Iraq were also under way. Smith's attack on the government after Black Wednesday confirmed what had long been known: that he was a sharp parliamentary performer. More broadly, he set out to heal divisions in Labour ranks that had persisted throughout the Kinnock era. In particular, he responded to the criticism that 'spin doctors' had been allowed to make too much of the running. The so-called shadow Communications Agency was abolished, and the influence of the arch spin merchant, Peter Mandelson, director of party campaigns in the late 1980s, was greatly reduced. Smith earned respect across the party, including among former enemies on the left, for his willingness to adopt a more inclusive approach, one that promised to listen to all points of view.[4]

There was criticism of Smith's leadership, especially in private, from Labour 'modernizers' who believed that the party needed to reform itself drastically if it were ever to regain a wide appeal. The leader's rather staid image and the absence of a 'big idea' meant there was little to excite the electorate. It would not be enough, the argument ran, simply to rely on Tory unpopularity and 'one more heave' to bring Labour back to power, since past experience had shown that economic recovery was likely to precede any future election, persuading disenchanted voters to return once more to the government fold. One such critic, the shadow Home Secretary Tony Blair, frequently told friends: 'John is just so cautious. It's a disaster.'[5] Smith believed – partly as a result of the attacks made on his own shadow budget in 1992 – that it would be a mistake to saddle Labour with too many specific policies years ahead of an election. He also felt that following Kinnock's policy review in the late 1980s it was not necessary to start from scratch. But, contrary to what critics alleged, he did recognize the need for some eye-catching initiatives, and as a result he announced the establishment of a Commission on Social Justice in December 1992 – exactly fifty years after the publication of the Beveridge Report. The Commission drew its membership from among academics, pressure-group leaders and business people, and its task was to examine how the welfare state could be modernized to face the challenges of the 'global' economy. Smith was no longer alive when it reported nearly two years later, but its work was a testimony to his willingness to contemplate major policy changes in social welfare.[6]

Smith was also prepared to move on issues of internal party reform. In an effort to increase the miserably low proportion of women MPs, he backed the adoption, confirmed at the annual party conference in 1993, of all-women shortlists for parliamentary candidatures in half of all vacant Labour-held and marginal seats. In the most dramatic moment of his leadership, Smith persuaded the 1993 conference to take up 'one member, one vote' (OMOV) for candidate selection, rather than relying on an electoral college for such selections. In 1989 Neil Kinnock had managed to establish the principle that trade unions should have a maximum of 40 per cent of votes in the candidate selection process, with OMOV applicable to the remainder of the party membership. Smith had given a commitment in his leadership campaign to seek ways of reducing the influence of union block votes, and in consequence he pushed forward proposals to make all members' votes of equal value. Resistance from some union leaders meant that the vote at conference was on a knife-edge until the last moment. Smith told his private office staff that he would resign if defeated. It required much persuasion of union delegates behind the scenes, plus an impassioned if sometimes unintelligible call for loyalty by the rumbustious John Prescott, to win the day. A similar vote reducing union influence in future leadership contests reinforced Smith's victory and sent out the same message: the modernization of the Labour Party, first started by Neil Kinnock and aimed at removing any vestiges of 1980s' extremism, was still in progress.[7]

Smith had one further answer to those who felt he was not going far or fast enough. His strategy appeared to be working. From the time of Black Wednesday onwards, Labour advanced steadily in the opinion polls. Its average lead over the Conservatives throughout 1993 was close to 10 per cent, and this stretched further in the early months of 1994. Most polls at this time put Labour on 47–49 per cent support, while the Tories languished around 26 per cent. This was reflected in the local elections held on 5 May; Labour secured over 40 per cent of the vote, while the Tories polled a lowest-ever 27 per cent, causing them to lose control of eighteen councils and over four hundred seats. Labour did particularly well in London, an area where it had struggled to make any significant recovery in the 1980s.[8] Smith's credibility rose further and he looked forward with confidence to inflicting additional damage on the Conservatives at the European elections scheduled for June. Few could now question his strategy of 'playing the long game'. In spite of its great unpopularity, the government still possessed a workable parliamentary majority, and Smith knew that even if John Major was ousted a general election was still two or three years away. In the meantime, the Labour leader resolved to go on attacking the Tories over economic mismanagement while developing his own policy initiatives. He geared his whole approach towards victory in 1996 or 1997, though he was not, as it turned out, to live long enough to taste the fruit of his efforts. A week after the triumphant local elections in May 1994 he was dead.

*

When the news of Smith's death went out on radio and television on 12 May, it prompted an astonishing response. The sudden and unexpected death of prominent public figures is, of course, commonly followed by fulsome, often overblown, tributes. As the journalist Jon Sopel notes, there was a certain amount of 'humbug and hypocrisy' mixed in amongst what followed. Conservative ministers had attacked Smith fiercely during the local election campaign, and plans had been made to repeat such personal attacks in the forthcoming European elections.[9] The *New Statesman* reported that a few unnamed Tory MPs were heard laughing behind the Speaker's chair in the Commons when discussing rumours of Smith's death. It was not clear whether the laughter reflected a belief that pressure on the Prime Minister would dissipate, or whether it was because it was likely to ditch the leadership prospects of Michael Heseltine, who had himself suffered a heart attack in 1993.[10] Even so, most of the reaction was spontaneous and generous. It was widely agreed that the political classes were at their best in the hours after Smith's death, paying a series of warm compliments to the Labour leader.

Much of the nation's political life ground to a halt on 12 May. Within hours of the announcement, members of the public were laying flowers outside the Labour Party headquarters in Walworth Road, where staff openly cried. By the end of the day a room had been set aside for grieving visitors to come and pay their respects, and floral tributes were stacked a foot high. Flags flew at half-mast all over Scotland, and the Conservatives halted their annual Scottish conference which was taking place in Inverness. Television cameras caught the disbelief on the faces of Scottish Tory delegates when Smith's death was announced from the platform.[11] John Cole's successor as the BBC's political editor, Robin Oakley, later wrote that no death of a political figure in his time 'so devastated the Westminster community'. This was confirmed by Alistair Campbell, a leading journalist prior to his appointment as Downing Street press spokesman, who said he could not recall when a political death had caused such sadness, not just across the parties but among reporters, policemen, canteen staff and all those who worked in and around Westminster. 'Those who thought they liked' John Smith, Campbell said, 'learned that they loved him. Those who saw in him an average political talent appreciated the loss of a potentially great force for good.' All of this surpassed the reaction to the death of other leading political figures, such as Tony Crosland in 1977 and Iain Macleod in 1970; nothing comparable had been seen since the death of another Labour leader in his mid-fifties, Hugh Gaitskell, back in 1963.[12]

It was quickly agreed that campaigning for the European elections would be suspended until after Smith's funeral. Routine proceedings in the House of Commons were also cancelled on 12 May – the first time since the death of former Prime Minister Anthony Eden in 1977 that parliamentary business had been curtailed for a day as a mark of respect. MPs did gather together in the afternoon to hear forty minutes of public tributes, led by John Major. The Prime Minister called Smith one of the outstanding modern parliamentarians, fair-minded and a 'tough fighter for what he believed in'. Adopting a generous tone and sounding genuinely moved, Major concluded that when he thought of John Smith he thought of 'an opponent, not an enemy'. The *Guardian*'s parliamentary sketchwriter, Simon Hoggart, wrote that if the Prime Minister had always showed such a dignified and sure touch, his own authority would not have been under threat. Hoggart said that he could not recollect seeing the 'whole House of Commons grieve before'. Often, he added, when the Commons was said to be at its best, it was not. 'Yesterday for once they got it right.' Margaret Beckett, who as Smith's deputy assumed leadership of the party until a successor was agreed, recalled that his last words in public were at a fundraising dinner the evening before his heart attack: 'The opportunity to serve our country – that is all we ask.' This, Beckett said, should stand as his epitaph.[13]

In the days that followed, dozens of tributes were paid, on television and radio and in newspapers and journals. Many of these highlighted his particular political qualities, noting that he was a formidable figure in the House of Commons, capable on his day of bettering any opponent. There was also a consensus of opinion that he had been a 'brilliant success' as opposition leader, healing party divisions and presiding over the further transformation of Labour into a credible party of government. He had, it was agreed, squared the circle of achieving a balance between modernizers and traditionalists. As a modernizer, he had reformed the party's internal democracy; as a traditionalist, he had restored pride in Labour's history and outlook. Whereas his predecessor had alienated many on the left by facing them head on, Smith had carefully neutralized them by recognizing their legitimate place in the party.[14] His legacy was a Labour Party not only more united than it had been for a generation, but also better placed for victory. A common theme among obituary writers was that the nation had lost the man who would most likely have been the next incumbent of Number Ten Downing Street. Even the *Sun*, which boasted of its role in keeping Labour out in 1992, said that 'Britain's next Prime Minister died yesterday, cruelly robbed of the triumph he gambled his life for.'[15]

Over and above this, the most striking feature in the comments of friends and opponents alike was the emphasis given to John Smith's qualities as a person. At the moment of his death it became obvious, if it had not been before, that Smith was much more than a 'bespectacled bank manager'. He was a sociable and engaging personality, admired by all who knew him for his integrity and humour. For the *Times*, he 'epitomized the virtues of decency, vigour and authority which, well used, can turn politicking into statesmanship. He was, as Tennyson wrote of Wellington, "rich in saving common-sense".' Even die-hard opponents in the press such as the *Daily Telegraph* admitted that among Tories he was 'feared as a Labour leader precisely because he was respected as a man'.[16] Some journalists went so far as to eat humble pie. Writing in the *Independent*, Andrew Marr, later to replace Robin Oakley as political editor of the BBC, noted how the London-based political classes 'never quite understood this man'. They conceded his decency and seriousness but were almost blind to his huge and growing popularity in the country, poll ratings that only Wilson for Labour had matched at his zenith in the early 1960s. 'Yes, we got him wrong. We did not look closely enough . . . I contend that the reason why Mr Smith connected to voters was that they somehow saw through the cheery but cautious Westminster man, and grasped a little of the steeliness, the anger, the general grown-upness of the politician behind.'[17]

This was precisely the gist of the hundreds of letters, cards and messages of sympathy sent from all parts of the UK and from people of all ages to the Smith family. Many were from people who confessed to being Conservative voters or hitherto not interested in politics, but who saw Smith as 'a genuine man who practised what he preached', 'someone with integrity & foresight', a man 'with no hidden agenda'. One correspondent, Dr John Chisholm, addressed Elizabeth Smith: 'I am writing to you because I like countless others have been grieving and shedding tears after the death of your husband . . . Politics would again be seen as the high and honourable calling it is if it contained more men like John Smith.'[18] This type of reaction was widespread, and took some of those affected greatly by surprise. The broadcaster and columnist Laurie Taylor sheepishly admitted that he had been reduced to tears when he watched the television coverage on the evening of Smith's death, and had had the same reaction the following morning when tributes continued on the BBC's *Today* programme. Taylor said he 'bludgeoned' friends of various degrees of political cynicism into admitting that they had reacted in the same way; one even said 'it was nearly as bad as John Lennon'. Laurie Taylor confessed he was puzzled in retrospect, given that he had spent the last couple of years denouncing Smith as a bland Scottish lawyer devoid of radical intent. But, like his friends, he had to agree that Smith's honesty and decency had been taken too much for granted, and that his death 'prompted us to remember that there were still a few people left whose value could not be measured in simple terms of success or failure'.[19]

The funeral was held on Friday 20 May at Cluny parish church, only a short walk from the Smith residence in Edinburgh. The family were regular attenders at the Victorian Gothic church, which was packed with about nine hundred mourners. Television cameras were allowed to relay proceedings live around the country, giving the impression of a formal state funeral. In effect it was primarily a party occasion, with normal rules of protocol overturned. The Prime Minister and other members of the Tory Cabinet were allocated seats in the fifth row, behind family, friends and senior figures in the Labour Party. The *Guardian* described the funeral as a 'scorching exposition' of the 'Highland Christianity' that underpinned Smith's politics. According to the *Times*, Smith would have relished the spirit of the occasion, when 'solemnity of tribute and sorrow of loss were leavened by the laughter of memory'.[20] Eulogies were given by long-time friends such as Donald Dewar, the shadow Social Security Secretary, who said the 'people have lost a friend', and James Gordon, Smith's best man at his wedding and managing director of Radio Clyde:

You cannot become a Cabinet minister at 40, and be elected leader of a great political party, without unusual courage, judgement and intellect. His political skills, his mastery of his subject, his wit at the dispatch box, were all qualities which rightly commanded respect; but what won the hearts of so many in the nation and caused such an unprecedented outpouring of real grief at his passing were his more personal qualities, his transparent decency, straightforwardness, a keen sense of fairness and a willingness to fight for those not able to speak up for themselves; and, less obtrusive but underpinning all of this, a strong religious faith. John did not allow his undoubted abilities, which marked him out from the rest of men, to distance him from them, and his natural qualities shone through, so that he remained someone people could relate to and trust to understand their problems . . . He was one of us, not one of them.[21]

That evening, Smith made his final journey by car and ferry to the island of Iona, the legendary burial place of Scottish kings and saints, where he was laid to rest on Saturday 21 May in a private ceremony.

John Smith's death, and his funeral, were moments of immense political significance. One of the journalists who travelled to Edinburgh, Neal Ascherson, wrote in the *Independent* that Britain did not go in much for political funerals, and the notion that a funeral might be a new beginning as well as a farewell is a foreign one. 'But the death of John Smith has released a strange, very fresh gust of feeling. Like the cold wind blowing over Morningside from the sea, it carries a faint scent of something forgotten and remote: faith in a leader and trust in what he stood for.' Ascherson was struck by the way in which the eulogies seemed to rejoice in Smith's achievement more than mourning for a life brutally cut short when on the verge of triumph. 'It was as if the dead man had unlocked a rusty gate, so that a way ahead was open.'[22] In particular, Smith's death had done something to renew trust, if not in politicians as a class, then in the Labour Party. A few months earlier the government had launched an ill-fated 'back to basics' campaign, one that encouraged the tabloids to focus on ministerial sleaze. By contrast, Smith had shown that it was possible, as the BBC journalist James Naughtie said, to 'find a moral voice that wasn't sanctimonious', and in so doing he had struck a chord, 'like a memory from the past'.[23] This may have been only partially appreciated in his lifetime, but it was made obvious by the reaction to his death, and in turn generated a deeper empathy with Labour politics. For Labour, it made possible the restoration of a level of public trust that had been missing since the winter of discontent, if not before; lack of trust had lingered on in explanations of Labour's difficulties as recently as the 1992 election.

The columnist Martin Kettle picked up and elaborated on this point in the *Guardian* just two days after John Smith's death which, he said, had 'touched a remarkable chord within civil society generally . . . The evidence of the shared loss is all around us. It is a national experience.' The Thatcher years, Kettle argued, had been partisan and sectarian, underlining Labour's exclusion from political power. Besides the marginalization of the trade unions, Labour-dominated local government had been weakened, and those who were not considered 'one of us' had been excluded from key appointments, in Whitehall and on various public service bodies. But news of Smith's death had seriously undermined this 'exclusionary instinct', demanding as it did the full readmission of Labour into 'civil society'. Labour had been given, in other words, 'a legitimacy for which it has striven ever since 1983', not just in Scotland where it had remained strong but in southern England also, so that the election of a Labour government had become a stronger possibility than it had been for a generation. Hence for Martin Kettle, Smith's achievement in death went beyond the achievement of his life. But if this was a crucial moment, then it had its dangers. Any momentum in Labour's direction, Kettle noted, would not be continued – indeed would be reversed – if the search for a new leader was to be conducted in a 'venomous spirit' or if it ended 'in a narrowly judged choice of successor'. In view of the government's weakness, the most important Labour leadership contest for a generation was about to take place. The possibility of failure remained, yet a great prize beckoned. Martin Kettle concluded, with considerable foresight: 'A properly inclusive form of new Labour politics, a politics which speaks of and to one nation, could destroy and marginalize the divided Conservative Party in a way which has not seemed possible since 1945 . . . It is a grim, dark moment, still overshadowed by the death of John Smith. But tomorrow is also giddy with rare and marvellous possibilities.'[24]

Alongside the genuine outpouring of grief, speculation started almost immediately about who would be Smith's successor. 'Most politicians,' wrote Andrew Rawnsley in the *Observer*, 'suspended plotting for a decent interval – 24 hours.'[25] No contenders came forward to declare themselves before Smith's funeral, although this did not prevent widespread discussion in the press about the probable 'runners and riders' in the contest ahead. One name mentioned was Margaret Beckett, who had to continue acting as leader for several weeks once it was agreed that the voting process would take until July to complete. Beckett did eventually put her name forward, and was able to claim credit for her handling of Labour's strong performance in the European elections, held on 9 June. The party won sixty of the eighty-seven available seats, a net gain of fifteen, with the Conservatives again languishing below 30 per cent of votes cast. Another figure touted in various quarters was the sharp-tongued Robin Cook, who had served in senior shadow positions under both Kinnock and Smith. He was depicted as a possible representative of the traditional 'soft left', but after taking soundings he decided to stand aside from the fray. More attention still was given to Gordon Brown, who from early on after his election as MP for Dunfermline East in 1983, aged only thirty-two, was regarded as one of the brightest prospects in Labour politics. After only two years on the backbenches, Brown had been promoted to the shadow front bench, holding various trade and economic portfolios under Kinnock. John Smith rewarded his fellow Scot for coming top of the shadow Cabinet poll in 1992 by appointing him to the Treasury brief, a post in which he enhanced his reputation with a series of stinging attacks on the government's record. Brown was widely seen in 1994, as he had been for some time, as a serious contender for the leadership; like Smith he was a 'modernizer' on matters of party reform but also a traditionalist with obvious sympathy for Labour's roots and customs. He was, as the journalist Kevin Maguire says, 'New Labour family but Old Labour friendly'.[26]

In the days after Smith's death, however, it was another young member of the 1983 parliamentary intake, Tony Blair, whose name was on everyone's lips. Unlike Gordon Brown, Blair did not come from a conventional Labour background. His father had been a strong Conservative sympathizer, and while Brown had made a name for himself in Scottish university politics Blair was playing rock 'n' roll as a student in Oxford. As a barrister in the 1970s, Blair engaged in local London politics for the first time, and by good fortune was able to secure the nomination for the safe seat of Sedgefield in Durham at the time of the 1983 election. Once at Westminster, he was regarded as a rising star, gaining promotion to the front bench after only seven months. His close friendship with Gordon Brown was consolidated when they both served in Smith's shadow Treasury team in the late 1980s. Blair's name first became more widely known to the public after 1992 when he took a robust stance as shadow Home Secretary – 'tough on crime, tough on the causes of crime' – attracting media attention and increasing popularity among the electorate.[27] The 'tough on crime' soundbite was originally the brainchild of Brown who, being two years older and more cerebral, still regarded himself as the senior of the two friends. Although the leadership was not expected to become vacant for many years ahead, the two men were said to have a tacit agreement not to stand against each other, and allies of the shadow Chancellor firmly believed that Brown, not Blair, had the prior claim to run on the 'modernizing' ticket when the time came.[28]

In retrospect, the key moment of the Labour leadership contest was a non-event: the decision of Gordon Brown not to stand. Tony Blair showed little hesitation. Although he kept a low pro-file and made no early declaration of his intentions, paying a heartfelt tribute to Smith on the day of his death, Blair's mind was soon made up, whatever consequences it might have for life with his young family. He had dithered over whether to stand for the deputy leadership in 1992, and would not make the same mistake of allowing others to step in and make the running. Within days his instincts were confirmed when he received a mass of endorse-ments – from colleagues, from newspaper columnists and from the first opinion polls showing him to be the favoured choice of voters.[29] In contrast, Brown was slow off the mark. He had been closer to Smith than Blair and, as his biographer Paul Routledge notes, Brown's reaction to the unexpected loss was to behave more like a 'grieving friend' than an ambitious politician. He spent much of 12 May writing a long and eloquent tribute which appeared in the *Daily Mirror* the following day. John Smith, he said, 'treated everyone as his equal because he believed everyone was equal'.[30] By the time Brown began to gather together a small team of advisers, he was well behind in the leadership stakes. While the press speculated on his intentions, he was faced with a barrage of articles suggesting that his image as a dour Scottish bachelor made him less appealing to 'middle England' than his family-oriented, Oxbridge-educated colleague. Brown faced an uncomfortable choice: he could either back down and miss the prize he so coveted, or he could go ahead and risk accusations that he was splitting the 'modernizing' vote, possibly allowing another candidate like Margaret Beckett to come through the middle and take the leadership.

For a week after Smith's funeral various conflicting reports about Brown's intentions appeared. Many were inspired by Peter Mandelson who, having been forced to adopt a lower profile while John Smith was leader, now resumed, in the words of Andy McSmith, 'his old role as Labour's own Francis Urquhart of *The House of Cards*, wheeler-dealing in the corridors of the Commons and illicitly briefing journalists'.[31] He told some reporters not to write off Brown, others that the new leader would be Blair. Mandelson was hopelessly torn between two candidates whom he admired equally, although he did write a long letter to Brown warning him that his prospects were not looking good. Before long Brown reluctantly came to the same conclusion. He told his small campaign team that he would not stand on 30 May. The following evening this was confirmed at a brief and awkward dinner with Blair, held at Granita's in Islington – 'the kind of modern restaurant', according to Alan Watkins, 'which charges hefty prices for fresh pasta with shaved parmesan and wilted spinach'.[32] Brown's surrender to the apparent inevitability of a Blair victory was reported in the press as a selfless act, though he did receive in return assurances about his role as economic overlord in a future government. Brown also appears to have left the restaurant believing Blair would, as far as possible, support his eventual succession to the leadership, although Blair denies he ever intimated that he would stand down to facilitate such a development before the end of a second term in office. Whatever was agreed in the so-called 'Treaty of Granita', it was to leave deep scars. Gordon Brown never denied some years later that he continued to feel raw over the events of May 1994. His friends felt Brown had been let down by Blair who, it was said, had reneged on their earlier agreement, and his relationship with Peter Mandelson was permanently damaged. In due course, Blair and Brown were able to maintain a more cordial relationship than many Prime Ministers and Chancellors in the past. Even so, as the historian of Labour politics Andrew Thorpe notes, 'The very nature of Blair's elimination of Brown created a rift in the next Labour government three years before it was formed.'[33]

Part of the lingering bitterness of Brown's entourage stemmed from a feeling that the contest was manipulated by the media, with many pundits building up a bandwagon in favour of Blair. In reality, since 1992 Blair had overtaken Brown as the most likely successor to Smith. This may have been concealed from the general public during Smith's leadership, when no early contest was anticipated, but it was increasingly recognized in the political world. An instructive response to Smith's death was later recounted by Damien Green, working at the time in John Major's Downing Street Policy Unit: 'Our first thought after John Smith's death was, "How awful, a man only in his mid-fifties." Another second later the next thought followed: "Well, that's stuffed Hezza then" – a moment of satisfaction. But then a new idea struck. "Oh my God, it'll let Tony Blair in. He'll be even more difficult." It's what we all thought.'[34] In the days after Smith's death, journalists on newspapers as diverse as the *Sun*, the *Mirror*, the *Independent* and the *Daily Mail* were only making clear to a wider audience what had been evident in Westminster circles for some time – Blair was the obvious successor. This, combined with his willingness to act decisively at the critical juncture – just as Churchill in 1940 and Macmillan in 1956 had showed more steeliness than their rivals – meant that Blair was firmly in pole position. As Labour's focus group guru Philip Gould has written, the new 'political reality' was taking shape for many months before May 1994; it crystallized in the hours and days after John Smith's heart attack, 'and there was nothing anyone' – not Gordon Brown or even the arch-manipulator Peter Mandelson – 'could do about it'.[35]

After Brown's decision became public knowledge, what followed was certain to be an anticlimax. Tony Blair's biographer, John Rentoul, described the way in which the contest unfolded: 'For the first week, until John Smith's funeral, the campaign was conducted in secret, as decency almost completely suppressed open discussion in the party of the succession. Then there were three weeks of semi-secret campaigning, while the Labour Party fought the European elections. This was a period of self-imposed censorship during which the candidates still pretended not to be candidates. Only then did the official six-week campaign start. By that time, of course, it really was all over.'[36] Two other candidates came forward, but neither was able to mount a serious challenge to Blair. Margaret Beckett had acted competently as leader in the interregnum, but suffered from accusations of disloyalty, having shown herself lukewarm towards the party reforms carried through at the 1993 conference. The working-class background and no-nonsense manner of John Prescott won him support in some quarters, but he lacked Blair's broader appeal. In the event, Blair's victory was comfortable, if not overwhelming. He secured 57 per cent of the electoral college vote, as against 24.1 per cent for Prescott (who won the separate ballot for the deputy leadership) and 18.9 per cent for Beckett. In each section of the college, Blair took more than half the votes cast.[37]

John Smith's inheritance thus looked secure. The danger of a destructive, divisive contest had been avoided, and it became possible to see, as Martin Kettle had guessed, that a 'dark moment' could also turn into one of 'rare and marvellous possibilities'. The new Labour leader inherited a party united in its determination to return to power and confident after its strong performance in the local and European elections. He also faced a Tory government that continued to ignore Denis Healey's dictum that politicians, when in a hole, should stop digging. The economy, strangely enough, was no longer the problem. Unemployment was falling, interest rates and inflation were under control, and there were signs of recovery in the housing market. On past evidence, this should have been followed by a surge of support for the Conservatives. Instead, John Major continued to trail in the polls, beset by voter perception that his was an incompetent administration, sleazy and hopelessly divided over Europe. In late 1994 eight rebel MPs had the party whip withdrawn, and in 1995 the Prime Minister became so frustrated by the sniping of the Eurosceptic 'bastards' that he resigned the party leadership and challenged his critics to 'put up or shut up'.[38] Major saw off the challenge of John Redwood, the Welsh Secretary, but his failure to secure the backing of eighty-nine MPs underlined the weakness of his position inside his own party.

Tony Blair, by contrast, wasted no time in consolidating his hold over the Labour Party. In key respects his strategy was similar to that of his predecessor. He emphasized Tory failings, arguing that Labour would prove more effective in office. He also refused to develop many specific policies which might provide hostages to fortune. But in order to counter the charge that his party was not distinctive, and might not therefore inspire its core supporters or win over disaffected former Tory voters, Blair sought to capture the rhetorical high ground in a way Smith had not. As Labour's youngest leader, aged only forty-one, he began talking of the need to remake Britain as a 'young country', one that would be characterized by 'national renewal'. At his first party conference as leader, in October 1994, he unveiled the slogan 'New Labour, New Britain', and he spoke of the need to create a society 'rich in economic prosperity, secure in social justice, confident in political change'. There were similarities here with the approach taken by Margaret Thatcher in opposition during the late 1970s, arguing in very broad terms for a moral change in political life while relying on government unpopularity to maintain momentum. 'No one appeared to know what a "young country" was,' Andrew Thorpe notes, 'but it sounded good. "New Labour" seemed to sound better than "Labour."'[39]

There was, though, one early and decisive step that Blair took to demonstrate his commitment to the New Labour 'project'. It was obvious from his 1994 conference speech that he regarded Smith's process of internal party reform as incomplete. Labour had to avoid the danger of becoming 'a historical monument', he said, and so still required 'a clear, up-to-date statement of . . . objects and objectives'. This was Blair's way of preparing the ground for an attack on Clause Four of the party's constitution, still revered by many Labour traditionalists for its reference to 'ownership and control of the means of production, distribution and exchange'. By the spring of 1995 a new version of Clause Four had been approved by a special party conference. Many commentators made fun of its convoluted wording – with its reference to the need to create a community 'in which power, wealth and opportunity are in the hands of the many not the few, where the rights we enjoy reflect the duties we owe, and where we live together, freely, in a spirit of solidarity, tolerance and respect'. But when some 65 per cent of the party membership approved the change, it provided an important symbolic victory for the leadership. A majority of trade unions gave their support, and modernizers were keen to note that those, such as the TGWU, that were hostile had not balloted their members. Where Gaitskell had failed thirty-five years earlier, Blair had forged ahead in revising a key article of Labour's constitution; it gave substance to his charge that, in contrast to the Prime Minister, he led his party, he did not follow it.[40]

While there was muttering from traditionalists about the direction in which Blair was heading, his critics that had to concede that he made an immediate impression. In August 1994, after only a month in post, Labour's lead of 33.5 per cent over the Tories was the largest yet seen in Gallup's fifty-seven-year history of polling.[41] At the end of the year there was no sign of an early end to the 'Blair Bubble', with Labour touching the improbable level of 60 per cent support in some polls.[42] In the longer term, John Major was left clinging on to office hoping, Micawber-like, that something would turn up. But when the general election finally came in the spring of 1997, it served only further to highlight Tory divisions over Europe. All the evidence pointed to a comfortable Labour victory, though party activists with memories of 1992 refused to raise their hopes prematurely. It required the sight of Tory ministers tumbling out of their seats – most famously Michael Portillo at Enfield – before Labour workers began to celebrate what turned out to be a landslide. For the first time since 1970, Labour won over 40 per cent of votes cast in a general election, while the Conservative share of 30.7 per cent was the lowest since 1832. Labour's majority of 179 exceeded that won by Attlee in 1945. The Conservatives failed to win a single seat in either Scotland or Wales, and ceased to have a presence in most of the larger English cities. Labour's recovery was most obvious in southern England, where it captured fifty-eight seats outside Greater London south of the 'Severn–Wash line', in contrast to the mere three it had held at the 1983 and 1987 elections.[43] The 1992 parliament, which had witnessed first Black Wednesday and then the emergence of New Labour, had ended by bringing down the curtain on eighteen years of Conservative rule.

Tony Blair's victory in the Labour leadership contest has been described by his acolyte Philip Gould as 'the decisive moment in the 1992–97 parliament'. As a polling expert, Gould noted that Labour's lead in terms of 'political identification', a key measure of voting intention, jumped sharply and remained well ahead through to the 1997 election. On this basis, Gould concludes, Labour would probably have 'scraped home' under John Smith. 'But the majority would have been small, and a hung parliament not impossible. It was Blair who changed the political map.'[44]

There is no reason to doubt that Blair's triumph marked a critical turning point. His relative youthfulness, his presentational skills and his 'New Labour' rhetoric enabled him to maintain and extend support for his party, building it to levels sufficient not only to propel Labour to power in 1997, but also to ensure re-election four years later. The seeds of his achievement in becoming the first Labour leader to secure two successive full terms were laid in the summer of 1994, when Blair first displayed a dynamism that contrasted sharply with the tired leadership of the Tory government.

Yet for all this, Philip Gould's case is overstated. One weakness of his assessment is that he underplays the importance of John Smith's leadership. By placing so much emphasis on what comes after 'year zero', Smith is consigned to a historical role as the last representative of 'Old Labour' – a decent enough figure, but incapable of inspiring the nation in the way that Tony Blair did. It goes without saying that we cannot know what would have happened at the 1997 election if Smith had lived. But there was evidence before and during 1994 that Smith's Labour Party was heading for a solid victory, if not a landslide, whenever a general election came. After the immense trauma of Black Wednesday, Smith enjoyed a bigger and more prolonged lead in the opinion polls than any opposition since the war. This was not simply because the Tory association with economic well-being had been damaged beyond repair – well before Blair came on the scene. It was also due to the image of Smith as a leader who was both caring and decisive. The local elections of May 1994 underlined the extent to which he was capable of reaching out to 'middle England' as well as to the party's heartlands. As Labour regained ground in areas where its presence had been negligible in the 1980s, so it became obvious that there was no way back for Major's government.[45] In terms of the percentage of votes cast for each party, the result in May 1994 turned out to be strikingly similar to that of the general election of 1997.

Nor should it be forgotten that the emergence of New Labour

was possible only because of John Smith's unexpected death and the enormous depth of public sympathy it evoked. Smith's admirers were left to reflect on what might have been. Some looked backwards, claiming that his achievement was greater than that of Labour's other 'lost leader', Hugh Gaitskell. Whereas Gaitskell was followed by one of his leading enemies, Harold Wilson, who secured only a narrow win in 1964, Smith bequeathed a leadership that was no longer a poisoned chalice – a party with few factional tensions, in which all the potential successors promised to uphold his legacy, and which went on to secure the largest majority in Labour's history. Other friends turned to hypothetical questions, not just about whether Smith would have won had he lived, but also about the type of administration he might have led. The consensus here was that it is likely that differences would have been most apparent in terms of presentation, with Smith less concerned about 'spin' and more determined than Blair to maintain a close relationship between party and government.[46] All agreed that Smith's sudden death in May 1994 left the nation a poorer place. 'We are,' Andrew Marr wrote in perhaps the most eloquent tribute, 'missing someone special. We are missing a version of the future, a chance that has gone . . . Had he lived, he would have entered our lives, affected our wealth, altered our morale, changed how we thought about our country, influenced the education of our children . . . For good or ill? The question is now meaningless. That Britain won't happen.'[47]

The Britain that did happen was, of course, Tony Blair's Britain. In office after 1997, the key figure apart from the Prime Minister has been Gordon Brown as Chancellor: 'chief executive to Tony Blair's chairman', bestriding Whitehall and intervening in many aspects of government policy. As 'Red Gordon', he took the lead in seeking to raise the incomes of the poorest in society, working for the abolition of child poverty and redressing the international debt burden. As the Iron Chancellor, he kept a tight rein on public spending until he felt a strengthened economy warranted major new investment in the public services.[48] Without

Gordon Brown's decision to stand aside in the summer of 1994, the New Labour project may never have been ushered in. Brown's enormous desire for the top job made the potential for disaster real enough; the acrimony between Kenneth Clarke and Iain Duncan Smith in 2001 illustrated that leadership contests can easily degenerate into divisive affairs, more damaging than beneficial to the party in question. Sensing that he and Blair would stand or fall together, Brown declined to put his name forward, though his associates believe he did so on the understanding that the succession would be his. The events of mid-1994 heralded the arrival of New Labour, the dominant force in British politics at the start of the twenty-first century; but they also sullied the once warm relationship between the chief architects of the 'project', however much Gordon might protest that Tony is his 'best friend in politics'. In his book *The Rivals*, James Naughtie records a Number Ten insider saying that with every day that passes during Blair's second term Brown 'will make another cross on the calendar. Day after day after day.' And, Naughtie adds, there was no need to ask why.[49]

Notes

Introduction

1 John Cole, political editor of the BBC from 1981 to 1992, notes in a letter to the author (9 April 2001) that while he helped to popularise this saying, it was unclear where it originated; he presumed from memory that it was first said by Macmillan to a journalist or political colleague sometime in 1963–4.

2 John Charmley, *Churchill: The End of Glory* (London, 1993), p. 521. For an extended discussion of this theme, see Niall Ferguson (ed.), *Virtual History: Alternatives and Counterfactuals* (London, 1997), pp. 1–90.

1 'In the name of God, go', 1940

1 Alan Bullock, *The Life and Times of Ernest Bevin*, Vol. II, *Minister of Labour 1940–1945* (London, 1967), p. 1.

2 Clive Ponting, *Churchill* (London, 1990), p. 138; Charmley, *Churchill: End of Glory*, p. 2.

3 L. W. Fuchser, *Neville Chamberlain and Appeasement* (New York, 1982), pp. 190–91.

4 David Reynolds, 'Churchill in 1940: The Worst and Finest Hour', *in* Robert Blake and Wm Roger Louis (eds), *Churchill* (Oxford, 1993), p. 241. For the development of this theme see Kevin Jefferys, *The Churchill Coalition and Wartime Politics 1940–45* (Manchester, 1991), chapters 1 and 2.

5 David Carlton, *Anthony Eden: A Biography* (London, 1981), pp. 145–6.

6 Richard Cockett, *Twilight of Truth: Chamberlain, Appeasement and the Manipulation of the Press* (London, 1989), especially chapter 3.

7 R. J. Minney, *The Private Papers of Hore-Belisha* (London, 1960), p. 230.

8 Cockett, *Twilight of Truth*; Colin Cross (ed.), *Life with Lloyd George: The Diary of A. J. Sylvester 1931–45* (London, 1975). Sylvester records (p. 238) that Lloyd George was busy at this time creating the impression that 'we had damned well lost and that we should come to terms . . .'

9 Paul Addison, *The Road to 1945: British Politics and the Second World War* (London, 1975), pp. 56–60; Hansard, *Parliamentary Debates*, 1 February 1940, column 1336.

10 Neville to Ida Chamberlain [sister], 20 January 1940, quoted in Lord Butler (ed.), *The Conservatives* (London, 1977), p. 395; Bracken interview with W. P. Crozier of the *Manchester Guardian*, 29 March 1940, in A. J. P. Taylor (ed.), *Off the Record: W. P. Crozier, Political Interviews 1933–44* (London, 1973), p. 156.

11 Minutes of the Watching Committee, 16–29 April 1940, Paul Emrys Evans MP papers, British Library, London, Add. MSS 58270.

12 Robert Rhodes James (ed.), *Chips: The Diaries of Sir Henry Channon* (London, 1967), 1 May 1940, p. 244. On the relationship between Chamberlain and Churchill see Graham Stewart, *Burying Caesar: Churchill, Chamberlain and the Battle for the Tory Party* (London, 1999).

13 Ben Pimlott, *Hugh Dalton* (London, 1985), p. 273; Dalton feared Chamberlain might call an election which would wipe Labour 'further out than in 1931'.

14 Neville to Hilda Chamberlain, 4 May 1940; Margesson note to Prime Minister, 6 May 1940, Neville Chamberlain papers, Birmingham University Library, NC8/35/47.

15 Nigel Nicolson (ed.), *Harold Nicolson: Diaries and Letters 1939–45* (London, 1967), 7 May 1940, pp. 76–7.

16 Lord Home [Alec Dunglass, Chamberlain's PPS], *The Way the Wind Blows* (London, 1976), p. 74; John Barnes and David Nicholson (eds), *The Empire at Bay: The Leo Amery Diaries*

1929–1945 (London, 1988), 7 May 1940, p. 592.

17 Hugh Dalton, *The Fateful Years: Memoirs 1931–45* (London, 1957), p. 305.

18 *Channon Diaries*, 8 May 1940, p. 246. Lloyd George's words are in Hansard, *Parliamentary Debates*, 8 May 1940, column 1283.

19 'Memorandum on Events Leading to the Downfall of Neville Chamberlain', no date, Clement Davies papers, National Library of Wales, Aberystwyth, 1/2/8; Emrys Evans diary, 8 May 1940, Evans papers, ff. 125–6.

20 *Channon Diaries*, 8 May 1940, pp. 246–7.

21 Spens to Chamberlain, 9 May 1940, Chamberlain papers, NC7/11/33/162.

22 Cited in C. E. Lysaght, *Brendan Bracken* (London, 1979), p. 174. See also Ben Pimlott (ed.), *The Political Diary of Hugh Dalton 1918–40, 1945–60* (London, 1986), 9 May 1940, p. 343: 'The Old Man was telephoning from 8.00 onwards, trying to conciliate opponents of yesterday. He seems determined himself to stick on – like a dirty piece of chewing gum on the leg of a chair.'

23 e.g. Earl of Birkenhead, *Halifax: The Life of Lord Halifax* (London, 1965), pp. 453–4.

24 For detailed accounts of this episode see Carlton, *Anthony Eden*, pp. 161–2, and Robert Blake, 'How Churchill Became Prime Minister', *in* Blake and Louis (eds), *Churchill*, pp. 265–9.

25 *Dalton Political Diary*, 10 May 1940, p. 345.

26 Ben Pimlott (ed.), *The Second World War Diary of Hugh Dalton 1940–45* (London, 1986), 16 May 1940, p. 9 Harold Macmillan explained the action of the service MPs to Dalton along the lines that 'in the Army their loyalty to the King overcame their loyalty to the Old Man and Margesson. When they saw the mess in Norway, some at first hand, they made up their minds.'

27 J. S. Rasmussen, 'Party Discipline in Wartime: The Downfall of the Chamberlain Government', *Journal of Politics*, 32, (1970), 380–82.

28 Stuart Ball (ed.), *Parliament and Politics in the Age of Churchill and Attlee: The Headlam Diaries 1935–51* (London, 1999), 10 May 1940, p. 197. See also Chamberlain diary, 11 May 1940, cited in Keith

Feiling, *The Life of Neville Chamberlain* (London, 1947), p. 440.

29 Emrys Evans diary, 8 May 1940, Evans papers, f. 126; Boothby to Churchill, 9 May 1940, cited in Martin Gilbert, *Winston S. Churchill*, Vol. VI, *Finest Hour 1939–41* (London , 1983), p. 303: 'I find a gathering consensus of opinion in all quarters that you are the necessary and inevitable Prime Minister . . . '

30 Cited in Tim Clayton and Phil Craig, *Finest Hour* (London, 1999), p. 16.

31 Churchill to Chamberlain, 10 May 1940, cited in Gilbert, *Finest Hour*, pp. 314–15.

32 *Channon Diaries*, 11 May 1940, p. 251; Feiling, *Neville Chamberlain*, p. 443.

33 Jefferys, *Churchill Coalition*, pp. 35–9.

34 Cited in Clayton and Craig, *Finest Hour*, p. 29.

35 Sir John Colville, *The Fringes of Power: Downing Street Diaries 1939–1955* (London, 1985), 10 May 1940, p. 122.

36 *Channon Diaries*, 13 May 1940, p. 252.

37 Churchill to Lloyd George, 6 June 1940, cited in Gilbert, *Finest Hour*, p. 474; *Sylvester Diary*, 29–30 May 1940, pp. 264–6. Lloyd George's secretary reported that 'he thinks we are beaten. The whole point is that he hates Neville and the Government so much he would like to see them beaten.'

38 David Reynolds, 'Churchill and the British "Decision" to Fight On in 1940: Right Policy, Wrong Reasons', *in* Richard Langhorne (ed.), *Diplomacy and Intelligence during the Second World War* (Cambridge, 1975), pp. 147–66. On this episode see also John Lukacs, *Five Days in London: May 1940* (New Haven and London, 2000).

39 *Dalton Second World War Diary*, 28 May 1940, pp. 27–9.

40 Patrick Wilson, 'Dunkirk: Victory or Defeat?', *History Review*, September 2000, pp. 18–22; Angus Calder, *The People's War: Britain 1939–45* (London, 1969), p. 127. For a detailed account see Norman Gelb, *Dunkirk: The Incredible Escape* (London, 1990).

41 *Daily Herald*, 5–6 June 1940; Neville to Hilda Chamberlain, 2 June 1940, Chamberlain papers, NC18/1/1159.

42 Hugh Cudlipp, *Publish and Be Damned!: The Astonishing Story of*

the Daily Mirror (London, 1953), pp. 144–5.

43 *Amery Diaries*, 18 June 1940, pp. 625–6. On the so-called 'Under-Secretaries' plot' see also Addison, *Road to 1945*, pp. 109–10.

44 Hansard, *Parliamentary Debates*, 18 June 1940, columns 51–61.

45 *Dalton Second World War Diary*, 18 June 1940, p. 42.

46 Lord Beaverbrook to Samuel Hoare, 6 July 1940, Beaverbrook papers, House of Lords Record Office, C/308.

47 Rab Butler to Samuel Hoare, 20 July 1940, Lord Butler papers, Trinity College Cambridge, E3/8, f. 114.

48 'Cato', *Guilty Men* (London, 1940), p. 125: 'Let the guilty men retire . . . of their own volition, and so make an essential contribution to the victory upon which we are implacably resolved.'

49 Gilbert, *Finest Hour*, p. 924, quoting the words of a Downing Street official, John Martin. See also Paul Einzig, *In the Centre of Things* (London, 1960), pp. 209–20.

50 Churchill to Sir Roger Keyes, 30 July 1940, quoted in Gilbert, *Finest Hour*, p. 697; Chamberlain diary, 9 September 1940, cited in Feiling, *Chamberlain*, p. 451. Hugh Dalton's cruel description of Chamberlain was the 'Old Corpse Upstairs'; see *Dalton Second World War Diary*, 4 July 1940, p. 53.

51 Ralph Ingersoll, *Report on England* (London, 1941), p. 165.

52 Isaiah Berlin, *Mr Churchill in 1940* (London, 1964), p. 27.

53 Geoffrey Best, *Churchill: A Study in Greatness* (London, 2001). See also Phil Craig on the 'finest hour' in the *Guardian*, 30 August 2000.

2 'The turn of the tide', 1942–3

1 Cited in Michael Sissons and Philip French (eds), *Age of Austerity 1945–51* (London, 1963), p. x.

2 Addison, *Road to 1945*, p. 188.

3 *Channon Diaries*, 1 and 6 June 1941, p. 307.

4 Colville, *Fringes of Power*, 18 August 1941, p. 428.

5 *The Economist*, 1 November 1941.

6 Angus Calder, *The People's War*, p. 313.

7 *Dalton Second World War Diary*, 4–5 February 1942, pp. 360–62.

8 James Stuart, *Within the Fringe* (London, 1967), p. 120.

9 Kevin Jefferys (ed.), *Labour and the Wartime Coalition: From the Diary of James Chuter Ede, 1941–45* (London, 1987), 24–5 February 1942, pp. 54–8.

10 *The Economist*, 28 February 1942.

11 Lord Hankey to Samuel Hoare, 12 March 1942, Lord Hankey papers, Churchill College, Cambridge, HNKY 4/34.

12 Morgan Philips Price, *My Three Revolutions* (London, 1969), p. 279. Philips Price, Labour MP for the Forest of Dean, was initially supportive of the censure motion but eventually decided to abstain. A full account of the debate is given in G. M. Thomson, *Vote of Censure* (London, 1968), pp. 192–207.

13 Addison, *Road to 1945*, p. 205; W. S. Churchill, *The Second World War*, Vol. IV, *The Hinge of Fate* (London, 1951), pp. 354–6.

14 *Channon Diaries*, 6 May 1941, pp. 302–3. On 25 June 1942, p. 353, Channon wrote that he for one would never 'vote against Winston to make Anthony King'.

15 *Channon Diaries*, 1 July 1942, p. 354.

16 *The Times*, 4 July 1942, reported that the minority vote consisted of eight Conservatives, eight Labour, two Liberals, six Independent MPs and three Independent Labour Party members (twenty-seven in all, including two tellers).

17 *Headlam Diaries*, 2–3 July 1942, pp. 323–4.

18 G. S. Harvie-Watt, *Most of My Life* (London, 1980), p. 93.

19 Walter Elliot, broadcast of 8 August 1942, quoted in his book *Long Distance* (London, 1943), p. 74.

20 Typed diary notes, July 1942, Butler papers, G14, ff. 58–60; *Dalton Second World War Diary*, 24 August 1942, pp. 479–80.

21 Ivor Thomas MP to Tom Jones, 13 August 1942, Viscount Astor papers, Reading University Library, MS1066/823.

22 *Dalton Second World War Diary*, 8 September 1942, p. 490.

23 James Stuart memo to the Prime Minister, 9 September 1942, Public Record Office (PRO) PREM 4 60/4; *Chuter Ede Diary*, 20

September and 27 November 1942, pp. 97 and 110.

24 Cripps to Churchill, quoted in Colin Cooke, *The Life of Richard Stafford Cripps* (London, 1957), pp. 298–9.

25 Bracken, who said Churchill found the suspense of waiting 'almost unbearable', was in conversation with the Prime Minister's doctor; see Lord Moran, *Winston Churchill: The Struggle for Survival 1940–65* (London, 1966), pp. 91–6.

26 *Dalton Second World War Diary*, 8 November 1942, p. 515.

27 *Chuter Ede Diary*, 31 December 1942, p. 115.

28 *Channon Diaries*, 23 June 1942, p. 353.

29 Correlli Barnett, *The Audit of War: The Illusion and Reality of Britain as a Great Nation* (London, 1986), p. 340.

30 Kevin Jefferys, 'British Politics and Social Policy during the Second World War', *Historical Journal*, 30/1 (1987), 123–44; Stephen Brooke, *The Labour Party during the Second World War* (Oxford, 1992).

31 Dalton, *The Fateful Years*, p. 410.

32 Lord Butler, *The Art of the Possible* (London, 1971), p. 90.

33 *Chuter Ede Diary*, 27 November 1942, p. 110.

34 Hansard, *Parliamentary Debates*, 12 November 1942, column 138.

35 Notes by R. A. Butler, no date [1941], Butler papers, G16, f. 100.

36 Jose Harris, 'Social Planning in Wartime: Some Aspects of the Beveridge Report', *in* Jay Winter (ed.), *War and Economic Development* (Cambridge, 1975); *William Beveridge* (Oxford, 1977).

37 Harvie–Watt, *Most of My Life*, p. 117; War Cabinet minutes, 15 February 1943, PRO CAB 65/33.

38 Charmley, *Churchill: The End of Glory*, pp. 523–4.

39 Secret Conservative Committee, 'Report on Beveridge Proposals', 19 January 1943, Conservative Party archive, Bodleian Library, Oxford, 600/01.

40 Hansard, *Parliamentary Debates*, 18 February 1943. The amendment calling for immediate implementation was defeated by 338 votes to 121; the minority consisted of ninety-seven Labour MPs joined by Liberals, Independent MPs and members of the Independent Labour Party.

41 *Dalton Second World War Diary*, 18 February 1943, p. 555.

42 James Griffiths, *Pages from Memory* (London, 1969), p. 72.

43 Home Intelligence Weekly Reports, 10 December 1942 and 11 March 1943, PRO INF 1/292; 'Public Feeling about the Beveridge Proposals', Home Intelligence Special Report, 13 May 1944, INF 1/293.

44 On local trends in opinion see Jefferys, *Churchill Coalition*, chapter 6, 'Finding one's way in the country'.

45 Addison, *Road to 1945*, p. 227; W. P. Crozier interview with Churchill, 26 March 1943, *in* Taylor (ed.), *Off the Record*, p. 345.

46 Diary notes by Butler, 9 September 1943, Butler papers, G15, f. 81.

47 Beveridge to Barrington-Ward, 14 December 1943, quoted in Jefferys, *Churchill Coalition*, p. 133.

48 'Agents' Electoral Forecasts 1945', Conservative Party archive, CCO4/2/61.

49 Home Intelligence Weekly Reports, 8–15 January and 26 February–March 1941, PRO INF 1/292.

50 Tom Harrisson, 'Who'll Win?', *Political Quarterly*, 15 (1944), 21–32.

3 'The end is Nye', 1951

1 The key sympathetic works are Kenneth O. Morgan, *Labour in Power 1945–51* (Oxford, 1984), Alec Cairncross, *Years of Recovery: British Economic Policy 1945–51* (London, 1985), and Peter Hennessy, *Never Again: Britain 1945–51* (London, 1992). For left-wing critiques, see Ralph Miliband, *Parliamentary Socialism* (London, 1961) and John Saville, *The Labour Movement in Britain* (London, 1988). The 'wrong turning' notion is developed in Correlli Barnett, *The Lost Victory: British Dreams, British Reality, 1945–50* (London, 1996).

2 John Campbell, *Nye Bevan and the Mirage of British Socialism* (London, 1987), p. 245.

3 Peter Hennessy, 'The Attlee Governments 1945–51', *in* Peter

Hennessy and Anthony Seldon (eds), *Ruling Performance: British Governments from Attlee to Thatcher* (Oxford, 1987), p. 28.

4 Douglas Jay, *Change and Fortune: A Political Record* (London, 1980), p. 135.

5 For reassessments of the careers of Bevin and Morrison see the chapters by Robert Pearce and Greg Rosen respectively in Kevin Jefferys (ed.), *Labour Forces: From Ernest Bevin to Gordon Brown* (London, 2002).

6 Morgan, *Labour in Power*, p. 184.

7 The joke was recalled in a letter from R. C. Fairhurst to the *Guardian*, August 2000. For a detailed account of the introduction of the NHS see Charles Webster, *The Health Services since the War* (London, 1988).

8 Quoted in Alex Robertson, *The Bleak Midwinter, 1947* (Manchester, 1987), p. 113.

9 Susan Cooper, 'Snoek Piquante', *in* Sissons and French (eds), *Age of Austerity*, pp. 51–3.

10 Hugh Dalton, *High Tide and After: Memoirs 1945–60* (London, 1962), p. 347. See also H. G. Nicholas, *The British General Election of 1950* (London, 1951), pp. 296–305.

11 Quoted in Henry Pelling, 'The Labour Government of 1945–51: The Determinants of Policy', *in* Michael Bentley and John Stevenson (eds), *High and Low Politics in Modern Britain* (Oxford, 1983), p. 278.

12 *Dalton Political Diary*, 25–6 February 1950, pp. 470–71.

13 Quoted in Morgan, *Labour in Power*, p. 412.

14 Jonathan Schneer, *Labour's Conscience: The Labour Left 1945–51* (London, 1988), pp. 196–8.

15 Philip Williams (ed.), *The Diary of Hugh Gaitskell: 1945–56* (London, 1983), 4 May 1951, p. 257.

16 Philip Williams, *Hugh Gaitskel: A Political Biography* (Oxford, 1982 edn), p. 181.

17 Quoted in Morgan, *Labour in Power*, p. 450.

18 *Gaitskell Diary*, 30 April 1951, p. 246.

19 *Channon Diary*, 10 April 1951, p. 458; Williams, *Gaitskell*, p. 176.

20 Quoted in Michael Foot, *Aneurin Bevan*, Vol. II, *1945–60* (London, 1973), p. 330.

21 Robert Pearce (ed.), *Patrick Gordon Walker: Political Diaries 1932–71* (London, 1991), p. 194.

22 *Dalton Political Diary*, 19 April 1951, p. 533.

23 *Tribune*, 20 April 1951.

24 *Gaitskell Diary*, 4 May 1951, p. 255.

25 Barbara Castle, *Fighting All the Way* (London, 1993), p. 190.

26 *Gaitskell Diary*, 4 May 1951, p. 256; *The Times*, 22 April 1951.

27 Morgan, *Labour in Power*, p. 455.

28 Williams, *Gaitskell*, pp. 173–4 and 279–80.

29 Foot, *Bevan*, pp. 318–20; K. O. Morgan, *Labour People: Leaders and Lieutenants from Hardie to Kinnock* (Oxford, 1987), pp. 244–5.

30 *Dalton Political Diary*, 5 April 1951, p. 518; Jay, *Change and Fortune*, p. 205.

31 Castle, *Fighting All the Way*, p. 193.

32 *Dalton Political Diary*, 5 April 1951, p. 518; Dalton, *High Tide and After*, p. 365.

33 Campbell, *Bevan*, p. 246.

34 *Gaitskell Diary*, 30 April 1951, p. 244.

35 Campbell, *Bevan*, pp. 247–8; Brian Brivati, *Hugh Gaitskell* (London, 1996), p. 117.

36 Foot, *Bevan*, pp. 314–15.

37 Pimlott, *Dalton*, p. 600.

38 *The Times*, 26 April and 2 May 1951.

39 Jay, *Change and Fortune*, p. 207; Cairncross, *Years of Recovery*, pp. 228–33; David Butler, *The British General Election of 1951* (London, 1952), pp. 13–20.

40 Jay, *Change and Fortune*, p. 210.

41 Butler, *General Election of 1951*, pp. 239–42.

42 Jay, *Change and Fortune*, p. 210.

43 *Dalton Political Diary*, 'End of October 1951', p. 567.

44 Harold Macmillan, *Memoirs*, Vol. III, *Tides of Fortune 1945–55* (London, 1969), 21 September 1951, p. 355.

45 Colonel J. R. Hutchinson MP to Rab Butler, 21 November 1951,

Butler papers, B17, f. 153.

46 Viscount Chandos [Oliver Lyttelton], *The Memoirs of Lord Chandos* (London, 1962), p. 341; Geoffrey Lloyd MP to Sidney Butler, 28 October 1951, Butler papers, B17, f. 180.

47 Chandos, *Memoirs*, p. 344.

48 *Dalton Political Diary*, 5 April 1951, p. 518; Williams, *Gaitskell*, pp. 182–5.

49 David Howell, *British Social Democracy: A Study in Development and Decay* (London, 1980 edn), p. 177.

4 'The best Prime Minister we have', 1956

1 David Butler, *The British General Election of 1955* (London, 1955), p. 15.

2 *Yorkshire Post*, 7 April 1955.

3 *The Guardian*, 27 November 1999.

4 The most sympathetic biography is Robert Rhodes James, *Anthony Eden* (London, 1986); other more critical assessments are cited below.

5 Sir Anthony Eden, *Full Circle* (London, 1960), p. 272.

6 Eden to Churchill, 8 April 1955, Public Record Office (PRO) PREM 11/864.

7 Samuel Brittan, *Steering the Economy: The Role of the Treasury* (Harmondsworth, 1971), p. 201.

8 *Dalton Political Diary*, 26 May 1955, p. 671; Butler, *General Election of 1955*, pp. 67–92.

9 *New Statesman*, 4 June 1955; *Manchester Guardian*, 28 May 1955; *The Times*, 28 May 1955.

10 Conservative Research Department, 'Report on General Election 1955', Conservative Party archive, CRD2/48/54.

11 Macmillan diary, 6 April 1955, Bodleian Library, Oxford, quoted in Peter Hennessy, *The Prime Minister: The Office and its Holders since 1945* (London, 2000), p. 212.

12 *Dalton Political Diary*, 1 April 1955, p. 658; Alistair Horne,

Macmillan, Vol. I, *1894–1956* (London, 1988), p. 376.

13 Lord Kilmuir, *Political Adventure: The Memoirs of the Earl of Kilmuir* (London, 1964), p. 308; Nigel Nicolson MP, quoted in A. Thompson, *The Day Before Yesterday: An Illustrated History of Britain from Attlee to Macmillan* (London, 1971), p. 121.

14 Cabinet Minutes, 21 September, 4 and 25 October 1955, PRO CAB 128/29.

15 Eden diary, 2 October 1955, Lord Avon papers, Birmingham University Library, AP20/1/31.

16 Butler, *Art of the Possible* p. 181; Macmillan, *Tides of Fortune*, pp. 658–92.

17 *Daily Telegraph*, 3 January 1956.

18 *Manchester Guardian*, 9 January 1956.

19 *The Times*, 19 January 1956; 'Notes of Prime Minister's Meeting with Newspaper Editors', 23 January 1956, PRO PREM 11/1539.

20 Drew Middleton of the *New York Times*, quoted in David Carlton, *Anthony Eden: A Biography* (London, 1981), p. 399.

21 Nigel Nicolson (ed.), *Harold Nicolson: Diaries and Letters*, Vol. III, *1945–62* (London, 1968), 26 July 1956, p. 305.

22 *The Times*, 1 August 1956.

23 Keith Kyle, *Suez* (London, 1991), pp. 163–5.

24 W. Scott Lucas (ed.), *Britain and Suez: The Lion's Last Roar* (Manchester, 1996), pp. 49–70.

25 Kyle, *Suez*, pp. 245–8.

26 Lucas, *Britain and Suez*, pp. 76–7.

27 Peter Rawlinson, *A Price too High: An Autobiography* (London, 1989), pp. 68–71.

28 Kyle, *Suez*, pp. 378–9 and 429–30.

29 Lucas, *Britain and Suez*, pp. 54–5; Kyle, *Suez*, pp. 430–33.

30 *The Observer*, 4 November 1956. See also Tony Shaw, 'Government Manipulation of the Press during the 1956 Suez Crisis', *Contemporary Record*, 8/2 (1994), 279.

31 Quoted in Rhodes James, *Eden*, p. 657.

32 Kyle, *Suez*, pp. 464–5.

33 *The Economist*, 8 December 1956.

34 Hennessy, *Prime Minister*, p. 247.

35 D. R. Thorpe, *Selwyn Lloyd* (London, 1989), p. 256.

36 Edward Heath, *The Course of My Life: My Autobiography* (London, 1998), p. 176.

37 Randolph Churchill, *The Rise and Fall of Sir Anthony Eden* (London, 1959), p. 121.

38 Butler, *Art of the Possible*, p. 194; diary notes, n.d. [1957], Butler papers, G31, ff. 96–100.

39 Quoted in Patrick Cosgrave, *R. A. Butler* (London, 1981), p. 119. See also Lewis Johnman, 'Defending the Pound: The Economics of the Suez Crisis', *in* Anthony Gorst, Lewis Johnman and W. Scott Lucas (eds), *Postwar Britain 1945–64: Themes and Perspectives* (London, 1989), pp. 166–79.

40 Enoch Powell, quoted in Anthony Howard, *RAB: The Life of R. A. Butler* (London, 1987), pp. 240–41.

41 Bracken to Lord Beaverbrook, 7 December 1956, quoted in Carlton, *Eden*, p. 463.

42 Quoted in Kyle, *Suez*, p. 514.

43 Quoted in Thompson, *Day Before Yesterday*, p. 160.

44 Victor Rothwell, *Anthony Eden* (Manchester, 1992), p. 245.

45 Bracken to Beaverbrook, 23 January 1957, quoted in Carlton, *Eden*, pp. 463–4.

46 Bracken to Beaverbrook, 4 February 1957: quoted in Carlton, *Eden*, p. 465.

47 Kilmuir, *Political Adventure*, p. 285.

48 Foreign Secretary Selwyn Lloyd refused to give an opinion. Enoch Powell, a Butler supporter, says he was not asked; see Andrew Roth, *Enoch Powell: Tory Tribune* (London, 1970), p. 159.

49 Gerald Sparrow, *RAB: Study of a Statesman* (London, 1965), pp. 138–48.

50 Harold Macmillan, *Memoirs*, Vol. IV, *Riding the Storm 1956–59* (London, 1971), p. 184; Kyle, *Suez*, p. 533.

51 Henry Fairlie, *The Life of Politics* (London, 1968), p. 61; Butler's diary account of the succession, February 1957, Butler papers, G31, ff. 70–73; Memorandum of 'Confidential Exchange with Chief

Whip', 21 February 1957, Butler papers, G31, f. 76.

52 D. R. Thorpe, *The Uncrowned Prime Ministers* (London, 1980), p. 209.

53 Rab note on relations with WSC, March 1957, Butler papers, G31, ff. 89–91.

54 Fairlie, *Life of Politics*, p. 61.

55 See John Darwin, 'The End of Empire', *Contemporary Record*, 1/3 (1987), 51–5.

56 Hennessy, *Prime Minister*, pp. 208, 223 and 246.

57 Kyle, *Suez*, p. 557; W. Scott Lucas, *Divided We Stand: Britain, the US and the Suez Crisis* (London, 1991), pp. 324–5.

58 Quoted in Horne, *Macmillan*, Vol. I, p. 376.

59 Tony Lambton MP to Selwyn Lloyd, 22 November 1956, Selwyn Lloyd papers, Churchill College, Cambridge, SELO 1/88; John Ramsden, *The Age of Churchill and Eden 1940–57* (London, 1995), pp. 318–19.

60 Edward Boyle to Hugh Trevor–Roper, 20 November 1956, Lord Boyle papers, University of Leeds, MS 660/3871.

61 Michael Pinto-Duschinsky, 'Bread and Circuses?', *in* Vernon Bogdanor and Robert Skidelsky (eds), *The Age of Affluence 1951–64* (London, 1970), pp. 68–9.

62 Quoted in Alistair Horne, *Macmillan*, Vol. II, *1957–1986* (London, 1989), p. 7.

63 Heath, *Course of My Life*, pp. 181–2.

5 'Sexual intercourse began in 1963'

1 Clive Irving, Ron Hall and Jeremy Wallington, *Scandal '63: A Study of the Profumo Affair* (London, 1963), p. 1.

2 Wayland Young, *The Profumo Affair: Aspects of Conservatism* (London, 1963), p. 14.

3 Janet Morgan (ed.), *The Backbench Diary of Richard Crossman, 1951–64* (London, 1981), 5 March 1963, pp. 983–6.

4 Horne, *Macmillan*, Vol. II, p. 471.

5 Arthur Marwick, *A History of the Modern British Isles, 1914–1999* (Oxford, 2000), pp. 238–46.

6 Philip Larkin, 'Annus Mirabilis', *High Windows* (London, 1974).

7 Rawlinson, *A Price too High*, pp. 91–4.

8 Harold Macmillan, *Memoirs*, Vol. VI, *At the End of the Day 1961–63* (London, 1973), p. 437; Macmillan diary, 22 March 1963, quoted in Horne, *Macmillan*, Vol. II, pp. 475–6.

9 Richard Lamb, *The Macmillan Years, 1957–63: The Emerging Truth* (London, 1995), pp. 461–2.

10 Rawlinson, *A Price too High*, pp. 95–101. See also Robert Shepherd, *Iain Macleod* (London, 1994), pp. 294–5, Macleod, the Leader of the House, later claimed he had been extremely blunt, saying 'Look Jack, the basic question is, "Did you fuck her?",' to which Profumo reportedly replied that he had not.

11 James Prior, *A Balance of Power* (London, 1986), p. 28.

12 Irving et al., *Scandal '63*, pp. 108–10.

13 Phillip Knightley and Caroline Kennedy, *An Affair of State: The Profumo Case and the Framing of Stephen Ward* (London, 1987), pp. 162–6.

14 Young, *Profumo Affair*, p. 25.

15 Irving et al., *Scandal '63*, p. 135.

16 Knightley and Kennedy, *Affair of State*, pp. 184–6.

17 Harold Evans (ed.), *Downing Street Diary: The Macmillan Years 1957–63* (London, 1981), 9 June 1963, p. 271.

18 *Daily Mirror*, 6 June 1963; *News of the World*, 9 June 1963; *Sunday Mirror*, 9 June 1963; *Sunday Telegraph*, 9 June 1963.

19 Macmillan diary, 7 July 1963, quoted in *End of the Day*, p. 442.

20 *Evans Diary*, 9 June 1963, p. 271.

21 *The Times*, 11 June 1963. The leading article was greatly resented by Macmillan, who dubbed the *Times*'s editor Sir William Haley 'Halier than Thou'.

22 The Cabinet minutes for 12–13 June are extensively quoted in Lamb, *The Macmillan Years*, pp. 470–71.

23 Quoted in Young, *Profumo Affair*, p. 36.

24 Ben Pimlott, *Harold Wilson* (London, 1992), pp. 294–6; *Crossman*

Backbench Diary, 22 June 1963, p. 1001.

25 *Evans Diary*, 23 June 1963, p. 275.

26 Macmillan diary, 7 July 1963, quoted in *End of the Day*, p. 442.

27 *Daily Mail*, 18 June 1963; *Daily Telegraph*, 18 June 1963; *Private Eye*, June–July 1963.

28 Account by Paul Channon MP of 1922 Committee, 27 June 1963, Butler papers, G41, ff. 21–4.

29 *Evans Diary*, 23 June 1963, p. 278; Channel 4 *Secret History* programme, 'The Duchess and the Headless Man', August 2000. See also the *Guardian*, 10 August 2000.

30 Quoted in Knightley and Kennedy, *Affair of State*, p. 8.

31 Quoted in Anthony Howard and Richard West, *The Making of the Prime Minister* (London, 1965), p. 51.

32 *Evans Diary*, 28 July and 4 August 1963, pp. 284–6.

33 Macmillan diary, 7 July 1963, quoted in *End of the Day*, p. 444.

34 Lamb, *The Macmillan Years*, pp. 479–81.

35 Macmillan diary, 19 September 1963, quoted in Horne, *Macmillan*, Vol. II, p. 490.

36 *Daily Telegraph*, 27 September 1963, *The Times*, 27 September 1963; *Daily Mirror*, 27 September 1963.

37 Howard and West, *Making of the Prime Minister*, chapter 4.

38 Macmillan diary, 17 October 1963, quoted in *End of the Day*, p. 514.

39 Maudling interview with Anthony Howard, 21 November 1963, quoted in Howard, *R. A. Butler*, p. 399.

40 Iain Macleod, 'The Tory Leadership', *The Spectator*, 17 January 1964.

41 Macmillan diary, 19 October 1963, quoted in Horne, *Macmillan*, Vol. II, p. 571.

42 See Christine Keeler with Douglas Thompson, *The Truth At Last: My Story* (London, 2001), chapters 10 and 11.

43 Knightley and Kennedy, *Affair of State*, pp. 243, 254 and 260.

44 Horne, *Macmillan*, Vol II, pp. 484–95.

45 Confidential typed note, 12 July 1963, Butler papers, G40.

6 'They think it's all over', 1966

1 Richard Crossman, *The Diaries of a Cabinet Minister*, Vol. 1, *Minister of Housing 1964–66* (London, 1975), 24 July 1966, p. 581.

2 Howell, *British Social Democracy*, p. 245. Another hostile view of the period is found in Clive Ponting, *Breach of Promise: Labour in Power 1964–70* (London, 1989). See also Ben Pimlott, *Harold Wilson* (London, 1992) and Philip Ziegler, *Wilson: The Authorised Life* (London, 1993).

3 Scott Newton and Dwilym Porter, *Modernisation Frustrated: The Politics of Industrial Decline in Britain since 1900* (London, 1988), p. 120.

4 James Margach, *The Abuse of Power* (London, 1978), p. 177.

5 Jim Tomlinson, *Public Policy and the Economy* (Oxford, 1990), p. 242.

6 James Callaghan, *Time and Chance* (London, 1987), pp. 159–64.

7 Ponting, *Breach of Promise*, pp. 44–54.

8 Chris Cook and John Ramsden (eds), *By–Elections in British Politics* (London, 1973), pp. 228–9.

9 Lord Wigg, *George Wigg* (London, 1972), p. 329.

10 *Crossman Diaries*, Vol. I, 3 April 1966, pp. 492–3.

11 Tony Benn, *Out of the Wilderness: Diaries 1963–67* (London, 1987), 26 April 1966, p. 405.

12 Edward Short, *Whip to Wilson* (London, 1989), pp. 266–7.

13 *Benn Diaries: Out of the Wilderness*, 6 June 1966, pp. 421–2; 13 June 1966, p. 425; 21 June 1966, p. 437.

14 *The Seaman* [Journal of the NUS], 7 July 1966.

15 *Crossman Diaries*, Vol. I, 21 June 1966, p. 544.

16 *Daily Mail*, 20 July 1966.

17 *The Economist*, 16 July 1966.

18 Pimlott, *Wilson*, p. 411.

19 Pimlott, *Wilson*, p. 415.

20 *Crossman Diaries*, Vol. I, 18 July 1966, p. 575.

21 *Crossman Diaries*, Vol. I, 12 July 1966, pp. 567–8; diary note by Wilson, 'The Economic Crisis of July/August 1966, 9 August 1966,

quoted in Pimlott, *Wilson*, p. 418.

22 Barbara Castle, *The Castle Diaries 1964–76* (London, 1990 edn), 14 July 1966, p. 74.

23 *Crossman Diaries*, Vol. I, 18 July 1966, pp. 573–4; *Castle Diaries*, 18 July 1966, pp. 75–6.

24 *Castle Diaries*, 19 July 1966, pp. 76–7.

25 *Crossman Diaries*, Vol. I, 20 July 1966, p. 579.

26 David Marquand MP, quoted in Austin Mitchell and David Wiener (eds), *Last Time: Labour's Lessons from the Sixties* (London, 1997), p. 196.

27 George Brown, *In My Way* (London, 1971), pp. 107–8.

28 *Crossman Diaries*, Vol. I, 24 July 1966, pp. 581–2; *The Economist*, 6 August 1966.

29 Peter Shore, quoted in *Benn Diaries*, 6 August 1966, p. 466.

30 Kenneth O. Morgan, *Callaghan: A Life* (Oxford, 1997), pp. 244–5.

31 Cecil King, *The Cecil King Diary* (London, 1972), 10 August 1966, p. 84; Pimlott, *Wilson*, p. 421.

32 *The Economist*, 23 and 30 July 1966.

33 William Howie, assistant government whip, quoted in Mitchell and Wiener (eds), *Last Time*, p. 202.

34 Newton and Porter, *Modernisation Frustrated*, p. 155.

35 Tim Bale, 'Dynamics of a Non–decision: The "Failure" to Devalue the Pound, 1964–67', *Twentieth Century British History*, 10/2 (1999), 192–217.

36 This view was expounded by the Labour minister Tony Crosland in *Socialism Now* (London, 1974), pp. 15–58.

37 Richard Crossman, *The Diaries of a Cabinet Minister*, Vol. II, *Lord President of the Council and Leader of the House of Commons* (London, 1976), 11 December 1966, p. 160.

7 'Who Governs?', 1974

1 Hennessy, *Prime Minister*, p. 332.

2 John Charmley, *A History of Conservative Politics 1900–96* (London

and Basingstoke, 1996), p. 193.

3 R. Bacon and W. Eltis, *Britain's Economic Problems: Too Few Producers* (London and Basingstoke, 1976), p. 56.

4 Anthony Seldon, 'The Heath Government in History', *in* Stuart Ball and Anthony Seldon (eds), *The Heath Government 1970–74: A Reappraisal* (London, 1996), pp. 1–19.

5 John Campbell, *Edward Heath: A Biography* (London, 1993); Robert Taylor, 'The Heath Government and Industrial Relations: Myth and Reality', *in* Ball and Seldon (eds), *Heath Government*, p. 162; Hennessy, *Prime Minister*, p. 334.

6 John Ramsden, *The Winds of Change: Macmillan to Heath, 1957–75* (London, 1996), p. 368.

7 Douglas Hurd, *An End to Promises: Sketch of a Government 1970–74* (London, 1979), p. 108.

8 Campbell, *Heath*, p. 561.

9 Joe Gormley, *Battered Cherub* (London, 1982), pp. 122–4.

10 *The Economist*, 1 December 1973.

11 Quoted in Campbell, *Heath*, pp. 565–6.

12 Heath, *Course of My Life*, p. 506.

13 James Prior, *A Balance of Power* (London, 1986), p. 89.

14 Campbell, *Heath*, p. 573.

15 *The Economist*, 22 December 1973.

16 *New Statesman*, 4 January 1974.

17 *The Economist*, 12 January 1974.

18 *Sunday Times*, 6 January 1974.

19 *Daily Mail*, 10 January 1974.

20 David Butler and Dennis Kavanagh, *The British General Election of February 1974* (London, 1974), p. 34.

21 *The Miner*, April 1974.

22 *The Miner*, April 1974.

23 Campbell, *Heath*, pp. 580–84.

24 Prior, *Balance of Power*, p. 92.

25 For a detailed account of the campaign, see Butler and Kavanagh, *General Election of February 1974*.

26 Heath, *Course of My Life*, p. 512.

27 Andrew Rawnsley, *The Observer*, 5 November 2000.

28 Cited in Martin Holmes, *The Failure of the Heath Government* (London and Basingstoke, 1997 edn), p. 118.

29 Campbell, *Heath*, p. 619.

30 Taylor, 'Heath Government and Industrial Relations', p. 189.

31 Stuart Ball, 'The Conservative Party and the Heath Government', in Ball and Seldon (eds), *Heath Government*, p. 350.

32 Dennis Kavanagh, 'The Heath Government 1970–74', *in* Peter Hennessy and Anthony Seldon (eds), *Ruling Performance: British Governments from Attlee to Thatcher* (Oxford, 1987), pp. 231–2.

33 Hennessy, *Prime Minister*, p. 356.

34 Vernon Bogdanor, 'The Fall of Heath and the End of the Postwar Settlement', *in* Ball and Seldon (eds), *Heath Government*, p. 389.

8 'Crisis? What crisis?', 1979

1 Denis Healey, *The Time of My Life* (London, 1989), p. 433. On the IMF crisis, see Kathy Burk and Alec Cairncross, *'Goodbye, Great Britain': The 1976 IMF Crisis* (London and New Haven, 1992).

2 The comment of an ex-Permanent Secretary at the Department of Employment, quoted in Denis Barnes and Eileen Reid, *Government and Trade Unions: The British Experience 1964–79* (London, 1980), p. 212.

3 Bill Rodgers, *Fourth Among Equals* (London, 2000), p. 179.

4 James Callaghan, *Time and Chance* (London, 1987), p. 517; see also Morgan, *Callaghan*, pp. 639–46.

5 Quoted in 'The Winter of Discontent: A Symposium', *Contemporary Record*, 1/3 (1987), 37.

6 Quoted in John Cole, *As it Seemed to Me* (London, 1995), p. 180.

7 *The Sun*, 11 January 1979.

8 Joel Barnett, *Inside the Treasury* (London, 1982), p. 170.

9 Ruth Winstone (ed.), *Tony Benn: Conflicts of Interest: Diaries 1977–80* (London, 1990), 11 January 1979, p. 433.

10 Cole, *As it Seemed to Me*, p. 183.

11 Bernard Donoughue, *Prime Minister: The Conduct of Policy under Harold Wilson and James Callaghan, 1974–79* (London, 1987), p. 211. Bill Rodgers said, 'It was the only time I remember the Prime Minister saying, "What do I do?"'; see 'Winter of Discontent Symposium' p. 43.

12 *Benn Diaries: Conflicts of Interest*, 30 January 1979, p. 446.

13 *The Guardian*, 23 January 1979; *New Statesman*, 26 January 1979.

14 *Benn Diaries: Conflicts of Interest*, 22 January 1979, p. 443.

15 *Daily Mail*, 2 February 1979; Channel 4 *Secret History* programme, 'The Winter of Discontent'.

16 *Daily Mail*, 1 February 1979; Roy Hattersley, *Who Goes Home? Scenes from a Political Life* (London, 1995), p. 202.

17 Anthony King, 'Politics, Economics and the Trade Unions 1974–79', *in* H. R. Penniman (ed.), *Britain at the Polls, 1979* (Washington and London, 1981), p. 83.

18 *Benn Diaries: Conflicts of Interest*, 1 February 1979, p. 449.

19 *Daily Mail*, 15 February 1979; *The Economist*, 17 February and 10 March 1979.

20 *The Guardian*, 7 March 1979.

21 Quoted in Cole, *As it Seemed to Me*, p. 186.

22 *The Observer*, 4 February 1979.

23 'Winter of Discontent Symposium', pp. 42–4.

24 Colin Hay, 'Narrating Crisis: The Discursive Construction of the "Winter of Discontent"', *Sociology*, 30/2 (1996), 265.

25 *Daily Mirror*, 30 January 1979; *The Guardian*, 23 January 1979; *Secret History* programme, 'The Winter of Discontent'.

26 S. Kessler and F. Bayliss, *Contemporary British Industrial Relations* (London, 1995), p. 227. See also Robert Taylor, *The Trade Union Question in British Politics: Government and Unions since 1945* (Oxford, 1993), p. 261; John McIlroy, Nina Fishman and Alan Campbell (eds), *British Trade Unions and Industrial Politics*, Vol. II, *The High Tide of Trade Unionism 1964–79* (Aldershot, 1999), p. 101; Chris Wrigley (ed.), *British Trade Unions 1945–95* (Manchester, 1997), pp. 23–9.

27 Phillip Whitehead, 'The Labour Governments 1974–79', *in*

Hennessy and Seldon (eds), *Ruling Performance*, p. 264.

28 M. Artis, D. Cobham and M. Wickham-Jones, 'Social Democracy in Hard Times: The Economic Record of the Labour Government 1974–79', *Twentieth Century British History*, 3/1 (1992), p. 58.

29 Healey, *Time of My Life*, p. 463.

30 Callaghan, *Time and Chance*, p. 540; William Rodgers, 'Government under Stress: Britain's Winter of Discontent 1979', *Political Quarterly*, 55 (1984), 177.

31 David Butler and Dennis Kavanagh, *The British General Election of 1979* (London, 1980), pp. 336–48.

32 McIlroy, Fishman and Campbell (eds), *British Trade Unions*, pp. 95 and 117.

33 Cole, *As it Seemed to Me*, p. 179; *Secret History* programme, 'The Winter of Discontent'.

34 Healey, *Time of My Life*, p. 462.

35 Martin Holmes, *The Labour Government 1974–7: Political Aims and Economic Reality* (London, 1985), p. 139; Whitehead, 'The Labour Governments', p. 263.

36 Hay, 'Narrating Crisis', p. 253.

37 Nick Tiratsoo, 'You've never had it so bad: Britain in the 1970s', *in* Nick Tiratsoo (ed.), *From Blitz to Blair: A New History of Britain since 1939* (London, 1997), pp. 189–90.

9 'Rejoice, Rejoice', 1982

1 Lawrence Freedman, *Britain & the Falklands War* (Oxford, 1988), p. ix.

2 John Smith, *74 Days: An Islander's Diary of the Falklands Occupation* (London, 1984), 1 and 2 April 1982, pp. 20 and 25.

3 Quoted in The *Sunday Times* Insight Team, *The Falklands War: The Full Story* (London, 1982), p. 22.

4 Ion Trewin (ed.), *Alan Clark Diaries: Into Politics 1972–82* (London, 2000), 2 April 1982, p. 310.

5 *New Statesman*, 18 June 1982.

6 *The Economist*, 10 April 1982.

7 Sir Geoffrey Howe, *Conflict of Loyalty* (London, 1994), pp. 245–6.

8 Cecil Parkinson, *Right at the Centre* (London, 1992), p. 190.

9 *Clark Diaries*, 3 April 1982, pp. 312–13; Margaret Thatcher, *The Downing Street Years* (London, 1993), p. 28.

10 Parkinson, *Right at the Centre*, pp. 190–91.

11 *The Economist*, 10 April 1982.

12 *Clark Diaries*, 7 April 1982, p. 317.

13 Parkinson, *Right at the Centre*, pp. 199–201.

14 For an anti-government view of the incident, see Desmond Rice and Arthur Gavshon, *The Sinking of the Belgrano* (London, 1984).

15 Parkinson, *Right at the Centre*, pp. 203–4.

16 *The Economist*, 15 May 1982.

17 Peter Clarke, *A Question of Leadership: Gladstone to Thatcher* (London, 1991), p. 284.

18 Clive Christie, 'The British Left and the Falklands War', *Political Quarterly*, 55 (1984), 288.

19 Bernard Ingham, *Kill the Messenger* (London, 1991), pp. 288–9.

20 Derrik Mercer, *The Fog of War* (London, 1987), pp. 104–39; BBC Radio 4 programme, 'The Falklands War', broadcast 1986.

21 *New Statesman*, 9 and 16 April 1982.

22 Thatcher, *Downing Street Years*, p. 223.

23 Max Hastings and Simon Jenkins, *The Battle for the Falklands* (London, 1983), p. 163.

24 Quoted in Hastings and Jenkins, *Battle for the Falklands*, pp. 254–5.

25 For a full description of these encounters see Martin Middlebrook, *Operation Corporate: The Story of the Falklands War 1982* (London, 1985).

26 Smith, *Islander's Diary*, 12–14 June 1982, pp. 231–43.

27 Borges, quoted in *Time*, 14 February 1983; Freedman, *Britain & Falklands War*, pp. 1, 66 and 105.

28 Quoted in Thatcher, *Downing Street Years*, p. 235.

29 Hastings and Jenkins, *Battle for the Falklands*, pp. 315–16.

30 Thatcher, *Downing Street Years*, p. 173.

31 Hastings and Jenkins, *Battle for the Falklands*, p. 335.

32 *New Statesman*, 18 June 1982; *Clark Diaries*, 25 June 1982, p. 329.

33 *Sunday Times*, 23 January 1983.

34 Thatcher, *Downing Street Years*, p. 264. See also Nigel Lawson, *The View from No. 11* (London, 1992), p. 138.

35 Christie, 'British Left and the Falklands War', pp. 303–6; Ivor Crewe and Anthony King, *The SDP: The Birth, Life and Death of the Social Democratic Party* (Oxford, 1995), p. 246.

36 David Sanders, Hugh Ward and David Marsh, 'Government Popularity and the Falklands War: A Reassessment', *British Journal of Political Science*, 17/3 (1987), 281–313; 'The Falklands Factor', *Contemporary Record*, 2/1 (1988), pp. 28–9.

37 Mark N. Franklin and Lawrence Freedman, 'The Falklands Factor', *Contemporary Record*, 1/3 (1987), 27–9; Harold D. Clarke, William Mishler and Paul Whiteley, 'Recapturing the Falklands: Models of Conservative Popularity 1979–83', *British Journal of Political Science*, 20/1 (1990), 63–81.

38 David Butler and Dennis Kavanagh, *The British General Election of 1983* (London, 1984), pp. 112–13.

10 'I fight on, I fight to win', 1990

1 *The Observer*, 19 November 2000.

2 *The Guardian*, 22 November 2000.

3 This theory was supported only months before Thatcher's downfall by the political scientists R. K. Alderman and M. J. Smith, 'Can British Prime Ministers Be Given the Push by their Parties?', *Parliamentary Affairs*, 43/3 (July 1990), 260–76.

4 See Alan Watkins, *A Conservative Coup: The Fall of Margaret Thatcher* (London, 1991); Robert Shepherd, *The Power Brokers: The Tory Party and its Leaders* (London, 1991); Mark Wickham-Jones and Donald Shell, 'What Went Wrong? The Fall of Mrs Thatcher', *Contemporary Record*, 5/2, (1991), 321–40; R. K. Alderman and Neil Carter, 'A Very Tory Coup: The Ousting of Mrs Thatcher', *Parliamentary Affairs*, 44/2, (1991), pp. 125–39. The

numerous autobiographical accounts by leading Conservatives involved in the crisis are cited in the notes that follow.

5 Kenneth Baker, *The Turbulent Years: My Life in Politics* (London, 1993), p. 365.

6 *The Spectator*, 1 December 1990.

7 Quoted in Peter Hennessy, *Prime Minister*, p. 425.

8 Ingham, *Kill the Messenger*, pp. 380–81.

9 Quoted in Hennessy, *Prime Minister*, p. 408.

10 Quoted in John Major, *The Autobiography* (London, 2000 edn), p. 168.

11 Thatcher, *Downing Street Years*, p. 644.

12 Lawson, *View from No. 11*, p. 574.

13 Michael Crick and Adrian Van Klaveren, 'Mrs Thatcher's Greatest Blunder', *Contemporary Record*, 5/3 (1991), 414.

14 Allan McConnell, 'The Recurring Crisis of Local Taxation in Post-War Britain', *Contemporary British History*, 11/3 (1997), 55–6.

15 Danny Burns, *Poll Tax Rebellion* (London and Stirling, 1992), pp. 87–104.

16 *Daily Telegraph*, 6 March 1990.

17 Hugh Macpherson, *Tribune*, 6 April 1990.

18 Crick and Van Klaveren, 'Thatcher's Greatest Blunder', pp. 398 and 415.

19 Cole, *As it Seemed to Me*, p. 314.

20 Thatcher, *Downing Street Years*, p. 642.

21 Alderman and Carter, 'Very Tory Coup', p. 128.

22 Howe, *Conflict of Loyalty*, pp. 643–5.

23 *The Times*, 2 November 1990; *The Guardian*, 2 November 1990.

24 Michael Heseltine, *Life in the Jungle: My Autobiography* (London, 2000), p. 355.

25 *The Economist*, 10 November 1990.

26 Heseltine, *Life in the Jungle*, pp. 355–6; Howe, *Conflict of Loyalty*, pp. 659–60.

27 Watkins, *Conservative Coup*, p. 151.

28 *The Spectator*, 17 November 1990. The full text of Howe's speech is reprinted in *Conflict of Loyalty*, pp. 697–703.

29   Hennessy, *Prime Minister*, p. 433.

30   Alan Clark, *Diaries* (London, 1993), 13 November 1990, p. 347.

31   *The Economist*, 17 November 1990.

32   Cole, *As it Seemed to Me*, p. 369.

33   Parkinson, *Right at the Centre*, p. 25.

34   Heseltine, *Life in the Jungle*, p. 362.

35   Baker, *Turbulent Years*, p. 390.

36   Hugo Young, *One of Us: A Biography of Margaret Thatcher* (London, 1991 edn), p. 584.

37   *Clark Diaries*, 17–18 November 1990, pp. 349–52.

38   *Clark Diaries*, 20 November 1990, p. 358.

39   Heseltine, *Life in the Jungle*, p. 368.

40   John Sergeant, *Give Me Ten Seconds* (London, 2001), pp. 10–16; Baker, *Turbulent Years*, p. 397.

41   *Clark Diaries*, 20 November 1990, p. 363.

42   Baker, *Turbulent Years*, pp. 398–9.

43   Quoted in Anthony Seldon and Stuart Ball (eds), *Conservative Century: The Conservative Party since 1900* (Oxford, 1994), p. 87.

44   Andy McSmith, *Kenneth Clarke: A Political Biography* (London, 1994), p. 175.

45   Thatcher, *Downing Street Years*, pp. 851–5.

46   Watkins, *Conservative Coup*, p. 18.

47   McSmith, *Kenneth Clarke*, p. 173.

48   *Clark Diaries*, 21 November 1990, p. 366; Young, *One of Us*, p. 590.

49   Quoted in John Gibson, *The Politics and Economics of the Poll Tax: Mrs Thatcher's Downfall* (London, 1990), p. 256.

50   Baker, *Turbulent Years*, p. 414.

51   *The Observer*, 9 December 1990.

52   Baker, *Turbulent Years*, p. 417; Biffen, quoted in Watkins, *Conservative Coup*, p. 213.

53   Thatcher, *Downing Street Years*, p. 855.

54   Parkinson, *Right at the Centre*, p. 4. See Hennessy, *Prime Minister*, p. 433: 'For it was the Cabinet which undid her . . . '

55   Young, *One of Us*, p. 588.

56   Quoted in Watkins, *Conservative Coup*, p. 17.

57 Thatcher, *Downing Street Years*, p. 845.

58 Cole, *As it Seemed to Me*, pp. 355–6.

59 Cole, *As it Seemed to Me*, p. 315.

60 Michael Brunson, *A Ringside Seat: The Autobiography* (London, 2000), p. 173.

61 Baker, *Turbulent Years*, p. 414.

62 Ingham, *Kill the Messenger*, p. 381; McSmith, *Kenneth Clarke*, p. 165.

63 Quoted in Hennessy, *Prime Minister*, p. 403.

11 '. . . an extremely difficult and turbulent day', 1992

1 Philip Stephens, *Politics and the Pound: The Tories, the Economy and Europe* (London, 1996), p. xii.

2 Major, *Autobiography*, pp. 662–4.

3 *Sunday Times*, 12 April 1992.

4 See the columns of William Keegan and Will Hutton in the *Observer*, April 1992.

5 Major, *Autobiography*, pp. 162–4.

6 Major, *Autobiography*, pp. 317–18.

7 Norman Lamont, *In Office* (London, 1999), pp. 225–6.

8 Anthony Seldon with Lewis Baston, *Major: A Political Life* (London, 1997), p. 310.

9 Major, *Autobiography*, p. 232.

10 Quoted in Seldon, *Major*, p. 312.

11 Penny Junor, *John Major: From Brixton to Downing Street* (London, 1996), p. 258.

12 Major, *Autobiography*, p. 327.

13 Seldon, *Major*, pp. 313–14.

14 Seldon, *Major*, p. 314; Lamont, *In Office*, p. 246.

15 *The Observer*, 20 September 1992.

16 *The Times*, 17 September 1992; *Independent on Sunday*, 20 September 1992.

17 Stephens, *Politics and the Pound*, pp. 253–5.

18 Quoted in Hennessy, *Prime Minister*, p. 465.

19 Lamont, *In Office*, p. 249.

20 Junor, *John Major*, p. 265, for the evidence of Sarah Hogg and others; the term 'wobbled' was first used by Simon Jenkins in the *Times*.

21 Lamont, *In Office*, p. 250.

22 On this crucial meeting, see Stephens, *Politics and the Pound*, p. 250.

23 Heseltine, *Life in the Jungle*, pp. 431–2.

24 Lamont, *In Office*, pp. 251–2.

25 Hennessy, *Prime Minister*, pp. 463–4.

26 Quoted in Stephens, *Politics and the Pound*, pp. 246 and 252.

27 Lamont, *In Office*, p. 254.

28 Gyles Brandreth, *Breaking the Code: Westminster Diaries 1990–1997* (London, 1999), 16 September 1992, p. 115.

29 Quoted in Hennessy, *Prime Minister*, p. 464.

30 Seldon, *Major*, p. 318.

31 Quoted by Geoffrey Wheatcroft in the *Guardian*, 12 March 2001.

32 *The Sun*, 17–18 September 1992.

33 *Daily Mail*, 17 and 19 September 1992.

34 *The Observer*, 20 September 1992; *New Statesman*, 25 September 1992.

35 *The Independent*, 17 September 1992.

36 *The Times*, 17 September 1992.

37 Lamont interview with Max Hastings, quoted in Seldon, *Major*, p. 318.

38 Lamont, *In Office*, pp. 234 and 267–8.

39 Seldon, *Major*, pp. 318–19.

40 Major, *Autobiography*, pp. 334–6.

41 Teresa Gorman with Heather Kirby, *The Bastards: Dirty Tricks and the Challenge to Europe* (London, 1993), p. 71.

42 *The Times*, 21 September 1992.

43 *Brandreth Diaries*, 24 September 1992, p. 117; Major, *Autobiography*, p. 339.

44 Gorman, *Bastards*, p. 44.

45 *Brandreth Diaries*, 17 and 25 September, pp. 116 and 119.

46 *Sunday Times*, 20 September 1992; *The Observer*, 20 September 1992.

47 Ivor Crewe, 'Electoral Behaviour', *in* Dennis Kavanagh and Anthony Seldon (eds), *The Major Effect* (London, 1994), pp. 107–9.

48 Daniel Wincott, Jim Buller and Colin Hay, 'Major and European Integration', *in* Peter Dorey (ed.), *The Major Premiership: Politics and Policies under John Major, 1990–97* (London, 1999), pp. 100–101.

49 Major, *Autobiography*, pp. 312, 315 and 341.

50 Wincott, Buller and Hay, 'Major and European Integration', pp. 102–3.

51 Major, *Autobiography*, p. 324; Lamont, *In Office*, pp. 234–8.

52 Stephens, *Politics and the Pound*, pp. 259–62.

53 *The Economist*, 19 September 1992.

54 Quoted in Dorey, *Major Premiership*, p. 200.

55 Lamont, *In Office*, p. 393.

56 *The Times*, 17 September 1992.

57 *The Times*, 17–18 September 1992. The MORI poll in the *Sunday Times*, 20 September, found that more voters blamed the government than the Bundesbank for the crisis.

58 *New Statesman*, 16 October 1992.

59 *Spectator*, 26 September 1992.

60 Heseltine, *Life in the Jungle*, p. 432.

61 *The New Statesman*, 25 September 1992.

12 'The people have lost a friend', 1994

1 Andy McSmith, *John Smith: A Life 1938–1994* (London, 1994), p. x.

2 McSmith, *John Smith*, pp. 266–7.

3 L. P. Stark, *Choosing a Leader: Party Leadership Contests in Britain from Macmillan to Blair* (London, 1996), pp. 94–7 and p. 205; Andy McSmith, 'John Smith 1992–94', *in* Kevin Jefferys (ed.), *Leading*

Labour: From Keir Hardie to Tony Blair (London, 1999), p. 203.

4 Paul Routledge, *Mandy: The Unauthorised Biography of Peter Mandelson* (London, 1999), pp. 122–32.

5 Quoted in James Naughtie, *The Rivals: The Intimate Story of a Political Marriage* (London, 2001), p. 45.

6 The report was finally published in 1994 with the title *Social Justice: Strategies for National Renewal.*

7 McSmith, *John Smith*, pp. 294–5.

8 Ivor Crewe, *The Guardian*, 5 May 1994.

9 Jon Sopel, *Tony Blair: The Moderniser* (London, 1995 edn), p. 172.

10 *New Statesman*, 20 May 1994.

11 McSmith, *John Smith*, p. x.

12 Robin Oakley, *Inside Track* (London, 2001), p. 160; *Today*, 13 May 1994; *Sunday Telegraph*, 15 May 1994. See also McSmith, *John Smith*, p. x.

13 *The Guardian*, 13 May 1994.

14 Anthony Howard, *The Times*, 13 May 1994; Hugo Young, *The Guardian*, 13 May 1994. See also John Rentoul, *Tony Blair* (London, 1997 edn), pp. 349–50.

15 *The Sun*, 13 May 1994.

16 *The Times*, 13 May 1994; *Daily Telegraph*, 13 May 1994.

17 *The Independent*, 13 May 1994.

18 Examples of the correspondence, including Dr Chisholm's letter, are reproduced in Gordon Brown and James Naughtie (eds), *John Smith: Life and Soul of the Party* (Edinburgh, 1994), pp. 179–206.

19 *New Statesman*, 20 May 1994.

20 *The Guardian*, 21 May 1994; *The Times*, 21 May 1994.

21 Reproduced in Brown and Naughtie (eds), *Life and Soul*, p. 57.

22 *The Independent*, 21 May 1994.

23 James Naughtie, 'A Political Life Observed', *in* Brown and Naughtie (eds), *Life and Soul*, pp. 52–3.

24 *The Guardian*, 14 May 1994.

25 *The Observer*, 15 May 1994.

26 Paul Routledge, *Gordon Brown* (London, 1998), chapters 6–8; Kevin Maguire, 'Gordon Brown', in Greg Rosen (ed.), *Dictionary of*

Labour Biography (London, 2001), p. 88.

27 Rentoul, *Blair*, chapters 7–13.

28 Routledge, *Brown*, pp. 190–91.

29 Rentoul, *Blair*, pp. 351–2.

30 Routledge, *Brown*, pp. 191–2.

31 Andy McSmith, *Faces of Labour: The Inside Story* (London, 1997 edn), p. 328.

32 Alan Watkins, *The Road to Number 10: From Bonar Law to Tony Blair* (London, 1998), p. 177.

33 Andrew Thorpe, *A History of the British Labour Party* (Basingstoke, 2001 edn), p. 222; Routledge, *Brown*, pp. 345–8. On what was agreed, or not agreed, at Granita's see Naughtie, *The Rivals*, pp. 70–5.

34 Quoted in Donald Macintyre, *Mandelson and the Making of New Labour* (London, 2000), p. 290.

35 Philip Gould, *The Unfinished Revolution: How the Modernisers Saved the Labour Party* (London, 1999 edn), p. 195.

36 Rentoul, *Blair*, p. 353.

37 Stark, *Choosing a Leader*, p. 6.

38 Major, *Autobiography*, pp. 608–47.

39 Thorpe, *History of Labour*, pp. 224 and 228. See also P. Anderson and N. Mann, *Safety First: The Making of New Labour* (London, 1997).

40 Tudor Jones, *Remaking the Labour Party: From Gaitskell to Blair* (London, 1996), pp. 134–46.

41 *Daily Telegraph*, 5 August 1994.

42 Rentoul, *Blair*, pp. 403–5 and 423.

43 For a full assessment of the campaign see David Butler and Dennis Kavanagh, *The British General Election of 1997* (London, 1997).

44 Gould, *Unfinished Revolution*, pp. 208–9.

45 Ivor Crewe, *The Guardian*, 5 May 1994; Anthony King, *Daily Telegraph*, 13 May 1994.

46 Brian Brivati, 'Conclusion', *in* Brian Brivati (ed.), *Guiding Light: The Collected Speeches of John Smith* (London, 2000), pp. 283–7.

47 *The Independent*, 13 May 1994.

48 Maguire, 'Brown', *Dictionary of Labour Biography*, pp. 88–9.
49 Naughtie, *The Rivals*, p. 75. Brown's comment that Blair was the 'best friend I've had in politics' was made in his interview with the *Times*, 22 November 2001.

Further Reading

1 Chamberlain, Churchill and Britain's 'finest hour', 1940

Geoffrey Best, *Churchill: A Study in Greatness* (London, 2001)

Robert Blake and Wm Roger Louis (eds), *Churchill* (Oxford, 1993)

John Lukacs, *Five Days in London: May 1940* (New Haven and London, 2000)

Graham Stewart, *Burying Caesar: Churchill, Chamberlain and the Battle for the Tory Party* (London, 1999)

Malcolm Smith, *Britain and 1940. History, Myth and Popular Memory* (London, 2000)

2 El Alamein and Beveridge, 1942–43

Paul Addison, *The Road to 1945: British Politics and the Second World War* (London, 1994 edn)

Correlli Barnett, *The Audit of War: The Illusion and Reality of Britain as a Great Nation* (London, 1986)

Stephen Brooke, *The Labour Party during the Second World War* (Oxford, 1992)

Kevin Jefferys, *The Churchill Coalition and Wartime Politics 1940–45* (Manchester, 1995 edn)

Jose Harris, *William Beveridge* (Oxford, 1977)

3 The demise of Attlee's government, 1951

Brian Brivati, *Hugh Gaitskell* (London, 1996)
John Campbell, *Nye Bevan and the Mirage of British Socialism* (London, 1987)
Peter Hennessy, *Never Again: Britain 1945–51* (London, 1992)
Kenneth O. Morgan, *Labour in Power 1945–51* (Oxford, 1984)
Charles Webster, *The Health Services since the War*, Vol. 1 (London, 1988)

4 Eden and the Suez crisis, 1956

David Carlton, *Anthony Eden: A Biography* (London, 1981)
Kevin Jefferys, *Retreat from New Jerusalem: British Politics 1951–64* (London and Basingstoke, 1997)
Keith Kyle, *Suez* (London, 1991)
Robert Rhodes James, *Anthony Eden* (London, 1986)
W. Scott Lucas (ed.), *Britain and Suez: The Lion's Last Roar* (Manchester, 1996)

5 The Profumo affair, 1963

Alistair Horne, *Macmillan*, Vol. 2, *1957–1986* (London, 1989)
Clive Irving, Ron Hall and Jeremy Wallington, *Scandal '63: A Study of the Profumo Affair* (London, 1963)
Christine Keeler with Douglas Thompson, *The Truth At Last: My Story* (London, 2001)
Phillip Knightley and Caroline Kennedy, *An Affair of State: The Profumo Case and the Framing of Stephen Ward* (London, 1987)
Richard Lamb, *The Macmillan Years, 1957–63: The Emerging Truth* (London, 1995)

6 The July crisis, 1966

Barbara Castle, *The Castle Diaries 1964–76* (London, 1990 edn)

Richard Crossman, *The Diaries of a Cabinet Minister*, Vol. 1, *Minister of Housing 1964–66* (London, 1975)

Ben Pimlott, *Harold Wilson* (London, 1992)

Clive Ponting, *Breach of Promise: Labour in Power 1964–70* (London, 1989)

Austin Mitchell and David Wiener (eds), *Last Time: Labour's Lessons from the Sixties* (London, 1997)

7 The three-day week, 1974

Stuart Ball and Anthony Seldon (eds), *The Heath Government 1970–74: A Reappraisal* (London, 1996)

David Butler and Dennis Kavanagh, *The British General Election of February 1974* (London, 1974)

John Campbell, *Edward Heath: A Biography* (London, 1993)

Edward Heath, *The Course of My Life: My Autobiography* (London, 1998)

Martin Holmes, *The Failure of the Heath Government* (London and Basingstoke, 1997 edn)

8 The winter of discontent, 1979

James Callaghan, *Time and Chance* (London, 1987)

Denis Healey, *The Time of My Life* (London, 1989)

John McIlroy, Nina Fishman and Alan Campbell (eds), *British Trade Unions and Industrial Politics*, Vol. II, *The High Tide of Trade Unionism 1964–79* (Aldershot, 1999)

Kenneth O. Morgan, *Callaghan: A Life* (Oxford, 1997)

Nick Tiratsoo (ed.), *From Blitz to Blair: A New History of Britain since 1939* (London, 1997)

9 The Falklands war, 1982

Iain Dale (ed), *Memories of the Falklands* (London, 2002)
Lawrence Freedman, *Britain & the Falklands War* (Oxford, 1988)
Max Hastings and Simon Jenkins, *The Battle for the Falklands* (London, 1983)
Martin Middlebrook, *Operation Corporate: The Story of the Falklands War 1982* (London, 1985)
Margaret Thatcher, *The Downing Street Years* (London, 1993)

10 Margaret Thatcher's downfall, 1990

Michael Heseltine, *Life in the Jungle: My Autobiography* (London, 2000)
Sir Geoffrey Howe, *Conflict of Loyalty* (London, 1994)
Robert Shepherd, *The Power Brokers: the Tory Party and its Leaders* (London, 1991)
Alan Watkins, *A Conservative Coup: The Fall of Margaret Thatcher* (London, 1991)
Hugo Young, *One of Us: A Biography of Margaret Thatcher* (London, 1991 edn)

11 Black Wednesday, 1992

Peter Dorey (ed), *The Major Premiership: Politics and Policies under John Major 1990–97* (London, 1999)
Norman Lamont, *In Office* (London, 1999)
John Major, *The Autobiography* (London, 1999)
Anthony Seldon with Lewis Baston, *Major: A Political Life* (London, 1997)
Philip Stephens, *Politics and the Pound: The Tories, the Economy and Europe* (London, 1996)

12 The emergence of New Labour, 1994

Gordon Brown and James Naughtie (eds), *John Smith: Life and Soul of the Party* (Edinburgh, 1994)

Kevin Jefferys (ed.), *Leading Labour: From Keir Hardie to Tony Blair* (London, 1999)

Andy McSmith, *John Smith: A Life 1938–1994* (London, 1994)

James Naughtie, *The Rivals: The Intimate Story of a Political Marriage* (London, 2001)

John Rentoul, *Tony Blair. Prime Minister* (London, 2001 edn)

Index